The South African War (1899–1902) is no longer treated as 'a white man's war' by historians. Black South Africans were drawn into service by both sides, and the war affected the black communities in a variety of complex ways. Dr Nasson has written a closely focused regional study of the conflict in the Cape Colony, describing the dramatic participation of black people in the conduct of the war, and their subsequent exclusion from the fruits of peace. (The Abraham Esau of the title, a patriotic Coloured artisan, was murdered by Boer guerrillas.) Dr Nasson sets the conflict in the context of Cape political culture and social life at the turn of the century. This is a major contribution to South African and imperial history.

ABRAHAM ESAU'S WAR

AFRICAN STUDIES SERIES 68

GENERAL EDITOR
J. M. Lonsdale, *Lecturer in History and Fellow of Trinity College, Cambridge*

ADVISORY EDITORS
J. D. Y. Peel, *Professor of Anthropology and Sociology, with special reference to Africa, School of Oriental and African Studies, University of London*
John Sender, *Faculty of Economics and Fellow of Wolfson College, Cambridge*

Published in collaboration with
THE AFRICAN STUDIES CENTRE, CAMBRIDGE

A list of books in this series will be found at the end of the volume

The Calvinia martyr: Abraham Esau, the Coloured man lashed and murdered by the Boers. From *The Cape Times Weekly*, 13 March 1901.

ABRAHAM ESAU'S WAR

A Black South African War in the Cape,
1899–1902

BILL NASSON

Department of Economic History
University of Cape Town

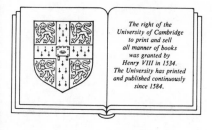

The right of the
University of Cambridge
to print and sell
all manner of books
was granted by
Henry VIII in 1534.
The University has printed
and published continuously
since 1584.

CAMBRIDGE UNIVERSITY PRESS

CAMBRIDGE

NEW YORK   PORT CHESTER   MELBOURNE   SYDNEY

Published by the Press Syndicate of the University of Cambridge
The Pitt Building, Trumpington Street, Cambridge CB2 1RP
40 West 20th Street, New York, NY 10011 USA
10 Stamford Road, Oakleigh, Melbourne 3166, Australia

First published 1991

Printed in Great Britain at the University Press, Cambridge

British Library cataloguing in publication data
Nasson, Bill
    Abraham Esau's war: a black South African war in the
    Cape. 1899–1902. – (African studies series; v. 68).
    1. Boer War
    I. Title II. Series
    968.0481

Library of Congress cataloguing in publication data
Nasson, Bill
    Abraham Esau's war: a Black South African war in the Cape.
    1899–1902 / Bill Nasson.
        p.   cm. – African studies series: 68)
    Includes bibliographical references (p.   )
    ISBN 0 521 38512 1
    1. South African war, 1899–1902 – Participation, Black. 2. South
African War, 1899–1902 – Campaigns South African Calvinia Region.
3. Esau, Abraham, 1884–1910. 4. Calvinia Region (South Africa) –
History. I. Title. II. Series.
DT1896.N37 1990
968.04'8 – dc20   90–1538   CIP

ISBN 0 521 38512 1 hardback

WD

To the memory of Joe Nasson

I hope you will not mind, I am a coloured boy of 18. My skin is coloured but my heart is bold . . . my master is very good to me but I am going to leave him just for the sake of our Empire and Queen. I will take the rifle in my hand and the bandolier round my body.

Letter to the Prince of Wales' Light Horse, from Pieter Albertus, Caledon:
Umtata Herald, 20 April 1901

Even now at night, one wakes up in horror, fancying the native town guard are all about the house, and are firing at you.

Olive Schreiner Letters, UCTL, MMPUS/BC16/D.60/241,
O. Schreiner to F. Schreiner, 30 June 1902

Panic in him and round him
like a wind-flapped tilt –
only the sable sons of Ham
cram Death's dark veld.

from Tony Harrison, 'Voortrekker', *The School of Eloquence*
(Rex Collings, London, 1978)

Contents

List of illustrations and maps   *page* xvi
Preface and acknowledgements   xvii
Abbreviations   xxiii

1   Introduction: perspectives and place   1

2   Colonial state, imperial army and peacekeeping   12
    Attitudes and policies   12
    Formation of African levies   16
    Auxiliaries and social confrontation   19
    Imperial army and auxiliary service   22
    Skills and service conditions   23
    Military mobilisation and the labour market   26
    Political imbalance and class assertion   29

3   The politics of patriotism   32
    A patriotic consensus   32
    J. T. Jabavu and the pacifist dilemma   34
    Imperial hopes and misgivings   38
    Patriotism, class consensus and class insecurity   39

4   Arms and patriotism: town guards and district militia   41
    Mobilisation and organisation   41
    Class composition and hierarchy   48
    Paternalism and discipline   52
    Leisure and action   55
    Conditions and opportunities   58
    A soldiering community   61

Contents

5 Moving Lord Kitchener: military transport and supply work   64
   Transport mobilisation   65
   Geographical origins and social composition of auxiliaries   67
   Peasant suppliers and contractors to the imperial army   70
   Remount labour   74
   Working communities, leisure and culture   77
   Labour independence and labour control   86
   Conclusion   90

6 The Republican guerrilla war in the countryside   96
   Blacks on commando   96
   Fighting retainers: *agterryers*   95
   Labouring conditions   102
   Conscription, expropriation and control   105
   The Leliefontein incident   108
   Political belligerence   113
   Conquests and oppositions   117

7 Martyrdom, myth and memory: Abraham Esau's War   120
   Background and identity   121
   War crisis and war preparation   122
   British collaborator   126
   Invasion and occupation   128
   Resistance and martyrdom   130
   A memory and tradition of Britishness   133
   Myth, history and representation   139

8 Treason offenders and their antagonists   142
   Treason: definition and responses   143
   Witnesses, infiltrations and grievances   149
   Popular politicisation   157
   Missionaries and malcontents   162
   A forum for a 'counter-culture'   166

9 Peace and reconquest   169
   Social peace   170
   Demobilisation and the return of labour   172
   The decline of skilled and migrant independence   176
   Compensation and relief   179

Contents

Population, segregation and mortality   182
Political aftermath   186
Conclusion   189

Notes   193
Bibliography   225
Index   238

Illustrations

Frontispiece The Calvinia martyr: Abraham Esau, the coloured man lashed and
murdered by the Boers
1 Indian cavalry at Green Point Military Camp, Cape Town *page* 15
2 Garrison of No. 29 blockhouse, Sterkstroom 23
3 Imperial yeoman and camp follower 25
4 The 'Black Watch': African militia, Somerset East 49
5 Transport conductor with boy remount servants, King William's Town 67
6 Group of British officers' servants and water carriers, Victoria West 75
7 Fortified outpost, Namaqualand 109
8 African men and women and colonists surrendering weapons under
martial law regulations, Worcester 149
9 Grave of Constable James Kobe Madlaila, Steytlerville 185

Maps

1 South Africa *page* xxvi
2 Transkeian Territories *c*. 1900 17
3 Cape Colony, magisterial districts 1897 43
4 The Cape Colony 72
5 British blockhouses and fences: Smuts' invasion of the Cape Colony 96
6 Commando movements of Commandant William Fouché and General
Wynand Malan 104
7 Calvinia and neighbouring districts 123

Preface and acknowledgements

In Anthony Sher's novel, *Middlepost*, two roving characters, Issy and Smous, stumble upon a corpse lying in the open. It is shortly after the end of the South African War, and in the rusting silence one of them makes an instinctive connection. ' "Mmm" . . . said Issy, his mind elsewhere, "this was a Boer district. Killed in the war, I suppose." Ahead on the left, a man was lying in the gutter . . . "You seen one before?", asked Issy. "A dead body?" . . . Issy laughed. "No, I mean a Bushman." ' [1] The 'Boer district' could be anywhere in the Cape; it could be Mafeking or Kimberley. It is, however, Calvinia. A remote spot not known for sieges, diamonds or the prototypical Boy Scout movement, it has its share of 'Bushman' corpses in the war years. It was also the source of a complex of black reactions and responses to 'the white man's war', which found expression in a certain village radicalism and a pugnacious folklore: its hero was a wily Coloured blacksmith, Abraham Esau.

This Cape artisan's historical identity crystallised in the moment of war; it hardened in his bluff attachment to British imperialism and Cape liberalism, in his anti-Boer agitation and conspiratorial intelligence organisation against threatening Boer Republicanism, in his capture and execution by an invading commando in 1901. For the local black population, death invested Abraham Esau with martyrdom, and his experience and actions generated an abiding mythology. In sum, the martyring of a Coloured patriot encapsulated a memory of the distinctive pressures and conflicts of a Cape colonial war experience. For the myth-making of the Abraham Esau episode has meaning in that it represents what Roland Barthes has termed 'an instantaneous reserve of history', [2] here a regenerative memory of a South African War which was a crisis of identity for black people and classes in the Cape. The core of Esau's experience and the active engagement that flowed from it were firmly rooted in local conditions of existence; the ordinary blacksmith may be assimilated to a tumultuous world in which ordinary men and women were extraordinary men and women, living in defence of their rights and everyday concerns as Cape citizens in tough times.

The story of Abraham Esau and the significance of his claim upon our historical consciousness of the South African War are therefore of central relevance to this book. He is an important presence here because, to gloss the ideas of Marcus Rediker, Robert Skidelsky and others, the impersonal larger movements of warfare and the 'logic' of social crisis found a coordinate in a particular human life, and in the historically grounded dispositions that made up that life. This book is therefore called *Abraham Esau's War* not just on account of the individuality of the figure whom readers will encounter in chapter 7, but because of its typology; an appreciation of the ways in which Abraham Esau understood the meanings of the South African War and sustained wartime actions begins to reclaim not only one subject's individual experience, but the 'intellectual present'[3] in which so many rural Cape artisans, workers and peasants thought and acted.

It remains to us, then, to look more closely later in this book at the sort of figure Abraham Esau was, and the impact he had on politics and society in his time – and after. For in this attempt both to write a regional history and to tell a story, I hope that it is clear that in a good deal of what follows it is the presence of Abraham Esau that matters. But before exploring the thick texture of wartime social experience for black people in the Cape Colony, we need to consider briefly the broader historical boundaries of our subject. In this respect, an appropriate starting point is perhaps a dual question: why another study of the South African War? What does the social interpretation which follows have to add to the existing historiography on the war?

The South African War of 1899–1902 seems to hold a perennial fascination for historians, and rightly so. As a major colonial war of British imperialism against the Boer or Afrikaner Republics, it has produced and can still provide essential evidence for continuing discussion and debate over imperial needs and ambitions and the development of an alliance between state and capital as a central, directive force in the capitalist integration and development of Southern Africa after 1910.[4] While the scholarly social – as distinct from the economic or political – history of the war has long been a virtually fallow field, more recently stones have been turned, ploughs have been busy and furrows have appeared. The 'internal' social and economic data of the conflict has begun to ripen for harvesting; thanks to some of the contributions to the war historiography we can move beyond those abiding images of the concentration camps or imperial military disasters at Spion Kop or Modder River to some appreciation of such varied elements as the position of African mineworkers on the Rand, the day-to-day relations of working-class British troops, or the class composition of Boer National Scouts.

If we now have an improving picture of the general social landscape and human matrix of the South African crisis, the definition and meaning of the war experience remains an important question. What was the content, and what were the divisions and terms of the South African War? In great measure the answer depends on *whose* war one means and in which sector it was located – the burden of the war effort differed sharply in the way in which it pressed upon regions. Whatever the answer – which might reveal relations between Boer landlords and *bywoners* (non-landowning rural poor whites) or agrarian dislocation and food shortages as crucial issues in the social history of the war – informed historians now know that any definition of the conflict exclusively in terms of 'a white man's war' is a distortion of historical reality. Its course and outcome cannot be fully appreciated outside the context of the engagement of black South Africans with developments.

This interpretation stresses the centrality of the experiences and material conditions of black people in the war, and it tries to do so through studies of a specific people in specific relations and situations. This history is therefore in no sense an attempt at a 'totalising' history of the black population in the war. Several years ago, Peter Warwick published his pioneering synthetic survey, *Black People and the South African War 1899–1902* (Cambridge, 1983), which opened up many of the dimensions of the topic, and without whose example I could probably not have written as I have. Where appropriate, I have tried to situate the formation and self-activity of Cape African and Cape Coloured people within the wider national context sketched so admirably by Warwick's *Black People and the South African War*. But this book remains emphatically a regional or local study, imbued with the indigenous life, culture and consciousness of a locality. If this account of the Cape 'people's war' can help to illuminate something of the fullness of popular human experience in these years of upheaval and transition, then Abraham Esau and his kind will, one hopes, have provided impetus for possible further micro-studies. And their lives and dramatic struggles will have been at least partially rescued from the relative 'condescension of posterity', in a radical South African historiography which still provides very largely the Witwatersrand side of the story of the transformations of these years.

To appropriate a useful expression from that vintage Marxist historian, Gwyn Williams, following Georges Sorel, this book might best be described as a 'diremption': a selection of essential movements, practices and patterns which I hope represent a living conjuncture of wrestling historical forces. My principal purpose in producing this book is to assess the meaning of the South African War for the black population of the Cape Colony and to subject its most characteristic dynamics there to historical examination. The book is an attempt to reconstruct something of the *atmosphere* of the Cape dimensions to the war; for the atmosphere in a generalised crisis is, as Ronald Fraser has suggested in his Spanish Civil War study, 'a social emanation ... never more than at a time of extreme social crisis does the atmosphere become a determining factor in the way people respond to events. For, however intangible, it is never abstract or distant. It is what people feel. And what people feel lays the ground for their actions.'[5] Here, above all, the war assumed the image of a claustrophobic social crisis; its intensely localised tensions and loyalties were multiple and sharp. Much concerning the particular momentum of events in the Cape will be related here; but that momentum of conflict also reveals a good deal else. As war-fever rocked the colony, the social, economic and cultural tonality of the area became highlighted, as did the rippling ideas and beliefs which lent purpose and cohesion to the efforts of communities and individuals to survive and defend their interests and identities. In short, social turmoil, agrarian clashes and the mushrooming of militia and other British auxiliary forces helped to shape the Cape's distinctive turn-of-the-century history; they also expressed much of, and explained much about, the historical inheritance of that area which did not dissolve in the massive capitalist transition and realignment of this formative era.

I believe, then, that the topic of this book raises issues which are relevant to an understanding of the diverse and influential cluster of forces which have assisted in the making of a layered black experience, as subject societies were blanketed in the present century by the spread of an integrated, settler-dominated capitalist state. What follows, therefore, is also intended as a modest contribution to a writing of South African history which sees that history as a contested site for meanings and experiences from below as well as from above; or, as John Iliffe has recently put it, the 'rewriting of South African history as the product of struggle between all the elements in society, rather than as a design imposed by dominant settlers or capitalists'.[6] What this points to is treatment of a spectrum of evolving relationships, radiating both inward and outward as South African society underwent dramatic material transformations. As depicted by Shula Marks and Richard Rathbone in their edited collection, *Industrialisation and Social Change in South Africa*, a major representation is the question of the 'interrelationships between the political economy, imperial and local, and class formation, between different sections of the working class and different classes, between class, culture and consciousness'.[7] I hope this book conveys some sense of one interesting strand in that history.

Sources for the social history of the South African War are plentiful. For all that, records concerned directly with the conduct of African or Coloured people are rather uneven in quality and are very widely scattered. For example, we do not have a statistical record of their war service; it is no exaggeration to state that there are probably better figures for draught animals purchased by the transport brigades of the Grenadier Guards than for that regiment's contingent of Mfengu, Sotho and Coloured scouts and transport riders. Any statistical illuminations in this study are therefore limited and no more than elementary. The following account of war experience accordingly rests squarely upon a bedrock of qualitative source material. Naturally, the overwhelming bulk of this material was produced by British or white colonial participants and observers. Most especially because they were produced in the heady atmosphere of war crisis, these varied letters, reports and other papers have needed a particularly critical appraisal of the reliability of their picture of black behaviour.

Yet, while such limitations need to be acknowledged, by following Raymond Carr's injunction to 'quarry in the outworks' of historical archives, this book has been based on a rich store of new material. Much of the most illuminating source material comes from British military collections which have never been used before; indeed, these manuscript papers, along with contemporary printed material, provide evidence on topics of central concern to social historians, such as peasant activity, or the ideological resources of tenants on scattered settler farms. While military history should preferably be left to military historians, the same surely cannot be said for its 'social' sources: these can serve a far wider historical purpose, and serve it very profitably. Here I would endorse Michael Howard's insistence that for historians, 'wars are not tactical exercises writ large. They are, as Marxist military analysts quite rightly insist, conflicts of *societies*, and they can be fully understood only if one understands the nature of the society fighting them.'[8] Colonial administrative records have also been of considerable value. Scarcely a district magistrate's archive is without some relevant material, however scrappy, and I have tried to sample these collections as widely as possible. Among collections of unofficial papers, missionary archives provided useful data on labour and other activity in the countryside. Newspapers and journals have been another essential source. On the other hand, the proportion of relevant available material written by the colony's educated African and Coloured elites is not large; there are hardly any contemporary printed sources apart from the newspapers, *Imvo Zabantsundu*, *Izwi Labantu* and the *South African Spectator*. In view of this, and of the book's central focus on 'popular' rather than petty-bourgeois class experience, a range of manuscript letters, statements, formal affidavits and depositions all carry considerable weight in the text. Many of these surface in police and army intelligence files, and appear in translation in the voluminous papers concerned with treason investigations. Others are to be found scattered in correspondence papers, as the disclosures of informers or as demands and grievances lodged with military officers and district officials. These documents are evidently the *only* literate expression of labourers and peasants which has survived the war. As their statements and affidavits throw important light on particular situations and individuals, I have tried wherever possible and appropriate to cite this material in the text. I have done the same with the small cluster of oral sources collected for this book.

In the course of research and writing I have incurred many obligations and in acknowledging them I naturally take full responsibility for the result. This book originated as a doctoral thesis for the University of Cambridge. Although its shape, tone and texture have since altered somewhat, my first considerable debt is undoubtedly to my supervisor and friend, John Lonsdale, who has long been generous with his time and thought. I owe him a special note of gratitude for his guidance and constructive advice and criticisms both regarding the thesis and its preparation for publication in book form. As a postgraduate student I was supported financially through the generosity of the Master and Fellows of Gonville and Caius College, Cambridge, who elected me into a Gonville Research Studentship; and I received some additional help with travel monies from the managers of the Smuts Memorial Fund for Commonwealth Studies in the University of Cambridge, and from the Trustees of the Ernest Oppenheimer Memorial Trust in Johannesburg, South Africa. For allowing me time off from employment as a research assistant several years ago, in order to work on this topic, I am also grateful to Francis Wilson of the Southern Africa Labour and Development Research Unit (SALDRU) in the School of Economics of the University of Cape Town.

I also profited from having an opportunity to present material from this study to seminars or conference workshops at the Universities of Cambridge, London, York, Oxford and Cape Town, and at Yale University. To those who offered helpful advice and challenging criticism, I wish to record my thanks. The original thesis was examined by Professor Shula Marks and Professor D. K. Fieldhouse and I am grateful to them for their suggestions and corrections. Thanks are also due to the archivists and librarians of various record offices, libraries and museums who have given me both assistance and hospitality; Major W. H. Mahon of the Irish Guards and the staff of the reading room in the National Army Museum deserve special mention for going out of their way to aid me in gaining access to deposits of rarely examined military records. Barbara Conradie, formerly of the Cape Archives, must also be thanked for being particularly helpful. I am also grateful to Mrs Sue Wright, Mrs Veronica Tregurtha and, most especially, Mrs Gill Curling, who typed portions of the manuscript with care and good humour. Leonie Twentyman-Jones compiled the index.

One of the pleasures of writing is surely the opportunity to record in a public place one's debts to those who have offered essential encouragement, interest, advice and support over some years of dabbling in both the subject and the discipline. These individuals are as wide ranging as the debts. While I cannot hope to record everyone, I wish to acknowledge Ian Phimister, Colin Bundy, Vivian Bickford-Smith, Patrick Harries, Christopher Saunders, Nigel Penn, Albert Grundlingh, Peter Warwick, Andre Odendaal, Stanley Trapido, Charles van Onselen, Brian Willan, Jan Fredrickson, Shamil Jeppie, Kitty Kiernan, Linda Chisholm, Tessa Fairbairn, Stephen Watson, William Beinart, Taffy Shearing, Gary Mead, Laurie Jaffe and Navlika Ramjee. I should also like to acknowledge Bernard Porter and the late Alan Lee, who helped to ensure that I withered into history rather than literary studies. At Cambridge University Press, Jessica Kuper has been a friendly and supportive editor and Wendy Guise and Jean Field have my appreciation. And finally, to Ann and Leah in particular, I owe a special tribute. Though they did no proofreading, they helped, among other things, to persuade me that history is too important to be left to professional historians.

I would like to offer one personal concluding reflection or, probably more accurately, admission. Born in Cape Town in the early 1950s, I have spent most of my years here experiencing, and recoiling from, the utter ghastliness of a Nationalist South Africa, with its reliance upon an appalling combination of authoritarianism, lunacy and mediocrity. I suppose that such a personal formation leaves a mark on one's work. It has probably affected the manner of this book's deeply felt historical obsessions. It is, in consequence, undoubtedly longer on moral economy than on political economy; it has been my good fortune to work in a Department of Economic History which accommodates both concerns. I suppose that in ways that one may not ordinarily find easy to acknowledge, some of the threads which run through *Abraham Esau's War* make up history as an imaginative survival. To Ian Phimister a candid and generous perception of this is due; to me the consequential errors and deficiencies.

Acknowledgements

The substance of chapters 5, 7 and 8 appeared in earlier versions as articles in the *Journal of Imperial and Commonwealth History*, 12, 1 (1983) (Frank Cass and Co. Ltd), the *Journal of Southern African Studies*, 11, 1 (1984) (Oxford University Press), *African Affairs*, 87, 347 (1988) (The Royal African Society and Oxford University Press), and as a chapter in P. Thompson and R. Samuel (eds.), *The Myths We Live By* (Routledge). I am grateful to the editors and publishers for kind permission to reproduce that material here. I would also like to acknowledge the following for permission to use illustrative copyright material in the text: Weidenfeld (Publishers) Ltd (map 5), Tafelberg Publishers Ltd (map 6), Royal African Society and Oxford University Press (map 7). I also wish to thank Rex Collings Ltd for permission to quote from Tony Harrison's poem, 'Voortrekker', from *The School of Eloquence*, 1978.

Abbreviations

ACG	Archives of the Coldstream Guards
Admr	Administrator
Ag	Acting
AG	Attorney General, Cape Colony
AGG	Archives of the Grenadier Guards
Agt	Agent
AIG	Archives of the Irish Guards
CA	Cape Archives: a full list of abbreviations of individual manuscript series appears in the bibliography
Cape Hansard	Cape Colony, *Legislative Assembly Debates, Hansard, 1899–1902*
CBBNA	*Cape Blue Books on Native Affairs*
CC	Civil Commissioner
CDO	Chief Detective Officer
CM	Chief Magistrate
Cmdt	Commandant
CO	Colonial Office
conf.	confidential
Const.	Constable
desp.	despatches
encl.	enclosure
IOL	India Office Library
JP	Justice of the Peace
LHC	Liddell Hart Centre for Military Archives, King's College, University of London
LMS	London Missionary Society
MCA	Methodist Church Archives
MMPUS	Murray Parker, Ursula Scott Collections, UCTL
MMS	(Wesleyan) Methodist Missionary Society
NA	Native Affairs Department, Cape Colony
NAM	National Army Museum
NCO	Non-commissioned officer
NMM	National Maritime Museum

Abbreviations

OC	Officer Commanding
P/MMS	Primitive Methodist Missionary Society
PRO	Public Record Office
RAMC	Royal Army Medical College
RFA	Royal Field Artillery
RHF	Royal Highland Fusiliers
RM	Resident Magistrate
RO	Regimental Orders
RSR	Royal Sussex Regiment
SAL	South African Public Library
SGR	Scots Guards Records
SLD	Secretary to the Law Department, Cape Colony
SM	Special Magistrate
SNA	Secretary for Native Affairs, Cape Colony
SO	Staff Officer
Spl	Special
tel.	telegram
UCTL	J. W. Jagger Library, University of Cape Town
UFCS	United Free Church of Scotland
USPG	United Society for the Propagation of the Gospel
WCL	Westfield College Library, University of London
WO	War Office
WSCRO	West Sussex County Record Office, Chichester

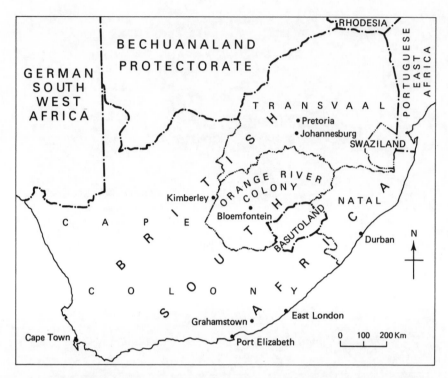

Map 1 South Africa. Compiled by F. Stemmet (1982), from *British South Africa* (Maskew Miller, Cape Town, 1905).

1

Introduction: perspectives and place

Although this book is a case study of the minutiae of experiences and events in a dramatic period in the history of a limited area of colonial Southern Africa, it is the major reorientation of South African historical writing in recent years which provides its 'totalising' context. It is, to adapt another of Gwyn Williams' imaginative illuminations, an ear in other people's corn. One of the defining features of this field of contemporary South African social history is a central concern with the daily life and culture of those who have been oppressed and excluded by race and class in South African history. 'Whose story?' is the question which has animated the seminal essay collections on pre-industrial and modern South Africa edited by Shula Marks, Stanley Trapido, Anthony Atmore and Richard Rathbone, the peasant studies of William Beinart and Colin Bundy, the social history of the industrial-revolution Witwatersrand by Charles van Onselen, and the multi-essay volumes emerging from the University of the Witwatersrand History Workshop.[1] The answer to 'whose story?' provided by these and other works too numerous to list here, is naturally not 'everyone's', but primarily that of subordinated, relatively voiceless classes and sectors

The common theme is that South Africa's black workers, peasants and petty bourgeoisie need to be represented historically as self-aware and self-activating actors in their own right; not only structured by the historical process but partly structuring its shape themselves. From this perspective, it is the human achievement of men and women and their imbrication in innumerable conflicts and accommodations which contest or sustain the historical terms of social development under capitalism. In place of the cruder, more instrumentalist kinds of economic determinism in which, in the words of E. P. Thompson, people figured merely as 'vectors of ulterior structural determinations',[2] the 'new' social history has been exploring the story of social domination and struggle in South Africa as one undoubtedly bounded by changing relations of production but also conditioned by cultural, political and other factors located in class relations and social consciousness.

Largely gone is an interpretation of the South African past as the sullen or barely-comprehending capitulation of dominated classes to the harsh dominion of industrial or agrarian capital.[3] Instead, there is increasing attention to the class, cultural, ideological and other forces operating upon and around African peoples and other communities, to encompass classic 'clashes between real subjects, amid the heat and thun-

1

dering noise of cultural, political, and material production'.[4] While it is obviously not the purpose of this introduction to treat in any detail the full and diverse historiographical context which informs this book, it is the general significance of this conception of the historical experience of South Africa's plebeian classes which needs to be stressed.

Thus, the best recent work on the entrenchment of capitalist agriculture and the dispossession of peasant holdings comprehends the importance of the continuing 'struggle for land, as well as for better conditions of work', into the twentieth century. As Beinart and Peter Delius have observed, that struggle 'could become infused with changing local identities which recalled the former, more independent status of African people'; while 'scope for defensive responses remained open ... the thrust of African defences' has had a formative impression upon the state segregationist order of post-Union South Africa.[5] Similarly, van Onselen's study of working-class activity and consciousness on the industrialising Witwatersrand carries an insistence on the significance of different class and cultural mediations of exploitative economic experiences. Fundamental to *New Babylon* and *New Nineveh* is a treatment of historical experience as 'the warm, vibrant and intensely human struggle of people seeking to find a place of dignity and security within a capitalist world' in a period in which 'mine owners did not always enjoy a free hand in their conflict with the subordinate classes'.[6] It is this approach, essentially derivative from the British History Workshop tradition of social history, which this book tries to incorporate and to extend in its analysis of a moment of particularly acute crisis in the everyday life of the Cape region. This book will have served some purpose if it helps to tell the history of how peasants, artisans or labourers made sense of their experience and grappled to act upon it, in one of the most energetic, creative and robust popular engagements in modern South African history.

New work on South African history appears today with the pace and regularity with which the 1980s regime renewed its State of Emergency rule. A few of these chronicles and reinterpretations which are relevant to Cape history, such as those on the development of Coloured politics and the 'making' of Coloured identity,[7] provide settings to which the war experience explored here provides a concentrated contribution, providing greater depth to part of the historical puzzle. Others, taking their cue largely from Warwick's overall revision of the South African War, have sought to accord appropriate recognition of the position of blacks in the conflict as active participants who struggled, suffered and were disillusioned by its dismal outcome.[8] Albert Grundlingh's most recent exploration of black South African involvement in the First World War represents a slim but lively elaboration of that experience in terms of 'war and society' analysis.[9] Grundlingh's book confronts the difficulty of conceptualising and demonstrating the military connections between society, economy, politics and ideology. And it does so in a context in which there are few directly relevant African 'war and society' models available to show how to clarify and assess linkages.[10] At another level, South Africa certainly provides little confirmation of the validity of the now ageing concept of the military participation ratio first developed by Stanislav Andreski.[11] The presumption that participation in war can lead to an improved market position and other benefits for previously subordinate or 'underprivileged' groups in society would come as a considerable surprise to veterans of the South African Native Labour Contingent.

2

In terms of adding knowledge of the interrelationship between war and black South African society to the overall historical map, there is a link between social-historical work on the South African War and contributions on the experiences of black auxiliaries in both the First and Second World Wars.[12] But it is more the contrasts and discontinuities between the 1899 to 1902 conflict and the later wars which need to be stressed, rather than any discernible similarities and continuities in the attitudes and behaviour of various communities. The world wars brought inflation, shortages, intensified industrial class conflict and labour-contingent recruiting drives for service abroad, but they did not bring warring imperial and settler troops marching and counter-marching through the countryside. While social tension was present, these wars were essentially external and distant happenings. Moreover, the parameters of African service were uniformly set by a consolidated settler state which had acquired political control over its own destiny; for its rulers, the political force of the imperial connection was limited and growing increasingly negligible. For white dominions, co-operation in wartime did not, as Bernard Porter has put it, 'necessarily signify that they wished to be shackled in peace'.[13] These factors rooted the terms and texture of black war experience in a universe of power and structure of national life which have very little in common with the consciousness and discourse which governed popular life in the earlier South African War.

For the movements of this war were located and fought out deep *within* the formations of settler and black societies of Southern Africa; though international by definition as an imperialist war, its ramifications were profoundly local, grounded in colonial relations of conflict, division and association. As a South African – as distinct from an 'Anglo-Boer' – war, it received some of its sharpest civil expressions in the conquered Boer states.[14] But, if 'civil war is the continuation of politics – internal class politics',[15] then it is the Cape region which slithered into it most meaningfully. It is in the lived experiences of black people in the Cape Colony that a sense of the complex actualities, course and meanings of this civil war between black communities and a fractured settler population can best be grasped.

While I have tried to include all important material relevant to fundamental themes and issues of the Cape war experience, there are inevitable omissions and biases. In some cases, the decision to pass over topics has been eased by the availability of works by other scholars which have made pointless any further retelling here. Thus, there is no discussion of the Cape's celebrated sieges of Kimberley and Mafeking; the latter engagement is probably among the best researched examples of how a community of African and Coloured civilians weathered the strains and bore a good deal of the destructive costs of conventional warfare.[16] On the same ground, despite the significance of African dockers' position in a key strategic supply sector, I have little to say about dock labour; there are informative contributions on relations between workers and port employers, and on strategies of labour containment and control in the early 1900s, which are relevant to the war period.[17] These, then, are the intentional omissions. There is one other limitation to my subject. Largely because black women rarely if ever figure in South African War records, but undoubtedly also because of my conditioning in the traditional mould of social or labour history, women's war experiences are noted only fleetingly at some points in this study. I hope that any further

3

analyses of the impact of the war upon black communities will be able to incorporate a greater sense of the position and activity of women, possibly drawing on local oral tradition.

The nature of South Africa towards the end of the nineteenth century has been adequately, indeed abundantly, explored by modern historiography:

> In the 1870s at the beginning of the mineral revolution, South Africa was a geographical expression. Precapitalist and capitalist modes of production existed side by side, as did state forms of varying size with their own ruling groups and systems of exploitation. There were two British colonies, two ostensibly politically independent republics and numerous still autonomous African polities. All of these were multiethnic and multilingual ... Colonists of British and European descent lived side by side in the colonies with large numbers of indigenous peoples ... African kingdoms were equally heterogeneous entities, composed of people of different origin.[18]

Marks and Trapido's recent succinct characterisation moves us from introductory perspectives to a brief consideration of place. It was the post-1870s carapace of capitalist growth, quantitative and qualitative, which was transforming human relations in this patchwork of regions, against which the ferment of war constituted a critical eruption. The Cape, as one of those British colonies, was riveted to the engrossing core structure of capital accumulation resting on the Witwatersrand goldfields. But, as Alan Mabin has noted, 'the effects of the gold discoveries' were not 'almost instantaneous on the whole economy of Southern Africa'.[19] For if Cape economy and society were an interconnected part of South Africa's 'distinctive historical mesh', they were a far from fully *integrated* part. The unevenness of the development of capitalist social forces was reflected in uneven development not only between urban and rural areas and within classes,[20] but between the discrete social and cultural ecologies of regions. Most prominent was a profound divergence between the historical experience of the northern hinterland and the self-conscious British inheritance of the south.

Of no less significance is the fact that, as Beinart and Bundy have stressed, 'the intensity and pace' of local change under colonial domination in a large area like the Transkei region was limited rather than breakneck; the vaulting thrust of 'thoroughgoing industrialisation took place in a restricted zone'.[21] Kimberley, of course, imposed its own brutalising style upon African workers racked by the uniformity of compounds and by wage reductions.[22] But in the Cape's peasant territories and also elsewhere, in rural villages, on mission lands or among tenant communities on white farms, an inherited sense of independent identity, community and tradition provided a common rural frame of reference for modes of thought and action.

While social development here was relatively slow and molecular in character, this region was also the oldest and much of it the most deeply colonised settler area of Southern Africa. By the turn of the century, the Ciskei was solidly incorporated country under colonial authority; even the partially excluded Transkeian Territories, consolidated and administered separately from the Cape Colony itself, were experiencing the tightening embrace of the colonial state, expressed through the depreciation of client–patron relations of control in favour of the 'harder coin ... of bureaucratic magisterial authority'.[23] Periodic panicky rumour and disaffection continued to send minor

4

tremors through the stomachs of local Cape officials, but by the end of the 1890s no further decisive challenge to the 'peace' of colonial pacification was anticipated.

This had implications for the role and status of Cape allies and collaborators as irregular auxiliaries or 'loyalist' levies in the service of British strategies of conquest or confiscatory methods of reprisal against intractable communities. With a stable and confident colonial state enjoying the fruits of 'a full transformation from conquest to control',[24] the need and opportunity for mobilised and armed Bhaca or Mfengu 'loyals' had evaporated. Stressing the vastly superior firepower with which even small colonial forces could overawe or, if need be, overcome mostly unarmed peasants, Beinart has quite correctly argued that the military dominance of the colonial state rested in its 'capacity . . . to subdue any challenge', rather than in 'the number of troops and police in the districts'.[25]

Yet the practical significance of this was that the Cape's defences rested on a very small professional military establishment which was better suited to routine policing than the fighting of any major colonial war. The Cape Mounted Rifles, which in the guise of the Cape Regiment or Cape Mounted Rifle Corps (known more commonly as the Cape Corps) had embodied Khoi horsemen and other 'mixed race' regulars early in the nineteenth century,[26] was reconstituted in 1894 as a 1,000-strong settler cavalry squadron. This force was posted to keep guard over East Griqualand and the Transkei generally. Augmenting the Cape Mounted Riflemen was a Native Affairs Department Police Force of some 600 men and small local constabularies of white and African police. To these fell 'the day-to-day policing of the farms and locations'.[27] Able-bodied colonists took a healthy interest in rifle associations and the like in rural areas, with bodies like the East Griqualand Mounted Rifles becoming a useful adjunct to standing forces in the event of any local disturbance; by 1894, there were an estimated 6,000 volunteer riflemen in the colony.[28] All this was fine if things went well. It was the thought of them going badly which provided occasional cause for concern. Thus, in May 1899, the British military tactician J. F. Owen remarked that, 'the forces of the Colony are now evidently no more than sufficient to cope with isolated disturbances on the frontiers . . . should it be faced with invasion from without, and major tribal unrest from within, the dangers will be very great'.[29]

If Mfengu and Bhaca groups no longer had the liberties of service and action as 'native levies', for Africans generally there was an additional important curtailment of other ordinary liberties of weapons ownership. In the 1870s, white anxieties over the accumulation of firearms in black hands, mainly through transactions on the Griqualand West diamond fields, led the Cape administration to curb a process which 'clearly raised the potential stakes in any future war between black and white'.[30] In 1878, the promulgation of the Peace Preservation Act enforced the disarmament of Cape blacks and sparked off the 1880 to 1881 'War of the Guns' with Basutoland, in which the colonial authorities were forced into a humiliating withdrawal by a resistant Sotho polity. 'It was', as Marks and Atmore have suggested, 'both the new abundance of firearms, and the skill with which Africans were now using them, that led to the increasing clamour in the Cape Colony that Africans be totally disarmed.'[31] Henceforth, the legitimacy of gun ownership was to be a settler monopoly; with it went protection and the ultimate sanction for enforcing colonial authority and control.

If the defences of the Cape colonial state ensured peace and stability, that security was seen to rest in part on the free soil of bourgeois liberal ideology, or 'Cape liberalism'. Its ideal was the incorporation of a narrow base of 'respectable' black citizens into the colonial order: a settler-dominated and directed colonial class consensus, with rough proletarians or traditional tribesmen controlled on its edges. For the Cape's liberal leadership, as well as for its 'progressive' peasantry, educated elites and better-off artisanry, the virtues of this social and political order were quite clearly displayed when they looked northwards. The contrast there was chilling, and seen as greatly to the credit of the liberal Cape's obvious moral superiority over neighbouring settler-state systems. For instance, from the point of view of the Western Cape Coloured elite at the turn of the century, as portrayed by Gavin Lewis, in 'stark contrast to both the principles and practices of the neighbouring Boer Republics . . . which from the start had excluded all blacks from franchise and citizenship rights and duties, Cape liberalism bore some reality'.[32]

For those who met literacy and property standards, the best measure of that reality was not just the rule of law in a Victorian, liberal capitalist free society, or formal common equality before the law, which was not nearly so equal for black citizens as the foremost liberals liked to pretend; it was the non-racial franchise. Conceived in a mid-1850s period when the ideological dominance of liberal merchant capital and its convergence with the interests and purposes of missionaries and colonial officials made the incorporation of a free peasantry and independent artisan class the preferred option, the basis of the franchise did not survive the next four decades intact. The class logic of the non-racial franchise was as much differentiation and exclusion as incorporation; to ensure the continuing minority character of the black vote in the composition of the colony's electorate, qualifying levels were raised in 1887 and 1892. African voters, who had comprised 25 per cent of the electorate in 1892 saw their representation slump to some 15 per cent by the late 1890s, although their votes still carried some weight in one-third of pre-war constituencies.[33] Urban and rural Coloured voters were estimated to comprise around 11 per cent of the electorate in 1893.[34]

While, for most of the nineteenth century, British imperialism assumed the incorporation of the Boer settler population into the Cape colonial order, this binding was always partial; identification and willingness to work within its framework of relations and values tended to be limited to wealthier landed farmers in highly commercialised areas like the Western Cape and the established merchant bourgeoisie. But for other Boer interests beneath and around this strategic marriage, such as poorer farmers and squatters, there was discrimination rather than accommodation. The introduction of responsible government speeded up political organisation among settlers, with Cape Boers 'the first to form organisations beyond simple pressure groups'. The 'first political organization with a nationalist programme', the Afrikaner Bond, was formed in 1880, ending a period when Cape politics had been free of party-political divisions. Drawing together different sections and organisations of the Cape Boer population, the Bond pursued 'a parliamentary existence based on pragmatism, patronage and the development of Afrikaner nationalism within the British Empire'.[35]

The original fears of English-speaking colonists at the time of the 1853 Constitution, that they might be swamped by an alliance of Boer and Coloured voters, were never realised. Instead, there were new anxieties by the 1880s that the Afrikaner Bond would be excluded from influence by an electoral coalition between English-speaking settlers, Coloured men and Eastern Cape peasants.[36] The Bond had its own defenders of the entitlements of the Cape franchise and liberal rights of private ownership and legal equality; as it moved up in the scales of influence, interest and patronage it also cornered some African support, notably in the shape of the Mfengu journalist and political agent, John Tengo Jabavu, and his newspaper, *Imvo Zabantsundu*. But it also had vociferous and increasingly powerful farming elements implacably opposed to the Cape order. As Trapido has shown, the emergence of a Boer nationalist movement was a major factor 'which hastened the undermining of the franchise'. Since this meant that the 'very existence of an African peasantry was under attack', a consequence was that peasants became involved in electoral politics with a greater feverishness than ever before.[37] With the Afrikaner Bond popularly acknowledged as the greatest institutional threat to liberal political rights, African protests against settler politicians' moves to tamper with the franchise in the 1890s were inseparable from a hardening of sentiments and attitudes towards Boer political activities. In defence of their threatened position, enfranchised citizens made full use of whatever lean political muscle their vote afforded them. And, by and large, it was English-speaking white politicians who gained their preferment; in the words of Trapido, 'the defence of the franchise was closely related to the defence of the peasantry, and although only a minority of English members of Parliament were involved in this dual defence, the conflict was portrayed as being conterminous with a rigid English–Afrikaner divide'.[38]

And yet the posturing of the Bond was not the only, nor necessarily the most 'illiberal' factor endangering the class texture of patrimonial liberal political and social relations. The 'civilising' mission in Cape high politics was also waning 'because the demands of monopoly capital, first on the diamond fields of Kimberley, then in the gold mines of the Witwatersrand, for vast quantities of unskilled, cheap labour, and the speed with which that labour had to be conjured up, conquered, and coerced left little room in the long run for an enfranchised black peasantry and artisan class'.[39] Or, in Saul Dubow's summation of the ideological shift in the late-nineteenth-century Cape, 'the combination of administrative difficulties and the new conditions occasioned by the mineral revolution, combined to rob the classical liberal vision of its practical force'.[40]

Under the spur of industrial capitalism, new social, political and ideological relations began to make the running. With mercantile capital being 'shouldered aside by industrial capital, it was increasingly labour, rather than agricultural produce, that was required from African "reserve" areas like the Transkei'.[41] Accordingly, the attachment of Transkeian societies by the Cape colonial state came to be conceived not in terms of liberal incorporationist strategy, as the moving of an independent peasant sector into paternalist political structures, but as the management of controlled proletarianisation in a segregated bloc of rural reserves. The 'useful safety valve' of drawing peasant producers into the colony's representative institutions was not an appropriate mechanism for the control of a mass African labour force.[42] By the turn of the century, according to Martin Legassick, 'while defending what it had achieved, Cape liberalism had moved from a concern with equality before the law and with the non-racial franchise, to a study of the means of . . . administration of Africans who would not be incorporated on equal terms in the common society'.[43]

Yet, while the material basis and content of liberalism in the late-Victorian Cape was undergoing social reformation and ideological realignment, classic colonial liberal ideology and rhetoric lived on as an article of faith within subordinate black communities. The forces of Southern Africa's advancing industrial capitalist transition were now dominant, but its segregationist social relations within political and civic life were far from fully articulated; older practices and styles associated with the hegemony of merchant capital's liberal political culture persisted. In subjective spirit, if not in objective reality, a conserving liberalism continued to provide a fund of legitimating beliefs for Cape African and Coloured inhabitants to draw upon. Its roots, and the thinking and emotional responses to which it gave rise, forged the moral imperatives of being a Cape citizen and a British subject around which classes formed a regional identity.

We now know an increasing amount about the ascendance of segregationist theories, the hardening of the colour line and the increasing application of racially discriminatory measures in administrative practices in the post-1870s Cape.[44] But the striking point is that these displacing pressures coexisted with other settled modes and realities of living as a Cape inhabitant. While there were segregatory codes of law and administration for the Transkei, there were no racially differentiated Cape Colony laws, with the minor exception of restrictive liquor legislation. It is important to recall that there was no pass law for Africans. And non-racial male suffrage, fixed individual property rights and the axiom of equality before the law represented constitutional liberties which, while trampled upon, were still standing in 1899. 'There is little doubt', as Trapido has shown, 'that the Cape's political system brought non-whites a wider range of civil liberties and a larger share of the Colony's resources than that which accrued to the African and Coloured populations in the other territories of white settlement in South Africa.'[45] The self-image which this generated produced a 'freeborn' mentality; carrying its popular resonance from Cape civil society's liberal 'moment of consent', it drew a frontier across the northward face of the colony.

General consideration of the ticklish questions of ethnic identities and class formation and consciousness obviously falls outside the scope of this book. Here it is merely appropriate to point out that many strands of consciousness, stemming from an array of work situations, differing experiences of exploitation and levels of social expectation and cultural realisation went into the 'making' of classes or other social forces in Cape colonial black society. There was little approaching homogeneity of condition or experience. A spread of colonised communities, ranging from proletarianised Coloured labourers and servants in the west to African accumulators in the northeast, were pursuing livelihoods in their own particular environments, which could be anything from the 'small master' micro-economies of workshops to the rural pattern of mission families yoked to the agricultural cycle and having varying degrees of migrant participation in labour markets.

Each realm of social life, within its own terms of domination, authority, resistance or acquiescence, was finding its own way to cope with the relations of the colonial era. To this process people brought traditions, acquired or inherited social identities, practices and skills, and whatever they could marshal from their native cultures and the colonial cultures to which they were now continuously exposed.

In their interactions with the dominating classes, African and Coloured inhabitants invariably found that 'the majority of settlers made little distinction between colour and class'.[46] Goldin, for instance, has noted a stratification of the Cape population by 1900, 'in a manner which entrenched an ethnically hierarchical ordering of social status and employment'.[47] The lines of racial domination, subordination and exclusion moulded social consciousness in a bewilderingly complex set of transactions and evocative meanings; there is only space here to hint at one or two substantive variants. In Cape Town, white artisans kept skilled Coloured workers at arm's length, while on the docks, a 'Cape Boy' minority could usually count on holding down skilled jobs, with African migrants consigned to the heaviest, unskilled labour. In the agrarian sector, impoverished colonists who, as *bywoners* or roving proletarians, were distressingly short of 'a status commensurate with their colour',[48] confronted the nightmare of a breed of middling-to-comfortable African competitors. Bested by the productive capacity of peasants and looked upon with disdain by Coloured artisans or mission-school-educated African constables or skilled transport riders, the white labouring poor in the countryside increasingly gave racist expression to their class discontents over 'subsidiary economic struggles'.[49] Traces of racial fluidity among the Cape underclass poor were present, as Bundy has illustrated.[50] But in general, racial enmity and social distance between white and black labourers was widespread. These tensions were to be exacerbated by the competitive pressures of war conditions.

As the 1890s drew to a close, the Cape was in transition. For its ruling bloc, the integrating ideological integument of evolutionary liberalism was breaking up under the pressure of new forces. Beneath its shrinking shadow could be found the vexing, unresolved question of producing labour to meet the intensifying needs of mining and agrarian capital. With an estimated 45,000 men leaving the Transkeian Territories by 1899, labour migration was established as an element of increasing importance in the economic life of the region.[51] But if the cheap labour requirements of mining and settler commercial agriculture dominated, they did not yet fully confine the lives and allot the roles of all communities of working-class Cape citizens. Thousands of Cape migrants were still able to give the low wages and long, regimented hours of mine work a wide berth; and they likewise strove to evade the miserable terms of farm wage employment. Railways, roads, transport work and harbours continued to provide preferred employment options for workers. Historically, the Cape colonial state as employer had always paid better than the settler sector. And even where remuneration was not substantively greater, in these services a crucial consideration was awareness that 'workers were likely to be able to maintain greater control over their life at work'.[52] Mine owners and commercial farmers were still fuming over labour scarcities on the eve of war, with the outbreak of that conflict about to provide further aggravation.

The outbreak of the South African War on 11 October 1899 saw a Coloured and African population which outnumbered settlers by over three to one, tipped into a crisis whose resolution was to be of pivotal importance for the development of South Africa in the twentieth century. While they had a common interest in keeping the Cape black population contained and peaceable, English and Boer settler factions were bitterly divided, a sure sign that power and legitimacy would be a contested area. At first, the trajectory of the war remained unclear. On the morning of 12 October there were few obvious and reliable portents of things to come, particularly that for the people of the Cape the war's dislocations were to be so severe. Meanwhile, from farms, missions, mines, homesteads, artisan villages and offices, blacks entered the war with their own distinctive aspirations, resentments and social visions. For dominant settler-class forces and the colonial state, there was an early shiver of apprehension at the thought of war-induced discontinuity and instability jeopardising structures of control. With Africans viewed as potential predators and aggressors, the mood at the outbreak of war was one of uncertainty and anxiety.

A brief word on the organisation of this book. The structure adopted is a thematic, analytical narrative with chronological threads. This seems to be the most useful form in which to depict immersion in the war experience as a *process*. For that reason, rather than cramming all post-war perspectives and concerns into the conclusion, I move beyond the war years in some earlier chapters, in order to touch on issues which flow naturally from a particular wartime focus.

And a last reflection or two on the material which follows. A central purpose of the book is to examine the ways in which the momentum of war swung towards an imperial incorporation of the labour, services and products of black communities and individuals on generally favourable terms. In approaching this human engagement, a basic question has been: how did the Cape's inhabitants respond to, make sense of and act upon unprecedented conditions of colonial crisis? The domestic impact of the war generated a spirit of assertion from below. Its broad, swirling dimensions were indicative of the depth of underlying social antagonisms and fears stirred by the shock of Anglo-Boer confrontation; while its challenges and resolution significantly shaped the order of wartime relations and the restoration of peace in 1902.

Particularly important for the actualities of common life and struggle was peoples' sense of gaining footholds for collaboration in the operations of the colonial state and tactics of British imperial forces in the region. Town guards, district militia and regular army auxiliaries emerged in many instances as instruments of popular allegiance and popular will, affirming an identity and place all their own. Their incorporation raised a dilemma for authority: how could they engage in armed activity without becoming dangerously entangled in already brittle relations between imperialist and nationalist settler populations? For the consciousness and enthusiasm of bodies of armed African and Coloured men not only gave pause to rampaging Republican guerrillas; it also made rural colonists queasy. A proliferation of Cape 'specials' of various kinds ushered in a rough period of confrontation between themselves and colonists, and between colonists and military authority, over subversions of customary relations of hierarchy and obedience.

Other groups with pride in their skills or the capacity to market their product also had reason to cheer; ample work and good wages augured well for skilled migrant workers as transport riders and enlarged opportunities for others as ancillary workers. New favourable short-term conditions breathed life into labouring associations, solidarities and cultural idioms of self-esteem. Greatly expanded local commodity markets enabled favourably located African peasant producers to make a killing. For the Cape's

10

cultural accumulators, its petty-bourgeois intelligentsia and coteries of other enfran-chised interests, the opportunity to fit old ideals to new openings enabled the virtually unanimous assertion of clearcut imperial aspirations and allegiances. Initially at least, there was general optimism in the future of a gradualist imperial politics of incorpor-ation and secure or expanded relations of full citizenship.

Other themes represent the opposite side of this coin. Republican incursions and local rebellion had brutalising consequences for affected communities and individuals, with agrarian settlements laid waste and resisters trampled down. Everywhere Repub-licanism faced a hostile environment; in time of war a mobilised Cape black population was not only indispensable but unavoidable. And with this went the increasing salience of an active citizenship. Away from the hysteria and ferocity of Boer conquest, hun-dreds of belligerent labourers, servants and tenants were locked in desperate scuffles with emboldened Boer masters. With transactions becoming increasingly trouble-some, the degeneration of these rural relationships reflected another layer of civil war – its hostilities permeated through the cultural appropriations of law and legitimacy.

To those who faced the hostility of Boer Republicanism, the war in the Cape was a battle to preserve rights, liberties and customs as citizens and subjects under an existing colonial order. Their diffuse forms of organisation and struggle represented a defence of social identity, ways of common life and an older historical autonomy. They walled themselves in against the intrusive force of a new historical presence – an illegitimate order of Republican control. It was this outlook which helped to give the Cape war its characteristic inner quality of creeping menace and compulsive defiance.

When hostilities ceased, settler leadership looked to a smooth restoration of the forces of order. Social peace returned to the Cape, but there remained a burdensome legacy of costs to be tidied up. The strength with which the war had endowed sections of the black population made them less than eager to submit tamely to white demands. And while the political outcome of the conflict was hugely dispiriting for black aspir-ations, ordinary citizens had nevertheless reaffirmed their collective historical defi-nition and hardened it with a sense of a fuller, more independent and assertive life. Bringing groups to heel in order to reappropriate their labour and reduce their inflated position involved a contested process of post-war 'reconquest' for ruling colonial forces. But to begin, we examine why, how and with what effect Cape blacks began to service the peacekeeping and combat needs of colonial state power and imperial military force.

2

Colonial state, imperial army and peacekeeping

Well over a decade ago, Donald Denoon published a pioneering interpretative essay on the race relations of the South African War, in which he stressed that 'in Southern African history, in war as in "peace", the communities do not belong to discreet historical compartments', and suggested that if Africans 'were supposed to behave like an animated geographical background . . . they did not always accept that role'.[1] More recently, Warwick's work has of course come to represent a substantial elaboration of these themes, emphasising that it 'soon becomes evident . . . once one begins to question seriously the popular image of the war as one confined to white participants, that black people played an indispensable part in military operations'.[2] And Basil Davidson has joined Warwick in seeing African activity and consciousness as of primary significance in the waging of the war. 'The British', Davidson has argued, 'could scarcely have fought the war at all if they had refused African assistance, non-combatant or otherwise'.[3]

With the broad contours of the territory already well laid out, this chapter is not intended to provide another general account of the ideological tone and adaptations of the principle of keeping the South African conflict 'a white man's war'. What will be considered is the specific local formation of black people's involvement in colonial and imperial military forces, the processes, relationships and institutions which impeded or advanced their interests as recognised parties to the struggle, and the tensions and conflicts of their relationship to antagonistic sectors of settler society.

Attitudes and policies

From the War Office, the main line of British policy was clear: the use of non-white troops in a white South African War was politically and socially unacceptable. A secret War Office memorandum of February 1901 confirms that almost all officials there concurred in the belief that the stability and legitimacy of British imperial interests in Southern Africa was best served by entrusting war service duties to white soldiers.[4] This assumption meant a bar not only upon the use of local African levies but also upon the deployment of non-European forces normally available to the War Office, like the West India Regiment, Central African Regiment or the West African Frontier Force. As V. G. Kiernan has noted, the strategic contrast between the South African War and the First World War, when non-white imperial contingents were readily transferred to a European theatre of war, is therefore very striking.[5]

Fear that the arming of local African collaborators would menace settlers and state authority with social insurrection also coloured Colonial Office attitudes. In September 1899, for example, Chamberlain, Milner and senior officials argued for keeping blacks out of military arrangements; district administration in South Africa would ensure order by directing Africans to remain passive and peaceable, and police administration in African areas would support this by seeing to it that African police duties did not venture into militaristic organisation.[6] In the Cape Colony, as elsewhere, Britain would obviously have preferred not to use black troops or auxiliaries on day-to-day service; this reluctance offers a clear example of the way in which a dominant political culture acted as a constraint on the style of colonial warfare and peacekeeping. But Britain was hardly her own mistress in this matter. Practical limits to ideological inclinations soon obliged the imperial government to dilute principle with pragmatism.

In February 1900, Lord Cromer despatched a token force of some 450 Egyptian soldiers to the Cape, where they performed a number of transport service functions at remount depots in Queenstown and De Aar.[7] As early as December 1899 and again in June 1900 and February 1901, several companies of Indian cavalry were also landed in the colony and assigned to local remount work. Although turbaned Bengal Lancers were regarded as a colourful curiosity by some, to anxious Boer minds the Indian presence was most disturbing. Although they were unarmed and kept in a strictly non-combatant capacity, there were hostile outbursts in the pro-Republican press that Bengal and Madras Lancers were to be unleashed against Boer forces in the Cape.[8] Typical of objections was that of the Revd W. P. de Villiers, reporting from Carnarvon in January 1900 that 'our towns and villages will be garrisoned by Indian sepoys'.[9]

Highly disciplined and proficient cavalry fighters resented being shunted into menial support tasks; in this they attracted the active sympathies of many British troops. A common indictment of military administration was its restraint on the operational independence of Indian contingents. Officers complained that major tactical opportunities were being squandered, in addition to pointing out that as grooms, grass-cutters and water-carriers, Indian servicemen were at risk and needed their arms.[10] As a Scottish corporal at the Stellenbosch remount depot recognised:

> The Bengal Lancers . . . at this place are a hardy lot of men, and are splendid horsemen. They have fine, regular features, just like white men, only their colour is different. They are as much soldiers of the Queen as we are. We often go over to their tents where they receive us very kindly, and give us cups of tea, and discuss their schemes for cutting up the Boers, should they be given the chance. Like them, I hope this will be soon.[11]

Local official advice was antagonistic to any such intervention. Both wartime Cape administrations under W. P. Schreiner and Sir Gordon Sprigg found the use of black imperial troops objectionable; in December 1900, for instance, Sprigg forced the demobilisation of a company of Maori scouts, prior to their embarkation for the Cape Colony.[12] This zeal for excluding categories of combatant was not to extend to rejecting the involvement of Cape African auxiliaries, but for petulant settler politicians a hollow precept was clearly still better than no precept at all.

African communities in the Cape Colony and Transkeian Territories constituted a potential threat to social peace only in the most qualified and limited sense. As Beinart and Bundy have suggested, the 'demonstrable strength of the colonising power and its ideology of progress, modernisation and Christianity'[13] had stimulated the growth of diverse groups of African collaborators, allies and various subsidiaries or 'loyals'; these were sufficient to ensure general stability and control, and the containment of discontented elements. While war unrest in the Cape created a major opening for possible African insurrection against the colonial state, such an outcome was never very likely; short of any conflagration caused by a rash Republican invasion of Transkeian districts, what confronted authority was a more rumbling kind of crisis: rumour, tensions and local instability and disturbances.

Nevertheless, uncertainty about the inclination of rural Africans and fear of their independent, forcible intervention in Anglo-Boer struggles, became the subject of urgent general debate in both imperial and colonial ruling circles. One of the most widespread and deeply rooted beliefs was that Africans were, in their primary motives, basically vengeful towards whites. In the context of Cape security, the natural pugnacity of 'Basutos' and 'Pondos' would, if left unchecked, plunge the colony into disorder at a time when a divided settler community would be least able to ward off African hostilities.[14]

Concerned white observers were divided over how best to deal with the possible threat of African rebellion. The pressing question was what strategy would best ensure that Africans kept their peace and their place. One opinion was that it would be unwise to consider any mobilisation of African levies as the arming of auxiliaries might lead them to realise their own strength, commit excesses and threaten the protective ideological barriers of settler society. The *Scottish Review* caught the excitable dilemma of these racist arguments perfectly in April 1900:

> With native races, war is so entirely a joy and a pastime, that if not allowed to fight on the side they favour, it is not unlikely that they may take service on the other, rather than not fight at all. Many persons, therefore, recommend the employment of a limited number of disciplined natives within the [Cape] districts overrun by the Boers . . . There were however, two insuperable obstacles to the employment of armed natives. One was the danger of their getting out of hand and committing the atrocities of barbarous warfare; the other, more serious still, was a . . . shock which would have been given to every section of South African society, by the sight of the uncivilised blacks and English soldiers, shoulder to shoulder in a war against a white race.[15]

The other view was incorporationist. A measure of licensed African participation in the conflict would assist the maintenance of social and political stability. Arming levies in the middle of a white-settler crisis was risky; but not half as risky as giving Africans the impression that they were mistrusted or leaving them aggrieved at being excluded from a legitimate role in defending the Cape Colony. Incorporation would contain social danger. Giving African groups a material stake in the imperial war campaign and engaging their loyalties would diminish the chances of suspected or known dissident chiefs currying favour with Boer Republicans, or making some other challenge to the colonial status quo.[16] Indeed, there was an intrinsic attraction in enabling Africans to undertake some policing role, at least in defence of their crops, herds and homesteads.[17]

14

An interventionist approach appealed not only to British soldiers pushing for 'militarisation' and impatient of 'civilian' controls, but also to the prevalent liberal assumptions of the British missionary establishment. Cape African civilisation had left behind its old brutalisations; its virtues of honesty and self-control deserved appropriate social recognition. Missionaries thus condemned the 'maudlin sentiment' and 'sentimental sop' which denied Africans the right to war service. 'Natives educated by the rule of the Cape Colony', according to one Anglican, 'are not the savages the Boers describe them as . . . Fingoes, Basutu – ay, even *all* our Natives . . . could be trusted . . . very thoroughly.'[18] In April 1900, the Presbyterian *Foreign Mission Chronicle* argued that Cape Africans 'would make excellent and devoted soldiers, and could of course . . . be trusted thoroughly'.[19]

The political minds of the colonial state clung to fragile hopes of segregating Africans from the upheaval of war, mostly in the teeth of logical evidence to the contrary. In October 1899, Prime Minister Schreiner appealed to Africans to remain calm and peaceable and went on to express the hope that hostilities would not become serious enough to push 'the native factor into this deplorable war'.[20] Schreiner's successor, Sprigg, who served as premier from 1900 to 1904, underlined government thinking when he advised Milner in December 1900 that his administration wanted it 'clearly established that the rights and liberties of the people of this Colony are not dependent upon the support of the Native population'.[21] Uncomfortably for Sprigg,

1 Indian cavalry at Green Point Military Camp, Cape Town.
(Courtesy of the Cape Archives Department)

15

this assumption did not seem to reach the locations, where inhabitants were not at all averse to sharing in the defence of rights and liberties.

There is little doubt that Schreiner regarded the formation of African levies as something to be feared like the plague. Writing in December 1899, he argued that the 'upheaval and atrocity' associated with the conduct of African belligerents provided the 'best proof' against raising levies.[22] 'I do not hesitate to say', the prime minister told Milner, 'that the idea of approving of any violence by natives to whites in South Africa is abhorrent to me.'[23] In response to nervous apprehensions among rural settler communities in the northeast, Schreiner swiftly despatched J. W. Sauer to the troubled Dordrecht locality, his task during November and December 1899 'to denounce the vile rumour that Britain would utilise Native forces against the Boers'.[24] Other establishment political warriors echoed him. 'There is', insisted J. X. Merriman, the Colonial Treasurer, 'no truth in the claim that Natives are being armed.'[25]

Like Gladstone, who pretended that Britain had not really invaded Egypt when it had, Schreiner did his best to discount the signs. The problem was that hostile interests were becoming increasingly aware of them. In November 1899, for instance, Marthinus Steyn, President of the Orange Free State, cabled Schreiner to protest at the presence of Coloured auxiliaries in border areas. Demanding that they be stood down, he threatened to incite Cape Boers to civil disorder unless quick action was taken.[26] Floundering, the premier advised J. H. Hofmeyr, the Afrikaner Bond leader, that the use of armed auxiliaries was a blunder by heavy-handed district administrators or commandants which would be checked.[27] Magistrates at Barkly East and Aliwal North were reminded that African escorts for arms shipments were 'scarcely prudent' and implored not 'to disturb the minds of the farmers' by giving credence to a 'mistaken idea that the natives are being armed'.[28] Acutely sensitive to a rapidly deteriorating settler political climate, Schreiner's abiding fear was that any apparent legitimising of African military roles might provoke social turbulence among the Cape Boer population.

Formation of African levies

The Cape Colony stood to lose from getting itself entangled in war; it also stood to lose something from adequate preparation for war. This factor bedevilled Schreiner's term of office. When he was eventually forced to take measures to enlist African assistance to strengthen the colony's defence, they were taken with little enthusiasm. In response to uncertainty about Republican intentions towards the Transkeian Territories and security concerns over the safety of neighbouring Eastern Cape regions, the British Army recommended the formation of standing African levies as the only means of forestalling continuing Boer aggression. Settler volunteer contingents (the Cape, East Griqualand and Transkei Mounted Rifles) did not command much confidence.[29] Schreiner's characteristically nervous and vacillating response to Milner's suggestion in November 1899 that Walter Stanford be transferred from the Native Affairs Department to raise a peasant militia in East Griqualand, was to 'record [his] view plainly that nothing but immediate and urgent necessity for defence could justify arming or organising native forces in this contest now'.[30] In the view of an infuriated High Com-

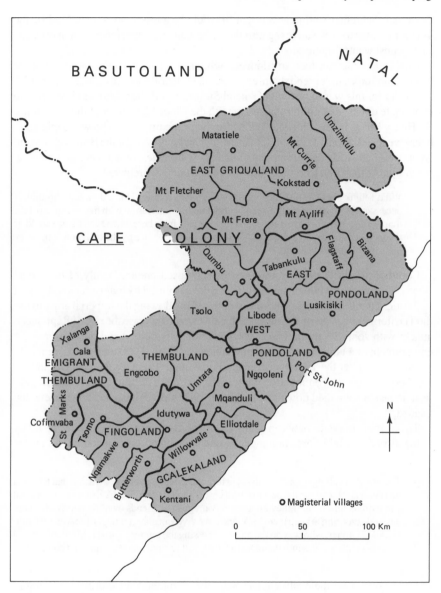

Map 2 Transkeian Territories *c*. 1900 (F. Stemmet, 1982).

missioner, Schreiner's attitude was that 'it would be a less serious matter to lose the Territories, than to arm Natives against the white man, even in defence of their own district against wanton aggression'.[31]

Unable to drag his feet any longer, Schreiner relented to the organisation of Transkeian forces to 'defend themselves and their districts against actual invasion'.[32] Authority for this was to rest with General Sir Redvers Buller, who was instructed to coordinate day-to-day military planning with the Chief Magistrate of the Territories, Sir Henry Elliot. It was a miserable time for the prime minister, who was depicted as being 'very sick about the arming'.[33] But Milner had achieved for the British command what it wanted: wide discretion in its relations with levies, unhampered by political meddling. As the High Commissioner impressed upon Schreiner:

> What I think about arming Natives is, when we have said 'Don't do it until absolutely necessary', we have said all we can, without unduly interfering with the discretion of the man-on-the-spot . . . To go further and try to decide from here when such a step should be taken, is certain to lead to fiasco. Moreover, it is interference by the civil power in a pure question of military defence.[34]

Commencing in December 1899, levies composed predominantly of traditional Bhaca, Thembu and Mfengu colonial allies were mobilised by magistrates and posted as frontier guards. Elliot was vigorously opposed to allowing the imperial army to use the Territories as a base, on the grounds that this would increase the risk of Republican attack; with John Scott, the Chief Magistrate of East Griqualand, he favoured the embodiment of a large force of drilled volunteers.[35] Over 4,000 men were eventually embodied in either the Thembuland Field Force under Elliot, or the East Griqualand Field Force under the command of Walter Stanford.[36] But the initial alert about Republican invasion soon died down and by March 1900 most Transkeian levies were disbanded.

The keeping of peace between Transkeians and Boer forces was credited by many to the display of Field Force plumage. As one relieved observer recorded in January 1900:

> The effect of calling upon the natives to turn out to resist and repel invasion had the most marvellous effect upon the peace of East Griqualand . . . The Dutch . . . seeing what a great danger threatens them if they invite or encourage their friends over the border are every day endeavouring to keep them back, and have given an undertaking on the word of Commandant Olivier, who was on the point of crossing the border . . . that if Mr Stanford will not cross with Natives into their District, they will scrupulously refrain from coming this way.[37]

In Cape Town a scrupulously vigilant Schreiner commended Elliot for his restraint, informing parliament that 'not more than 500 natives had actually touched matchlock'.[38] Between 1900 and 1901, Mfengu, Thembu, Bhaca and also local Sotho levies were revived on a smaller scale in response to periodic scares about invasion or seditious plots.[39] But the only noteworthy incident in the Transkeian region was an altercation in November 1901, when a small detachment of Boers under Commandant Bezuidenhout penetrated the Maclear district in East Griqualand and clashed with a large African force. The weaker Republican commando was routed.

For the authorities, these and other alarms were momentarily worrying, occasionally time consuming, and always irritating; but they were not a concrete threat to stability and order. Tensions and hostilities between various Transkeian communities and the Cape colonial state were not new; but neither did they necessarily become inflamed because of the war. Self-conscious separations and rivalries between diverging rural communities, to which must be added the newly nervous circumstances of threatening Republican encroachments, tended to concentrate African minds on the inward importance of conserving their local standing and spheres of influence over rural resources. Even the specific anti-colonial impulse of Ethiopianism seemed to lose some of its edge in areas where it had influence; as Beinart has observed, while at 'the turn of the century . . . Cape politicians and officials were nervous about the spread of Ethiopianism', the war actually 'defused the position for a couple of years'. [40] Other sources of intermittent settler alarmism seem to have concerned Elliot very little. So confident was he of Transkeian stability that panicky colonists in Pondoland and in the Butterworth and Elliot districts were dissuaded several times from arming and moving 'into laager, owing to fear' as this was considered likely needlessly to inflame peaceful relations. [41]

Auxiliaries and social confrontation

Outside the Transkeian region, auxiliary forces for home defence were also a principal concern for the colonial state. For the Cape was weakly held, vulnerable to Republican penetration from the north and to the internal corrosions of its Cape Boer allies. Despite fears of creating something akin to a black 'standing army', the use of mounted auxiliaries was accepted as an essential way of maintaining security and order in tracts of the countryside which were most exposed to disturbance. In the northwestern Cape, the combined strength of the Namaqualand Border Scouts, Bushmanland Borderers and Border Scouts reached 1,900 by the beginning of 1902; on the colony's northeastern flank, bordering the Orange Free State, the Herschel Defence Force consisted of some 1,300 Mfengu, Thembu and Sotho mounted scouts and special police. [42] These and other mobile forces served as an adjunct to the defensive system of local town guards and district militia which is considered in a subsequent chapter.

The political confrontation between Cape Boers and British imperialism was further aggravated by relations between Africans and the colonial administration. Farmers, for example, did not take kindly to having their guns impounded by British commandants under martial law while many Africans still in possession of rifles merely had theirs registered. [43] And the sight of armed auxiliaries turned their stomachs. From a flurry of angry resolutions at the 1900 Afrikaner Bond Congress, we can single out one, which deplored the 'criminality' of British conduct as 'the day was approaching when white men had to stand shoulder to shoulder and back to back to uphold their position in this Colony against the Coloured Races'. [44]

The whole atmosphere of Cape Republican politics was clouded by the experience of rural colonists whose fear of African auxiliaries sometimes reached hysterical levels; the striking dimension is that these local social and class tensions provided the spur for numbers of particularly poorer farmers and other marginal Boers to rebel and join the Republican military campaign. In Lemoenfontein, Potfontein, Strydfontein and Platkopdrift, which contained small communities of landless settlers living in the Herschel and Aliwal North districts, the aggressive conduct of Herschel 'specials' reportedly sent many local Boers scurrying to enlist in the Myburgh commando, which was fighting near Lady Grey between October and December 1901.[45] Commenting, the De Aaar commandant, F. G. Parsons, reminded a correspondent of a 'former occasion' when he had 'pointed out... the effect on the mind of the Dutch of the vision of the inferior black race getting ascendancy over them. This . . . has got much to do with the increase in the number of rebels.'[46] At Piquetberg, near Tulbagh, the commandant emphasised that the ease with which rebels were being recruited was largely due to 'a good deal of ill feeling between the Dutch and our Coloured men';[47] these relations were mirrored in places like Prieska, Aberdeen, Murraysburg and Jansenville.

Tensions produced by the sight of parties of armed Africans touched the code of colonial social behaviour at a most sensitive point; as an anonymous correspondent advised George Boyes, the Victoria West magistrate, 'Sir, just a few lines to you. I and my brother is leaving this night to go to the Boers. We is not angry with the soldiers, but we can't stand no longer under the Black Watch . . . we can't stand under the black.'[48] British officers were well aware of the obtrusiveness of black military organisation and the impact this was having on relations but, as one of their number observed in January 1900, this was 'the price we shall have to pay for our use of loyal Natives'.[49] Another was equally blasé, concluding that black auxiliaries were 'striking fear into the hearts of these idle and degenerate whites from the gutter... recruitment by Boer leaders in these parts [Lady Grey and Albert] seems to be directed by no system but engineered by the spontaneous reaction of low class Boers . . . there is bad feeling between them and our "specials" '.[50]

What whaped poor whites' incendiary feelings was the bold movement to and fro of African 'specials' whose offensive conduct was now buttressed in law. *Bywoners* and others who took up arms were obviously attracted by the material gains to be made from participating in commando operations against various communities and settlements;[51] but a further decisive factor appears to have been fear of displacement – weak Boers were propelled into Republican ranks by the urge to stave off the threat of African ascendancy. Under the polarising conditions of war, Republican rebellion against an increasingly partial colonial state provided an explosive answer to the class insecurities and status predicament of unskilled or destitute colonists fearful of further falling. Wartime forces therefore narrowed the gulf between poor Boers and landed commando leadership, as shared animosities towards the enlarging role of African 'loyals' welded them together; their joint social thrust was that of an aggressive sense of racial superiority. Whatever the strains and contradictions of their precarious position in the class structure of rural settler society, the landless rural poor of the midlands and other areas moved to embrace wealthier, landed Republican guerrilla leaders. Identification under these conditions was spontaneous and easy; real unity was provided not by economic and social convergence but by the compelling forces of fear and hostility. With the colonial state increasing its consolidation of power on racial lines during this wider period, poorer whites were eventually to cement 'a niche, through the vote, in the dominant political alliance'.[52] In the South African War, their insertion into that niche was temporarily cemented through the bearing of a Mauser rifle.

While the colonial state came to terms with the incorporation of African and also Coloured volunteers into the imperial war effort, the political costs of inflaming relations with its Boer settler constituency were high. But there was no option but to endure the divisions and discontents which its peacekeeping strategies had produced. Disturbances in the vulnerable localities of Barkly East, Rhodes, Herschel, Lady Grey and Aliwal North provide a classic illustration of the dilemmas confronting colonial authority. Justifiably nervous about stability in the northeast, the government at first tried to use the spectre of African civil unrest to deter Orange Free State forces and local Republican allies from threatening order. Sauer reminded farmers in November 1899 that 'any invasion will presumably occasion and justify strong resistance by the Natives, and the Free State will have forced the Native factor into prominence'.[53] The Aliwal North commandant advised the Jamestown authorities to let it be known that Africans would 'not remain passive while their huts are being burned and their stock destroyed or captured, even if they are asked by the authorities to do so . . . in the event of the Enemy appearing . . . the Natives should harass them in every possible manner'.[54] In Herschel, on the other hand, perceptions differed; officials were urged not to play up the 'Native factor' and especially to avoid any high-handed use of the Herschel Defence Force which might be used as a pretext for Orange Free State invasion.[55]

In the event, it was not in Herschel that peace was to be most disturbed, but in the disaffected districts which ringed it. In Barkly East, Aliwal North and Rhodes, farmers were agitated by arms supplies to Herschel Africans and by the impounding of their own weapons. The match which set the area alight appears to have been provided by the visit of the Sotho chief Moiletsie to Barkly East on 22 November 1899. An eager ally from the border district of Quthing, Moiletsie is supposed to have said to Campbell, the Barkly East magistrate, 'why do you allow all these Boers to stay in this town? Let me go for them and I will soon clear the town of them.'[56] Four days later, a Free State commando under Olivier occupied Barkly East, attracting the support of an estimated 90 per cent of the local settler population.[57] Invasion and colonial rebellion to turn Barkly East into a fortified Republican *laager* were legitimised as emergency measures against African interference. In the days that followed, commandos continued their advance through Dordrecht and Lady Grey, all the while invoking the threat of African lawlessness as a justification for seizures. In bringing the occupations to a peaceful end early in 1900, colonial officials trod warily. At a meeting with Olivier outside Lady Grey on 27 January, D. B. Hook assured the guerrilla leader that Herschel 'specials' would not menace occupying forces in Barkly East and Lady Grey.[58] And when a small draft of Mfengu and Thembu constables was used to hasten the commando withdrawal from Lady Grey, it did not stay long. 'It was deemed inadvisable to retain them in Lady Grey in deference to the feelings of the Dutch population of the town.'[59]

Fear of settler turbulence did not cause the imperial army in the Cape to lose much sleep over the political risks of embodying auxiliaries in its ranks. Field Marshal Lord Roberts was initially cautious, but his request that scouts and despatch riders remain unarmed and not be provided with uniforms was a dead letter; his subordinates in the field simply disregarded the instruction. Horatio Kitchener, who replaced Roberts as Commander-in-Chief at the end of 1900, was much less squeamish than his predecessor about arming auxiliaries. And his position was strengthened by a Republican decision of July 1901 in which General P. H. Kritzinger warned the British that any auxiliary, whether combatant or non-combatant, would be shot if taken by the Republicans; this was followed by a further threat that any black persons suspected of spying or of informing upon the Boers would be similarly treated.[60]

Imperial army and auxiliary service

If Kitchener was keen to arm auxiliaries against the Republicans, he was not keen to inflate the importance of the services they provided or to provide numbers. It was not until March 1902 that St John Brodrick, the British Secretary for War, increasingly anxious for up-to-date information, was able to extract statistics on blockhouse guards in the Cape. Kitchener's reply can at best be credited with a certain lack of candour:

> You have asked me a rather difficult question about black men who are stated to be actually garrisoning blockhouses, etc. In Cape Colony, Cape Boys and Bastards are separated by Act of Parliament from Natives. Of the latter, we have some as watchmen between blockhouses. Of the former, Cape Boys, I believe French has recently allowed some to occupy intermediate blockhouses out west. Of the Bastards, there has always been a corps at Uppington [sic] on the German frontier, to guard roads and water holes; they may be said to be police . . . I will try to get accurate numbers, but it means a vast amount of telegraphing.[61]

This rambling, dismissive reponse did not help Brodrick in fielding awkward Commons questions, and he continued to press the Commander-in-Chief, remarking:

> One thing I am troubled about viz. employment of Kaffirs as *soldiers* . . . I can't help having a suspicion that on some lines of country, the COs are so reduced in men that Kaffirs are possibly doing soldier's work – I don't want – for your credit as well as my own – to go back on anything I may say in the H of C, and though I have taken a pretty high line, the letters that come through hardly seem to square with our official assertions.[62]

Pointing out that 'the temptation on the spot to relieve our men of hard work is no doubt very great', Kitchener finally conceded that 10,053 auxiliaries had been armed. Of this total, 2,496 Africans and 2,939 Coloured men were reported as bearing arms in the Cape.[63] Kitchener's figures so grossly underestimated the actual situation that they might as well have been plucked out of thin air. Given the Commander-in-Chief's past record of evasiveness on this question, it is quite conceivable that they were.

The role played by British Army auxiliaries was both diverse and considerable, for their mixed skill levels supplied the essential needs of the imperial army. And military work provided a focus for energies and a new sense of prestige and economic reward for substantial numbers of Cape workers. African and Coloured recruits worked as runners, despatch riders, scouts, guides, sentries, blockhouse guards and in a variety of other non-labouring capacities in communications, intelligence and defensive work.

By far the greatest complement of men was enrolled in transport divisions and in remount depots and departments, and the mobilisation and work experience of these auxiliaries is illustrated in some detail elsewhere in this study. As official camp followers, workers were also employed as regimental cooks, catering assistants, servants and as horse 'boys' for cavalry officers.[64] At base camps, labourers undertook cleaning and sanitary work and there was a constant demand for fit and strong men to work on blockhouse construction, earthworks, sangars (low stone-built parapets), trenches and other defensive redoubts.

Skills and service conditions

Auxiliaries played a key supportive role in the imperial army's regular military campaign. Although some observers were sceptical of the abilities of black scouts, regarding them as untrustworthy, unreliable and indisciplined ('mostly swollen with bravado and drink'),[65] British commanders, as Warwick has rightly emphasised, were generally able to count on accurate scouting and intelligence work.[66] Friendly local intelligence was crucial if the army was to have any chance of matching Boer intelligence, which always seemed to be one leap ahead of cumbersome, plodding, British columns. Even small, mobile detachments, while moving more swiftly than larger forces, were unable to do so competently without the aid of reliable African or Coloured scouts and trackers. Some tightly organised contingents, like the Bushmanland Borderers and Namaqualand Border Scouts, were welded into disciplined bodies, providing not only intelligence to British troops, but fighting hard against commandos in difficult, rocky and arid terrain in the northwest.[67] Smaller bands of mounted scouts were also sent into action against rebels at night. These were high-risk operations, but they could be

2 Garrison of No. 29 blockhouse, Sterkstroom.
(*Army and Navy Illustrated*, 8 March 1902)

extremely effective. Thus, on several occasions during 1902, Mfengu and Baster scouts with the Coldstream Guards put rebel forces near Williston and Carnarvon to flight. These audacious bodies were described by Colonel Codrington, the senior Guards officer at Victoria Road, as 'quite topping, having good ideas, much originality, and not being the least afraid to act on their own against the Boer'.[68]

'The Scots Boys', a party of eighty Coloured and Sotho scouts provisioned from blockhouse lines in the northeastern Cape, also built up a reputation as a crack force, shadowing commandos and often spearheading offensive operations by the Scots Guards against rebel forces. A Lieutenant Beale of the Royal Sussex Regiment undoubtedly spoke for many intelligence officers when he wrote in September 1901:

> On the question of arms, by the way, I see a chap had the damn nerve to ask a question in the House about arming Natives. I should awfully like to see that chap out here and told to go to a farm fifteen miles off to see if there are any Boers skulking there . . . I always send a dozen or so of the Native scouts with rifles at the ready . . . simply because [they] . . . can see the country and what's in it 3 or 4 miles off as you can read a book, also they can ride 50% better than any soldier . . . for the job of scouting, the black man has no equal.[69]

Given the hazards facing scouts, guides and despatch carriers in high-risk areas like Namaqualand in the northwest and Molteno and Aliwal North in the northeast, it proved difficult at times to hire an adequate number of auxiliaries. An intimate knowledge of the local countryside was necessary for sound intelligence work; shortages could not be eased by drafting in men from elsewhere. Nor was it feasible to persuade transport riders to transfer to intelligence departments to undertake scouting. Remount officials and transport officers flatly refused to permit transfers and relations between intelligence and transport divisions were generally cool on account of the former's attempts to poach able men.[70]

Threats to the survival chances of so strategically essential a group of auxiliaries had the effect of significantly improving their bargaining position. In a number of centres service attractions were increased in a variety of ways. Special rations and generous clothing and forage allowances were offered, in addition to paid leave (two weeks in every three-month contract), and a special bonus payable to auxiliaries who could supply a fit man to replace them while on leave, or provide a new recruit to fill their place once they had terminated a period of service.[71] For Mfengu headmen in Alice, Fort Beaufort, Peddie and Alexandria for instance, the bonus system was said to be working especially well. From Alexandria, it was reported in August 1901 that influential local Mfengu, serving as mounted scouts, were insisting that British Army paymasters pay them in Krugerrands.[72] To Colonel Cooper of the Namaqualand Field Force the solution to recruitment difficulties was simple. 'We will', wrote Cooper in January 1902, 'have to provide better pay and better weapons, if we are to keep our force of black scouts at a reliable strength.' To intelligence officers Cooper later telegraphed, 'Whatever is wanted by runners and riders, you are authorised to pay.'[73]

Data on the earnings and rewards of intelligence auxiliaries is especially fragmentary, but there seems little doubt that in a number of localities these were very considerable indeed. Real wages in Calvinia, Kenhardt, Prieska, Upington and Carnarvon, were highly inflated, with scouts of the 5th Lancers and East Surrey Regiment earning

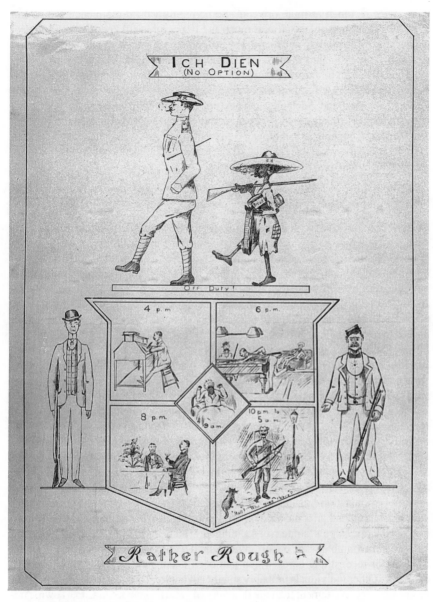

3 Imperial yeoman and camp follower.
(Courtesy of the National Army Museum, London)

up to twice as much as mule drivers.[74] Some highly valued regimental scouts and despatch riders were able to clear as much as £10 per month. Although earnings elsewhere were more modest, and marked by differentials, many mounted men were paid well above the official rates of £4–£5 per month. Thembu and Mfengu employed by the Highland Light Infantry in the northeastern region of the Cape during 1901, earned extra pay and increased gratuities for longer contracts of six or nine months. In Somerset East, Bedford and Adelaide, some Africans involved in intelligence operations were earning as much as £7.10s. per month during 1901. Namaqualand Basters, described by Cooper as 'totally loyal . . . excellent scouts', were able to command an average monthly wage of £6 and, while manning isolated pigeon-post stations, received advances on wages of £2 per month.[75]

Military mobilisation and the labour market

Army recruiting in the colony was in some respects chaotic. Neither Roberts nor Kitchener appointed a customary inspector-general for recruiting and there was no provision for examining the fitness of black volunteers. Military departments and regiments vied with each other for men, with the transport division enlisting its own labour independently. Shortly after the outbreak of war, the first army labour depot was created at De Aar in the northern Cape. Under the command of Lieutenant-Colonel Percy Girouard,[76] several smaller depots were subsequently set up in the Eastern Cape, well located to recruit migrants from the labour markets of the Transkei and Ciskei, and able to draw upon the assistance of magistrates, white civilian labour recruiters and licensed African labour agents. During the course of the war the De Aar labour depot attracted close on 10,000 African recruits, drawn from nearby areas like King William's Town and Queenstown and from more distant Transkeian centres.[77]

The army became a refuge for many unemployed migrant labourers who were streaming back from industrial labour markets on the Rand and for men from impoverished communities in Transkeian districts whose worsening situation on the land was being exacerbated by drought and crop failure during 1899–1900. In Peddie, for example, it was recorded that 'numbers were engaged by contract to the military authorities to such an extent that few able-bodied men were left', while the proportion of the male population enlisting from Bathurst soared to 72 per cent in 1900.[78] But there were reasons other than acute need for army enrolment. What Beinart and Bundy have described as the Cape's 'stratum of accumulating and "improving" peasants'[79] eagerly grasped at favourable wage opportunities which would enable pastoralists to expand holdings or reconstitute herds which had been decimated by the 1890s rinderpest epidemic. Other individuals probably sought adventure; some form of soldiering life promised more excitement than the drudgery of wharfside work in Cape Town. And for entrenched loyal Christian communities of peasants and workers, imperial military service offered something appropriate to the consciousness which had conditioned their 'making'; they could therefore attach themselves to it as the obvious course of action in disturbed times.

Across the Cape it is evident that auxiliary recruitment was a major cause of labour shortages in sectors of the colonial economy. The British Army wanted regular

26

supplies of able-bodied men and was willing to pay well above the market rate to obtain this. This directly threatened settler farming which feared that military competition in the labour market would inflate the price of labour and undermine local relations of authority between master and servant. Thus the reaction of white producers and land-lords to the arrival of army recruiters was generally one of hostility or despair; already plagued by chronic labour shortages, settlers saw production constantly hampered by military poaching of wage and tenant labour.

In the western and southwestern Cape, in districts such as Tulbagh, Malmesbury, Caledon, Robertson, Uitenhage and Oudtshoorn, where normal wages for Coloured male farm servants ranged from 10s. to 15s. per month, the local labour market was virtually transformed overnight. As new and more generously paid opportunities pre-sented themselves to poor rural workers, farmers were left cursing as the flight of labour from their lands left crops rotting in the fields and herds untended.[80] Bethune and de Lisle's columns incited labourers to desert farm service, promising them indemnity against any possible civil criminal action for breaking labour contracts.[81] Johannes van Breede, a fruit farmer from Robertson, was moved to write angrily to Colonel de Lisle, 'Our labourers have up to now been honest and contented men. Now you have given them big ideas as to what they should be worth.'[82] A similar denunci-ation came from the Western Province Fruit Growers' Association which, at its 1900 Annual Congress in Stellenbosch, complained that 'boys were receiving very high wages, which was the reason why their servants were growing so independent and overbearing'.[83] In the Eastern Cape there were complaints from Cathcart, Alice, Fort Beaufort and Albany that shepherds, shearers and reapers were becoming alarmingly 'independent' and 'bold' in their demands, with many 'haughtily refusing to work for anyone but the soldiers'.[84] Others, according to the *Cape Mercury*, were 'demanding food and wages to equal the generous terms offered by the imperial forces'.[85]

The major problem faced by settlers and the colonial administration was the main-tenance of normality. For the social consequences of the imperial army's presence amounted to something much more significant than the payment to Cape workers of a few extra pounds per month above their normal wage. What rapidly became an issue in the countryside was the continuation of a stable colonial social hierarchy, and the security of personal relations of domination between master and man. Detecting 'a spirit of greater independence than heretofore', the East London magistrate reflected that this was due:

> in a large measure to the high wages paid to Native Labourers by the Military Authorities and the Natives associating with the English soldiers. The fact of a native drawing 3 or 4 shillings a day while the European soldier has only drawn his modest shilling has con-tributed towards this end. It is hoped that something will be able to be done to bring about a state of affairs that existed prior to the outbreak of hostilities. Regulations will have to be introduced to bring home to the ordinary Native the fact that he is not the equal of the white man.[86]

A growing climate of settler insecurity reduced confidence in the colonial govern-ment which deepened as labour discontents spread through the rural possessing classes. Deputations and petitions from farmers and farmers' associations conveyed a dismal picture of depressed and suffering producers, all of whom felt they were having to bear the costs of the military's 'pampering' of the agricultural labourer. In parliament, rural members attacked Schreiner for the state's lack of protection against the encroachment of army needs.[87] Citing the plight of Middelburg farmers, the Prime Minister grumbled to Milner that 'farmers . . . find it most inconvenient that their servants leave them without completing their service' and pleaded for 'some arrangement . . . to obviate a grievance which is probably felt in numerous districts'.[88]

But no solution was possible. In some districts, civil commissioners who were attentive to farmers' needs tried to restrict army activity, but their authority was weak and their coercive powers over runaway workers doubtful.[89] The state's role in trying to balance the claims of competing military and civil sectors was clearly an unenviable one, as its hesitant, mostly floundering attempts at regulation simultaneously irritated settler employers and British recruiters. Moreover, the fact that the conduct of the war was as much a political as an economic struggle meant that in places district administration also intervened in labour distribution, to enforce sanctions against dissident colonists. Far from intervening as the instrument of settler accumulation, magistracy officials at Herschel barred Africans from labouring on Barkly East and Rhodes farms between 1900 and 1901, in an attempt to impede the production of landowners suspected of secretly provisioning Orange Free State commandos. And at Britstown and Victoria West, Coloured workers were officially directed away from employers whose Republicanism was too vocal.[90]

Mining, ports, railways and public works also encountered severe difficulties in securing adequate labour. Harbour Boards at East London and Port Elizabeth, which offered less attractive terms than the Cape Town port authority, found their working capacity weakened during 1901, as workers opted for alternative employment. The De Beers Company found itself drastically short of workers for Kimberley, as did the New Cape Collieries at Stormberg and Diepkloof. At Somerset West, the De Beers Dynamite Works found its labour supply reduced dramatically in comparison with pre-war levels. Despite increasing wages in 1901, and offering agricultural allotments to contract labourers, the Indwe Colliery faced crippling shortages which the management blamed squarely on the military. By 1901, its workforce had been roughly halved from its pre-war level, and coal production had slumped from 18,000 tons in October 1900, to 11,000 tons in June 1901.[91] In an injured outburst in 1901, George Dugmore, managing director of the mine, deplored Indwe's continuing labour losses:

> The inducements to natives of military employment are that the work they have to do is so light as to practically be no work at all, while the natives are at the same time rationed with meat daily, and receive other delicacies . . . Many have gone, nearly all of whom have entered the service of the military have forfeited some portion of wages due to them, in some instances as much as 20s, rather than remain and perform the hard manual labour of mining, as they prefer the indolent and well-fed occupation of military employment . . . After they have worked for only a few days – ten sometimes – they hear of the inducements of military service and leave the Co. for such work.[92]

While Cape harbours, railways and roads preserved their traditional position as more favoured sectors of employment for migrant workers than mining and agriculture, even these areas found that labour supply was less regular and predictable.

Despite money wage increases between 1899 and 1902,[93] the imperial forces remained a more attractive prospect, with their higher earnings providing a more secure insulation against general price inflation, in addition to other material and social satisfactions. Inevitably, what looked to the dominant political culture like an erosion of proper order and control was experienced by those below as a sudden increment of strength, freedom and self-worth for Cape workers. Localised, small-scale forms of organisation grew. Even the British Army found itself having to deal with skilled, time-expired scouts who, working together in small groups and with close contacts with each other both on service and after duties, would exploit competition between intelligence departments to bid up their prices when re-engaging. This was sometimes met by steps to counter differential earnings rates by equalising terms and conditions of service.[94] But these uneven arrangements were never fully harmonised.

Political imbalance and class assertion

Mobilisation and engagement linked both to economic and political conjunctures also disturbed the balance of forces in other crucial ways. By intervening so drastically in economy and society, the imperial army ensured worsening relations between itself, colonists and local district administration. The growing role of British district commandants, intelligence officers and secret agents produced bitter wrangling between soldiers and officials over a diffuse command structure, particularly in relation to unresolved areas of authority and control over black communities. Poor communications, the alternating paralysis and interference of the civil authorities and constant rumour contributed to confusion and tensions between magistracy officers and soldiers who acted without consultation.[95] But if dealings with Africans were thought too delicate to be left to unknown and often capricious Lieutenants or NCOs, Cape officials had little choice in the matter.

Officials in areas like Aliwal North, Bedford, Adelaide and Vryburg expressed concern about the political practice of British commandants who, by not observing established sanctions, rights and obligations, were undermining stable relations of colonial authority through their actions. For instance, Captains Carter, Stallard, Sullivan and Bonham-Carter, who controlled sectors between De Aaar and the Orange River border from 1901 to 1902, were a thorn in the side of magistrates and farmers. At their insistence, numbers of Africans 'with a good record of loyal service' were freed from tax obligations and encouraged to occupy white farmland regardless of owners' objections.[96] The chief intelligence officer of the Namaqualand Field Force, Captain Charles Christie, was another problem entirely. In April 1902, he freed Coloured thieves from Williston prison and armed and enrolled them as despatch runners at £4 per month. Conceding that this was a 'bone of contention' between himself and Williston police authority, Christie was nonetheless well pleased, reporting, 'I am sending [them] . . . through from here to Upington and Kenhardt. I know that several of them have done eighteen months and more for offences such as sheep-stealing, but I know they will do their best for us as ten of their friends are still in jail, and I promised them that I would have them also released if they performed their duties diligently'.[97] Other officers repeatedly refused travel passes to railway labour agents to recruit workers in districts such as Bedford, Adelaide and Hofmeyr where local populations seemed to be regarded as private labour dormitories for the army.[98]

Implementing the most obvious means of control and policing of increasingly restless communities – pass controls under Martial Law – met with varying degrees of uncooperativeness or passive obstruction from military administrators. An examination of the conduct of NCOs, who were generally put in charge of issuing travel passes, reveals a good deal of casual bribery. Eggs (which on some local markets were sold to officers for as much as 2s. *each*), were bartered freely for passes, and there was an equally flourishing exchange in poultry and goats. In August 1901, the *Household Brigade Magazine* reported of one Grenadier Guardsman in Barkly East that 'any man or woman wanting a pass from Bertie just has to produce a pig or chicken'.[99] Some commandants considered pass regulations not worth the effort. Black families in Victoria West, for example, were allowed to move about freely by the local administrator, who declared in November 1900, 'these infernal passes they are supposed to have are a colossal nuisance'.[100]

In an intensifying segregationist climate hostile to the uncontrolled growth of informal locations for African workers, Cape officials were aghast at the cavalier attitude taken by the military towards the congestion of labour in unpoliced locations which sprang up around field hospitals and veterinary stations in such places as De Aar and Naauwpoort. The Imperial Yeomanry Hospital at Deelfontein in Richmond seems to have constituted a particular affront. According to one J. A. van Zyl, a neighbouring farmer, it was an eyesore, and 'of these hundreds . . . wandering about there, only a fourth of their number are employed while we suffer for want of labour'.[101] George Boyes, the Richmond magistrate, also wrote urgently to the Native Affairs Department in October 1900, pointing out that the Deelfontein hospital:

> employs a great number of Coloured servants and labourers with the result that a location has sprung up close to the Hospital, where these coloured people stay freely. Wages paid at the Hospital are very much higher than the wages paid by farmers, consequently hundreds of Coloured people have flocked to Deelfontein in the hope of obtaining employment . . . and farmers in these parts are complaining very much at not being able to obtain servants. Allowing such locations to grow is folly . . . [102]

Local officials and the Native Affairs Department in Cape Town continually pressed for blacks who were surplus to imperial army labour requirements to be dispersed and encouraged to migrate to take up work in the civilian sector; the retention of workers who are 'not *bona fide* and continuously employed' was judged 'a technical breach of the law by the military'.[103] Soldiers invariably were deaf to the clamour.

Recognition of the utility of using black army auxiliaries and other volunteer forces in peacekeeping and in providing security for the lives and property of Cape communities was the acknowledged basis for their incorporation. But it was precisely the character and limits of incorporation which made these forces a troubling basis for stabilisation of the Cape colonial order; with settler factions split, the issue of black participation became a struggle of interests and ideologies within the dominant class, with legitimacy in question and control over resources at stake. At a lower level, the most visible consequences of new activities and alignments were the mostly alarming explorations into the meaning of new freedoms and arrogated powers of workers with high wages and few inhibitions.

British commandants made extensive use of auxiliaries as petty constables and the vigour and presumption which many of them brought to this office clearly rattled colonists. Tulbagh, Malmesbury, Clanwilliam, Humansdorp and Barkly East were typical of places where settlers felt the full brunt of constabulary power, as auxiliaries not only sniffed around their properties at will but stopped them and conducted undignified body searches in the streets.[104] From Somerset East, W. M. Moolman bemoaned 'this daily annoyance' of Africans 'in khaki, demanding that I show them my pass'.[105] 'Armed Natives trespass on every part of my farm, doing whatever they please', spluttered William Bain from Caledon.[106] And from Aliwal North, an indignant N. J. de Wet shrilled:

> An armed British Native, one of these nights came to my house, demanding to see a residence permit from my family in a most insolent manner, a Native who according to all probability was not even able to read. I don't mind showing a permit to a white military person . . . at any time, but consider that these armed Natives have become a nuisance, promoting ill-feeling.[107]

During these years of heightened tension, the outlook and demeanour of colonial 'loyals' pointed to increasing social distance between predominantly Boer farmers, employers and proprietors and numbers of impudent subjects from downtrodden locations and villages. Freed from the civil wage discipline and accountability of subordinate to master or mistress to enjoy considerable discretionary power in their military policing duties, auxiliaries basked in the social space for individual harassment and other new mediating powers in relations with unfriendly colonists. Notions of accountability were now dramatically in conflict.

Sustained activism and independence on this scale grew out of a temporary and unique conjuncture of colonial stability and colonial hierarchy; if it did not result in wholesale assaults upon settlers, it did bring – a frequently quite ferocious – toughness to the texture of everyday peacekeeping transactions. It was this which expressed and clarified the expanded presence and strength of many black citizens. Their perceptions of themselves and others' perceptions of them changed radically through their associations with the imperial army. The tangled interventions in daily life of that army tended, according to the chief intelligence officer of the Somerset Light Infantry, 'to rather coarsen dealings between our "specials" and a goodly number of Europeans'.[108] But his was perhaps no more than confirmation of how some disorder and general social nuisance was the price imposed by mobilised blacks for their role in the preservation of civil order and social peace. For in these years there was no socially neutral ground.

3

The politics of patriotism

At the time of war, black colonial petty-bourgeois politics was lodged squarely within the incorporationist structures of Cape liberalism. Its political and cultural expressions provided a general social location and constitutional identity which almost inevitably assigned to educated African and Coloured elites their role as a bastion of imperial loyalty in crisis. For it was an imperial tinge to thinking and relationships which provided a political and social tradition to which educated and small-propertied blacks attached themselves, and through which they developed a distinctive consciousness in relation to settler interests and the colonial state. The idea that well-ordered, socially advancing black citizens should see representation to imperial interests as the most patent means to their protection and reward was of course as old as the first stirrings of 'modernist' African protest politics in the Cape.

A patriotic consensus

For members of the classic petty bourgeoisie and minor salaried professionals, the war was clearly, among other things, a war for the defence of the empire, in the sense that if Boer Republicanism triumphed, the 'liberalising' presence of imperialism would be endangered in the south. Cape liberalism's labour-market freedoms, property rights and formal equality before the law, already being undermined from within, would be toppled from outside. Second, the petty-bourgeois stratum was emphatically for war as a crusade for Cape rights and liberties for Africans in the Republics. Like Liberal or Conservative Russophobia traditions in nineteenth-century Britain, there existed in the Cape a climate of what might perhaps be termed 'Boerophobia', a recognition that Boer areas of the interior were areas of racial tyranny. Thus, the opportunities which a successful imperial military campaign might open up were thought at the time to be considerable. As Andre Odendaal has underlined, the African elite:

> hoped that a British victory would result in the extension of idealised British non-racial ideals over the Afrikaner Republics. Applied to South Africa, these ideals were best exemplified by Cecil John Rhodes's dictum of 'equal rights for all civilised men south of the Zambesi' – words used in the 1898 election campaign for political gain rather than out of conviction – and in the non-racial constitution of the Cape Colony.[1]

32

Dominant definitions of imperial concerns and aims worked to strengthen such beliefs. During the later 1890s, the British government expressed its irritation with certain racially discriminatory measures being adopted in the South African Republic; in 1897, for instance, Milner raised the issue of pass laws being applied to Cape Coloured citizens residing in the Boer state, and turned on Kruger again towards the end of 1898, in support of the Cape-based South African League which was taking up the grievances of Coloured workers being brutalised by police in Pretoria.[2] The outbreak of war saw a number of British politicians and imperial officials continuing this rhetorical commitment to justice and protection. 'The treatment of the Natives has been disgraceful; it has been brutal; it has been unworthy of a civilised power', Chamberlain informed the House of Commons on 19 October.[3] In February 1900, Lord Salisbury told Parliament that following a British victory, 'there must be no doubt that . . . due precaution will be taken for the kindly and improving treatment of those countless indigenous races of whose destiny I fear we have been too forgetful'.[4]

Early in 1901, Milner advised a deputation representing 'the Coloured people of the Western Province' that their desire to have the Cape 'colour-blind' franchise implanted in the Orange River and Transvaal Colonies was a sound one, as he 'thoroughly agreed . . . that it was not race or colour but civilisation which was the test of a man's capacity for political rights'.[5] The downward transmission of these appealing imperialist virtues helped to mould an imitative, deferential response. Thus, the Cape Town *South African Spectator* fluttered a confirmation that with 'the assurances of Mr Chamberlain and Lord Milner', a British victory in the interior would enable enslaved blacks to 'pass from the rod of oppression to the glorious heritage of free men'.[6]

A number of wider historical studies have observed that the war immediately became a lively issue among the Cape black elite.[7] With imperialism gusting strongly after the onset of hostilities, small urban bodies flaunted their subaltern patriotism, expressed through a constant stream of loyal petitions and pro-British resolutions. As early as September 1899, a large meeting of Coloured people in Cape Town had expressed support for Milner's South African policy, confident in its resolve that 'no basis for peace will be accepted . . . that does not secure Equal Rights for all civilised British Subjects, irrespective of colour'.[8] A meeting of Africans in Cape Town, affirming the signatories' 'warm and loyal devotion to her Majesty the Queen', noted with approval that, 'the Chief Minister of the Queen has mentioned the welfare of the Native people as one of the things he is bearing in mind'.[9]

Typically, Cape resolutions established a national dimension; a clear example of their sense of mission and identity was a petition of January 1900 which assured Milner of the 'firm and unalterable loyalty of the Coloured population of South Africa', and observed, 'we trust that everything will be done . . . [in the Transvaal and Orange River Colony] to secure liberty and freedom for all civilised people . . . we feel that only under the British flag and British protection can the Coloured people obtain justice, equality and freedom'.[10]

With petty-bourgeois patriotism firmly identified with England's duty to spread the Cape liberalising model beyond its frontiers, a consequence was a militarist agitation of impressive proportions. In Cape Town, Kimberley and Port Elizabeth, branches of

33

the Coloured People's Vigilance Society and the Coloured Men's Political and Protectorate Association issued messages in support of imperialist aims, bolstered Coloured military recruitment and raised relief funds for wounded troops.[11] For the Coloured Men's Political and Protectorate Association, founded in 1900, the war was a galvanising force, pushing it into a relationship with the British military. In the Western Cape, some school-teacher members were invited to address assemblies of troops at camps and enjoyed the hospitality of army officers who found them 'serious, respectable and always up to the call of service'.[12] Coloured speakers portrayed the Boers as savages, Kruger as a mindless tyrant and the British as fighting a just war.

By January 1900, almost thirty branches of the Coloured League had constituted themselves as war action committees and had set about raising 'Khaki' Corps and Coloured Volunteer Corps in various districts. At the League's annual congress in October of that year, resolutions exhorting citizens to defend the empire and attacking 'Boers, who are the sworn enemies of the Coloured people', clogged the agenda.[13] A number of *ad hoc* organisations also vaulted into being during 1900. In Port Elizabeth, East London, King William's Town and Queenstown, scratch councils of 'Loyal Native Subjects' sprang up from February onwards, providing food hampers for troops at nearby camps. 'Coloured War Councils' and small Coloured and African vigilance or defence committees or associations provided another temporary base for war propaganda and political mobilisation. The argument that support for the imperial war effort was essential if civil rights and the rule of law in the Cape were to be preserved became the staple fare of many meetings.[14]

Of the three black newspapers, two, *Izwi Labantu*, edited in East London by A. K. Soga and the *South African Spectator*, produced in Cape Town by F. Z. S. Peregrino, conducted a boisterous pro-British campaign. Even the third, the dissenting *Imvo Zabantsundu*, was loyal to the British Army. Apart from reporting on the impact of the war upon African civilians, *Imvo* regularly carried military recruitment notices for workers and applauded the patriotism of those volunteering for service, emphasising that 'the greatest credit is due to those who evince a wish to help the Imperial Forces; and in this respect we are proud to think that our countrymen have been behind their white fellow countrymen'.[15] A feature of the *Spectator*'s reporting was sensational accounts of Boer troops' atrocities against black civilians.[16] Even when misgivings about the intentions of imperial policy in the conquered Republics began to creep in, Peregrino urged patience, continuing to proclaim his 'most explicit confidence in the Imperial Government'.[17] And his involvement in the war went beyond sabre-rattling in the pages of the *Spectator*. In 1902, Peregrino was appointed Secretary of a Coloured Refugees Commission in Cape Town; in this capacity, he concerned himself with the needs of over 5,000 'Cape Boys' and other Coloured refugees deported from the Boer states who had taken up residence in the city, arranging papers and travel permits for those wishing to return to their homes upon the establishment of peace.[18]

J. T. Jabavu and the pacifist dilemma

If there was no distinct – or distinguishable – strain of elite opinion opposed to the prospect of war and later to the war itself, there was, as we have noted, one isolated dissenting voice in the form of *Imvo Zabantsundu*. Owned, published and edited in King William's Town by John Tengo Jabavu, *Imvo* introduced a querulous note into the sphere of imperial moralism.[19] Throughout the war, Jabavu consistently attacked British policy, declaring at the commencement of hostilities that 'forcing the Transvaal at a moment's notice, in one day, to make their conservative state as liberal as any Utopia', was the 'very quintessence of unfairness'.[20] His indignation sprang from a solid conviction that the war had been deliberately provoked and that the British government's alleged reformist political and social motives for going to war with the Boer Republics were specious. For *Imvo*, pious British resolutions about improving conditions for Africans were fraudulent. The paper asserted in December 1899 that 'Natives in the Transvaal have no vote; nor is the war being waged, intended to give them the vote.' African interests, Jabavu observed, were 'outside and distinct from the conflict' and what was much to be preferred was a settling of the question of those interests in the peace as a non-partisan issue.[21] As *Imvo* put it, 'the duty rests upon those interested in our people, to see that in any settlement, the rights of the Natives should be quite specifically safeguarded'.[22]

Jabavu was convinced of the necessity of peaceful negotiation and arbitration as a substitute for violence. Apart from what Leonard Ngcongco has defined as his 'basic pacifism', he appears to have been genuinely disgusted by the spectacle of a nasty and wasteful war. Declaring that crushing the Republics for the purpose of establishing British hegemony in Southern Africa was morally illegitimate, *Imvo*'s editor claimed that accommodation with the Republicans might be won by conciliation. For conciliation between Boer and Briton was always *Imvo*'s object. Not surprisingly, Jabavu's anti-war disposition and appeal to educated commonsense and enlightened rationality therefore echoed the rhetorical style of British Radical Liberals; not surprisingly, *Imvo* carried the anti-war speeches of prominent Radicals like Lloyd George, Harcourt, Morley and Campbell-Bannerman.[23] The tough test for Jabavu was, as J. R. Scott of the *Manchester Guardian* once put it, 'to make readable righteousness remunerative' in a highly unfavourable climate.[24]

Jabavu's radical rejection of what he termed 'the war option' of unconditional Republican surrender was shaped by a number of instincts and inhibitions. Clearly, he was against the war because his instincts were humanitarian and pacifist – his polemic was emotional and moral as well as political. A further crucial factor was undoubtedly the classic stance of Victorian newspaper enterprise: prominent proprietorship, the ideal of public duty and the utility of the newspaper as a link between voters and parties or other political interests. Here, Jabavu's established political allegiances and attitudes were anti-Rhodes and anti-Progressive; he enjoyed the patronage of leading South African Party liberals such as J. X. Merriman and J. W. Sauer and, in the later 1890s, his strengthening affiliations with Anglo-Boer conciliationists saw him urging African voters to spurn the Progressives in the 1898 election and even toying with the notion of an African electoral alliance with the Afrikaner Bond.[25]

Jabavu's pro-South African Party loyalties and endorsement of Merriman and Sauer's dissenting position against imperial intervention got him into immediate difficulties. His 'independence' became a focal concern of the loyalist A. K. Soga,[26] editor of the rival Eastern Cape *Izwi Labantu*, who heaped a torrent of abuse upon him;

backed by capital provided by Rhodes and the Progressives, *Izwi* was already locked in a fierce circulation battle with *Imvo* and relations between the two editors deteriorated from cool to acrimonious. *Izwi*, whose stock message was the innate bestiality and primitivism of Boers, took particular delight in portraying Jabavu as a creature of the Bond and a villain.[27] Despite the *Imvo* editor's insistence that an anti-war position did not imply any approval of Republican native policy, this did nothing to temper the formidable propaganda campaign against him. With the African press accorded a political prominence that it probably lacked at more usual times, Jabavu was to find himself increasingly isolated and estranged from mainstream assimilationist African opinion in the colony, which remained wedded to dominant imperial ideology.

Jabavu's opponents used both *Izwi* and other outlets in the Argus press group. For example, Robert R. Mantsayi, an *Izwi* director, used the columns of the *Cape Mercury* and the *Cape Daily Telegraph* to telling effect, noting icily that despite his 'pro-Boer policy . . . it is not our desire to crush Mr Jabavu or *Imvo*, but we would like to see him made to . . . mend his ways.'[28] According to the *Telegraph*, whereas at one time 'colonists did regard *Imvo* as the true exponent of Native opinion . . . it has become the exponent of Bond policies'.[29] There were further sensational allegations that Jabavu was in the pay of the Transvaal Secret Service, had accepted bribes from the Transvaal Volksraad and would be standing as a Bond parliamentary candidate for Tembuland – embarrassed by the last concoction, he issued a hurt denial in July 1901.[30]

As reaction to *Imvo* mounted, sentiment that Jabavu's conduct was near-treasonable was exploited to the full by his many critics. In the view of the *Umtata Herald*:

> Undoubtedly, *Imvo* did great mischief by persuading the Natives that the English Progressive Government was oppressing them; and that from that time it has served to embrace the politics of the Bond Party . . . a native correspondent in a recent issue of the *Cape Mercury* declares that but for the existence of another organ, *Izwi Labantu*, the mass of the aborigines would have been led away by *Imvo* into the Boer camp, and would have taken up arms against the British Government. If there was one thing we thought we could certainly expect of the natives, it was that in a war in which the Dutch element is striving for mastery, British rule would have the active sympathy of every native. It has been left to *Imvo* and its misguided followers to undeceive us in that matter.[31]

The question of Jabavu's patriotism and therefore fitness to run a newspaper was, naturally enough, taken up by liberal imperial spokesmen. James Rose Innes, for instance, warned him in December 1899 that his views were 'disloyal and seditious, and were martial law in force in this district [King William's Town] would subject [him] to immediate arrest and imprisonment'.[32] The *Mercury*'s editor, Thomas Kyd, joined Rose Innes in berating *Imvo*'s editor for failing to have 'preached loyalty and faithfulness to the *Natives* . . . to one and all', declaring in January 1900 that 'he stands convicted of an unfitness for his post . . . his first text should ever have been that of fealty to the Crown'.[33] When one muckraking correspondent, William Lord, accused *Imvo* of 'constantly belittling the efforts of the Imperial Government, and spreading falsehoods among our Native population', Jabavu entered a successful civil indictment against him for defamation, obliging Lord to withdraw his allegations, apologise publicly and pay damages and costs.[34]

There was no shortage of African contributions to the polemical excesses of the anti-

Imvo press. The *Cape Mercury, Cape Daily Telegraph* and *Umtata Herald* all provided numbers of self-styled 'Loyal Natives' with outlets for their expansiveness.
'God forbid that through his writing he must pose as the organ of Native opinion, and
thus earn a lasting disgrace . . . upon our people, of turning upon the British people, their
benefactors',[35] is an excellent example of this brand of lament. And as an irate correspondent to *Imvo* itself quizzed its editor:

> Have you read Livingstone's Mission story? Has the Boer changed, think you? . . . is there
> not an eternal hatred in the heart of the Boer towards the aborigines of this country? Are
> the Natives allowed to own and possess land in the adjoining States? Are there Native
> institutions there? Is there a Native editor of a newspaper in either state? Would it be
> allowed, think you? Would you like such a state of things here?[36]

A flavour of injured righteousness and an insistence on upholding what was correct
conduct pervaded the correspondence of the African intelligentsia; there is only space
here to convey a hint of its tone.

As the war intensified, *Imvo*'s position worsened. *Izwi*, which had tacked successfully into the war wind, increased its edge as Jabavu's readership shrank. While it was
losing circulation among the African elite of the Eastern Cape and the Ciskei and
Transkeian Territories, African army auxiliaries acted as additional enforcers of a
patriotic consensus, shredding and burning *Imvo* on the streets.[37] In parts of the Eastern
Cape, district military press censors instructed magistrates and postmasters to withdraw *Imvo* from postal circulation; in several districts under martial law, it joined the
British socialist paper, *Reynolds News*, as proscribed reading matter.[38] To add to its
misfortunes, the paper suffered the withdrawal of subsidisation by its wealthy white
patrons, notably Rose-Innes and J. W. Weir. In January 1900, a bitter Jabavu condemned what he termed 'a deplorable campaign of boycotting', calling it a severe hardship 'to take bread from the mouths of a number of innocent beings who depend on the
Imvo business for a living'.[39] A further blow followed in July, when the paper's King
William's Town printing shop abruptly terminated its contract, forcing the transfer of
production to another firm in East London; this seriously disrupted *Imvo*'s distribution
system and burdened it with higher production costs.[40]

It was the eventual extension of martial law to the King William's Town district in
January 1901 which brought complete collapse. With the threat of prosecution for
sedition now immeasurably nearer, Jabavu trimmed his sails. Although he stuck to his
conciliationist stand, *Imvo* editorials became notably more muted. Thus, while he
cared little for autocratic martial law practices, Jabavu described the regulations as
'moderate' and urged Africans to observe them conscientiously. Indeed, as a passionate liquor abolitionist, Jabavu welcomed the martial law suspension of liquor sales and
closure of canteens to King William's Town Africans.[41] But despite its more accommodating stance, *Imvo* remained a provocation to the military authorities and publication was stopped in August 1901.

Imvo's demise produced widespread satisfaction. Soga, who had been urging the
military administration to muzzle it, was exultant, applauding the appearance of
'Nemesis' which had 'found out our Native contemporary at last'.[42] Equally smug was
the *South African Review*, which concluded that 'the line taken up during the war has

been such that no one can dispute the suspension'.[43] The paper was only to reappear again after the war, in October 1902. Obviously, *Imvo Zabantsundu* was bound to have become a casualty of the war; apart from facing white hostilities, any pro-peace black paper stood little chance against the strongly British identity and imperialist temper which coursed through the veins of Cape black political culture. The petty-bourgeois radicalism of this period, driven by the forces of aspiration and anxiety, was not pacific but warlike and demagogic in tone; from within an imperial heritage it was simultaneously and aggressively defensive and expansionist. It was polarisation, disruption and struggle between settler factions, not white conciliation, which provided orientation and identity for the core values of citizenship and an ideology of rights.

Imperial hopes and misgivings

The existence of a real point of juncture between a local British patriotism and its cross-border mission against Republican racial 'enslavement', meant that wartime interest in the fate of African people in the Boer territories was strong. Reports that Africans there were still subject to coercive measures even after imperial annexation in 1900 were received with considerable dismay. While conceding in September 1900, that 'representative' Cape political practice and administration could not be rooted 'wholesale' in the Transvaal, a Native Vigilance Committee in Alexandria nevertheless voiced its concern that African workers were still languishing under 'despotic laws' and asked why the imperial administration was displaying no desire to liberate Africans from repressive controls.[44] The unity imposed by the establishment of 'legitimate' British authority in the interior moved other association speakers to call in unison for 'an expansion of just rights for all classes of native'.[45] In July 1901, African army interpreters in Adelaide, Alexandria and Bedford drew up a fifty-signatory letter (including those of clerks and teachers) which called upon the imperial authorities to lend a more sympathetic ear to 'the voteless and rightless Transvaal Natives, whom neither education nor British civilisation has touched'.[46] Increasing hardship for industrial workers on the Rand even moved *Izwi* to appeal to imperial interests to curb capitalist exploitation of labour and to resist its imposing political power; in September 1901, Soga declared that 'while we recognise the advantages of capital so long as it is subservient to the interests of the state, we are equally alive to the terrible consequences of its unrestrained power which threatens to ... enslave the people by the sweating process, to undermine the stability of governments, and to dictate the policies of states'.[47] Such rumblings, however muted, led one British intelligence officer in Prieska to acknowledge at the beginning of 1901 that it was 'becoming clear that our victory over the Boers is not the embodiment of all ... [Africans] ... could hope for. Some complain that the rights of their ... brethren are being neglected.'[48]

Yet these troubled sentiments did not add up to any unified anti-imperialist political feeling in the Cape. Despite growing anxiety that African interests were being sold short, the Cape elites maintained their dominant and encompassing political alignment and continued to back the British. For faith in metropolitan Britain's moral willingness to do justice to African aspirations was deep and hard to shake. It is in this sense, then, that for groupings of professional and other incorporated Africans it was not British ascendancy over the former Republics but its conservative methods of administration that constituted a problem.

Ultimately, it was of course John Tengo Jabavu's sceptical attitude towards the initial imperial message of the protection of 'Native rights' and the attainment of 'justice', which proved to be the most realistic, hard-headed assessment of British policy intentions in South Africa. For the 'civilised', 'cultured' and educated Cape elite, Britain's deeds were not to correspond with its wartime promises and pledges. The implications of peace on the terms of the Treaty of Vereeniging for the formation and transformation of consciousness and more coherent black political organisation in Cape society and elsewhere in South Africa have been well covered by other historians. We need stress only that the imperial political act which proved the hardest to stomach and one which became the real *bête noire* of the Cape elite, was Clause Eight of the May 1902 Peace Treaty. This stipulated that 'the question of granting the franchise to Natives will not be decided until after the introduction of self-government'.[49] It was this discriminatory basis to the unification of settler South Africa which ensured that the Cape petty-bourgeois strata would emerge from the reconstruction years somewhat chastened. They were to enter Union with the threat of probable curbs upon their most prized 'civilised' right, the franchise, hanging over them.

For this and other reasons, the elite constituency became more wary of the style and substance of white politics after 1902; it was post-war disillusion which led to more independent formations of their political interests in the colony, such as the Coloured African People's Organisation and the South African Native Congress. And it is in this period that we see the stirrings of an Africanist politics in the Cape, seeking freedom from constraining settler manipulation and colonial control, cautiously constructing idioms of independent political representation, willing to fight more independent battles, and with a diminishing interest in docile flirting with 'friends of the natives'. What developed out of the post-war decade was what Bundy, in the context of his study of Headman Enoch Mamba as a 'populist moderniser', has termed 'more considered exercises in supratribal politics';[50] or what Marks has identified as the beginnings of 'an inclusive, liberal-democratic nationalism . . . in part a challenge to the exclusive nationalism being forged by the Afrikaner petty-bourgeoisie at the time'.[51]

Patriotism, class consensus and class insecurity

The exceptional historical 'moment' of the war years represented the achieving of a fully formed loyalist consciousness by the educated elite within black society. Among the Cape's outstanding African 'political communicators', John Tengo Jabavu's anti-war rhetoric certainly made him a minority of one. If patriotism as an organised, deliberate and purposeful phenomenon represented the consciousness of a minority, it was a vocal minority of somewhat contagious individuals. With no discernible ideological anti-militarism among the colonial peasantry and working classes, the defensive, conservative sensibilities of Cape British patriotism struck a responsive chord well beyond the social expression of specific petty-bourgeois concerns. However different the social experiences of the war for rural workers, peasants and urban petty bourgeoisie, there was a pronounced sense of a general integration into a patriotism centred on

British stability and British survival. The popular temper of 1899 to 1902 might thus be fruitfully contrasted with the experience of the later, and more remote, imperialist Great War, when, as Grundlingh has observed, 'the loyalist rhetoric from the educated elite' never had the reality and meanings to appeal much to the everyday life of the African working class.[52]

The Cape colonial 'Englandism' of the elite was certainly not created by the war, nor did it evaporate when it ended: what war did was to magnify its repertoire enormously. At this level of generality, it cannot be properly understood if the patriotic role of 'educated men' is regarded as simply representing the passive adoption of hegemonic imperialist values. A more fruitful approach might be to adopt the 'status-anxiety' thesis which social historians such as Richard Price have used to explain the roots of lower-middle-class patriotism and jingoism in late-nineteenth-century Britain.[53] In this case, the argument that economic insecurities and social and cultural pressures and tensions produced by 'broader social structural and political shifts of the later nineteenth century' could make militarist and imperialist outbursts the 'ultimate assertion' of 'respectability, duty and sacrifice' for beleaguered lower-middle-class elements, has an undeniable appeal. The analogy with the Cape is tempting. There, after the 1880s, fears and insecurities over land tenure issues like Glen Grey, attacks on African franchise rights and discriminatory designs in education policy all served to accentuate the vulnerability of the social position and ideology of the black petty bourgeoisie. It is this broader context of nagging social fear that may partly help to explain why *Izwi Labantu* and the *South African Spectator*'s patriotism was so feverish an expression of priorities and values. The watchful, shifting conditions of life for self-improving subordinate groups arguably helped to propagate a deepening identification with the security of an imperial liberalism which seemed to reassure.

For an imperial patriotism quickened by wartime was an implicit answer to colonial pressures upon the ethics of 'improvement' and 'responsibility'. It allowed the edgy black elite an association with the presumed beliefs and intentions of the winning side. In short, the attraction of the patriotic message for groups plagued by status anxieties was in essence its defensiveness and protectiveness; for a brief time, it even seemed to hold the promise of pushing the margin of 'civilisation' and safety as far north as Pretoria. This was to be an unattainable objective. But whatever the defeats and role constraints for the Cape's black elite, whatever the living patterns which shielded most of the political intelligentsia from direct exposure to the pathological rural feuding between Boers and blacks, what emerged was a record of wartime survival and a continuing cohesion of interests and outlook. Men such as A. K. Soga and J. T. Jabavu passed on to the post-war generation the message and the lessons of a struggle rooted in the dignity of enfranchisement.

4

Arms and patriotism: town guards and district militia

'What we need now', reflected a Colonel C. B. Donald in November 1899, 'is to get native town dwellers interested in local defence. My own view is that mustering respectable men together in a native militia will be most beneficial.'[1] Donald's hopes were to be speedily fulfilled as African and Coloured townsmen required little prodding to enlist in volunteer rifle corps. In many areas of the colony there was a general rush to arms, with organised, regular town guard forces soon growing tremendously in both number and size. Garrisons in turn varied in size, equipment, military efficiency and social composition. Some were composed of special constabulary (mounted or on foot) under black sergeants and corporals; others of barely trained barefoot irregulars, armed with ancient muskets, sticks, pitchforks or spears. Local auxiliary forces assumed a rich diversity of forms. In some appropriate instances, colonial commandants took the collaborative 'Native levy' system as their model. In other cases, such as localities in the midlands or the northwest, more indiscriminately chosen quotas of able-bodied men were signed up for duty. Consolidation was rapid. Black militia units, under British or colonial military command, were a prominent public presence over a large part of the Cape by 1901.

If we are to appreciate the implications of broad black involvement in local military defence, it is important to consider the circumstances surrounding the raising of militia forces. Which interests supported and which opposed the formation of garrisons? What military and policing functions were assigned to volunteers? What were their terms and conditions of service? How effective were they in combating invasion and disorder? And what were the political and social consequences of their recruitment?

Mobilisation and organisation

In the early months of the war, the deficiencies of a small and frightened settler constabulary, a paralysed magistracy and an overstretched army were all too evident. Officials in several isolated localities suddenly found themselves imperilled as Boer forces broke through gaps in defences and threatened the security of small rural towns. Magistrates were bound to call upon the assistance of Coloured townsmen and hastily improvised squads were posted to confront mounted guerrillas in the streets. In Griqualand West, Alfred Harmsworth, the magistrate of Klipdam, equipped an eager party of

41

Coloured and African mine labourers to defend the magistracy during October 1899.[2] The brunt of the early defence of Kuruman fell upon a small guard of Coloured men, officered by white policemen. John Brown, the local Anglican missionary, recorded that the magistrate and 'twenty natives and at least thirty half-castes' barricaded themselves in a mission chapel in November 1899 and held out against Boer sharpshooters for almost a week. In a further skirmish later that month, a number of Baster guards were killed defending their territory.[3] Elsewhere in the northwestern Cape there was similar haste to engage the services of volunteers. In Kenhardt, some thirty riflemen were recruited to defend the town during March 1900. When it fell, the local police chief was imprisoned by the occupying commando, incensed by his having armed Coloured auxiliaries against it.[4]

Jumpy magistrates were also quick to use their powers to form labour levies for the construction of defensive fortifications. In Sutherland, Somerset East, Victoria West, Fraserburg and Britstown, for example, labour gangs were set to work digging trenches, erecting earthworks, constructing barbed-wire perimeter fences and laying mines. The availability of fortification work provided many hundreds of agricultural labourers with opportunities for additional casual employment, particularly as they were frequently better able than unskilled urban servants to meet heavy demands of strength and fitness, and to work long hours. Wages and patterns of work varied considerably from place to place. Some authorities paid a miserly and most-exploitative 8d. per day, while others stretched to 2s. And while some magistrates preferred to spread what work was available, others opted to keep a smaller number of men fully employed on a regular basis. Fluctuating labour demands also encouraged a tramping pattern of local migration. If things were slack after the completion of barricades, gangs of workers would take to the road, moving on to nearby settlements in the hope of picking up similar jobs.[5]

Labour was sometimes also drafted to perform a day's task without pay. Army Service Corps officers reported encountering great difficulty in trying to persuade Africans to dig trenches in return for tins of bully beef, pork pies (mostly decayed or toxic after being shipped over from Britain!) or brass buttons. 'The days of beads and blankets', one soldier observed rather ruefully, 'are no more.'[6] The Graaff-Reinet magistrate was typical of several conscription-minded district officials who made use of captive labour. He compelled convicts to dig trenches and authorised the military to detail 'loiterers' and 'renegades' in the area; a group of forty were forced into heavy labour during February 1901.[7]

If compulsion was occasionally needed to bring the poorest hands out of doors, this was fairly insignificant when compared with solid and independent popular agitation from below for combat duty. The pressure of popular demand upon the administration to admit fit black volunteers to militia service graphically illustrates the extent to which communities perceived the Republican war effort to be a direct threat to their own interests and security. Restlessness about defence and fear of invasion produced a self-assertive demand for rights to associate under arms and to fight. During October 1899 rural Coloured communities, led by the propertied, called public meetings in Uitenhage, Bredasdorp, Swellendam, Caledon and Tulbagh, at which noisy support was expressed for the formation of 'Coloured Corps'. A journalist noted that 'speeches were strongly in approval of Coloured citizens being given the same privileges of defending their homes and property as Europeans'.[8] In Hope Town, a resolution was passed calling upon the authorities to recruit coloured militiamen, 'as Coloured men had already shown their loyalty in a practical way, in past Native troubles'.[9] Here and elsewhere, there were sharp calls for political boycotts if demands for weaponry were not acceded to. Declaring it to be 'truly a Coloured man's question', the secretary of a hastily constituted Williston Vigilance Committee hinted sourly in November 1899 that if a local guard was not assembled, property owners in the district might abstain from voting for government supporters in the next general election. In the following month, an army intelligence report noted that in both Kenhardt and Carnarvon, the cry among many Coloured residents was one of 'no rifle, no vote'.[10]

Correspondents also took up their pens against the recruitment of poor whites to district forces; 'respectable' Coloured citizens evidently glared in horror at the sight of ragged colonists suddenly patrolling the streets. In the eyes of one writer, it was

Map 3 Cape Colony, Magisterial Districts, 1897 (F. Stemmet. 1982).

politically risky and socially undesirable to recruit 'from a lawless class of low Boer', comprised overwhelmingly of poor 'non-respectables' like lime-burners and wood-cutters.[11] There was also an unfavourable response to the enlisting of other non-British immigrants. They were repeatedly resented as unwelcome and undeserving interlopers in whose favour colonial society discriminated unfairly. Such attitudes were clearly not without a material base. As one aggrieved writer declared in May 1901, 'we Coloured people have no chance to join an organisation such as the Town Guards, but outsiders are allowed in such as Greeks and Lebanese, some of whom can hardly speak English ... yet the Coloured man is promised equal rights and is told to shout "hurrah" for the flag'.[12]

Popular feeling that Coloured men had a perfectly legitimate right to bear arms in defence of their lives and property was of fundamental significance. Some spokesmen skilfully portrayed the demand as one which linked the needs of security with the responsibilities and established rights of citizenship. Citing as a precedent the raising of an Oudtshoorn Coloured Town Guard comprising 'many of our class of people, such as respectable property owners', a Graaff-Reinet correspondent fumed, 'we are told by our white neighbours that this is a white man's trouble and, as such, must be settled by them, but it is also our trouble. The Boers are at our doors, and we are entitled to defend our families.'[13]

There is abundant evidence from dozens of small towns and villages to suggest that resident communities displayed a remarkably well-ordered and well-directed capacity to press directly for the establishment of armed units. In Colesberg and Steynsburg, for instance, 'Coloured War Councils' were formed spontaneously during May and June 1900 by propertied inhabitants, including teachers, carpenters, tailors and other arti-sans. Squads of up to a hundred able-bodied men were offered to the authorities in both municipalities; rough attestation forms drawn up by the 'War Councils' gave the name, age, height and occupation of every volunteer.[14] Between February and May 1900, Appollus Snyders and Adam Dampas toured Hofmeyr, Middelburg, Tarkastad and Murraysburg on horseback and by bicycle, urging 'principal Coloured residents' to set up registers of loyal and reliable volunteers.[15] Numbers of vigilance committees, war councils and various associations for the defence of peace, property or liberty supplied the authorities with lists of able men who should be called upon to serve. A dramatic gesture of popular feeling took place on 15 September 1900, when around 250 Coloured men marched on the magistracy at night to demand uniforms and weapons. When met by the commandant who promised to give sympathetic consideration to their call, they dispersed in good order, their path home illuminated by the flickering effigy of Paul Kruger hung from a ladder on the back of a wagon.[16]

The immediate impetus for the raising of forces in Cradock and Richmond was the experience of fierce, running conflict between local inhabitants and commandos which broke out during the early months of 1901. There were sporadic disturbances involving refugee squatters and at least two armed raids upon the Cradock native location in which a number of youths were hauled off as forced commando labour. On 24 February, several African army scouts and police constables were shot on the northern outskirts of Cradock, having been posted there by the Cape Police merely a week pre-viously.[17] Writing to *Imvo* in March, a headman, T. N. Nanquela, declared that this loss of African lives 'arouses our blood to a great extent, because our people are excluded from this war'.[18] A further aggravation to townspeople was the close proximity of gangs of local 'low, rough Europeans' who, having been armed by Boer guerrillas, intimidated railway workers, robbed Indian pedlars and periodically interfered with district trade and labour movements by confiscating travel passes issued to Africans by the Cradock magistracy.[19] When Adam Oliphant and E. Swarts led a deputation to the commandant early in April, to insist upon places for blacks in the Town Guard, the mood they represented appears to have been solid. It was certainly sufficiently solid to override the remaining objections of the Cradock authorities and the apprehension of white merchants and employers. Colonel A. S. Henniker was stationed on 20 April to advise the Cradock commandant on the levying of a militia. Satisfied at 'having armed a good number of black boys properly', Henniker was subsequently incensed to discover that the 'Chamber of Commerce, the damn rebels, have had the nerve to complain about this'. He tried unsuccessfully to have members of the Chamber interned for treason.[20]

Richmond was another focal point of clashes early in 1901. Scattered incidents of violence involving commandos and black civilians indicate a similar set of tensions and confrontations to those obtaining in Cradock. The worst fears of the population were realised when a Boer force briefly seized control of Richmond's streets; Boer riflemen blazed away wildly at houses, sniped at townspeople and got into bloody scuffles with unarmed youths. After the commando withdrawal, Klaas Ambral, Kameel Erasmus and Jafta Steurberg presented a 150-name petition to the authorities, declaring:

> We, the undersigned Coloured residents of Richmond beg to petition that the Government may supply us with arms and ammunition, so to place us in a position to defend the Town, ourselves and families. We beg respectfully to bring to the notice of the Government that in February last when the Boers attacked Richmond, they shot two unarmed Coloured men, and if reports are correct which we continually hear, a Coloured man who falls into the hands of the Boers receives most brutal treatment from them; in view of this we shall only be too glad to assist in our own protection; moreover, we hear that at other Towns in this colony, Coloured Defence Forces are being raised. Consequently, we conclude that you should now forward this petition to the Government with your favourable recommendation.[21]

Stung into action, the magistrate lost no time in obtaining the approval of the Attorney General for the recruiting of Coloured town guards. Despite some opposition from members of the existing settler volunteer guard, the first squad commenced drill on 16 April 1901.

By no means all officials were so speedily convinced of the necessity for the establishment of regular forces. Among magistrates and colonial commandants there was hesitancy and unease about the formation of black militia. In many districts there was already widespread settler discontent over auxiliary recruitment into the British Army and over the raising of armed magistracy scouts and district mounted police. Local colonial commands were reluctant to run the political risk of being seen to be sanctioning the establishment of potentially wilful militia forces. British Army officers, on the other hand, had little or no patience with the timidity of colonial officials with whom they had to liaise. In Cradock, for example, the magistrate was initially scorned as a 'milksop' for dragging his feet over the issue of raising 'a strong native corps'.[22] And from Philipstown, in December 1899, a Lieutenant Phillips charged that the commandant was pandering to 'the prejudices of pestilential Europeans' in not immediately forming 'squads of well-armed native specials'.[23]

Military imperatives generally overrode local political preferences. While larger, secure cities like Cape Town could appease racist sentiment by blocking the entry of Coloured men to its Town Guard,[24] magistrates in more vulnerable spots faced times of continuing disorder and crisis, demanding urgent and effective action with all the resources they could possibly muster. The army might patrol the countryside, but id did not have the reserves to commit detachments of regular troops to garrison small towns.

Nor were there sufficient politically reliable colonists to bring town guards up to adequate strength in every settlement. Apart from the difficulty of encouraging rural Cape Boers to turn out on behalf of the imperialist cause, there were disquieting signs that those who did volunteer could be vulnerable to Republican pressure and subversion. Incorporation did not necessarily produce a trusting alliance; proletarianised Boers were not easily lured into an identification with the law-and-order concerns of dominant local social elites of state officials, small employers, merchants and shopkeepers. In January 1900, for example, an intelligence agent in Burghersdorp reported some riflemen ('low-class malcontents') to have gone over to the Republican side.[25] In March of that year, it was suspected that surreptitious offers of looted African stock were inducing white guards in Steytlerville to secretly switch allegiance to the Republics.[26] In Hanover an exceptionally meddlesome and bossy town commandant received a fright when his sergeant ('van Niekerk, a malicious degenerate') refused an order, telling him that soon the Cape government would be overthrown and his throat would be slit.[27]

The fact that the loyalty of white volunteers could not be automatically assumed everywhere served only to strengthen argument for recruiting blacks. With guards not billeted in barracks and therefore exposed to Boer agents, the problem of settler reliability was very marked in parts of the midlands and the northwest; here, the inclination to rely on potentially more loyal African or Coloured men was marked from the very outset.

The Cape government allowed officials considerable latitude over when and how guards were to be formed; initially, it also issued no guidelines as to the numbers or the duties and powers of any militia force. Responding to a request in November 1899 from the Upington magistrate for authorisation to mobilise a force of 200 Coloured men in the Gordonia district, John Graham, Secretary of the Law Department, advised, 'if you are satisfied attack is to be feared and you can now arm a sufficient number of reliable men, you are authorised to do so. It is most important to check the spread of invasion or rebellion wherever we can.'[28] The Attorney General advised magistrates that they had full discretionary powers to deal with defence as a purely local matter. The more zealous amongst them did not need much encouragement. In February 1901, the Martial Law Administrator at Adelaide despatched a confidential circular to magistrates in the eastern and southeastern Cape urging them to act energetically in enlisting 'Native specials'.[29] Several weeks later, A. Shuter, the Assistant Resident

Magistrate of Graaff-Reinet, announced, 'I beg to state that I entirely approve of arming Natives in towns and villages to repel an invasion of the enemy. The Natives as a whole are thoroughly loyal and will, I am sure, fight stubbornly . . . in Graaff-Reinet, there is a considerable number of Coloured persons who would also contribute to the strength of the Town Guard.'[30]

Limitations of source material made it impossible to determine precisely the numbers of men who served in local defence forces or to consider properly such relevant questions as average length of service and the share of war casualties borne by these garrisons. Muster Rolls for Native and Coloured town guard detachments were either not maintained by commandants or have not survived in the archives, so the overall proportion of black guards to colonists is unclear. What can be suggested is that there was considerable variation between districts for a host of local reasons. In places like Steytlerville and Jansenville, for instance, where a substantial section of the settler population was disaffected, a very large proportion of recruits would have been drawn from the black population.[31] Levels in more 'loyalist' settlements would have been lower.

Manning levels also fluctuated significantly. Town guards which recruited heavily among agricultural workers lost men during sowing and harvest seasons, unless defence needs were pressing. Migrant sheep shearers in the Karroo and the northeast still drifted off into the countryside as had always been the custom. But in localities where enemy forces posed a constant threat to everyday security, large squads of volunteers were on active duty for lengthy periods of unbroken service. Here they came to resemble a full-time standing militia.

On the reasonable assumption that virtually all small rural towns and villages in the interior employed town guards, and allowing for the flimsy basis of available statistical evidence, we may conclude that there were somewhere between 5,000 and 6,000 men under arms by the middle of 1901.[32] Garrisons also employed a further, unknown number of individuals as armed scouts, despatch runners and riders, and as messengers in cycling corps, as well as stepping up enlistment of police specials with new powers of search and interrogation.

Scattered figures for Coloured town guards and Native specials for the period July to October 1901 provide a sample indication of the local distribution of forces enrolled at this time. Companies raised under Colonial Defence Order No. 11 of 1901, in a cluster of six small towns, were as follows: Prince Albert – 54; Hope Town – 86; Willowmore – 106; Hanover – 119; Jansenville – 182; Steytlerville – 234. In northwestern districts, scattered company returns indicate that the proportion of Coloured militiamen in town garrisons was particularly large. Colonel White of the Namaqualand Field Force reported in April 1902 that of the Garies contingent of 471, 'only 90, are white men, the remainder Bastards'. They consisted of 239 Namaqualand Border Scouts ('mostly of the better class of agriculturalists') and 142 'intelligence specials and armed Bastard refugees'. Combined Battalion strength for Concordia, Na'babeep, Port Nolloth and Lambert's Bay was listed as 800 during February 1902; of these, 642 were described as 'loyal Coloureds'. In the copper-mining settlement of O'Okiep, the town guard employed 312 regulars, of whom 255 were Coloured riflemen. A further corps of 240 'native irregulars' was posted to guard mine workings and outlying blockhouses from January to May 1902. When Republican forces advanced into the district in March 1902 and began to menace O'Okiep, the hard-pressed military command equipped further large numbers of Coloured miners. During the major Boer offensive from 4 April to 3 May, the town guard complement was raised to over 660 and an additional 130 armed specials were recruited to secure heliograph and carrier-pigeon stations.[33]

The meagre evidence on the social class and ethnic composition of militia forces allows little more than a few observations about general trends. In certain instances, commandants were able to exercise a preference for traditional groups of colonial military collaborators; in Dordrecht, Aliwal North and Jamestown, various Mfengu, Thembu and Bhaca volunteers answered this requirement well enough. To British officers newly posted to town garrisons, Sotho men (the colony was, unfortunately, short on Zulu soldiers) were often thought to be best fitted to martial needs. Colesberg Town Guard, it was noted, employed 'very many Basutos of excellent character', while at Stormberg, 150 armed 'magnificent and muscular Basuto watchers' assisted in the patrolling of town perimeters and in preventing the pilfering of railway goods.[34]

Imperial preference seems to have been keenly appreciated by canny Africans who profitably redefined themselves in new identities. Thus, in Tarkastad in 1901, a large party of Ngqika and Gcaleka agricultural workers volunteered for service, breezily declaring themselves to be Sotho migrants from Mafeteng. When asked why by a puzzled Cape Mounted Rifleman who knew them well, they are said to have replied, 'Because it is the Basutos who are most wanted for the war.'[35] Lonsdale's observation that in colonial Africa, 'tribes were often born on the way to work' seems peculiarly apposite here.[36]

Outside those eastern and northeastern areas which had identifiable African communities with internal traditions of military collaboration, garrisons generally recruited men without ethnic distinction. Although there was some feeling that it was preferable not to recruit indiscriminately from local populations – from those of 'unruly habits and uncertain dispositions' – in practice there was little alternative.[37] In western, southwestern and northwestern districts, Coloured communities furnished the bulk of militiamen, while in the midlands, the routine formation of segregated Coloured town guards and Native detachments suggests that Coloured and African men shared military burdens and, occasionally, equally if separately.

Class composition and hierarchy

A significant feature of town guards is that riflemen were drawn mostly from that section of the working class which was more or less in regular wage employment. Recruits came from a variety of unskilled and semi-skilled job sectors; for example, there were concentrations of railway workers, miners, agricultural labourers, sanitary workers, house servants, building labourers and general casual labourers. Artisans also featured prominently in certain ranks. Blacksmiths, wheelwrights, masons and carpenters, 'an intelligent class of Cape Boy' were apparently well represented in the Sutherland Coloured Town Guard, while the Williston garrison was described as being 'very much of the artisan type'.[38] Displaced peasants who thronged many settlements after fleeing fighting in the neighbouring countryside also swelled militia ranks; service was one way of dealing with the increasingly worrying problem of protecting livestock or grain reserves.

NCO posts were generally filled by clerks, interpreters, government messengers, professionals like teachers, others involved in civil administration tasks and small masters in shops, like butchers or tailors.[39] The ideal force to drill and equip was self-evidently that comprised of 'respectable men', by which was meant those classes – skilled labour elites and petty-bourgeois owners – most thought to embody instinctive loyalty towards the imperial war effort, along with a solid commitment to uphold colonial authority and peace, property and order. However, those drawn from a small proprietorial milieu were only rarely present in sufficient numbers to constitute a numerically dominant and 'respectable' controlling element. Indeed, contrary to the fond aspirations of officials (to say nothing of the pride and expectations of some Coloured NCOs) town militia came to represent labourers, rather than property owners, under arms. The only reliable comprehensive occupational breakdowns which we have for Willowmore in January 1901 and Cradock in August 1901 provide some confirmation of this trend (see tables 1 and 2).

Militia companies were also young. Cases of men serving at relatively advanced ages were rare, and guards were overwhelmingly men in their twenties, thirties and early forties; here and there there were instances of middle-aged or older recruits or juvenile volunteers. Concern about the shortage of settlers to defend towns was

4 The 'Black Watch': African militia, Somerset East.
(Courtesy of the Greater London Record Office, Middlesex Records Division)

Table 1. *Occupations of the Native guard in Willowmore, January 1901*

Town labourers	59
Agricultural labourers	36
Gardeners	3
Government employees	2
Lime burners	2
Woodcutters	2
Harness makers	1
Total	105

Source: 'A Typical Native Levy', *Highland Light Infantry Chronicle*, 3/4, 8 (1901), pp. 558–9.

matched by worry that many of those who were volunteering were in fact unfit for combat duties owing to age and poor health. Of the ninety-seven colonists in the Garies Town Guard, sixty-six were judged completely non-effective, being 'old and weak', by Colonel White who added caustically that 'men over seventy are surely unfit for war service'.[40] In Port Nolloth, a 5th Lancers officer observed, 'The European men are fairly worn out, even after light piquet duties ... most are well over sixty years old, and not a few over seventy, and can't stand this work much longer.'[41] From other districts there were similar sorry tales of the obvious inadequacy of white riflemen to withstand the rigours of service and of disconcertingly low levels of morale.

In the opinion of advisory officers of the Army Medical Corps, the obvious solution was to weed out unfit colonists ('such as those who are half blind or crippled') and to restock companies with younger and abler black volunteers who were 'generally of superior fitness and physique'.[42] For colonial commandants, the recruiting of younger men rapidly became a primary concern; at Graaff-Reinet, to cite one instance, M. J. Slabbert, a recruiting officer, was advised to enlist 'only natives who are well under the age of thirty'.[43]

In April 1901, Colonial Defence Force headquarters in Cape Town belatedly issued a circular instruction to district commandants, sanctioning the formation of Coloured town guards under separate commands, and encouraging them to bring company strengths up to at least a hundred riflemen. This was no more than a lame attempt to impose a modicum of central scrutiny and bureaucratic direction over the ragged build-up of forces already undertaken as local initiatives. The achievement of some uniformity of structure between numerous separate forces was never within grasp. An issue of new Lee Mitford or Martini Henry rifles was authorised for companies of one hundred or more guards, which were assigned the same complement of officers stipulated for settler riflemen.[44] Town guards were to be led by white captains and preferably white NCOs and to have black sergeants and corporals as intermediates in the chain of disciplinary authority.

This was the ideal, but it was not always attained. There were some isolated – yet quite extraordinary – occurrences when those subordinate sergeants and corporals actually dislodged their superiors. At Dordrecht in January 1901 and at Victoria Road during June of that year, 'first-class Native NCOs', with the backing of regular British officers, replaced settler officers.[45] A captain and two NCOs at Prieska were dismissed

Table 2. *Occupations of the Coloured town guard in Cradock, August 1901*

Town labourers	98
Agricultural labourers	81
Railway labourers	13
Government employees	7
Tailors	1
Blacksmiths	4
Carpenters	2
Stonemasons	5
Total	211

Source: NAM, 6807/187, W. M. Eustace, Report on Employment of Native Companies, No. 4 Region, 2 Sept. 1901.

for inefficient management and 'poor understanding' of their detachment of African specials, and were replaced for a time by a bellowing Sotho sergeant known as 'John Impi', and two corporals, Ezekiel Dodwane and John Kabindline. 'John Impi' was favourably described as a 'huge black man and a crack sharpshooter, with a wonderful command of barrack-room English'.[46] Given the constant pressure from British army regulars to enlarge the military roles and policing powers of district auxiliaries, it was inevitable that such promotions would be viewed as a threat to the retention of firm and stable white authority and control. The integration of local peacekeeping interests between colonial commandants and British officers was always riven with divisions in both temperament and intent. With relations often fragile, the elevating of African NCOs brought consternation to colonial officials. 'To elevate the native so breeds disrespect for properly constituted authority and will lead to mischief', declared a typically worried and indignant Captain Halse of the Cape Police in February 1901.[47]

The national context of ideological ferment and flux, social and political challenges and reciprocities, and creative popular engagements produced by the war, took on its own shape and meaning in the local locus and experiential texture of identities of class and in the strands of culture, position and security. A striking characteristic of social relationships in town guards was interminable friction and even open squabbling between skilled and proud African volunteers and marginalised poorer whites who were now sometimes suddenly slotted into positions of lower authority. Not merely respected social leaders but also a wide mix of respectable working men felt aggrieved, even humiliated, at being made to defer to casual white navvies appointed over them as NCOs. When disciplinary relations brought blacks and coarse, rough-house Boers face-to-face, tensions and antagonisms could become especially acute. In Somerset East, it was said, 'these Piets are mostly useless because the Natives will always punch their heads when they get them off-duty'.[48]

The problem from a disciplinary point of view was that the authority exercised by unskilled whites as NCOs was not derived, to any degree, from their civilian rank. Ideally, that authority would have mirrored it. A consequence of the lack of unifying class continuities of power and authority was that the structure of militia control sometimes offended men's sense of self-respect and of external recognition of themselves as self-reliant bodies, capable of running their own affairs. One long-faced guard told an army officer in March 1901 that 'civilised native specials' were loath to drill and submit to the barking of 'European loafers'.[49] From Vryburg and Sutherland there were reports of restlessness, animosity towards white NCOs and stoppages on duty. The *Household Brigade Magazine* noted, with somewhat mixed relief, that 'troopers' there were 'not plotting mutiny', but were irritated at 'having to doff their caps to whites of the lowest class'.[50] Mutterings of discontent were not without effect. The more astute of commandants made efforts to appoint officers who would be more socially and politically acceptable to African privates. Men with the right kind of local standing could make all the difference. One such instance was at Pearston, in Griqualand West, when a point was made of appointing to the Native Volunteer Guard, 'local English farmers with a sound record of opposing the Bond at Elections'.[51] Such provision, a Colonel Levey suggested, would make Africans 'more amenable to receiving commands, issuing as they do from Europeans who share the natives' distaste for the Boer'.[52]

Paternalism and discipline

The general settler response to the authorities' call for officers requires some further examination. Patricia Morton, among other historians, has emphasised the late-Victorian view of the traditional role of the militia or volunteer home guard as 'the People's Army'. As a model of institutional co-operation and class collaboration, it was a general axiom of militia thinking that employers should undertake military obligations and accompany workers into the ranks.[53] Conditions in the Cape certainly conformed to this pattern. It was clearly recognised that employers were most naturally suited to fill company vacancies as officers and the class composition of those accepting commissions was invariably a solid reflection of local, propertied settler interests. Thus, in Tarkastad in August 1901, a Captain Vale appealed for 'better class Europeans, preferably with experience of dealing with . . . labourers'[54] to accept commissions. Agricultural labourers in western and southwestern districts found themselves under the command of colonists on whose lands they toiled. By 1901 it had become fairly commonplace for employers to exhibit recruiting notices at places of work and to move in and out of town guard ranks themselves. White merchants, traders, farmers and other businessmen of varying substance were firmly interlocked with structures of control in the militia.

The active involvement of settler-employers in local town guard affairs was a significant factor. In the newly unsettled world of the rural village and small market town, regulation of an orderly everyday life in the continued negotiation and consolidation of hegemony became a priority for the local ruling class. It was important to bind workers to employers at a time when the local economy was feeling the unwelcome and trying effects of labour redistribution and the breakdown of servile attitudes among workers. Accordingly, militia service offered its higher-ranking members more than brandy and a regimental cigar with visiting British Army officers; it brought an opportunity to connect worker loyalty to employers at a time when labour was adopting a more brash and independent posture.

Moreover, it was recognised that the commissioning of masters would, where necessary, greatly ease the recruitment of rank-and-file militiamen. Settlers who expected to officer armed members of the local labour force would be likely to provide encouragement for, perhaps even apply pressure on, reluctant workers to enlist. Finally, the actions of 'big' settlers in taking up commands enabled them to fulfil a notable symbolic role as the visible embodiment of constitutional British order, authority and duty. Through their involvement in the local drama of invasion scares they could not only reinforce their standing and leadership but also assert an identity of interest between masters and men in the face of an external enemy.

Where conditions required such action, commissioned colonists proved to be exceptionally persuasive recruiting agents, rarely exempting employees from military obligations. At the beginning of 1901, *Lloyds Weekly Newspaper* noted, 'the Town Guard movement is being enthusiastically taken up by all classes and grades of Cape colonial society. Employers of labour in particular are doing everything in their power to assist their native employees in joining the appropriate corps.'[55] Works managers, contractors and store owners were typical of those who gave a major fillip to recruitment by swearing in workers. From the Ciskei and elsewhere in the Eastern Cape, there were reports of traders cajoling African debtors into service as a means of getting their hands directly upon cash incomes. From anguished protests lodged by some African riflemen in places like Alice and Alexandria, it appears that with the collusion of commandants, some traders had little compunction in arbitrarily extracting debt repayments from wage packets.[56] As prospective NCOs, small masters and labour foremen sometimes brought along black recruits. On Namaqualand Railways, white platelayers and gangers brought, individually, 'on average, 6 to 9 Bastard navvies with them'.[57] At Cradock and Willowmore, railway foremen mobilised and commanded squads of Coloured railway workers, who were attached to town garrisons as railway guards.[58]

The desired end being employer hegemony over a disciplined and dutiful militia force, many companies were closely structured in ways which emphasised the subordination of black volunteers to a local settler command. More often than not, volunteers would find themselves in garrisons in which discipline and the control of units in action rested personally with colonists who were their immediate employers or taskmasters in civilian life. Men were frequently more likely to feel the impact of their own employers than the impact of a Mauser cartridge.

The paternalism of social leadership by militia 'honourables' was invariably the usual combination of firm discipline and benevolence. There were reserves of customary distribution and relations of deference which local ruling elites could draw upon to help weld men into a stable, reliable and loyal force. At Jansenville, a merchant and town guard officer issued free coffee and biscuits to African squads on night patrol. Several leading colonists ('gentlemen of means') supplied provisions for special garrison dinners, graced the table and made speeches about orderly community and duty to men in Willowmore. In Burghersdorp, officers opened a subscription to provide relief for distressed families who had lost breadwinners on active service. There were gratifying responses; in 1901 African sergeants at Dordrecht thanked farmer-officers of the district for 'helping those who are in need'.[59]

Garrison duty also helped to ensure that in their free hours away from normal employment increasingly impulsive workers would not snatch periods of release from the discipline and restraint of the wage relation to make public mischief. With relations of control firmly structured, there were great hopes that the militia experience would smoothly reinforce ultimate settler authority in daily life in immediate, visible ways.

In some companies industrial and military disciplines certainly seemed to merge, as prominent colonists utilised their civilian status as a means of controlling labouring militiamen. Here was the leverage to enforce their preferences. The trappings of effective personal authority and control of employers over workers was about as complete as it was possible to get. For example, workers at the Indwe Colliery mustered together in the Dordrecht Native Volunteer Guard were officered by Edward Allman, a labour superintendent at the mine. During 1901 Allman indicated that diligent militia service might gain miners credit with the Indwe mine management.[60] Namaqualand Town Guard Battalions in Garies, Concordia and O'Okiep were remunerated by paymasters of the Cape Copper Company (which retained rights of hiring and firing) and drilled by mine foremen. Coloured mine police and 'boss boys' from the O'Okiep labour compound were enrolled as corporals, further cementing the link between military and industrial discipline. On 2 April 1902 the O'Okiep copper mine ceased operations and turned its entire labour force over to Colonel J. S. Shelton, the town commandant, to help buttress local defences. The man appointed to manage the new recruits was the superintendent of the Namaqualand Copper Company, George Dean. Described as 'a great power over the Natives in Namaqualand', Dean was given the ludicrously inflated rank of major in the Namaqualand Field Force and was later commended for 'maintaining a good state of discipline in the Native ranks'.[61] In the context of such taut styles of authority, it is arguable that the authoritarianism of the labour regime in mining would have conditioned industrial workers to respond amenably to military discipline and drill, as V. G. Kiernan has suggested in his illuminating discussion of colonial army recruitment in Africa.[62]

Two key issues emerge from the establishment of these mechanisms of control. The first is that methods of control were indeed constructed by local dominant elites as a contribution to the stabilisation of the social order as a whole. The other point is that it is important to keep sight of the fact that while the propertied went to time, trouble and sometimes even personal expense to maintain order and discipline, reliance on formal methods of social control did not always make the militia a lubricant of harmonious or ordered relations. The assiduous extension of settler authority into the military sphere did not produce at every turn obedient conduct and a deferential demeanour on the part of uniformed employees.

For despite expectations that militia service would instil habits of employer-approved self-discipline, sobriety and orderliness, the conduct of certain companies was anything but tractable. For instance, in reporting on the conduct of even the Dordrecht Native Town Guard during February 1901, Colonel H. R. Kelham detected 'a deplorable tendency towards behaving like common street roughs'; several months later, the *Highland Light Infantry Chronicle* described a fracas involving guards and the Dordrecht Police, sparked off by the guard 'taking pot shots at the town clock. Their ideas of discipline are rather primitive.'[63] Garrisons were not always content to be passive until ordered to act by their officers; they relished making their own dramas to alleviate boredom. When districts were calm, idle riflemen amused themselves by spreading rumours that rebels were gathering on nearby farms. This invariably caused a great hue and cry as shops were boarded up, streets were cleared and gleeful guardsmen paraded about to the bang of drums and the tinny notes of bugles; the 'emergency' would also provide garrison scouts with exercise and extra pay as they were despatched to comb districts. The manoeuvrings of Bedford militia, tersely dubbed 'Fingoe force' by an ever-imaginative army intelligence staff, were apparently regularly led astray by 'feverish excitement' and 'wholesale recklessness'; their wayward behaviour reduced their exasperated attending officers to a frantic state.[64]

Leisure and action

Customary competing local identities and solidarities not only persisted in some places but probably intensified through new organisational ways of expressing popular communal rivalries. Thus, relations between African militia forces in Aliwal North, Lady Grey and Burghersdorp were flecked by boisterous triangular rivalries. Companies indulged in acts of ritual aggression to demonstrate their sense of military stature and self-pride. Burghersdorp riflemen ('dressed up very fantastically with black and yellow feathers') challenged their counterparts in Lady Grey to sham fights, at which large baying crowds gathered to support each side with partisan fervour.[65] Wagering in some form or other was widespread. Human wrestling and knife-edge scorpion and dog-fighting contests in Lady Grey led to squabbles between opposing camps and to occasional brawling between Sotho and Mfengu militiamen. Hardly a report of 'sports' in regimental journals does not contain some mention of the militia's love of violent and drunken sports.[66]

Forces undoubtedly exercised a powerful attraction upon civilians. They were home defenders *par excellence*, stalwart protectors of the citizenry who were both local and decorative. Aside from their purely military activities, as a new form of popular organisation they added variety to the social and recreational life of rural communities. In many places distinctive new kinds of popular entertainment and attraction matured in the town guard institution, for the militia offered men a break from work and a chance to take part in more exciting pursuits which could bring some sense of achievement and renown. At Garies, for example, there was a garrison brass band whose players were drawn from the Steinkopf German mission; by providing music, parading banners and a show of freshly minted military traditions, the guard drew affectionate crowds to its weekly processions and became an essential ceremonial part of any public function.[67]

Mustering for drill and rifle-shooting also took on an air of festivity, with gatherings of spectators, speeches by officials on the conduct of the war and patriotic addresses by local black proprietors or clergymen. Every garrison seems to have had its own revered sharpshooter, such as the mason Cornelius Arendse of Concordia, a man respected for his fists as well as his eye.[68] The following description of events in Aliwal North during March 1901 is a fairly typical representation of the atmosphere and actors:

> In addition to the Native Town Guard here, we have a further 200 Natives, mostly Fingoes and Basutos, who are dotted along at likely places on the perimeter. They are officially called Native Watchers, and are armed with Martini Henry rifles . . . a tough looking crowd, some wear Kaffir cooking pots on their heads, as their own local head-dress . . . Tin billies and handkerchiefs full of cow dung for fuel are slung at the end of the rifles and every man is swathed in two or three gaily-coloured blankets. The Watchers drill and train with the main native garrison on Saturdays, and such occasions provide an unprecedented treat for the native population, which attends the affair in vast numbers. There are prize shoots and mock battles, which are very popular. The assembled native throng partakes of music and singing, and one of the better educated native NCOs usually says a few suitable words.[69]

To volunteer was respectable but not necessarily respected by everyone in authority. Among a few regular army officers there was apprehension about perceived deficiencies of discipline and 'character' in Coloured companies. Generals Settle and French were in mutual agreement that absolute reliance could not be placed on north-western garrisons as 'most of these are Coloured, and may not offer much resistance'.[70] In the Namaqualand Field Force itself, Colonel Cooper was equally scathing, expressing his 'lack of faith' in the militia and concluding, 'one simply can't trust the Coloured men of the Town Guard without a considerable stiffening of reliable Fingoes'.[71]

However, such suspicions of the combat willingness of Coloured garrisons proved to be unfounded. First, as enemy offensives against small towns were mostly scrappy affairs, even half-trained militia forces were sometimes able to put up a respectable resistance. Second, and more crucially, mobilised men shared a set of well-founded expectations and beliefs about the violent and repressive consequences of any local Republican conquest. They understood well enough that if they took flight they would be hunted down mercilessly by hard-eyed *veldkornets*. For Boer malice was widespread, enduring and intense; it invariably ruled out retreat or contrite surrender for local defenders. Finally, the close identity, local solidarities and *esprit de corps* of the militia were self-conscious unifying forces, impelling men to stand firm and united in resistance.

And a number of enemy incursions were indeed repelled. When, for example, Somerset East was threatened early in March 1901, Coloured volunteers found that the commandant was unable to equip all of them adequately. Undeterred, they improvised their own weaponry and scrambled to man defences.[72] According to Brown, Kuruman labourers undertook prolonged and fatiguing periods of service; some privates were armed only with pitchforks and sharpened stones, while fifty men in the Somerset East forts had merely ten obsolete muzzle-loaders between them. Despite repeated raiding to try to dislodge them from their position, this motley force held together tenaciously.[73]

Although armed encounters were waged with considerable determination, fighting was seldom particularly bloody and casualties also tended to be relatively light. The numbers of combatants on both sides were small and confrontations mostly took the form of sporadic exchanges of gunfire. But it must again be stressed that militia service was highly risky. Where captured settler guards were liable to be roughed up at worst, their black subordinates were virtually certain to be severely assaulted or executed.

Reporting the capture of forty-eight militiamen at Pearston on 3 March 1901, the *Graaff-Reinet Advertiser* welcomed the release, unharmed, of five colonists, but added a worried note as 'the Coloured prisoners the Boers have taken off with them, and it is feared that something serious may happen to them, as the enemy seems to be very severe with them, using their sjamboks to drive them on'.[74] Early in April their corpses were found dumped in the veld. At Klipfontein, Muishond, Concordia and Na'babeep in the northwest, Boers did not maltreat captive white NCOs but summarily shot their small squads of 'native watchers'.[75] On a number of occasions audacious commandos raided Native locations at places like Willowmore and Molteno, abducting off-duty guards under cover of darkness and subsequently shooting them. Their bodies were left prominently displayed in an evident attempt to scare and intimidate local Africans.[76] The grisly fate of a squad of the Adelaide Native Guard which was seized by the Kritzinger commando during August 1901, only came to light six months later. Then, tipped off by an informer, the authorities dug up a crop field on an abandoned farm; called to examine the unearthed corpses, the Adelaide district surgeon recorded that each man had been shot through the back of the skull.[77]

In some areas, the identity and purposes of militia forces were as much internal patrolling as a special constabulary as external defence. Companies came to be incorporated as a reinforcement for hard-pressed regular police, battling to control the disorderly influx of refugees who were fleeing the turmoil of the countryside for the greater security of guarded settlements. Municipal administrations lacked sufficient manpower to wield effective authority over African squatters and turned to the militia to help to enforce control; magistrates, notably in the midlands and the northeast, commonly resorted to using town guards as special constables to apply emergency municipal regulations and to uphold both military and civil law.

In Bedford, Maraisburg and Steynsburg, trusted men were sworn in as Special Native Military Police, 'to maintain order and generally watch the natives'.[78] Under mounting pressure from irate farmers fuming about the disuse into which the Masters and Servants Act was falling, the Graaff-Reinet authorities used militiamen to locate and flush out labourers who had deserted their employers and secreted themselves in the native location.[79] Town guards doubling up as police specials also enforced demands from an overbearing and grasping magistrate, Anthony Garcia, for grazing fees from refugee stockholders, conscripted unemployed youths for sanitary work in the Army Service Corps and regularly patrolled the bulging location, 'to prevent unlawful itinerant Natives, chiefly washer women, prickly pear gatherers and lime burners, from entering or leaving'.[80] This last imposition must have created much bitterness amongst those trying to scratch a survival in the face of rising urban living costs.

A policing factor undoubtedly inserted some frictions into militia relationships with local communities as a whole. The operation of patrols presented an intrusion into locations not previously kept under such close routine surveillance. And snooping and interference was deeply resented – most strongly in the common enforcement of directives curbing free movement and assembly in public places. There is evidence to suggest that when they were used for close internal policing, rather than just maintaining security, town guards forfeited some of their popular standing. Thus, a police 'special' who wished to avoid crossing residents whose property and lives he defended as a militiaman, would prudently confine himself to picking upon visible 'outsiders' when exercising powers of search and dispersal.[81]

Conditions and opportunities

Permanent Town Guard Standing Companies were allocated regulation-issue equipment from ordnance depots and district stores which supplied Infantry Colonial Corps. Militiamen mounted on their own horses received a cash allowance for animals and saddle equipment (which fluctuated between one and two shillings per day) and horse rations. For many recruits, regulation dress did not run to adequate warm clothing for winter months. For example, the Royal Marines journal, *Globe and Laurel*, criticised the commandant of the Queenstown Native Town Guard for not providing warm stockings, blankets and boots for thinly clad riflemen; a Captain Stokes-Rees was one of a number of Marine brigades' officers who responded by donating surplus blankets.[82] Some bold and enterprising British officials creamed off local tax monies to help to fund small clothing workshops or allocated production to 'shops' to supply winter garments.A few knitters and weavers enjoyed a brisk trade, aided by the sweat of female domestic servants drafted in on miserably low day wages to cut material or sew buttons.[83] But supplies from these and other official sources were erratic and wholly inadequate; pilfered British infantry greatcoats remained much sought after.

Official colonial draft orders on wages for companies were issued early in 1901. Commandants were directed that all 'Coloured N.C. Officers and men, when actually called out for service, will receive half the rates of pay as issued to White men ... they will also receive 1s. 3d. money allowance when rations cannot be issued.'[84] This discriminatory pay scale caused some unhappiness among militia members and even provoked a protest or two from official quarters where there was worry about its possible impact on morale. But known custom and discriminatory practice prescribed that black wages be minimised. The Adelaide magistrate expressed what was probably the general view when he declared, 'less pay does not mean the Coloured man's services are less worthy. It is an incontrovertible truth that the white man is usually paid more. We cannot meddle with this custom, whatever the circumstances.'[85]

The official scale laid down for Coloured companies was as follows: men providing their own horses and saddles, 4s. per day, plus rations and forage allowance; men on foot without equipment, 3s. per day, plus rations. A sum of either 1s. 3d. or 1s. 6d. per day was distributed when full rations or hay were unavailable.[86] African garrisons received roughly the same entitlement although, inevitably, their ration allowance was inferior. In themselves, militiamen's official earnings tell us relatively little about their real standards of living during the war; local wage movements were not uniform in this period nor were rises in the price of food or fuel. What can be reliably concluded is that there were marked differences in income from place to place and that the fortunes of militia volunteers fluctuated accordingly.

For example, men in what became standing companies made virtually constant wages, while the earnings of those called out for watch duties on a day basis were naturally irregular. Moreover, some commandants reduced the real value of wages by deducting for equipment breakages, while others did not impose penalties. And finally, rates of discretionary payment administered at local level were highly complex and their determinations bore only a loose relation to fixed wage scales established by the Cape Law Department; they were complicated enough almost to merit a chapter to themselves. In some districts, special payments were widespread. Mounted riflemen who undertook additional scouting duties could be paid as much as 8s. per day plus their keep and an extra bonus in kind (such as milk, butter and live poultry) which not only insulated them from the pressures of wartime price inflation and shortages, but enabled them to accumulate savings. Where necessary, as in a tense and chronically insecure Namaqualand, supplements were paid for hazardous duties. And elsewhere, at a place like Middelburg in the northern Cape, regulars of a special crack platoon of Coloured riflemen received as much as 12s. per day when watches included night duty.[87]

There are also indications that guards could take advantage of their position to supplement earnings through various – mostly shady – kinds of petty entrepreneurial activities. Sergeants in charge of garrison supplies became an invaluable source of commodities for civilians chafing under shortages and rationing and willing to pay a suitable price to overcome them. Two Coloured quartermasters in Sutherland were prosecuted for secretly selling forage and biscuits to refugees on their own account. A sense of corporate loyalty led to men covering up for one another's misdeeds; one corporal, for instance, was disciplined for failing to report that another, William Josephs, had spent station duties selling beer. Exemption from martial-law pass controls on travel enabled men to roam districts where some of them bullied farmers and were able to exact protection payments by the mere threat of denouncing them as pro-Boer collaborators.[88]

Livestock and timber were sometimes also confiscated illegally, ending up as meat and fuel in local markets. For conveying illicit liquor from stills in native locations to army camps, scouts in the Stormberg district were rumoured to be clearing 2s. 6d. per night.[89] The authorities appear to have been largely helpless to check smuggling and other ways of milking official positions for private advantage. The fact that an entire company might have involved itself to a greater or lesser extent in petty criminality presented insuperable problems to any commandant seeking prosecutions, as the Alexandria magistrate woefully acknowledged in February 1902.[90]

Men also found themselves well equipped to profit from their uniforms and weaponry in unofficial protective relations with black residents. As a home guard they were the natural resort of anxious rural refugees desperately wanting protection for themselves, their stock and what household goods they had managed to rescue from Boer depredations. A coercive constabulary influence reflected only one side of what could be ambivalent relations; in another respect, there was pleasant and rewarding collusion for the militia. At Prieska, for example, a platoon under the command of a wily NCO called Joseph Mrara turned out as night cattle guards to protect the livestock of displaced peasants on open pasture land on the municipal outskirts. This off-duty service came at a price: owners paid retainers in cash or grain.[91] 'A regular battalion' of young boys was armed with heavy sticks and drilled by riflemen in Philipstown; a fee of 2s. 6d. per recruit was extracted from elder kinsmen.[92] And from Fraserburg,

Sterkstroom and Molteno in 1900 and 1901 there were reports of guards training small bands of refugees privately outside town limits and levying sums ranging from £5 to £10 on headmen for their services.[93]

In turn, such initiatives did much to fan the war mood in small settlements. And they flourished with some encouragement and contrivance from above; British Army officers billeted locally to advise commandants refrained from curbing the growth of unofficial 'specials', and in some instances actually encouraged the licensing of small bands of civilians to carry rifles 'for defence and security'.[94]

A principal concern of the authorities was the regulation of firearms. In certain towns, gun issue and gun practice were strictly controlled by commandants who were nervy about the potential, if not intention, of militia volunteers to stir up serious trouble if left unsupervised. Ammunition was either retained by officers or hand-picked sergeants and distributed prior to drill or active deployment; otherwise all rifles were deposited in the magistracy armoury when not in use. In Bedford and Alexandria, strict quotas were imposed for the distribution of live rounds and there were cartridge counts to try to ensure that African riflemen could not stockpile bullets for themselves.[95]

However, such curbs do not appear to have been very widely enforced; indeed, the control of some armouries was extraordinarily lax. It was not uncommon for volunteers to retain their firearms and only relinquish them at the end of the war; guns were simply stored in their homes. There is also evidence of the actual registration of guns being in complete disarray. The Middelburg commandant conceded privately that he was quite unable to tell how many rifles had been issued to Africans, adding, 'it is not unlikely that some of the more wily native specials now possess more than one Lee Enfield'.[96] A traveller arriving in Middelburg in September 1901 recorded his astonishment at the sight of 'hundreds of gun-carrying aboriginals, strutting up and down'.[97]

Slackness in the imposition of controls is at least in part a reflection of the administration's perception that militiamen were sufficiently dependable to be entrusted with weaponry on a continuous basis. As for the various individual militia bodies themselves, how far constant larking about with guns was genuine anxious vigilance and how far it was also a form of Dutch courage or masculine bragging it is difficult to know. What we do know is that town-guard volunteering, whatever its artifices, was a way of life with its own engaging camaraderie and with brandished guns its own cherished, ritual expression of territorial position and association.

There was little discussion of the role of town guards in the Cape legislature; the natural desire of the colonial government was to keep the political temperature down. It was not until the post-war period that the question was debated properly and by then the chief aim of the Sprigg ministry was to put the whole uncomfortable episode behind it. On 29 August 1902, the government conceded that 'in many cases Natives had to be employed . . . The military authorities were as much averse to the employment of Natives as anyone else. But the towns had to be defended.' The prime minister insisted that their use had been subject to strict conditions. He 'had laid it down as a rule that Coloured people were not to be allowed to join the defence forces, except in . . . exceptional circumstances . . . they were allowed to bear arms in self-defence, but they were not allowed to go outside the limits of the town'.[98]

Post-war reports that Coloured militiamen were still in possession of firearms alarmed some rural MPs who, while favouring the retention of guns by colonists, clamoured for the swift disarmament of militiamen. Disarmament duly took place, but in fairly leisurely and piecemeal fashion as there were no real signs that discharged riflemen were endangering the peace. Finally, in reporting to parliament in October 1902, Sprigg took pains to dispel rumours that the government was harbouring plans to enrol Coloured riflemen in a permanent colonial defence force.

A soldiering community

Militia organisation might aptly be seen as a late embodiment of some of the key values of the earlier, mid-Victorian expression of the Cape liberal tradition; townsman patriotism, local initiative and local worthiness, and class harmony in service based on a shared sense of place and obligation, were all promoted by the day-to-day tasks of defence and security. While there may have been persistent undercurrents of unruliness running through certain of the ranks, there was mostly approved discipline and order. Above all, town-guard volunteers were fiercely loyal to colonial authority.

But this is not to say that these bodies should be seen as merely representing another co-opted group, marshalled from above as an important stabilising force in the Cape's war emergency. In terms of the particular position and perceptions of riflemen themselves and their role in the shaping of their own adaptations to colonial rule's loss of local cohesion, there are a number of other factors which help to explain their stance. On one level, as garrisons were not subject to harsh or brutal military discipline, they did not develop any collective grudges against the military establishment: desertions, for example, were virtually unknown. There was also no serious discontent about pay and conditions. Not only were money wages relatively good in large, regular forces, but there were other perks and bonus benefits which enabled men to make gains. Like many of those who were contributing tangibly to the war effort, they were not abandoned to wartime inflation.

On a deeper level, patriotic soldiering brought status. Having won the trust of most officials and army regulars, town guards acquired a sense of endowed dignity and even self-importance. This pride was enhanced by interlocking workplace, family and other associations, and by the influence of paternalist engagement which had leading colonists and Cape officials gracing garrisons with their beaming presence, dispensing small-scale patronage and fanning the national interest. Furthermore, local forces were simply able to derive far greater advantage from their role in keeping the peace than in endangering it. For service was unquestionably a peculiar blend of duty, risk and popular pastime. Alongside the military staples of drill, parades and shooting, which were not inconsiderable backslapping attractions in themselves, all manner of small benefits, small freedoms and small discretionary powers accrued to enlisted men. They included the wielding of authority over both white and black civilians, unrestricted personal mobility between districts, the prestige of ostentatious gun ownership and opportunities and extra income margins to pursue recreational pleasures. Town guard organisation had something of the attractive element of a club; one could meet one's friends and relatives there, enrol in order to join them and pursue some undoubted enjoyment. Such practices contributed greatly to the status and self-image of the town militia.

A further decisive factor was the looming and violent presence of local Republican rebels or Orange Free State invaders. This ensured that militia volunteers concentrated their energies on arming against an external foe and digging in to protect their spheres of life. In the prevailing climate, struggles against new 'conquest' were struggles of substance in themselves. This preservationist impulse drew 'respectable' household-ers and common labourers into a coherent alliance of communal arms and vigilance. For there was an understanding that any threat to the fabric of stability and security would surely open the way to Republican advance; any disturbance of social peace was to give commando commandants their chance to step into the breach. Communities were acutely aware of what was at stake for the prevailing configuration of local cul-tures and relations of work, property and law.

It is commonplace for historians to emphasise the fervent pro-British patriotism of black communities in the Cape. The popularity of the town guard or militia movement certainly provides vivid confirmation of such sentiment; there can surely be few more obviously patriotic acts than to volunteer to defend your home country against enemy invasion. Yet, an equally significant contingent question remains to be asked: what *kind* of patriotism induced individuals to enlist? For what needs to be stressed here is the localised, self-assertive and indigenous nature of the patriotism of the Cape arti-sanry and working class; what needs to be noted is its distinctive appropriating force of common rights. What is apparent is the manner in which local residents imposed their own meanings of patriotism. These arose from the experiences and struggles of the war, as well as from culture and politics – the power of popular sociability, of kinship, neighbourhood and community securities could all shape a defensive yet also pugnacious kind of 'patriotic', folksily familiar district politics. While the militia may have represented patriotic expression, that should not be interpreted as the product of a simple, unmediated absorption of an imperial creed.

This chapter has argued that the emergence of town guards owed something to the determining demands and pressures of agitated communities in response to fears of disorder and breakdown, as well as to colonial initiative and prompting. And these bod-ies marched as a result of their own history and on some of their own terms. They were not essentially dragooned into service as Krupp-fodder in a baffling squabble between ruling factions. Their rush to arms was not just a rush to protect the lives of their masters or the security of big property, but the rights of a willed 'community' of citizens. For working-class volunteering exemplified a level of self-awareness of citizenship and represented a demand for the exercise of citizenship rights, and a recognition of its status, through the bearing of arms. In sum, militia formations presented an unusually pre-eminent expression of a civic culture of citizenship; with a strong corporate sense of identification with the interests of town or community, they might perhaps be seen as bearing some resemblance to the famous First World War 'Pals Battalions' formed in British industrial cities.[99]

Militia from very different localities, each with their own specific class and ethnic contours and their own level and style of combination, constructed a common yet locally self-conscious identity. Their dominant pose was keeping both feet in a rough-

and-tumble patriotism of the streets. And through their own initiatives, and the influence of the wide range of local interests from which they derived their support, they identified the battle with the Boer Republics as inescapably and intensely their own cause.

Association with these forces, and the attendant risks, reward, fears and resentments, served to reinforce participants' interpretation of their needs and obligations as that of sustaining law, order and loyal citizenship. For the quality of the war in the Cape provided otherwise divided workers, artisans or clerks with a common self-definition as *the* dependable law-abiding class. As the bearers of violence and lawlessness, it was Boers who were 'beyond the law', a threat not just to the props of colonial government but to the social defences and material interests of the lawful. This element provided, as we shall see in a later chapter, the individual ideological moorings of Abraham Esau's war. And it was in this sense that black resistance and struggle in an insecure world had its own vision. In its militia embodiment, that vision diverged somewhat from the simple 'men and masters'[100] nexus of Victorian volunteer peacekeeping. For 'these natives', as a British soldier observed in November 1900, 'think this war to be their own'.[101]

5

Moving Lord Kitchener: military transport and supply work

> Sir, we are willing at all times to do our duty for the Queen. Our great multitudes of waggons and beasts are already moving Lord Kitchener into battle against the Boer pestilence. I have several good waggons and loyal drivers to assist the soldiers in this war. Please accept our humble services. We are free and strong Native subjects, who will do the business of carrying and fetching today, tomorrow and many long days afterwards, until the British flag rules over all.[1]

These were the words of Paul Mahlungu, a petty-transport contractor to the Queenstown Remount Depot, on 22 August 1900, just a week after Kitchener's columns had launched a major sweep against Republican forces under Steyn and De Wet. Mahlungu's comments crystallised something of the mood and spirit of African transport auxiliaries at this time, when men everywhere were applying themselves imaginatively to a new situation of shifting work structures and expanding opportunities.

This chapter considers the experiences of Cape African and Coloured transport workers, allied service workers and produce and other commodity suppliers upon whose wheels, anvils, fields and backs the imperial war effort rolled forward. Its particular emphases are on the structure of wartime working communities, on the role of rank-and-file non-combatant auxiliaries, on the construction of workplace culture, on the nature of work relations and the pressing pace of work itself, and on the variety of responses and practices of the thousands of able-bodied men and youths who became contracted parties to the war. An exploration in microcosm of the buzzing innovation and variation of the world of military transportation can help us to see something of the dynamics of wartime relations of production and marketing and of the rhythms of the labour market for booted auxiliaries and barefooted remount servants. This exceptional moment of initiative, choice and creativity in occupational life is worth repossessing, not only in its own right, but because of its possible meaning to rural historians concerned with tracing the dipping fortunes of peasant communities in industrialising South Africa, as the extension of capitalist productive relations inched them remorselessly towards what Bundy has termed the eventual 'closure of the peasant option'.[2] For it is clear that if small independent transport carriers represented an overshadowed enclave in the turn-of-the-century colonial economy, the conjunctural circumstances of war enabled them to combine past experience and new strategic choices in a striking display of conscious organisation and independent social power.

Transport mobilisation

Long-range imperial military campaigning required the large-scale mobilisation of local resources and local labour, and from the commencement of hostilities British officers looked to the haulage skills and transport facilities of rural African and Coloured communities. Every transport officer and remount official everywhere was hungry for the typical mission muleteer and the pace of recruitment, particularly in the early months of war, was little short of breakneck. Army enlistment was voluntary: imperial forces did not depend on the conscription and forced labour of porters and carriers, as they were to do in other African campaigns; there is no Cape evidence to support Martin Murray's general contention that 'throughout the military campaign, the British Army depended upon forced African labour for . . . harness menders . . . guards, railway workers, oxen drivers and the like'.[3]

Initial imperial optimism over the ability of the Colony's single-track rail lines to sustain an abnormally large wartime freight traffic soon crumbled. Service along the narrow-gauge line running north, and along the small string of single-track feeder lines from Cape ports was from the start unreliable. Crippling rolling stock shortages – particularly of armoured locomotives – meant the running of little more than an erratic and skeleton supply service. Throughout hostilities, there was poor timing and scheduling of supply trains, and frequent stoppages due to line blockages, enemy sabotage and direct attacks on rolling stock.

The rail communications infrastructure was naturally not without its uses in sheltered parts: feeder lines from ports carried supplies to military railhead stockpiles at Naauwpoort, De Aar, Stormberg and Colesberg. But, for the most part, rail proved inadequate and unreliable under the strains of war conditions. And in critical areas it also lacked the necessary line extensions. The result was a sudden paradox. On the one hand, to apply Timothy Keegan's conclusion to the regional economy as a whole, by the turn of the century 'railway construction meant that the transport riding economy was doomed'.[4] On the other hand, a peculiar context of danger and opportunity ensured that for a brief period the lumbering Scotch cart and other animal-drawn services were once again unrivalled in capacity and efficiency.

The changing structure of transport and supply during the war did little to curb the growth of transport employment. Indeed, the sudden shift in February 1900 from the conventional War Office regimental or decentralised system to a general transport network had the effect of increasing auxiliary recruitment and multiplying black roles, as inexperienced brigade officers floundered around, trying to assemble new cart and wagon companies. Imperial Army transport emerged from its reorganisation under Roberts and Kitchener in far worse shape than before,[5] but for transport riders employment opportunities were greatly expanded. From the start, management presented great difficulties. Most army men on the spot lacked any prior experience or imported traditions of long-range haulage of military supplies. It is not surprising that the most chronic British military problem of the war was that of effective logistics.[6] With the exception of a few seasoned transport officers with some African or Indian service, British troops generally made heavy weather of the business of labour organisation, control and work discipline. The average regimental transport sergeant did not make a smooth transition to taskmaster and pacemaker over a civilian labour force. It was not surprising that working relationships were often soured by the clash of cultures; the West Kents' transport officer surrounded by Vryburg muleteers found himself with a workforce whom he often literally did not understand and who did not understand him.[7]

Frantic efforts to control an unruly labour force, to assert authority on the job and to speed up hauliers opened the way for a small intake of colonists who took up jobs as transport conductors. Following widespread advertising during 1900 for 'white men, with previous experience of the management of oxen and mules, and the control of native subordinates', several hundred settlers entered the Cape's twenty-four remount depots, and numerous field transport divisions.[8] Officials recruiting such conductors were also looked to for advice: the Stormberg Native Location Superintendent was described as 'rather an interesting chap who had lots of ideas on how we should control our Native and Cape Boy drivers'.[9] The ratio of conductors to drivers and leaders varied; a typical forward-battery company employed one for every ten wagoners, while Army Service Corps general supply transport placed a conductor in charge of every fifteen to twenty vehicles. Occasionally, squads of Australians (generally Queenslanders and New South Wales horsemen) were seconded as conductors; there was an eager belief that their rural occupational background (as horse-breakers, stock-men, and kangaroo hunters) and 'bush' experience of aboriginals would equip them to keep African labour in line. The only mark they made was to harden further Australian troops' notorious reputation for indiscriminate violence against labourers.[10]

Transport conductors were mostly Boers. A few were skilled supervisory men from white transport firms, but the bulk were drawn from the ranks of marginalised poorer whites in the countryside, some of them jobless rural drifters, others scratching out a precarious living by working intermittently in the casual labour market. For semi-nomadic, illiterate and impoverished white woodcutters, roadworkers, and lime-burners, transport work promised escape from the degradations and humiliations of casualised labour to good earnings and some job status. Among pockets of redundant and indigent *bywoners* there were also transportation skills to cash in on in a rising wartime market. And there were those non-landowning Boers whose livelihoods had been obliterated by the narrow gauge: formerly self-employed, undercapitalised long-distance transport riders who had been shunted by the 1890s railway expansion into a grim cycle of bankruptcy and joblessness. If the growth of mechanised transport had 'effectively drained the life blood from long distance transport riding',[11] the war brought a transfusion of sorts to some marginal whites as well as to blacks.

It is not possible to construct a full quantitative analysis of black participation in transport work. Of an estimated 100,000 men in military employment nationally, Warwick has suggested that at any given moment there were at least 14,000 men engaged in British transport riding.[12] This figure represents a conservative estimate, probably still well below the actual numbers working at busy times. While it is imposs-ible to provide anything like an accurate national or regional assessment of the number of transport workers employed, there are countless snapshots in military records which provide a fleeting sense of the proportions involved. At Kuruman for instance, 600 Mfengu and Coloured muleteers were enrolled on a single day in December 1899.[13] The mean daily total of migrant Coloured recruits arriving at Naauwpoort between February and June 1900 was 185.[14] Scattered figures from Namaqualand, late in the war, are even more emphatic; in less than a week, the Coldstream Guards enlisted 2,100 muleteers and wagon guards.[15] Around 7,000 African drivers and leaders helped move French's columns to Machadodorp in the Transvaal in 1900, while 5,000 transport auxiliaries in control of 11,000 mules drove Roberts to Bloemfontein in February

5 Transport conductor with boy remount servants, King William's Town.
(Courtesy of the South African Library)

67

to March of that year. A further feature of the growth of British transportation needs was the importation of several contingents of Indian cavalrymen. Debarred from combat service, Bengal and Madras Lancers chafed under the indignity of grooming horses and forking hay at Cape remount depots and base camps.

Geographical origins and social composition of auxiliaries

Although it seems that virtually all rural localities felt the pulse of the military labour market, for the most skilled transport auxiliaries two sources of supply were especially distinctive: first, the Coloured mission stations, dormitories of loyal skilled workers under obliging Anglican, Methodist and less sympathetic pro-Boer Moravian stewardship; and, second, the existing major seams of African migrant workers from the Eastern Cape and Transkeian Territories. The expanded market for labour sucked many men from rural and urban Coloured communities into long-distance labour migration for the first time. Normally locally centred muleteers or cab-drivers or immobile harness-makers, coachbuilders and smiths poured out of Moravian Hill in Cape Town and Moravian Hope in Port Elizabeth, hitting the road in their hundreds in search of army work; for those with equipment it meant an often heavy and always risky investment, while all faced long absences from home and unaccustomedly strenuous work.

In mission villages at Bredasdorp, Clarkson, Pniel, Elim, Mamre, Wupperthal, Genadendal, Riversdale and Douglas, the distant throb of Naauwpoort, De Aar and Queenstown also diverted much labour from domestic agricultural production and local wage labour circuits. These places witnessed high levels of self-recruitment, as men tramped or drove off in the hope of fattening themselves. Many of them had accumulated skills and practices as small hauliers, or had competence in some artisanal or semi-artisanal capacity, and came to form a hard core of independent and highly mobile transport riders, flitting from contract to contract as opportunities arose, hundreds of miles from their homes. It was not uncommon for mission stations which customarily produced surpluses for district produce markets to be fairly well stocked with mule teams and wagons.[16] And the open road beckoned.

In the sparse and bitter Rhenish and Methodist mission villages of the northwest, such as Kommagas, Steinkopf and Leliefontein, there was quite evidently some qualitative shift in small-producer awareness during these crisis years. Their Baster populations were small, diminishing and frequently on the edge of subsistence, but were nonetheless alert to market chances which seemed to offer the prospect of arresting their decline. Hundreds of men turned away from Leliefontein's thin and acid soil, disposed of small livestock herds to the military at inflated market prices and invested heavily in mule teams and wagons with which to contract to the Namaqualand Field Force. Mission drivers who had been stagnating for some years because of the Cape Copper Company's investment in rail transport from its inland colliery depots to west-coast port facilities were swiftly revitalised. In the short run, it was a fairly easy jump into relative and unevenly spread prosperity, but the brisk disposal of livestock assets as well as the sale of numerous wagons was clearly to have catastrophic long-term consequences for a community reproducing itself on the land.[17]

Mission lands also provided a fair complement of service workers. Self-employed and semi-independent individuals with craft skills in carpentry, masonry and harness-making joined blacksmiths, farriers and wheelwrights recruited from inland market towns in forming the skill base of remount depots. The trek also involved bands of young boys – some as young as ten or twelve years of age – who abandoned mission schoolrooms by the score, lured by the rumour of adventure and good earnings as army servants, grooms, grasscutters and veterinary attendants at such centres as De Aar, Stellenbosch and Worcester. Although war-related school losses are difficult to determine, at some schools over 50 per cent of enrolment was reported to be away in casual army employment.[18]

The dispersion of skilled labour drained lands of thousands of men. Between 1900 and 1901, an estimated 1,300 Coloured muleteers from Genadendal, Wupperthal and Elim were more or less permanently in service.[19] Writing in December 1901, R. M. Clark, a Bredasdorp Anglican Missionary, described the departure from his area of daily convoys of transport volunteers, each averaging 100 men, 400 mules and fifty wagons, in addition to sheep, goats, horses and packs of hunting dogs.[20] At the Belvidere mission in the Knysna region, 1,319 men, out of a total population of 3,290 persons, were reported away on transport duties in March 1900.[21]

Recruiting sergeants, magistrates and licensed labour agents in the Eastern Cape and Transkeian Territories helped to channel many thousands of African migrants into transportation work. And many journeyed to labour depots voluntarily and independently, the whiff of expanding opportunity strong in their nostrils. All manner of groups were well placed to exploit new demands for labour or materials or both, from temporary semi-skilled seasonal migrants who had picked up timber-working and portering techniques on the quaysides of Cape ports, and drifting adolescent youngsters with some equestrian or herding experience, to wealthy household heads with fields and wagons. Mfengu and Thembu communities in particular had a considerable history of expert involvement in the transport section of the nineteenth-century rural economy.[22] From an enlarging pool of mandatory wage labour in parts of the Ciskei and Transkei, many longer-term migrant workers, traditionally locked into port or railway or other transport employment, were quick to switch to military transport divisions and remount depots. There, attractions of higher pay, service perks and a continued opportunity to set the pace and shape the character of their labour far outweighed the risks of warfare.

In any assessment of the regional balance of labour recruitment, the increasingly impecunious condition and insecure position of particular communities who commonly combined labour migrancy with rural production also warrants emphasis. For the stability of some of the key source areas of migrant labour was seriously threatened by wartime disruption of the established lines of capitalist labour supply. Many districts with households living in deepening scarcity were feeling the shock of rural unemployment as migrants streamed back from closed or drastically contracted industrial labour markets on the Rand.[23] To compound matters, localised ecological disasters brought depression and dearth. The food supply in areas like Peddie, Bathurst, Keiskamma Hoek, Cathcart and King William's Town dwindled in 1899 and 1900, as drought and crop failures brought startling levels of famine.[24] Patchy regional agricultural collapses drained districts like Peddie and Bathurst of three-quarters and more of their adult male populations by 1900.[25] Migrants from affected districts undoubtedly sought more relief than opportunity in transport labour contracts. Thus, within a very short time of its establishment in November 1899 the De Aar remount depot attracted 2,000 recruits, with King William's Town and Queenstown being numerically significant supply areas.[26] Between November 1899, and March 1902, between 5,500 and 6,000 Africans left the King William's Town locality for De Aar.[27] In 1901, around 5,000 migrants were reported absent from Lady Frere district.[28]

It is extremely difficult to do proper justice to the scale and depth to which the lure of transport and supply work penetrated civil labour markets. For those nursing a desire to escape degrading conditions of employment on settler farms and mines, here was an opportune moment to move; new and realisable choices of service work freed Africans from the grip of existing employers. And exasperated and insecure employers found themselves confronting increasingly insubordinate and uncontrollable subject labour. Farmworkers in Clanwilliam, Tulbagh, Malmesbury, Caledon, Uitenhage and Oudtshoorn left herds untended and crops rotting in fields, breaking labour contracts to seek better pay and conditions at the Stellenbosch and Worcester remount depots, and in Bethune and De Lisle's sprawling transport columns.[29] Migrant African shepherds, goatherds, shearers and reapers in areas such as Fort Beaufort, Alice, Cathcart, Steytlerville, Willowmore, Hanover and Jansenville also spurned customary seasonal farm work, and banded together to turn out as remount workers and riders. Other quarters which felt the effects of outward movement and labour evasion were the colony's mine workings. De Beers at Kimberley and De Beers Dynamite Works at Somerset West, Indwe Colliery, the New Cape Collieries at Diepkloof and Stormberg and Namaqualand copper mines all lost unskilled and semi-skilled labourers of many different ranges of competence (including top-grade mine support workers such as hauliers, smiths and horse handlers) to the pull of war contracts.

Peasant suppliers and contractors to the imperial army

Discussion of those who entered directly into structures of military employment should be set against a broader picture of the response of peasant communities to wartime economic expansion. Within a mosaic of contracting, subcontracting and casual engagements, there were many who forged more independent links with the imperial army as suppliers of animals and produce, or as small, jobbing, service contractors. A working population of transport auxiliaries and suppliers must also be located within the wider context of class formation within colonial society as a whole. Communities, families and individuals could engage with the military in a number of different spheres. But pre-war forms of inequality and social differentiation were lifted into wartime job and supply markets. Those who entered the labour market as transport riders and suppliers did not always do so on equal terms and in equal capacities.

In addition to selling their skills, relatively prosperous peasant-household heads were able to amass greater returns from hiring out capital assets in the form of carts, wagons and draught animals. Many of them the fruit of mission living and mission education, these individuals were already plying Ciskeian and Transkeian regional commodity markets with Scotch carts and buck wagons, and were quick to combine loan and hire practices with discretionary participation in skilled, waged transport riding. Surplus vehicles with animal teams fetched inflated hiring fees and bonuses, and the military paid compensation for damage or loss of property at the current wartime market rate. Moreover, three-month labour contracts could conveniently be fitted into a seasonal cycle of cash-crop cultivation. For particular commodities and bodies of men, accumulation of fees and earnings reached substantial aggregate totals. To take just one example, the 20,000 Tlhaping of the Taung Reserve received a total sum of £25,490 for transport hire and services as a labouring elite of drivers and leaders.[30] Here and elsewhere, a characteristic pattern was for contractor riders to put accumulated war earnings to work, expanding livestock holdings and restocking herds shredded in the rinderpest scourge of 1896–7.[31]

There were also those, including big men of peasant communities concentrated in the Transkeian Territories, who devoted their resources very largely to keeping transport lines fed and provisioned. Market suppliers in East Griqualand and Emigrant Thembuland judiciously distanced themselves from the risks of war operations, hazarding neither their lives nor their assets by involving themselves in actual army transport riding. Considerable quantities of their cattle came to stock remount depots, having been sold at peak prices. Beasts changed hands at £25 to £30, while in some areas, like Albany, Bedford, Adelaide, Somerset East and Mount Fletcher, prime oxen fetched as much as £40 to £50.[32] For Sotho living both in Basutoland and in the north-eastern corner of the Cape, the export of ponies became a lucrative business. Basuto ponies which averaged £3 to £6 in the 1890s, soared in value to between £35 and £40.[33] Cavalry remounts fetched from £35 to £50, while top-quality trained horses were bringing peasant suppliers in Bedford, Adelaide, Alice and Victoria East as much as £60 by 1901.[34] Mule prices, for single beasts or as trained wagon teams, climbed to an average of £8 per mule, with top-grade animals fetching as much as £15.[35]

There was also a lucrative trade in pilfered haulage animals and remounts. Far from invoking action against African stock thieves, British officers were generally content to turn a blind eye upon any questionable legality in livestock transactions. Indeed, stock poached from Boer farms was often accepted with alacrity. Not surprisingly, the British found that this game could sometimes turn sour. On one typical occasion, a sharp gang of tramping sheepshearers from Adelaide was exposed as having bought up old army remounts for a song, fattening them up and then reselling them to inexperienced column transport officers as fresh stock.[36]

Military buying sparked off increases in production in a number of areas; evidence suggests that agricultural surpluses were produced specifically to meet military cash-crop requirements. Scarcity and price inflation stirred many independent producers to step up levels of commercial activity. Wheat was king, but barley and oat prices also soared, as did those of hay, vegetables and a range of dairy produce. In East Griqualand, there was much brisk activity as mixed herders and cultivators concentrated on grain production, some feverishly ploughing up new land in most unpromising situations. Groups of wealthier peasants in Albany concentrated on oat production;[37] during these years, the price of oat hay never fell below 7s. per 100 lb., and in 1901 reached a record peak of 10s. African producers also made spectacular returns on maize and on lucerne,

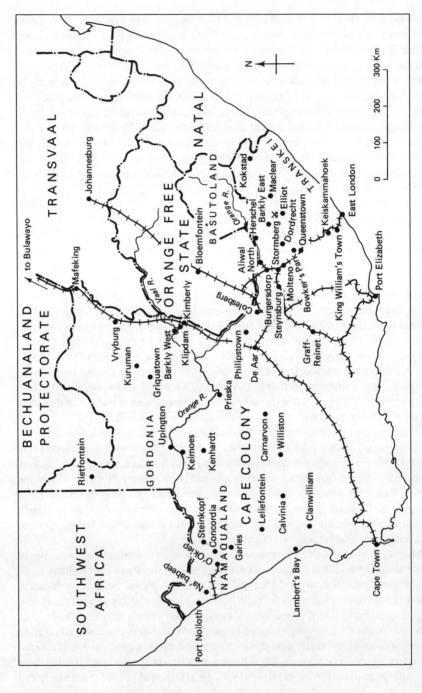

Map 4 The Cape Colony. Adapted from P. Warwick, *Black People and the South African War 1899–1902* (Cambridge University Press, Cambridge, 1983).

for which remount depots paid as much as 9s. per 100-lb. bag.[38] Increased wagoning activity boosted demand for wood for the building and repairing of vehicles, and in districts such as Adelaide, Queenstown, Sterkstroom and Molteno, woodcutting and the carrying of wood proved particularly remunerative, with traders well placed to exploit access to purchasing camps and stations.[39]

The most profitable export trade in cash crops rested in the hands of African entrepreneurs who possessed their own means of transportation, and could therefore bypass the snares of settler merchants and trading brokers in Eastern localities or comfortably squeeze smaller white middlemen out of local marketing chains. Larger peasants in East Griqualand and Thembuland were able to exploit good access to army bases in the region. In such situations, settler contractors and colonial traders were unable to cramp Africans' market access; producers generally negotiated food, fodder and livestock prices directly with British purchasing officers.

Good grazing land provided a further source of profitable income in Eastern Cape districts and the Ciskei. Towards the end of 1901, there were reported to be upwards of 20,000 remounts feeding on African land in the Eastern Cape, tended by men drawing fat army retainers.[40] The Grenadier Guards' grazing fees to a few groups of Ciskeian Africans amounted to £1,471 in 1901, while those of the Scots Guards to horse retainers in Albany, Bedford and Alexandria totalled £2,228 in the same year.[41] Typical of those who prospered were Silas Matesi and Joshua Damane of Bedford, who in 1901 received fees from the local Remount Agent of £86 and £104 respectively.[42]

Dozens of black hauliers also contracted to the military as independent civil carriers. In comparison with the well-capitalised settler trading and transportation interests which were expanding as a result of the wartime boom, their gains were modest. Established professional haulage firms which dominated local transport business obviously had the remount and draught animal reserves – and the access to ample pasture and water – to enable them rapidly to extend their range and speed as army carriers. White contractors were certainly able to corner the lion's share of the market along many road networks, and for firms such as Strachan and Co. in East Griqualand and Julius Weil and Co. in Mafeking there was unprecedented expansion.

Yet this settler growth was not necessarily entirely purchased at the price of independent black access to, and claims upon, the rewards of the transportation market. For wartime trade did not work restrictively. While there is no doubting the dominance of settler enterprises, it is also clear that the range of road haulage possibilities for small carriers, including the single man with his mule and wagon, expanded enormously. Established riding routes boomed with the advent of greatly increased traffic volume; where pre-war haulage demand had been slack, there was bustling activity. In addition, the war provided ripe conditions for the temporary carving out of new, irregular routes which ribboned out across rural districts, serving as the supply arteries of rural camps and garrisoned small towns and villages. For example, Coloured and Baster muleteers from Gordonia ran armed convoys carrying mission-station produce across entirely new routes linking stations with British regiments billeted in the Carnarvon, Prieska, Clanwilliam and Williston districts.[43] High commodity prices and haulage hire costs buttered the bread of these and many other black civilians working the new military routes which honeycombed the countryside.

Total earnings were high. Although income naturally fluctuated in real terms with the rising cost of wartime living, which varied from district to district, there were considerable numbers for whom wartime inflation was not so great as to wipe out newly acquired investment and purchasing power. By 1900, the army was paying independent Eastern Cape waggoners £1.15s. per day plus route bonuses for casual contracting. In 1902, Baster peasants were supplying mule-cart services at more than £2 per day.[44] African fodder hauliers at Aliwal North were reported, in September 1901, to be receiving 15s. per 100 lb. (on wagons which held three tons) for carrying loads to Albert.[45] In the west and southwest, the price of transporting fodder shot up to as much as 20s. per 100 lb., with some carriers also receiving mileage fees. A lively and prosperous casual trade developed around remount depots: Stellenbosch, for instance, was like a magnet to local Coloured muleteers, and drew many from as far afield as Caledon, Riversdale and Swellendam. Virtually any man with a horse and cart could pick up periodic light work with ease. Under-employed 'Coloured men of the cottager or herder type'[46] with little or no capital, hired equipment individually or entered into co-venturing partnerships, enabling them to add to casual earnings the proceeds from the carrying of small depot loads of fodder and manure or officers' laundry, or from the cart sale of skins, rabbits and dairy produce to troops. Better-off Coloured working-class market gardeners and allotment holders, who had been emerging as petty commodity producers in Stellenbosch in the closing decades of the nineteenth century,[47] hawked their produce to purchasing officers to secure the highest prices. Last, around transport depots and large Imperial Yeomanry veterinary hospitals there also developed a multiplicity of dispersed, small-scale trading and carrying transactions, involving such activities as liquor smuggling, and the carrying of small loads of firewood to camps. Laundry-women appear to have taken on a great amount of laundry work for the army and however mean the pay of 3d. to 6d. a day, these earnings lifted the family income of depressed rural households.[48]

Remount labour

Before turning to the transport rider 'labour aristocrat' who stood at the head of a clearly defined labour hierarchy, some attention needs to be paid to adjacent or neighbouring subsidiary remount workers. In general terms, the gulf that separated drivers and teamsters from remount labourers was wide in skill, status, pay, perks and work autonomy, but there were some striking exceptions. Depots at De Aar, Naauwpoort, Stellenbosch and Worcester employed Coloured carpenters, saddlers, harness-makers, farriers, blacksmiths and wheelwrights who formed an exclusive, specialised group of artisans and craftsmen, retaining rights to outside civilian jobbing and sometimes employing their own labourers on time rates, with remount paymasters subsidising pay. Their skills came at a startling high price; mid-way through the war, some farriers and wheelwrights were earning £11.5s. per month. Chiefs who accompanied and supervised larger migrant labour parties received £10 per month, with the military furnishing these representatives with a rifle, horse, groom, cook, interpreter and separate tent accommodation at remount depots. Rates for general labourers were far behind these and behind those of riders. Men toiling in field veterinary hospitals, depots and in the Army Service Corps earned from £2 to £3.15s. per month, while headmen serving as overseers were granted an additional monthly allowance of £1. Both wage rates and earnings in kind fluctuated considerably from place to place. Veterinary departments paid £2 per month, providing blankets, a daily ration of mealiemeal and salt and a weekly portion of meat, while cavalry terms of employment for much the same work were far more generous.[49]

A glance at remount and ancillary occupations reminds us of the great range of daily tasks. Boy labourers (who received staple rations and up to 1s. monthly as camp followers) worked as grooms, grasscutters, woodcutters and general servants. Men were employed in loading, cleaning and horse-breaking, and on the maintenance of mechanical transport like armoured steam tractors and locomotives, as well as carts, wagons and horse-drawn carriages. In perhaps the most striking instance of brute muscle power, gangs also laboured on railway projects as lumpers (timber loaders) and as coal-heavers.

In most places there was frequent switching around of labour from job to job. And the confines of the remount environment led to intensive work rhythms which could be excessively taxing. The often terrific pace of time-disciplined task routines and the onerous weight of transport conductors' demands led to a high incidence of casualties at large depots like Worcester or Naauwpoort, and much ill-feeling between labourers and officials over the vagaries of the compensation awards system for the injured or

6 Group of British officers' servants and water carriers, Victoria West.
(Courtesy of the Greater London Record Office, Middlesex Records Division)

sick. Accidents were so frequent that most of them probably went unrecorded. Inept handling of rearing horses and other animals by inexperienced camp followers resulted in a gruesome spiral of maiming and death. Pneumonia, rheumatism, bronchitis, muscular disorders and bone fractures were all conditions attributed by alarmed army doctors to prolonged and arduous work, with hours often running from sunrise to sunset, up to six and even seven days a week.[50]

Housing conditions for unskilled remount workers were also bad. Accommodation was invariably dilapidated and insanitary, with employees cramming themselves into rusty corrugated iron or tattered and filthy tarpaulin lean-tos, contrasting starkly with the sturdy regulation tents of transport riders.[51]

Unskilled workers were keenly aware of differentials in pay and conditions related to skill, and there were attempts by older camp followers and others to move up the occupational grade into the ranks of the skilled. Here and there, there was some structured labour mobility; any common manual labourer with a modicum of manual dexterity and strength could try to become an army transport rider. The Queenstown and East London Native Transport Departments, for example, held proficiency tests in mule handling, and there were some opportunities for aspirant riders to work a period of apprenticeship to experienced men.[52] But while the intake of 'apprentice' youths allowed for some transmission of skill within transport departments, this transition was not without its attendant tensions. Many transport riders regarded the use of casual labourers as an unwelcome encroachment. Apart from the aggravating and wearisome experience of working with raw youths, their presence on reduced wages and rations represented a dilution of high skill levels, threatening to undermine the autonomy of privileged 'master' workers and an elite occupational culture which exercised a strong stake in the maintenance of the existing gradation of labour.

Points of stress between remount conductors and the workforces of depots were common and often flared into open antagonism and disturbances. Wage fluctuations, for example, were a constant irritant, with Cape Government inspectors identifying this as a primary cause of labour dissatisfaction.[53] Moreover, at Stellenbosch, Worcester and Queenstown, African workers were aggrieved at the presence of lower-paid Indian ancillary labour, squealing that this would lead to a depressing of wage levels. Indian labourers themselves were agitated: at Veterinary Hospitals it was reported that 'Indian attendants have developed a habit of comparing wages with Natives employed alongside them, and many are becoming highly incensed at their lower rates.'[54] Other issues which stung workers into clamorous protest were the lack of adequate rest days, the prolongation of working hours without overtime rates, squalid accommodation, irregular rations, deferred pay and the high proportion of 'dirty jobs' and menial sanitary tasks which all were pressed to perform.

Much to their mortification, chiefs and headmen sometimes found themselves being overworked, assigned to rough jobs and subject to lapses in the maintenance of respectably wide perks and wage differentials between them and commoners. These provided compelling reasons for men of position, who objected to being treated like 'ordinary labourers . . . or Kraal boys',[55] to fall out with the military. Their self-respecting claim to differential treatment rested on the need to ensure that their workplace aspirations and prerogatives dovetailed with their positions of command in rural areas; as Beinart has put it, for late-nineteenth century Cape rural communities with established traditions of migration, patterns of authority 'in the rural districts and at labour centres interacted on each other'.[56]

Yet there were also disputes which cut across demarcations of authority and privilege between chiefs and headmen or their representatives, and ordinary labourers. A malcontent who may be singled out as illustration was Chief Mvuso Matanzima, a Thembu chief from Cofimvaba, who led a 200-strong squad of workers contracted to the Bowker's Park remount depot from October 1901. Relations between the chief and senior remount officers were prickly from the beginning. Upon arrival, Mvuso was adamant that a Lieutenant Flemmer, the recruiter at St Mark's, had promised wage increments, uniforms and blankets, and 'upon these promises we came here'. When these benefits failed to materialise, Mvuso proceeded to dog one of the officers, Major Etheridge, complaining bitterly of a gross breach of promise. A resentful Etheridge deplored the chief's 'ingratitude', concluding that his 'leniency' towards him had been 'subversive of discipline'. A fellow officer, Lieutenant Innes, added his piece, which was that Mvuso had 'not tried to help make his Boys work as much as he could have done'. Heartily disliked, Mvuso's three-month contract was not renewed. 'I gather', wrote F. J. Evens, a local Inspector of Native Locations, 'the whole Staff . . . will be pleased when Chief Mvuso's term expires . . . he appears to have been a most troublesome man'. The chief's annoyance took some time to fade. Weeks after his departure from Bowker's Park, he was discovered to be 'making mischief' by trying to obstruct 'the supply of native labour by spreading misstatements in native territory'. A furious Etheridge vainly urged action by the Native Affairs Department, alleging that Mvuso's conduct constituted 'a deliberate attempt to hamper the Government in a time of war'.[57]

Overlapping defensive interests impelled headmen to articulate workers' common grievances over such issues as the practice of splitting up migrant work parties between different remount depots, or the tendency to shunt men off to Bloemfontein abruptly whenever transport labour shortages arose there. Eastern Cape migrants had a strong, inherited regional inclination for non-industrial and non-agricultural Cape employment, for the northern states were acknowledged as a milieu in which workers would find themselves under more repressive controls. And labour conditions in the newly annexed British colonies remained bad. It was common knowledge among migrants that wages and conditions in British military employment in the Orange River Colony fell far short of Cape standards, and there were numerous desertions *en route* from work parties being ferried northwards. In the Transkeian Territories there was some fear of withdrawal of labour by chiefs, with labour recruiters and magistrates expressing concern about the consequences of unwitting misrepresentation placing them 'in a very false position as regards the Natives in the Territories'.[58]

Working communities, leisure and culture

The scale of the northwards movement of food, forage and ordnance was staggering. Pakenham is surely not far wide of the mark in calling this Britain's great trek.[59] We have already noted the numbers involved in rolling Roberts and French forward in 1900. For large columns, a formidable haul of De Aar, Colesberg or Naauwpoort to

Bloemfontein or Pretoria was not uncommon. One typical example of these long-distance supply columns was that which left Naauwpoort on 31 May 1900, under the command of Lieutenant-Colonel Frederick Maxse. This comprised seven companies of mule wagons – 550 vehicles, 4,700 mules, 1,600 drivers and leaders, and some 500 armed African wagon guards.[60] Such mobile transport companies were highly visible and made an imposing physical spectacle.

Some of the traces of that spectacle have naturally been laid down by those nineteenth-century Southern African travellers and other writers who have commented on labour and technological aspects of vehicle transport as an integral part of their portrayal of the veld in terms of a pastoral mystique of nomadic bullock-drivers, *voorlopers*, or other sturdy black bushmen.[61] Military accounts, detailed or impressionistic, splash further colour onto a broad canvas. Ox wagons, Cape carts and Scotch carts, which had a freight capacity of over three tons, had long spans of trained oxen ranging from ten to twenty in number. These were controlled by pairs of drivers wielding leather whips up to forty feet in length, and an energetic leading teamster, either mounted or running on foot, who supervised the leading bulls. In Namaqualand, water shortages and commando line sabotage saw large mule trains of up to seventy-eight mules (which used less water than locomotives) pulling linked trucks, replacing the railway as the pivot of military carrying from coast to interior. Elsewhere, heavy battery artillery was frequently transported by enormous teams of fifty to sixty oxen, handled by squads of drivers and leaders who used light sticks and fifty-foot long whips. Buck wagons, which carried up to 3,500 lb. of goods, were pulled by teams of six to twelve mules, controlled by two drivers (sometimes three) using short, thick, leather hunting whips. Heavy-baggage and munitions columns employed teams of twenty animals per cart, with two pairs of drivers and leaders, the latter scampering alongside swaying vehicles to assist in braking and in managing the lead mules.[62] In the army's most effectively run smaller transport companies, there was a seasonal switching in winter months from oxen to mules, as splayed ox hooves tended to provide better traction in muddy terrain which usually bogged down mules. Supplying pastoralists in many areas quickly adapted to this circulating livestock trade.[63]

The dexterity and judgement of transport riders prompted a great deal of glowing contemporary testimony. Drivers were often much admired for high standards of competence and steady nerve in keeping vehicles on the hoof, whether on the road or across rough countryside, braving accidents, poor visibility and the most inclement weather. When on the road, brigade companies and supply columns often worked in step to the blowing of horns and whistles or the beating of drums, not to mention more exotic rhythmic accompaniments such as the sound provided by three mounted Highland Infantry pipers for Sotho carters of the regiment's 1st Battalion.[64]

This provides an appropriate point at which to turn to a closer examination of the super-elite of skilled transport riders. A first consideration must be levels of earning as a primary criterion for determining their 'labour aristocratic' status. Although we lack consistent and thorough earnings data, there is a clear enough picture of income levels, contract benefits and job security, all subject to often minute incremental shifts and other movement. Within these bounds, minimum official levels ensured that a core strategic labouring elite of drivers and leaders was able to command regular levels of remuneration generally bettered only by the inflated wages paid to some scouts, and despatch riders and runners. As high-priced men, drivers earned a basic monthly cash wage of £4.10s., while experienced team leaders could draw £5.10s. Men on six-month contracts were paid monthly increments of 10s. after completion of twelve weeks' continuous service, and a terminating gratuity of £2. Monthly ration allowances were costed at between £2.5s. and £3. While the availability of food was subject to the usual wartime breakdown in supply, military rations at times included all or most of the following staple foodstuffs: meat, vegetables, meal, flour, sugar, salt, bread, tea and coffee. In good times, riders ate well. When employment perks extended to soups, stews, butter, biscuits, chocolate and condensed milk, they ate even better. Regiments supplied a standard clothing issue (costed at £3.3s.) of greatcoat, jacket, trousers, blanket, hat, boots and, sometimes, puttees. There were other discretionary and incremental work benefits, some of them universal and well formalised, others dependent on the random patronage and conscience of transport officers. Pay was not stopped for leave and there were overtime earnings for more than a ten- or twelve-hour day. Half pay and, occasionally, compensation, was given to a man hurt on duty and families of men killed in service often received assistance – perhaps £5 or more – from regimental subscription funds for native employees.[65]

Among highly mobile transport riders, fraud was widespread. Slippery employees rapidly became adept at outwitting the chaotic, cumbersome and poorly coordinated army pay system; time and time again, drivers were able to dupe overworked remount pay-masters with astonishing slickness. The paybook-and-chit method encouraged fraud, as auxiliaries were entitled to draw outstanding monies from whichever remount payroll happened to be most conveniently accessible. General dislocation and communications difficulties made the control of overlapping and double payment no easy task. In the 1st Cavalry Division, rough internal audits at the beginning of 1901 revealed that several companies had been overpaying heavily for months in succession – with some auxiliaries making off with anything from two to three times the average monthly wage. On one occasion, sixteen time-expired Mfengu muleteers forged paybook entries and defrauded the Coldstream Guards of £79.[66] Typically brazen was Andries May, a Field Artillery driver from Cradock, who milked his employers of more than £30 during September 1901. May, granted three weeks' leave to tend to his smallholding in Bedford, disappeared, only to surface in the records over two months later when it was uncovered that he had been drawing pay in Adelaide and Molteno.[67] Peasants who contracted vehicles and animals in addition to their labour were sometimes also remunerated for items on paper which never existed in practice.[68]

Within a framework of variable wages and prices during this time, the broad pattern that emerges is that the most skilled and pivotal transport workers were often able to obtain upward wage adjustments, while the least skilled and least organised remount ancillary workers experienced almost no wage movement. In May 1901, Cavalry Divisions advised officers that 'the pay of better Native Drivers in the Colony should not normally much exceed £5 per month, but the market rate is rising, and prices should be considered'.[69] In the same month, a Staff Officer of the Namaqualand Field Force concluded that 'it is prejudicial to the interests of recruiting among Natives if it is not made known that additional monies will be added to their pay packets, to match war prices'.[70] In April and July 1901, both the Naval Brigade and Scots Guards found that drivers were unwilling to renew contracts unless there were wage increases. The Naval Brigade dithered until Commander Robert Harris conceded the justice of the riders' case, pointing out to Transport NCOs that 'it would be contrary to all precedent to expect the terms and conditions of one contract should extend to other subsequent ones ... this is no time to play at the stony employer'.[71] Although inflation reduced the purchasing power of high military wages, price increases in the colony were uneven, patchy and localised; moreover, magisterial controls upon staple foodstuff prices in some Eastern Cape districts (such as Bedford, Fort Beaufort and Victoria East) drew much of the sting of market rises. There is no doubt that many skilled auxiliaries enjoyed dramatically increased real earnings. Levels were certainly of an order to provide surplus income which allowed for the investment of wages and fee earnings in stock, land and even labour.[72]

Riders did not always sit back and await the bestowal of wage adjustments. In surviving records of agitation it is evident that wages and contract conditions were sometimes flashpoints in localised labour conflicts. With the associational confidence of labourers who were often self-recruiting, transport riders were not lacking in militancy. This was sharpened by realisation of the strength of their strategic role and a consciousness of corporate working unity and common interests. During 1900 and 1901, there were small transport company strikes in pursuit of pay increases, cost of living bonuses, payment of wage arrears, and the fulfilment of agreed contract benefits. A typical strike leader's demand was that voiced in July 1900, by Solomon Seretlo, a literate mission recruit and leading carter with the Cheshire Regiment. Under the heading, 'A Cheeky Native Scribe', Seretlo's complaint actually made the pages of the regimental journal, *The Thistle*. Speaking for some eighty drivers, he wrote that 'the native men want boots which have been promised. Why also are we not given blankets for these cold nights?'[73] These strikes were mostly impulsive affairs, lasting a day or two or sometimes just a few hours. Good timing was essential to success. By choosing appropriate peak times for stoppages, groups of auxiliaries often hastened a placatory response.[74] Certain officers (such as those in the Household Brigades, Somerset Light Infantry and Royal Army Medical Corps) took some pains to maintain the morale and economic security of skilled workers, and on occasion went to considerable lengths to pacify aggrieved labourers and avoid labour troubles. Demands, after all, were small, and settlement invariably ensured an immediate return to normal work.

One must of course be wary of painting too rosy a picture; withdrawals of labour did not in each and every instance meet with a conciliatory response. There were senior British officers who adopted a hard attitude towards what they saw as provocation and impertinence. Although technically non-combatant civilian army employees, transport workers were under army regulations and strike actions smacked of mutiny. Irate officers were given to wild talk of mowing down workers, but when it came retribution and retaliation was selective. With skilled hauliers in short supply, there could be no impetuous mass firing of labour and nor could strikes be broken by introducing new hands. Instead, the army retorted by imposing smaller punishments such as fines and ration reductions.[75]

Transport riders' conditions of work and life – their distinctive habits of continuous association in workplace and community – were probably in themselves sufficient to produce levels of organisation adequate to handle strikes or deputations. Indeed, we occasionally see the flickering appearance of combinations which developed their own customs of work regulation and acknowledged regular leaders. In labour disputes, army victimisation and dismissals were generally confined to such apparent ring-leaders, often men with a known reputation for toughness and truculence. One such was Moeketsi, a Sotho wagoner, who was fired for leading a small strike at Steynsburg in November 1900. 'By all means get rid of him', a senior officer advised a colleague, 'I never cared about this insolent fellow one way or the other, and he already gets high wages, so I don't see why you should have to put up with his cheek.'[76] Labour unrest appears occasionally to have provided the army with a handy pretext for sacking or paying off individual drivers who were posing serious disciplinary problems.

It may well be possible to speak of the blossoming of a transport-riding 'culture' during this period, expressed in independence, leisure interests and sense of skills, pride and prestige. An important point about army transport riding companies is that they formed well-defined, *constructed* working and social communities, spawned by the war economy's broadening transport base. The crisis brought a sharp, qualitative change in social relations. While carters, wagoners and other peasant volunteers clearly drew on accumulated local community experiences of transport riding and inherited veterinary skills, war conditions produced entirely new contours of long-distance work opportunities and social experiences. Many shepherds and goatherds in poor proletarianised communities in the west and southwest were pitched into heavy haulage work for the first time. Seasonal migrants from Quthing in Basutoland, for instance, were drawn into close working relationships with Baster muleteers from Namaqualand. The common nature of skilled work, whether rooted in experience or recent apprenticeship, knitted men together rapidly.

There were momentous new forces acting upon workers, and shaping the world around them. The institutions of regiment, camp, depot and long-distance column were speedily woven into the patterns of everyday life, defining occupational and associational behaviour and activities. If transport riders became the labour aristocrats of the imperial forces, there was more to this aristocracy than high earnings. In work culture, drivers and leaders were strongly sectional and particularistic, distinguishing themselves from unskilled auxiliaries and actively asserting their own worth. Status, skill, pride, toughness, bravado and a florid public image were the warp and weft of transport riders' self-awareness. Skilled companies had cohesion and stability, as many volunteers gave months of unbroken service. Shared tasks and work burdens further deepened bonds of comradeship, already cemented in many instances by kin and local social relationships. Qualities of independence and self-reliance, and a perceptible *esprit de corps*, prompted much comment.[77] Occupational fraternity was a powerful force, manifested in a solid sense of corporate identity which drew many of its symbolic reference points from the prevailing military atmosphere.

Clearly any 'self-culture' did not exist apart from the realities of material life; as a description of lifestyle or aspirant standards it obviously rested upon buoyant earnings. That numbers of skilled workers 'invented' themselves as elite carriers is clear; that the attendant symbols and values were sometimes steeped in contradiction is equally apparent. For there were undoubtedly those committed to conspicuous consumption on the job, yet hopelessly indebted to farmers or traders, who were enjoying no more than a short but full break from bad times.

The urge to show their identity extended deeply into the workforce. For example, special clothing was a prized item; like town militiamen, workers eagerly donned distinctive dress. 'Cape Boy' muleteers were notably ostentatious. Brightly coloured slouch hats and black felt caps or sombreros adorned with ostrich feathers, worn with kilts or white duck trousers, appear to have been *de rigueur*.[78] Such attire enabled groups to identify themselves in public, particularly when off duty. To routine army issue were added gaudy blankets, gloves, caps, belts, puttees and military insignia. Many Coloured mission station muleteers appear to have sported some brightly coloured handkerchief or scarf to indicate the particular cluster of mission drivers to which they belonged. In off-duty processions, Herbert muleteers appeared in 'fantastic ribbons . . . with their faces painted', frequently with some kind of army helmet; in Williston and Carnarvon, wagon guards slit their trousers and pulled shirts through to represent a tail; ox carters from Aliwal North and Albert, in a bizarre display of carnivalesque, whitened their faces while their supervising British transport sergeants blackened theirs. Certain transport companies, such as those of the Household Brigades, drilled with dummy rifles, equipped their own amateur buglers to mimic reveille and habitually carried staffs in their vehicles, to which were affixed small, rough, flags or banners.[79]

Recreation and entertainment flourished, and came to occupy an extremely important space in transport riders' lives, lending vibrancy and rich colour to war experiences, and offering ritual consolation from, and defences against, the hazards, tensions and uncertainties of wartime living. It is arguable that recreational pastimes did not simply mushroom as a safety valve. They were a way of rolling with the punch: wartime disorder provided new spaces and opportunities for conviviality, ceremony and displays of skill. Although life could be rigorous, risky and chronically insecure, there was unquestionably a dimension to work which was bracing and exciting. This is not to romanticise the gamut of war experiences, many of which were harrowing. But there is surely more than a suggestion of the picaresque in riders' behaviour, in the sense of giddy public exhilaration in high prestige work; of pouring enormous energy into the handling of vehicles and animals during periods of peak activity; of great mobility; of leaving domestic routine and the solidities of neighbourhood and locality for risks, adventures and, possibly, violence, on a dangerous open road. Transport riders never stood still.

Certain recreational customs and ceremonies during these years had deep historical roots in pre-literate peasant oral culture, such as song and dance. Although we lack full and reliable descriptions of dance modes, there is evidence that bands of Bhaca, Mfengu, Thembu, Sotho and Mpondomise auxiliaries carried over traditions and continuities of improvised, communally evolved dancing and singing into a new world of action and imagination. Colour, dancing and ceremony were part of everyday routines at many camps. Among Xhosa-speaking Red migrants in the De Aar and Queenstown remount depots, new songs and war cries were composed and sung.[80] Migrants from Mount Fletcher, Mount Frere and Maclear were recovering the tang of military tradition in bursts and flurries of music, if they had ever fully lost it. The Muleteers from Moravian and Rhenish missions like Wupperthal, Elim and Steinkopf migrated with instruments, and their brass bands kept companies entertained with hymns and popular melodies. In return for dairy produce or tobacco, troops sometimes loaned Africans their fiddles, mouth organs and even their bagpipes. These were grafted to the threads of local rural musical idiom to produce sounds which, while making many British listeners blanch, nevertheless had some applauding their vitality.[81]

The ingrained roving habits of musically inclined Coloured men in 'labour and transport-riding for Afrikaner farmers' has been shown by David Coplan to have been an invigorating force behind the spread of popular music and dance culture in the latter half of the nineteenth century.[82] War conditions produced an efflorescence of such innovative musicianship and showmanship based on the use of brass and other western instruments; here was a further tenacious stage in the grafting of an independent work-ing class culture. Right across the Cape, the surge of musically based recreation was strong and compelling, drenching camps and depots in song and movement which drew their meaning and value from immediate military social relationships, popular perceptions of the defeats and triumphs of war and conventions of heroism and cowardice. Routines in which transport riders and remount labourers whitened faces to parody conductors, and aped and mimicked British remount officers, bear a striking resemblance to later wartime *Beni* and *Bom* dances elsewhere in Africa.[83] Shafts were directed against Kruger, Botha and Smuts, in much the way that Kenyan *askari* war verse was to cartoon the *Kaiser* in a later imperial war. Nor were the British exempt. A 'degraded' comic dance mocking General Gatacre's debacle at Stormberg (in which Gatacre was played as a hunted beast!) so maddened one Rifle Brigade Transport Officer that he docked his wagoners' monthly bonus.[84] These habits of farce and mockery represented more than mere reflex defensive mechanisms against varied symbols of white authority; they provided a solid base for a suggestive mentality of cocky resistance and levity.

The cultural constructs which marked relations between some army officers and transport riders carried very different meanings from the usual colonial black labour-commodity–white employer nexus. Stigmatising names of commodities or objects, commonly used by colonists to label male servants in what van Onselen has identified as the humiliating gesture of 'boy-commodity', were not much in evidence.[85] Instead, the names pegged upon leading African drivers were constitutive of an identity associated with masculine aggression and prowess. Transport riders acquired martial-sounding names such as Hannibal, Attila, Caesar, Napoleon, Alexander, Bismarck and Wellington. Captain Percy Clive ignored the Christian names (Absalom, Abraham and Joshua) of three of his leading teamsters and dubbed them Pathan, Rajput and Punjabi, after those most refractory of Britain's Asian colonial subjects.[86] Not to be wholly left out of the new game of status recognition, riders renamed team oxen and mules Kitchener, Roberts, Chamberlain, Kruger and Steyn, to note the most common usages.

Connections between war, soldiering and sports such as football, boxing, cudgelling and sham fighting were strong. Although non-military recreations among non-com-batant auxiliaries, they became encrusted with the vocabulary and material influences of war. As Keith Thomas has argued, 'manly' sports can be viewed as rehearsals of conflict, and as products of war organisation.[87] Transport riders took passionately to football (understandably, not cricket) as a 'manly' close-contact sport, which called for agility, fitness, daring and skill. Whether played as casual free-for-alls with pigs' bladders, or as structured inter-regimental contests, the game mirrored the values of their occupational self-image, and fitted well into a flamboyant, mutually admiring social world. Competitive team sport also fostered social cohesion and group unity, reinforcing the sense of solidarity of transport companies from which opposing players were drawn. In areas where football had established a presence by the end of the nineteenth century,[88] the war gave it a considerable boost. Regular regimental sports days were the seedbed of the game; the constant mobility of army hauliers dramatically extended its range and distribution. Teams of Coloured muleteers, enjoying some minor sponsorship or patronage from wealthier officers, played no small part in popularising the game. And the Ayrshires, Devonshires, Yorkshires and Wiltshires bear a novel historical responsibility. Their working-class troops introduced football to Coloured remount workers at depots in Green Point, Worcester and Stellenbosch, and many of the clubs that today dominate Western Cape amateur leagues retain those county names.

There were other popular games, such as scorpion and snake-baiting, meerkat-fighting, cocking and wrestling, which became boisterous match-play affairs, with a great many animal and human participants carrying African and British money. If some were drawn from rural culture, much was new. What is especially interesting is the way in which imported Victorian working-class leisure pursuits, such as bull-baiting and cock-fighting, were taken up by African auxiliaries. Suppressed in Britain, these sports rapidly gained an eager colonial peasant following at the end of the nineteenth century. Although it would be rash to make too much of this, the commercial fervour surrounding cash prizes, trophies and betting suggests that what can be seen here is the 'Victorianising' of peasant culture. With sharpening social fragmentation and differentiation undermining the base of communal peasant culture, the ground was ripe for the emergence of newly competitive sectional identities and highly individualised sporting antagonisms. War conditions seemed to provide a fertile environment for just this kind of expression.

Some especially skilled and favoured drivers and leaders achieved gentleman status at a stroke, taking on cavalry officers at pig-sticking and tent-pegging. At the Stellenbosch depot in 1901, regular triangular polo tournaments were held, involving Scottish Yeomanry, the Madras Lancers and a team of Mfengu and Coloured wagoners known as 'The Caledon Chiefs'.[89] Recreation was not always segregated. Officer involvement in the promoting and patronising of mounted sports also extended to other leisure activities. Pugilism, mule, horse, cycle and foot racing were all sports to which senior officers customarily made disbursements. For transport workers, such new pastimes also offered the prestige and prizes of victory. Blankets, boots and cash could be won. Bicycles (or more accurately, boneshakers) were prestigious prizes, as cycling was much in vogue, popularised by the Intelligence Department's practice of saddling despatch carriers on Sunbeams, Humbers and BSAs, and forming them into Native Cycling Corps. During 1902, the Namaqualand Field Force reported that numbers of its muleteers were investing sums of £3 to £4 in bicycles.[90] Unlike Victorian Britain,[91] cycles in the colonies struck more than purely recreational roots. They were also a flexible and cheaply maintainable means of transport.

Leisure and partial relaxation were fully embedded in the workplace, not divorced from but intimately associated with the labouring cycle. Like other skilled rural artisans or craftsmen, transport riders were imbued with pre-industrial concepts of work and time. Thompson has summed up those seminal characteristics as a 'deep-rooted folk memory' attached to a 'pattern of work and leisure which obtained before the outer and inner discipline of industrialism settled upon the working man'. There was a solid affection for the 'characteristic irregularity of labour patterns' which were distinguished by 'alternate bouts of intense labour and idleness whenever men were in control of their own working lives'.[92] The case of transport riders is a classic illustration, for their task – rather than time-orientated organisation of work – allowed them a very considerable degree of independence and control over their own everyday labouring lives. They believed that their skilled status gave them the right to set the pace and shape the character of their task habits and other labour routines.

Rituals of drinking and conviviality went a long way towards guaranteeing that work and leisure were never wholly separated. As a popular means of distraction and indulgence, drink was important: alcohol lubricated the rhythms of riders' work and recreational culture. Despite wartime prohibition, consumption could not easily be curbed, for the association between hard working and hard drinking proved to be a stubborn infection. Drinking on the job was common, and most transport riders seem to have kept themselves plentifully supplied with beer or spirits. It was not unknown for liquor to be an unofficial and illegal component of wages. The 5th Lancers paid its companies of muleteers £5.10s. per month, plus biscuits, chocolate and what beer and brandy the Chief Transport Officer quietly authorised.[93] Beer formed part of the staple diet of many auxiliaries; it provided not only sustenance but the necessary fluid that long and hot summer days demanded. The ambience of work-based drinking was also characterised by heavy off-duty consumption. Such hard drinking was occasionally pursued with extraordinary dedication. In one instance, feasting to celebrate the fall of Pretoria to Roberts in June 1900, thirty wagoners of the West Surrey Regiment drank sixteen gallons of 'Cape Smoke' in the space of a single night and morning.[94] In another episode, a transport officer's 'feast' for workers at which four oxen, eighteen sheep and fifty hogsheads of beer were consumed, reportedly resulted in 'no undue disturbance. All who wished to be drunk were drunk.'[95] There were many other equally awesome displays.

Paternalistic army officers who were prompted to provide such modest 'entertainments' for workers after a particularly arduous or risky spell of work, by supplying food and alcohol, frequently found that drinking got out of hand. It proved difficult to stem the seemingly inevitable decline from drinking to drunkenness. This pushed gatherings in directions which their army patrons deplored, as boisterous and rowdy auxiliaries jeopardised camp orderliness and slighted military authority and rank. Drinking formed not just a leisure pursuit away from the world of wage labour, but a custom *within* it, a bonding of work and leisure which could play havoc with routines and hamper discipline. Excessive drinking led to flying tempers, quarrelling and fighting, both within riders' ranks and between them and soldiers. Men working together in close proximity were reacting to changing conditions and to each other from dawn to dusk, often under great stress; sharpened by drink, simmering tensions simply boiled over. Sustained drinking was thus not all a matter of conviviality: a fat dossier of drink-related offences could be compiled from incident records in army journals, and from punishment books and court martial records. 'Cape Boy' muleteers, for instance, enjoyed a nefarious reputation for indiscipline, unruliness and a fearsome capacity for violence if provoked – conduct universally attributed to their absorption in the cama-raderie of strong drink.[96]

Riders were well steeped in traditions of *machismo* and were invariably eager to dis-play their prowess. For many companies, fiercely competitive mass drinking became virtually a way of life. Skill and district loyalties meshed with ethnic and social identity and status clusterings as townsmen or rural dwellers, staking out the boundaries of hearty rivalry. In larger mixed columns, it was not uncommon for carters and wagoners to drink against one another while on the move, while a team leader or British sergeant kept score. Similarly, Mfengu and Sotho drivers sometimes mounted impromptu beer-drinking contests. A group of Kimberley muleteers employed by the Scots Guards between 1901 and 1902 nourished a corporate identity as townsmen, treating rural and mission remount labourers with scorn and condescension at communal drinking sessions. This band of 'Kimberley Killers' (as they were dubbed by the Guards) con-tained a leading muleteer named Isaac Adonis who regularly boasted of being the British Army's beer-drinking champion.[97] With high levels of troop participation, drinking was certainly one of the most common (and time-consuming) pastimes which brought white soldiers and black workers together on fairly equal terms.

Transport riders' workplace conduct therefore throbbed with the tone and gesture produced by Thompson's typical pre-industrial labourer or peasant's confusion as to where work ended and leisure began.[98] It did nothing to endear them to those of a pro-ductive, orderly and disciplined cast of mind. Men certainly displayed expertise, skill and efficiency on the open road, but the work pattern was far from one of a dictated pace and rhythm of labour. Among British officers in charge of column inspections and fatigues, the repetition of complaints about drivers' 'loafing', 'rowdiness', 'reckless-ness' and 'abandonment' is too great for one to doubt their veracity. Work routines were not infrequently disorderly rather than disciplined, with much racing (mule carts could exceed twenty-five m.p.h.), falling asleep at the reins, and numerous driving mishaps caused by tippling.

Early in 1900, the Army Service Corps tried to instil some idea of order and temper-ate conduct. Field regulations prescribed speed regulations ('native drivers are for-bidden to drive at a trot when at camp'), a curb on the use of whips and a two-man limit on the number of drivers per wagon. But stiff penalties for infringements – fines and floggings – appear to have had little deterrent effect.[99] Riders came in for their fair share of abuse from infantrymen, frustrated by the din and disruption of camp life, and incensed by the spoilage of foodstuffs which sometimes toppled from careering buck wagons. Mule and ox drivers regularly raced one another, recklessly speeding around camps at risk to property and passers-by. Tents were damaged, and supplies repeatedly strewn in their dusty wake. Younger drivers delighted in storming rather than threading a path through camp lines, often provoking violence as harassed, irritable soldiers and jeering auxiliaries settled differences by means of fisticuffs.

Labour independence and labour control

One of the most enduring characteristics of transport riding was the fact that as well-organised riders possessed a critical skill, they were then able to hold the key to the control of the processes and pace of labour. For the military, handling endless fluctuations in work routines and movements and curbing unilateral stoppages became virtually the sum total of labour relations. Erratic practices coexisted with sustained bursts of masterly convoy work, sometimes at breakneck pace. What is important is that wagoners and carters clung to customary ways of pacing tasks. Sometimes, they had the muscle and power to preserve their ground completely, sometimes not; much depended upon the grip of supervision. Men had their own ways of attempting to regulate turn-around times, loading and unloading, inspanning and field maintenance. The 5th Lancers might have sounded reveille at 6 a.m. but its mule drivers were seldom mustered before 9 a.m.[100] In a typical summer working day of 6 a.m. to 6 p.m., it was normal to lose several hours through stoppages of various kinds.

Many columns had sheep, goats, horses and hunting dogs brought along by riders for safe keeping, and these required feeding and grazing, causing companies to lag behind schedule. Abrupt fluctuations in the skilled labour supply also hampered movements. Long-contract wagon crews granted paid leave would disregard return duty times, and rejoin at their leisure, or else pick up work elsewhere. Throughout the war, the Remounts Directorate at Stellenbosch was at loggerheads with Field Intelligence and Special Service departments over the poaching and subcontracting of men for casual despatch riding assignments. Transport NCOs of the Royal Field Artillery encountered frequent operational difficulties during 1901 when groups of African drivers took leave to appear as paid prosecution witnesses in treason trials in Adelaide and Bedford.[101] Deeply ingrained social demands, whether funerals or horse-racing, meant that still others helped themselves to shorter days; workers thought that they had a right to take time off if it was necessary, and considered demands that they secure permission for absenting themselves an impertinent imposition.

There were also numerous transport stoppages due to defiant disobedience of orders. Battle conditions induced fear, panic and flight. Unless armed (and only a small minority were), or accompanied by wagon guards, riders often refused to operate under heavy fire, or when there was probable danger of hit-and-run Republican attacks. If captured, British auxiliaries faced being summarily butchered by commandos, or else harsh treatment as captive labour. On countless occasions, men refused to perform duties, despite pleading, bullying and cajoling by British officers. While there were men who were cited in despatches for acts of extreme bravery,[102] the more widespread response to a guerrilla threat was to down whips and to sabotage transport. Traces were removed or slashed and teamsters outspanned oxen, after which men simply crawled under stationary vehicles until the danger had passed. When ordered into work at revolver point, cornered men either deserted or even turned on irate officers and NCOs, firing ancient muskets at their feet or thrusting bullwhips into their faces. Transport could sometimes be paralysed for days, with workers refusing to budge until routes had been made safe. What many employees were protecting were their capital assets as well as their lives, which explains some of their frantic stubbornness.

A critical factor behind disputes in the workplace was the controlling presence of non-military transport conductors who, as we have noted, came almost entirely from the ranks of casual, under-employed Boers drawn from places like old diamond fields and adjacent areas. Men from districts like Barkly West, Prieska, Upington and Burghersdorp formed a prominent group of white labour foremen in the military structure. Although drawing only several shillings per month more than the most highly paid auxiliaries, they maintained an aggressive superiority, distancing themselves from menial tasks (stacking, loading and unloading) and building a strong social exclusivity, living and sleeping in tents well segregated from workers' quarters. They themselves were tolerated but little loved by their army employers; 'tyrannical Dutch' or 'rough semi-Dutch' conductors were constantly berated for their lack of 'tact' in labour control.[103] While local conductors' utility in the crucial sphere of depot labour discipline was recognised, collaborating Boers enjoyed little social intercourse with soldiers, were treated with patrician contempt by senior officers and, with their political loyalties constantly suspect, were generally mistrusted. For example, while conceding that 'their local knowledge, and the fact that most of them speak a little Kaffir as well as Dutch, and some English, makes them of much material advantage', Commander Limpus of the Naval Brigade grumbled that 'these Boer conductors are of most dubious quality'.[104] Placed in a labour situation conducive to relations of intimidation and repression, conductors established a bawling, bullying presence in the workplace, although their effectiveness as taskmasters was sharply limited in certain circumstances. In many cases, conductors had little palpable impact on the mix of daily life and work, either because they were engaged in insufficient numbers, or because they were incapable of enforcing organisation and discipline upon pockets of skilled workers with defensive wit and strength. But where colonists were able to establish a firm hold over the less skilled and organised, their baleful presence was overwhelming. At Queenstown, De Aar, Naauwpoort and Worcester, for example, life could be made sheer misery for any remount labourer who stepped out of line; fines, floggings and beatings would be added to the frictions of daily work.

While the skilled transport-riding elite enjoyed a degree of real independence and bargaining muscle, unskilled and semi-skilled remount labour working in enclosed, small-scale employment structures, was far more vulnerable to relationships of exploitation and oppression. Many remount depots were enveloped by a miasma of corruption and petty abuses. There was a constant dribble of labourers' protests about the conduct of unscrupulous officials who were responsible for all manner of prickly impositions and extortions. Whenever conductors were short on competence and integrity, workers bore the consequences. Charges debited to time-expired men for equipment breakages were often well in excess of repair or replacement costs, with conductors doing very well by this. An official investigation at the particularly tense Bowker's Park depot in 1901 uncovered an unsavoury racket in which officials were defrauding migrants' families of earnings by remitting only a fraction and pocketing the rest. There were also refusals to grant men time to visit money-order offices to remit wages and pay obligatory taxes. The remitting of earnings accumulated by workers who had died in service caused heated and emotional disputes between claimants and officials, and feelings also ran high over the disposal of labourers' corpses, which were often callously dumped in the veld.[105]

The working atmosphere of field transport divisions and companies could be rendered especially brittle by collisions between transport riders' informal autonomy when carrying out their duties, and conductors' dogged attempts to assert supervisory directives. Not surprisingly, here was another set of circumstances in which the breach between poorer rural Boers and African competitors was widened. Glowering political hostilities, class and racial rivalries, prejudices and hatreds came boiling into the workplace. At Queenstown, for instance, mission-educated Africans from Lady Frere refused to take orders in Dutch from Boer foremen recruited in Cradock.[106] Similarly, at De Aar and Paarl transport officers were driven to despair by the discord between Boer and African employees whose antics led to regular brawling, as, according to the *Household Brigade Magazine*, conductors 'got into the most beastly rows with the native drivers over war affairs'.[107] A Divisional Transport Officer with the Medical Corps described a typical incident at Victoria Road in May 1900, noting that 'tempers are becoming increasingly ruffled. Today, six fellows, who spoke English, refused to inspan their mules because de Klerk had given offence. One of these drivers, Abraham, soon stirred up a spirit of revolt among the other natives, and they were very sulky, and deliberately worked slowly and very badly.'[108]

The impetus of the war certainly seems to have created bodies of militant peasant wage-earners and other skilled men fiercely conscious of their job status and standing as an almost self-contained migrant elite, and conspicuously unwilling to bend to the authority of colonists whom they considered their social inferiors in civilian and army life. Transport riders commonly took umbrage at being given orders in Dutch and did not mince words, execrating 'low-class Boers', 'back-veld Boers' and 'poor whites' in a stream of vituperative protest to their British employers. With workplace divisions so polarised, there were scores of running clashes between riders and conductors; driven too far, auxiliaries beat, flogged and stoned tormenting officials, smashed their property and fired their tents.[109] These antagonistic relations can perhaps be seen as prefiguring the later – and more one-sidedly oppressive and violent – transactions between controlling Cape Boer supervisors and Cape military workers in German South-West Africa in the post-war period; according to Beinart, these interactions constituted an 'explosive mix'.[110]

It must be recognised that auxiliaries did have access to official redress against victimisation, petty or otherwise. The legalistic forms of authority or control exercised by the soldier over workers' lives is clearly not of the same genre as that of the labour regimentation of the mining compound. The army penal code and military law ensured that transport management never had total, untrammelled power over labourers. Army disciplinary controls were by no means always a dead letter; labour grievances were cited at *ad hoc* hearings and courts martial, and when properly activated, these regulatory procedures undoubtedly offered some protection to abused employees. There were notable displays of firmness by senior officials anxious to maintain the duties and functions of military law: soldiers and settlers guilty of violent conduct or parasitic extractions were not treated lightly. In Prince Albert in December 1899, conductors were docked a month's pay and flogged for assaulting a muleteer. During May 1901, Trooper W. Davidson of the Coldstream Guards was sentenced to 100 days with hard labour for stealing chickens from an African ox driver; in August of that year, a transport NCO was reduced to the ranks and given 112 days with hard labour for striking two auxiliaries. The aggrieved parties were each awarded damages of £35.[111] In one extreme episode, two 'ruffian' conductors who had struck a team leader were spread-eagled across the wheels of a cart sent speeding across stony ground, before being stripped naked and held under water to the point of drowning. This kangaroo-court justice was authorised by the senior transport officer of the Somerset Light Infantry, a jaunty man called Percy Mordaunt. The hub of life for Mordaunt seemed to be his transport workers; so much of his time was spent buttering up the Somerset's company of Madras Lancers and African riders by cooking for them, eating with them and pitching his tent alongside theirs, that the regimental journal, *The Light Bob Gazette*, eventually dubbed him 'The Wog'.[112]

Although they have left little trace of themselves, small numbers of Africans were also contracted as regimental conductors. Small carriers, wagonmakers, clerks and interpreters, mission teachers (many of whom owned small Cape carts) who acted as recruiters and other schooled men from areas like East Griqualand, ached for employment as transport conductors. Animated by their own specific class aspirations and general consciousness of the torment of tightening segregation, such *kholwa* applicants emphasised their status as educated men, that as 'a better class of educated Native', they possessed the fitness, competency and pro-imperial loyalties required for army management tasks. 'Being Native', pleaded W. D. Soga in March 1900, 'ought not to debar one from appropriate employment.'[113]

Here was a compelling sense of socially aspirant men wanting to move freely in the upper notches of the labour market; no doubt British military employment practice was perceived to be attractively fluid. But only a trickle of Eastern Cape Africans appear to have gained entry at their desired level. Whatever the multiplying demands of war mobilisation, these labour wants were mediated by Cape officials who rarely neglected their imperatives to uphold sound and 'legitimate' customary colonial labour practices. Africans were not to lead but to be led. With anxious officials prying into labour divisions (including despatching detectives to snoop around transport companies), the social expectations and dispositions of the larger world penetrated into the military arena and strove to dictate its character. But these corrective interventions were not universally popular. Some senior officers were angered by interference with what they regarded as their autonomous domain. One such individual was a Major Dundas of the East Kent Regiment, who reported (with a gratuitous smear of anti-Semitism) a brush with the Hope Town authorities in 1901:

> Rubinstein, a detective from the local magistrate was here yesterday, poking his filthy Jew nose into affairs of what he called 'irregularities' . . . It happens that . . . my foremen, Lucas and Albert, are good sorts, and do for me very well, being well worth their £7 each

month. They understand English too. Rubinstein had the sheer impertinence to question my judgement in using these conductors. I told him this is my command, and turfed him out.[114]

The role of Cape officials as intermediaries was not without its tensions.

Conclusion

If independent and semi-independent transport riding represented an old and declining occupational staple by the turn of the century, the war undoubtedly gave it a sudden and fierce kiss of life. While the national picture presented by Warwick shows that the experience of material gains in the war was certainly not uniform, and that war conditions were directly injurious to the life chances of substantial sections of the settled rural population, there is nevertheless no doubt that many cultivators, herders and skilled rural migrants reaped particular benefits. For Cape migrants for whom skill specialisms, better-than-average wages and relative independence and choice formed the locus of self-definition, the grid of accumulation widened. And while semi-skilled and unskilled men fared less well, auxiliary labour service provided a better-paid and prestigious alternative to the known hardships and depressed wage levels of settler farms and mines.

For large numbers of migrants, even remount depots, despite the unpleasant rigour of their work regimes, superseded ports and railways as preferred employment options. And in these favoured pre-war labour preference sectors for established migrants, boom conditions also pushed up wage rates. If those caught up in conflict in exposed districts prayed for peace, transport workers might well be suspected of praying for the continuation of war.

Aggregate trends are essential to any understanding of the effects of the war on black people, but it is at the local level that the historian can best appreciate the intricacies of reward or deterioration, or the social calibrations of their mobilisation. As Beinart and Bundy have most recently demonstrated, rivers carrying the fragile freight of Cape migrant and 'peasant' independence may all have been tipping their cargo into the same capitalist sea, but they coursed at different speeds and there were significant diversions.[115] For an array of wealthier peasants, cycles of fortune were in the ascendant during the war years; accumulated wage and fee earnings were invested in productive assets of stock, land and agricultural supplies. Deft exploitation of market access provided those able to combine short-term labour migrancy with homestead production, with multiplying chances to strengthen their hedges. As a cavalry officer recorded three weeks before the end of the war:

> The natives have cunningly extracted every possible advantage from the present situation. Here at De Aar, they have been carrying on a feverish trade with Remounts, selling ponies, cattle, and forage at top war prices. Ever ready to work for good wages, they have enrolled in thousands for employment in the non-combatant branches of the army. And they are also becoming valued purchasers. Recently, large numbers of cattle, mares, and sheep have been purchased . . . from the Imperial Remount Department.[116]

Those who engineered and profited from some expansion of peasant economy must be numbered among the chief economic beneficiaries of the South African War.

If we lower our sights from these perspectives of strengthening, other social realities can be detected. Wholly proletarianised rural Coloured communities in the southwest or southeast breathed a different air. Here, the wartime surge in wages was spent primarily on consumption rather than in accumulative and productive investments. This stance reflected rooted social realities; each social sector on the land was affected by its own dynamics. With no resources and reserves in which to invest, many Coloured muleteers simply threw themselves into a hectic spending spree, making the most of a brief release from the humdrum toil, poverty wages and crushing degradations of life on settler farms. Full-stomached men developed a cyclical pattern of working very hard on short contract and enjoying a bout of leisure and breezy living until earnings were exhausted.

Without access to land or cash, wives and dependants (men had a habit of taking older sons or, perhaps, nephews into service with them) bore the heavy price of this ebullient phase. For households, there were months of wretched uncertainty and deprivation, with no remittance of muleteers' wages and the shock of total loss of contact. In some localities, like Tulbagh and Clanwilliam, a precipitous decline into destitution encouraged women to band together for sustenance and security. The importance of these bonds was strikingly visible when women besieged magistrates collectively for relief; in many cases it was only official grain doles and instructions to the army to make wage deductions as a direct remittance to households, that kept muleteers' families from starvation.[117]

To recognise and illuminate the social universe of Cape transport workers in the war, we must acknowledge its diversity, discontinuity and contradictions. Yet, out of this uneven combination, the demands of war were of key significance in also shaping a common, integrative experience of transport riding as a valued specialism. In a transitional phase of Cape working-class development, portrayed by Goldin as increasingly driven by the workings of an 'ethnically hierarchical' structuring of the 'racial and social division of labour' between Coloured and African people,[118] the axis of skill sustained a sociable community of interests between 'Cape Boy' muleteers from the Western Cape and African drivers from the northeast Cape and elsewhere. Moreover, the rough, raucous and resilient hours passed by migrant riders created areas of contested subordination, freedom and initiative; as this spirit spread beyond the ranks of the skilled, others absorbed it and, thinking it appropriate to the galvanising circumstances in which they found themselves, attached themselves to it. For what, following Thompson, we might term 'the whole culture'[119] of transport riding, these were years of frenetic and robust renewal, of insistent energies, and of demonstration through mobilisation of a self and labouring identity as a skilled and muscular migrant elite. 'Moving Lord Kitchener' or what a group of Western Cape Coloured muleteers described as 'riding the Guards',[120] meant more than labour to survive. It meant some control of working lives, the preservation of a customary lifestyle and the proud boast of status.

6

The Republican guerrilla war in the countryside

Blacks on commando

Between 1900 and 1902 there was, in the words of Lieutenant Charles Massey of the intelligence department of the Grenadier Guards, accumulating 'evidence of both armed and unarmed natives among our adversaries in the Colony'. Commandos observed in several Midlands districts, he wrote, 'all had some natives armed, and on horseback, wearing slouch hats and other Boer clothes'. He went on to remark, 'I have always believed what was said of the Boers as to their abhorrence of blacks, but now I know better.'[1] Massey's sightings were certainly accurate, despite indignant denials by scores of *commandants* and *veldkornets* that they were making use of African or Coloured retainers. Senior commandants in the region like Wessels, Kritzinger, Lötter, Myburgh, Malan and Theron trotted about swearing their allegiance to some inflexible conduct code of a white man's war. In the face of total British incredulity, Van Heerden and Conroy, for instance, issued specific rebuttals of imperial army allegations that their forces contained armed Africans. From Dordrecht during February 1901, Johannes Meyer, one of Van Heerden's *veldkornets*, 'denied most strongly that Kaffirs had been employed by him as armed Scouts in the district'. In a letter to the commander of a British column, he 'acknowledged that Kaffirs had been used by Van Heerden as cooks and cleaners, but said that on no occasion had they so much as even touched a rifle. As one white man to another, he was thoroughly disgusted by the accusation.'[2] British forces in Steynsburg and Molteno during 1900 also received regular assurances that as Africans were neither friend nor foe, there could be 'no concert' between Republican forces and blacks.[3] 'We do not permit', Commandant Conroy obligingly informed the Prieska garrison in February 1902, 'any Native under us to carry arms against Britain, neither in the Republics, nor here in the Cape Colony, nor are any Natives to be used as Scouts, in spite of the fact that Natives are employed by the enemy, not only as Scouts, but thousands are armed against us.'[4]

Probably no one tried harder than Jan Smuts to strike a persuasive and authoritative propaganda note. Early in 1902, he brazenly assured the pro-Boer journalist, W. T. Stead:

> The leaders of the Boers have steadfastly refused to make use of coloured assistance in the course of the present war. Offers of such assistance were courteously refused by the

government of the South African Republic, who always tried to make it perfectly clear to the Natives that the war did not concern them and would not affect them so long as they remained quiet . . . The only instance in the whole war in which the Boers made use of armed Kaffirs happened at the siege of Mafeking when an incompetent Boer officer [Commandant P. A. Cronje}, without the knowledge of the Government or the Commandant-General, put a number of armed Natives into some forts.[5]

The flurry of self-righteous accusations and counter-accusations between British and Boer officers appeared to represent little more than a dialogue of the deaf. For both parties to the conflict there was an awkward contradiction between intentions and actions. The movement of resources and men to different fronts at necessary speed was only possible through the appropriation of some level of external black aid.

Virtually all Republican commandants in the Cape pressed varying labour demands to service their operations. In character, purpose and intensity, these demands naturally differed from the requirements of the imperial and colonial forces. Apart from the fact that the light and highly mobile commando mode of warfare did not require the mobilisation of mass supplies of ancillary labour, Cape guerrilla leaders in any event lacked an administrative and logistic structure strong enough to coerce great numbers of labourers into war service. The customary machinery of Republican Boer control, worked by local commandants and their *burgher* militias, with *veldkornets, landdrosts* and other titular officials, simply did not exist. Moreover, Cape workers and peasants were not especially inclined to turn out on behalf of rebel insurgents who, for opportunism or political conviction, appeared to be seeking to depress their condition. But there was a constant demand for workers. And besides labour, Boers needed food, shelter and intelligence.

Bands of labour were secured at random, and men with skills were dragooned into servicing guerrilla needs. On commando, they filled a variety of agricultural, pastoral, domestic and combat requirements. In occupied districts or localities where guerrillas were able to roam with relative impunity, gangs of captive workers were put to work on rebel farms provisioning commandos and to maintain production on the lands of Boers whose labourers had absconded to join British forces. Larger bodies of forced labour were occasionally mustered together to carry out supervised acts of sabotage which involved heavy work, such as the digging up of railway track and shifting of trees and boulders to block mountain tracks. Farm servants and tenants were also frequently assigned as caretakers of the livestock and other property of farmers who were taking up arms against the British. Men also accompanied Boers in the field as grooms, cooks, cleaners, herders, muleteers, *voorleiers* (ox-team leaders), *agterryers* (after-riders), sentries, spies and scouts.

With the exception of the more reliable *agterryers* and a sprinkling of the most loyal scouts, blacks in Republican ranks were neither drilled in, nor entrusted with, firearms. We do not know, and cannot determine, how many *agterryers* saw service in the Cape or nationally; as they were not officially part of the Republican forces, no record of service was maintained. The most diverse estimates have been given, but the least inflated and most reliable aggregate figure, that suggested by Fransjohan Pretorius, indicates that roughly 15,000 may have served in the war.[6]

Fighting retainers: *agterryers*

Many British observers were initially perplexed by accounts of gun-bearing camp followers in Republican ranks, clearly victims of their own propaganda that every black person would distance themself from the Boer camp. 'It is inconceivable', wrote a smug Lieutenant Wayland in January 1900, 'that Natives would willingly ally themselves to the hated oppressors of their face.'[7] Corporal Albert Bowman snorted that 'nothing could be more ridiculous than to imagine that armed Kaffirs are aiding Johnny Boer'.[8] Dubbing them 'camp orderlies', *Under the Union Jack* reassured readers that 'the statements of several correspondents that the Boers are putting Kaffirs in the fighting lines against us, loses much of its seriousness when it is remembered that it is one of their customs, arising from the habit they have of appointing Kaffirs to attend upon the wants of each mess of up to six men'.[9]

In practice, there seems sometimes to have been none too sharp a distinction in certain commando ranks between support service and combat duty. Day-to-day expediencies in consolidating half-manned units and fighting tactics were unquestionably more decisive in moulding *agterryers*' roles than any high-command directive about maintaining their non-combatant status. Belligerent activity from *agterryers* there certainly was, and sometimes in good measure. Between February and April 1900, there were numerous sightings in the northeast of Boer camp followers who were all using firearms on their own account. Across to the west, Commandant Bezuidenhout used picked *agterryers* as marksmen, to bring down mounted Coloured scouts and despatch riders and runners employed by Carnarvon and Prieska garrisons.[10] In Namaqualand operations during 1902, the Smuts and Maritz forces were reliably reported to be employing some seventy black horsemen as sharpshooters.[11] For Smuts, this must presumably have been a most galling experience, in view of his passionate commitment to keeping the war a white man's affair. British troops in Concordia, Klipfontein, Garies, O'Okiep, Carnarvon and Williston all had bruising encounters with fighting Coloured *agterryers* who were skilled at infiltration and light skirmishing, and were often deadly shots. In Sutherland, during April 1900, forty Africans, 'fighting men, and not mere carriers of arms', were reported to be in the front line of an attack on a munitions convoy.[12] Observing operations around Colesberg in the early weeks of the war, an irritated Colonel R. S. S. Cobb noted that as part of a large Boer force of 1,300 men, there were eighty Coloured wagoners, a dozen armed scouts, and around 100 *agterryers*, all of whom were armed and were playing a prominent role in running engagements.[13]

Some of the most revealing reports of *agterryers*' military integration into guerrilla forces come from British soldiers posted to deal with Republican prisoners. These provide a suggestive picture of the social composition of rebel forces, with numbers of poor rural *burghers* clearly predisposed to join the armed rising. And in relation to our existing knowledge of the fragmenting class divisions within Cape settler society in the 1890s, with its 'ill-bred' poor-white underclass 'residuum', they also throw a little more light on the sometimes promiscuous state of class and ethnic relations at the very bottom of colonial society. As Bundy and Isabel Hofmeyr have respectively noted, conditions of life for the substratum of the poor tended towards a 'blurring of ethnic

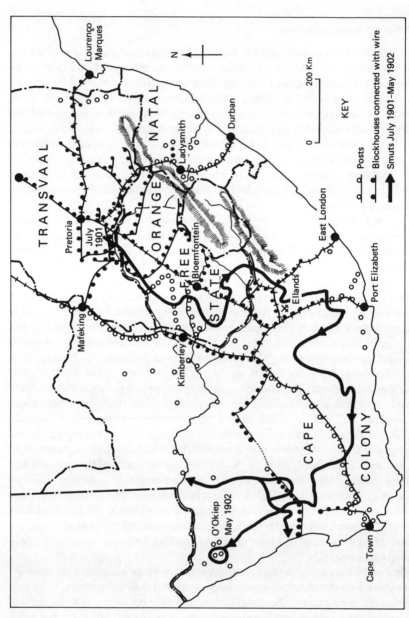

Map 5 British blockhouses and fences: Smuts' invasion of the Cape Colony. From J. Selby, *The Boer War: A Study in Cowardice and Courage* (Arthur Barker, London, 1969).

TRANSVAAL

ORANGE

FREE

STATE

NATAL

CAPE

COLONY

Lourenço Marques

Pretoria

July 1901

Mafeking

Kimberley

Bloemfontein

Ladysmith

Durban

Ellands

East London

Port Elizabeth

O'Okiep

May 1902

Cape Town

N

200 Km

0

KEY

Posts

Blockhouses connected with wire

Smuts July 1901–May 1902

identity', leading to 'jumbled racial communities'.[14] The war did not break every such association. From Carnarvon, in November 1899, Private Arthur Dye described the arrival of 'prisoners of a dreadful low class, composed of Dutch, half-castes, and also Kaffirs carrying Mausers'. He added wryly, 'perhaps these items are used in cooking, as the Dutchmen claim'.[15] In similar vein, an interrogating officer at Victoria West wrote, 'I talked to some of the Boer prisoners and found that there were Coloured men among the Boers, half Dutch, half Native. Also, a goodly number of Kaffirs. The Boers claimed they were only employing black men for digging, driving oxen, etc., but we know that some regularly used rifles.'[16] This same officer later handled another batch of captives, describing them as:

> A very mixed lot, several of them black or various shades of it . . . one of the native ones had been an after-rider and a scout for some considerable length of time, and I read extracts from his notebook, and some of the dossiers he had kept. There were details of his guns and ammunition, and also jottings of his visits to various Dutch rebel farms in Richmond and Fraserburg, and his doings among Dutch girls there.

This genial *agterryer*, Silas Damon, carried the expressive nickname 'Englisch', and certainly made himself remembered. His boastful personal record, written in a concoction of English and Dutch, meticulously listed the full names of eleven wives or daughters of farmers with whom he had liaisons, alongside a record of individual dates and places. In addition, it carried an inventory of items (clothing, clocks, furniture, food) he had liberated from farmhouses, with estimates of their market value.

Damon's other written contemplations – mainly resentment about the size of his commando allowances and planned transactions with stolen livestock – show him to have been a man of formidable appetites. He presented his history to his British captors, claiming descent from a family of Cape *dienstboden* (servants) who had accompanied Boer trekkers northwards earlier in the nineteenth century. When war broke out Damon was earning a pastoral living, tenant farming in the Winburg district of the Orange Free State; his relationship with an absentee Boer landlord was an amicable one. When captured, he was in possession of his personal cart and mule team, which he had brought with him when slipping into the Cape shortly after the outbreak of hostilities. Accompanying *burghers* operating along the northeastern flank of the Colony between November 1899 and February 1900, Damon led other *agterryers* in the field, once served as taskmaster over a forced local labour draft in Burghersdorp, and acted as 'quartermaster' in charge of captured English weaponry and kit.[17]

Many British observers glumly appreciated and admired the highly skilled horsemanship and weapons handling of *agterryers*, as well as the expert scouting, tracking and hunting abilities which they displayed. Although a small and subordinate service element in the Republican camp, these mounted servants and gun-bearers regularly played a vital logistical role during skirmishes, not only keeping firearms in constant working order, but also ensuring that riders and mounts were kept supplied with food and water while on the move. Different ranges of experience and practice and technical skills acquired through years of dependent service in the economies of Boer households were put to a key variety of uses. *Agterryers* undertook camp gun maintenance and repair, loaded rifles and carried ammunition, tended horses and serviced saddle equipment, transported rations, and were sometimes called upon to bear the wounded and bury the dead. Their exploits were – mostly grudgingly – celebrated in popular racist British verse, such as 'The Bravest After-Rider in Cape Colony', 'Kruger's Kaffir Kin', and 'Tale of a Stealthy Native Gun Bearer', the first verse of which ran:

> Tommy, Tommy, watch your back
> There are dusky wolves in cunning Piet's pack
> Sometimes nowhere to be seen
> Sometimes up and shooting clean
> They're stealthy lads, stealthy and brave
> In darkness they're awake
> Duck, Duck, that bullet isn't fake.[18]

A more sober description of their role was provided by the *Light Bob Gazette*, which noted 'each Boer, it seems, has a stout henchman, or it may be that two or three Boers have a henchman between them. In the event of an alarm, he rapidly catches and saddles up his Boer master's horse, while the Boer collects from him his rifle, bandolier, haversack and water bottle.'[19]

It was not only their proficiencies and internal discipline which set *agterryers* apart, but also their origins. Of those fighting in the Cape, most appear to have been conscripted externally, as surviving British prisoner-of-war rolls imply. Comparatively few seem to have been supplied by Cape Boer households, at least in part because commandants were unsure of the trustworthiness of their farm servants. The considered opinion of leaders such as Conroy and Van Heerden was that local servants were too unpredictable and insufficiently loyal to be trusted as gun carriers.[20] Here and there, as we have seen, some collaborators – rural drifters, unemployed casual labourers or discontented deserters from the colonial forces – made common cause with guerrillas and joined as armed camp followers. Relations between these individuals and commando *burghers* were intimate. Organised pilfering and theft was one nexus. In the Karroo, for example, the Van der Merwe commando contained several such Coloured men – John Aanhuizen, Jacobus April, Hans April and Hendrik Booysen[21] – but this kind of independently entered accommodation was rare. Skilled (and rewarded) *agterryers* like Silas Damon came principally from the trekker states, and often over very long distances. Coming from as far afield as Kroonstad, Potchefstroom, Pretoria and Lydenburg, these dependants rode south with their masters.

As is well known, *agterryers* were a peculiar creation of trekker society, drawn from that dependent class of clients and household servants which formed so striking a segment of the social structure of rural Boer communities. Coercive customs of clientage, apprenticeship or indenture created a supply of able labour at the disposal of farming households, consisting of individuals who had been wholly or partially socialised within rural Boer society, and who were physically as well as culturally close to the *burghers* to whom they were contractually bound. Numbers of these loyal *oorlams* and *inboekselings*, living their lives as domestic servants or farm overseers almost entirely through *burgher* culture, did not contest the authority of their Boer masters during the war crisis, unlike so many wilful rural tenants. As *agterryers*, they had for decades customarily played a key supporting role in burgher militia.[22] Thus, as Peter Delius and

Stanley Trapido have noted, '*Oorlams*, like their predecessors in the Cape, served in Boer commandos in the Z.A.R. [Zuid Afrikaansche Republiek] before the first British annexation, and it is well known that they played a part in sustaining Boer guerrillas in the 1899–1902 South African War'.[23]

Locked into service through clientage and other practices of control, some of these trusted farm servants provided lengthy stints of loyal service in demanding and dangerous conditions. Cornelius Klapper, for instance, served with the Naude commando from January 1900 until his capture in February 1902. Jacobus Plaatjies, Andreas Smit, Abel Sika, Frederick and Jacobus Maans fought with two commandos from November 1899 to 1901. Retainers did not always remain with their personal masters. Some men especially skilled in gun maintenance were switched between as many as five or six individual units within as many months. Others with a good grasp of medicinal herbalry were attached to various base camps, nursing Boer wounded in caves or tents.[24]

With subservient *agterryers* and *burghers* enmeshed in a common culture, there was evidently little visible distance between them; social distinctions between masters and dependants often appeared blurred, with the latter intimately assimilated into the guerrilla bands in which they lived and fought. 'The *agterryer* was invariably more than a servant', as Pretorius has so rightly emphasised.[25] The existence of a kindred sense of fraternity between masters and retainers was widely commented upon by British observers, who contrasted this with the ferociously harsh exploitation of commando labour gangs hounded into threshing and ploughing for rebel landowners. In 1901, the *Highland Light Infantry Chronicle* provided a detailed account of what it termed 'Boer familiarity with their Native Riflemen', noting that *agterryers* wore identical clothing to Boers, spoke some form of Dutch as well as, if not better than, their masters, shared the same food, and, sometimes, even the same tents.[26] At Molteno, an intelligence NCO remarked of an encounter with a batch of prisoners, 'I was very surprised at their familiarity with their black comrades . . . they laugh, talk, eat and joke with them like equals.'[27] Olifant, Nortje, Zwaartbooi and Witbooi, four *agterryers* seized by the Durham Light Infantry at Barkly East, were said to have freely shared clothing, utensils, rations, drink and songs with *burgher* companions who showed no evidence of observing racial boundaries.[28] This camaraderie prompted an interrogating British officer to conclude sardonically that the Boers might have benefited from 'proper training' in 'how to behave like white men'.[29]

In order to explain the apparently harmonious social relations and close identity of perceptions and interests between Boers and *agterryers*, historians have turned to the concept of an acculturating and incorporationist paternalism; in particular, emphasis has been placed on what Keegan has identified as 'the most explicitly paternalist imagery of the trusting and loyal retainer'.[30] Pretorius, for example has evinced an affection for a highly idealised picture of unifying social continuities, in which the 'relationship between a *burgher* and his *agterryer* was usually one of friendly understanding, based on a paternalism which the *agterryer* appeared to accept'.[31]

Commando working relationships do appear to provide a strikingly successful illustration of the attentive allegiances and quiescent accommodations that were mediated through the structures of ownership and labour in paternalist Boer households. Camps and small-wagon laagers provided the small-scale locations for face-to-face paternalist bonds of authority and deference to be effectively sustained, and the permanence of attachments between personal farm servants and masters supplied the 'well-defined personal relations' and 'clearly defined rights and duties' which, in David Roberts' general argument, 'formed the cement of paternalism'.[32]

Just how widespread and effective paternalism was in nurturing a snug symmetry between Boers and their mobilised dependants is not easy to determine. There were certainly cases of amicable interpenetration and a shared sense of obligations, of sharing for survival. Equally, however, the commando was an ambiguous social entity. For in its social relations, the embrace of a common humanity had its limits. The essence of a Boer paternalism anchored in a dominant culture and integrating relations of production (and style of warfare) was not benevolence and even less equality. It was a patriarchal authoritarianism, expressing control, leadership, hierarchy and ideological constriction. So, while relationships between masters and skilled retainers may have been free of a rigid distancing racism, and may have been friendly and sometimes even intimate, the latter always remained subservient to the will of the former. *Agterryers* were of servile status and in custom, if only rarely in writing, were regarded as bound by contract. In war, as in peacetime, the experience of such servants was determined by what Delius has referred to as 'contradictory processes of incorporation and exclusion' within Boer society.[33] Thus, commandos were habitually addressed as *Baas*, 'the classic term denoting racial and class superiority', to quote Hermann Giliomee.[34]

But these relations of hegemony were subject to fractures. Writing of the mid-nineteenth-century Transvaal, Delius has suggested that *inboekselings* and clients ought not to be regarded as 'mere ciphers for Boer culture'; despite the nexus which bound servants to masters, there was resentment of and resistance against their position and there were struggles 'to modify or escape it'.[35] War conditions compounded habits of contesting terms of compliance, for the paternalist colouring of Boer ideological hegemony held best in a stable, secure environment. Unsettling war experiences in the Cape both touched off internal conflicts and severely tested the rights and obligations of *agterryer* relationships, as well as the sanctions of their enforcement. Conditions put extraordinary pressures upon the structures of control; they stirred two processes, one ideological and more general, and the other more material and local. Both produced long faces and hurt among commandos. With so much now makeshift and arbitrary, life was experienced as an unbalancing series of continuities and discontinuities; the commando unit could be a closed arena or a sudden open gate to new mental horizons and a social and political world bounded by a different system. This interplay between old and customary and new and impulsive milieux was highly threatening to domesticated, reciprocal relationships between Boers and loyal dependants. Moreover, military engagements with well-armed opponents, supply crises and unexpected reverses which put guerrillas on the run across unfamiliar countryside all dented the standing of Boer leaders.

For many followers the first priority was covering their own hides. Desertion plagued units which were finding the war dismal. In other cases, finding their situation oppressive, numbers of restless servants seized opportunities to flee contract service, some attempting to sneak a niche for themselves in rural market sectors. Whether on the land, or as animal handlers for traders or transport contractors, ex-*agterryers* found a ready market for their skills. Boer concern to retain and control skilled dependants led several commandants to increase rewards for loyal service. In some cases, wealthier notables, like those with the Pijpers, Nel and Theron commandos, provided incentives to preserve long-term attachments; servants were allowed to retain some of their horses and livestock for their own use, were allotted a share of loot and were made handsome promises of land; the beneficiaries of this upturn were arguably doing considerably better than those bickering *bywoners* compelled to serve without agreed remuneration.[36] But the practice of conceding large perks to ensure retainers' loyalty was rare.

The more common line was to ensure that desertion or evasion would produce extremely unpleasant consequences. One requirement on which all commandants were agreed was that *agterryers* had no right to leave service in the field for any reason. Desertion was a risky tactic, as disloyal men were given short shrift if apprehended by Boer forces. Commandant Myburgh, with his usual ferocity, made a point of detailing trackers to hunt down servants who decamped, whom he generally had executed on the spot.[37] Kritzinger placed a bounty of 10s. on the head of any *agterryer* who absconded. The notorious Commandant Fouché of the Rouxville commando issued threats to blacks in his path that any person caught harbouring deserters would be treated as a British spy and shot. On one bloody occasion in December 1901, an irate Fouché careered through the homesteads of African tenants in Molteno, intent on flushing out several deserters who he was convinced were being sheltered there; men and women were flogged, huts were burned and crops were razed.[38]

One dramatic option open to a disgruntled *agterryer* was to change sides and become, in effect, a black 'henshopper' and 'joiner', as surrendered Boers who aided the British were called. For collaboration with the British attracted both white and black landless poor on the Boer side. Scores of servants surrendered to British forces in the Cape where, while not always sympathetically received (floggings were often administered and treason charges threatened), the many-sided skills and intimate intelligence they brought with them stood them in good stead. Those who offered themselves as informers and judicial witnesses were, as we shall see in a later chapter, generally favourably treated. Others redeemed themselves with different proofs of allegiance and friendship, creating a new identity for themselves; this was a cocky one, born of conflict. In Douglas, for example, Willem Jood and Willem Klein earned a considerable local reputation as crafty scouts.[39] Piet Mokana, who deserted Kritzinger's force, became a muleteer at Victoria West and earned praise as a proficient interpreter and hard-eyed interrogator of Boer prisoners.[40] April, a 'surly' ex-*agterryer* who, according to his British paymaster, 'could have passed as a white man', turned so venomously upon his former masters that he led an irregular squad of self-recruited horsemen against guerrillas in Beaufort West and Victoria West during 1901.[41] Some men took to a wandering life, putting on short spells as transport riders in various parts of the colony, undertaking remount work, and acting as casual scouts or spies for intelligence departments. Republican reprisals for such high treachery and defection were savage. In a harrowing incident, seven African drivers taken captive at Colesberg on

4 April 1901, were beaten with their own revolvers, whipped and subsequently shot. An officer who investigated the killings concluded, 'It turned out that all seven of the Native drivers were ones whom the Boers had recognised as having been after-riders who had earlier deserted from them. Why they thought they had a right to shoot them one doesn't know. They were not proper, enlisted soldiers, and so could not be guilty of desertion.'[42] Vengeful commandants naturally interpreted their rights over *agterryers* differently.

Trusted servants were occasionally also involved in the intricate and dangerous operations of spying, espionage, long-range scouting and district reconnaissance at night. Scattered commandos were rarely entirely isolated from one another, with regular communication at times dependent upon black riders or runners. There is evidence, for example, that some mounted African spies conversant in English tried to pass themselves off as British scouts in order to keep columns and camps under close observation and to get their hands on intelligence despatches. Alfred Malapi, a spy shot at Aliwal North on 15 December 1900, had, according to the British firing squad officer, 'been posing for some months as one of our Natives ... dressed exactly like one of our men, khaki coat, breeches, puttees, and an army cap'.[43] One or two identifications have surfaced to suggest that women may also have played some small part in these furtive penetrations of British security. As part of heterogeneous clusters of the casual labouring poor who teemed around camps and remount depots to eke out a living, numbers of women supplied both domestic and sexual services to troops. In the atmosphere of guerrilla war, the jump from anger about prostitutes picking the pockets of distracted clients to mild paranoia about snooping and spying, was swift and natural. There was concern that women might take advantage of the general immunity granted by both sides to do undercover work for Boer forces. The 5th Lancers assigned camp constables to watch suspects and carry out security checks of 'suspicious female Natives'. And the South Wales Borderers, for example, detained three of its laundresses for passing information to commando spies.[44]

Although individuals taken captive were generally eager and willing to inform on their masters in return for indemnity from prosecution, there are fleeting glimpses of quite fierce loyalty and intransigence on the part of spies who refused to betray Boer masters. At De Aar in June 1901, an officer recorded that 'several Natives just would not give the Boers away, despite being subjected to the most ferocious threats'.[45] 'Even after beating them and threatening to shoot them', Private S. Fearnside reported from Naauwpoort, 'two spies who were with Wessels would not tell us anything.'[46]

Labouring conditions

A major Republican objective being what it was – the assertion of local political dominance and social and labour discipline over the black labouring class and peasantry in the countryside – communities could expect to feel the sting of labour compulsion and property expropriation. Wholesale seizures of men caused a shock to rural society. Kritzinger, Smuts, Maritz, Hugo, Malan and Bezuidenhout – to name just a few – made no attempt to constitute labour resources through negotiating with local structures and interests, still less through bidding for friendship. Instead, taking charge of production and consumption on supplying rebel farms, they screwed down hard on any labour within reach. Forced labour gangs were sometimes augmented by returning Cape labour migrants from the Rand mines who, having been roughed-up and stripped of accumulated earnings, were muscled into work.

As Boer operations expanded, the costs of lengthening and spreading supply lines pressed on the backs of rural black property owners whose assets were commandeered at will. In Maraisburg, Steynsburg, Colesberg, Molteno, Albert, Dordrecht, Aliwal North and Barkly East, carts and wagons were wrested from Africans with owners frequently forced along as drivers. A classic victim was Jonas Mungawara, a prosperous Mfengu producer from Barkly East. Speaking in November 1901 of his harrowing period of capture, Mungawara testified that 'the Boers came here some time ago and took from me one mare, 19 horses, 35 bags of grain, my Cape carts and mule spans, and two of my servants. For four weeks they made me drive for them, saying they would shoot me if I did not do so.'[47] A somewhat perverse tribute to conditions on commando is provided by a Scottish infantryman who spent several weeks in 1900 as a prisoner of the Louwrens Geldenhuys commando:

> They impressed me greatly in the management of their transport. The Kaffir Drivers really did work when the Boers 'bossed' about. The British soldier on the other hand, fraternises too much with the Kaffir and fails to master him ... The fear of the Dutchman and his *sjambok* seemed to work wonders, and the waggons flew forward for all they were worth. We lack the Boer's experience, and in time we may profit ... Although we pay our Kaffirs £5 a month and more, we do not even get one half of the work out of them which the Dutchman does. He recompenses them with the *sjambok*, as the only payment, and makes them scavenge for their own food, and holds them in utter contempt as fellow creatures.[48]

Drivers and other forced workers suffered terrible privations. Often without even a regular crust at the end of the day, uncertain of when they might be released and saddled with punishingly hard work tasks, their lot was a miserable one. Prolonged fatigue, starvation diets, constant beatings and continual forced moving took a dire toll of health and fitness, as did biting winter frosts when little provision was made at camps to provide fuel and shelter.

Whenever opportunities arose, miserable and restive conscript workers fled, singly or in groups. Some managed to get safely clear of pursuit parties and return to homes from which they had been commandeered. Others, who had often been subsisting for weeks on a diet of boiled wheat, water and fruit, stumbled their way towards British forces in the hope of securing sustenance.[49] Those fortunate enough to run into relatively humane medical officers were nourished and treated in field hospitals. One exceptionally compassionate physician, Major Frederick Porter of the Royal Army Medical Corps, was so distressed by the weak and demoralised state of African labour fugitives that, in March 1901, he recommended increasing the number of native wards at field hospitals to cope with 'severely malnourished' deserters. Porter also devised a special protein diet to aid their recuperation. Like many of his fellow medical officers, he advised recruiting officers against enlisting fugitives and deserters because of their appalling physical state.[50] Injured *agterryers* sometimes also suffered medical neglect, finding themselves left to die in the veld without food or care. In one horrific case,

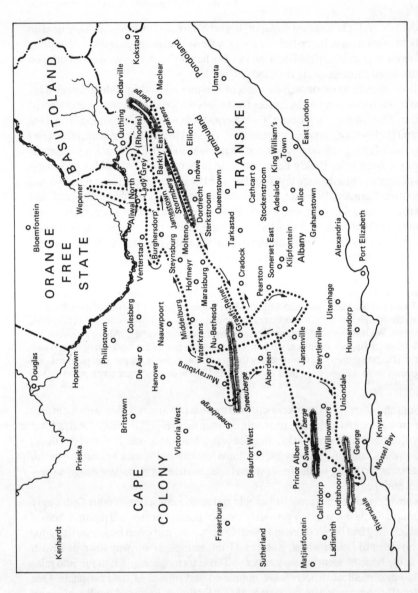

Map 6 Commando movements of Commandant Willem Fouché and General Wynand Malan. Such forces were typical of those referred to by Milner as a 'severed worm' wriggling about in the veld (Pakenham, *Boer War*, p. 526). Adapted from Ph. J. du Plessis, *Oomblikke van Spanning: Die Oorlog in die Kaapkolonie 1900–1902* (Nasionale Pers, Kaapstad, 1938).

Hendrik Setolane, his thigh shattered by a British bullet, was estimated to have dragged himself along for over ten miles to beg for help at a cavalry camp.[51] Something of the desperate plight of such men can be glimpsed through the text of a letter written by three wounded and abandoned servants in December 1900. Addressed poignantly to 'The Great Lord Roberts', and handed to Frederick Porter at Rouxville, it pleaded, 'Please sir, we three Native men wish loyalty to you as we can no more stay with Brink and his men we are hurt bad but Brink he say we are not White Men so there is no help. We are hurt and bleed bad and must now get help if soon we do not die.'[52] *Burghers*, in contrast, could mostly count upon some kind of makeshift provision.

Conscription, expropriation and control

Attempts to conscript labour created deep convulsions as settled communities experienced ordeals of raiding. Entire villages were sometimes depopulated of able-bodied men and boys. When mission station inhabitants at Wupperthal, Genadendal, Elim, Tulbagh and Riversdale spotted armed Boers in the vicinity, they fled into hills and ravines; once stations had been scoured unsuccessfully for labour by exasperated *veldkornets*, they filtered back gingerly. At times these settlements had their peace shattered two or three times a week. Through the midlands and to the northeast, Republican *veldkornets* and newly installed *landdrosts* pressed hard on heads of peasant settlements, demanding the supply of labour levies as *opgaaf*. Uncompliant headmen were dealt with violently. In Barkly East, Herschel, Richmond, Lady Grey, Adelaide, Molteno and Graaff-Reinet, there were countless floggings of recalcitrant village headmen. Whipping, that favoured form of punishment traditionally employed to symbolise and entrench trekker power and political authority,[53] became an instinctive answer to verbal resistance. In Gordonia, where guerrilla leadership was lethally impatient, rural smallholders who refused commando demands brought great violence down on their heads. Rhenish mission Baster leaders were shot, huts fired, and women and children seized as hostages to try to force communities into yielding labour tribute. In one incident, Boy Visser, a Baster goatherd in Upington, received fifty lashes and was tied between two horses and dragged along for several miles as punishment for refusing to locate labour for Niewoudt's force. Four other leading Basters, Willem Witbooi, Isaac Bok, Jacob Patties and Andries Visagie, were treated no less mercilessly in later encounters with Niewoudt's *veldkornets*.[54]

In districts where guerrillas were unable to consolidate control or scare the populace into docility, commandants tended simply to rampage onwards, spreading havoc. In some areas, the fabric of peasant communities was shredded as Boers razed crops, plundered stock and sacked homesteads. Not only were poultry and agricultural produce snatched as food and pigs and goats slaughtered on the spot to provide meat, but entire flocks and herds were liable to be scattered, driven off or wantonly butchered. It is difficult to gauge the full scale of losses at both community and individual levels; while the incidence of peasant calamity may have been heavy in settlements in Barkly East, the population in Engcobo would have escaped Republican depredation unscathed. In other words, the fleecing pattern of destruction and confiscation was highly uneven, with infinite local variation. Clearly, the patchy losses of the war for sectors of the black populace must be seen as a key determinant of the shifting mosaic of property, accumulation and survival in the colony in the early years of the twentieth century.

To appreciate the force of quantitative losses we can turn to some examples. During May 1902, for instance, Basters in Kenhardt lost over 3,000 sheep, watching despairingly from a distance as Maritz and Smuts drove them off.[55] In raiding in Carnarvon during March 1901, pastoralists lost 2,500 sheep, 893 cattle, 320 horses and 252 mules.[56] Jacob Kok and Hendrik Kieviet, two herdsmen in the Hay area, were typical of individuals who suffered cumulative losses from repeated raiding. Over a six-month period, Kok estimated that he lost 350 cattle, while Kieviet witnessed the slaughter of 80 of his goats and the seizure of 160 cattle and 178 pigs.[57] Many similar examples could be adduced.

The response of some stockowners was to try to preserve their herds by driving them into watered mountain recesses or behind natural hill ramparts. When guerrillas came after them – as happened at Stormberg in July 1901 – herdsmen could display exceptional tenacity and nerve. Efforts were made to try to beat off commandos, fighting with old single-shot rifles if they had them, but more commonly with rocks or spears. Others tried to protect their livestock by attaching themselves to British military camps and columns, driving their herds along for many miles under army protection, and snatching rest and pasturage whenever possible. In return for protection, followers were often called upon to donate some of their stock to army field kitchens and their labour to remount divisions.

Guerrilla campaigning naturally also involved black civilian casualties. Many individuals, whether or not they offered resistance to the Republicans, found themselves the victims of commando suspicion and malice. Anyone identified as actively serving the British war effort or as colluding in its operations was regarded as a foe and numerous civilian killings sowed great fear. In parts of the northeast, for example, settlements sometimes lost the struggle to keep life going in the face of Boer repression; turfed out of their homes by *veldkornets* who, after conducting fruitless searches for 'spies', vented their fury on bystanders, groups of Africans fled the countryside in terror. At Aliwal North, in January 1901, the Highland Light Infantry reported 'streams of Fingo and Basuto fugitives with their wives, families and all their belongings. To avoid being shot by the Boers was the reason they all give for their exodus. They certainly have been shooting a lot of natives simply suspected of being in our employ or of giving us information – murder is the right term.'[58] On 26 July that year, *veldkornet* Dirk Brits executed twenty-nine Mfengu residents in Dordrecht – men, women and children. The families were in league with the British, he asserted. After turning over the bodies to find kin and friends, the rest of the small Mfengu settlement bolted.[59]

British scouts, despatch runners and riders and other auxiliaries who were run to ground appear in most instances to have been shot, whether taken in arms or not. Black women who played a useful (and little acknowledged) part in British operations by providing intelligence auxiliaries with shelter and food and who stored despatches and signals, were not always spared either. Without casualty figures, the question of arriving at any estimate of mortality must of course remain elusive. What we do have are many firm indications of a sweeping policy of liquidating British collaborators.

106

Near De Aar, in the month of August 1901 alone, thirty-seven unarmed scouts were shot. In November of the previous year, a band of forty Mfengu and Coloured auxiliaries employed by the Argyll and Sutherland Highlanders and taken captive near Queenstown, were lined up and executed. The 17th Lancers lost sixteen of their despatch riders, 'cut to pieces' at Aliwal North in September 1901; several were shot, while others were disembowelled or 'otherwise dreadfully mutilated'.[60] As chilling glimpses of vengeance enacted by the commando leadership and its subordinates, examples like these could be multiplied endlessly.

Pacification rested on violence. From his Stormberg lair in 1901, Kritzinger authorised subordinates to shoot on the spot not only British auxiliaries but any black person of whom they were suspicious. Taking full advantage of such latitude, Jan Maree and Hermann von Doornek executed over fifty Coloured people, including children, as they cut a lethal path through Rietfontein, Matjiesfontein and Sutherland between August and December 1901. Maree claimed that they had been informing on Boer movements.[61] Louwrens Geldenhuys who, according to the British special intelligence agent at Williston, 'did not spare the life of any Native unfortunate enough to cross his path', testified upon capture that 'General Smuts personally gave me orders to shoot all unarmed Natives who might be working for the British who should fall into my hands.'[62] The response of some British officers to the wave of killings was firm and ferocious. Colonel White of the Garies garrison in Namaqualand was so incensed by Smuts' execution of an Andries van Wyk, brother of Petrus van Wyk who had guided British columns through Kenhardt, that he immediately ordered the shooting in reprisal of five Boer prisoners on 4 March 1902. 'Inform Smuts', White thundered, 'that if he continues with these murders more severe reprisals will be made.'[63] Two of the most dour and ruthless Republican commandants operating in the Cape, Johannes Lötter and Gideon Scheepers, were taken by the British and at hearings faced charges of having murdered 'half-caste scouts' and 'loyalists or Natives'. Both men were executed.[64]

In a number of districts guerrilla leaders moved almost at will, taking special pains to lay out their claims and sanctions across as broad a front as possible. Lötter and Scheepers, for instance, issued decrees and proclamations which made clear to rural inhabitants just what kind of harsh measures they could expect if they fell foul of Republican forces. In areas where if Boers did not have uncontested control they had at least the largest claim to it, commandants acted with unprecedented conceit and personal arrogance, imposing stringent curbs on movement along roads and across fields.

Conroy, for example, ruled in January 1901 'that no Native or Native girl will be allowed to move about the districts of Carnarvon or Prieska without a pass signed by him'.[65] Also threatened was anyone near a commando 'without proper reason'; anyone who had slipped their personal safe-conduct pass to another; and anyone who dishonestly requested a pass. Fouché and Kritzinger likewise sent their *veldkornets* galloping through settlements, issuing proclamations and ensuring that terms of obedience were known to inhabitants. Characteristically crushing and comprehensive was an expulsion decree issued by Fouché at Aliwal North on 14 October 1901:

Seeing that the British military authorities employ Kaffirs and other Coloured people against the combined forces of the Orange Free State and South African Republic as fighting parties, and also as spies, so it is that I, Willem Diedrich Fouché, herewith determine that from this date, to the 15th November next, all Coloured people on the farms of any of the inhabitants of the Cape Colony must immediately leave the said farms and return to their country. If the said Kaffirs or Coloured people do not act according to this proclamation, they will be dealt with . . . also that all shepherds and servants . . . must be provided with a pass. If this pass cannot be produced by the said shepherd or servant when any armed *burgher* meets him he will be regarded as an English spy and will be shot if he falls into our hands.[66]

The Leliefontein incident

The most searing conflation of property destruction and personal assault occurred at the Methodist mission station of Leliefontein, near the small towns of Kamieskroon and Garies in southern Namaqualand. Placed in the context of wartime struggles and envenomed relations between blacks and Boers, the experience of Leliefontein provides good evidence of the way in which intrusive divisions of purpose and interest between local populations and invading forces structured daily life, for running agrarian conflict had a particularly unhinging impact on this mission settlement. Events in Leliefontein are therefore worth following in some detail.

Here, as elsewhere, the war enlarged markets; as early as January 1900, the supply needs of the Namaqualand Field Force began tapping even the marginal pastoralism and cultivation of this 75,000 acre Baster reserve. After lean years of toiling away on increasingly exhausted soil and diminishing pasturage, an impoverished mission community received a sudden kiss of life. Cultivation marched higher up hillsides as army purchasing officers provided the money and motivation for a cycle of local accumulation. Good rains during 1900 and 1901 helped production. Corn and garden vegetable prices rose sharply. Some of the poorer residents abandoned precarious cultivation altogether after rationing Field Force patrols from small surpluses, and invested in animals. Large numbers of young men went out and contracted themselves to the Namaqualand military as scouts, despatch riders and runners and carriers at pigeon post and heliograph stations. Other inhabitants sold their only visible capital assets – cattle, sheep and goats – and purchased carts and mule teams with which to establish themselves in army transport riding.

On the vital supply route between Carnarvon and Williston, 275 armed guards and 180 muleteers were Leliefontein burghers; a further 250 wagoners worked supply lines between Lambert's Bay and Port Nolloth and British garrisons. From 1901 to 1902 there were also an estimated 300 'Leliefontein Boys', also known as 'Cooper's Camels', scouting for the Namaqualand Intelligence Department.[67] So many men were siphoned off that in January 1901 the governing mission council or *Raad* reported that it had been unable to hold sessions for several months, 'owing to so many of the *Raadsmen* and Burghers being employed as Scouts during the Great Boer War'.[68]

These activities provoked the enmity, and often also the fear of pro-Republican settlers. Farmers were in particular angered and frightened by the appearance of armed and uniformed Basters impertinently questioning them and impounding their cattle on

108

all manner of pretexts. Long-standing conflict over labour supplies was also sharpened by the Namaqualand Field Force habit of poaching workers whom farmers were desperate to obtain. Settler growers were already weak in the market and unable to put more land under the plough. However patchy its pasturage and scrubby its cultivable land, Leliefontein still enabled many of even its poorest residents to scratch out a living through subsistence production, hunting and gathering, and thus to resist full proletarianisation.[69] A further frustration for farmers was the unhelpful attitude of white Methodist staff who refused shrill demands to prod members of their congregation into wage labour at busy times of the farm year.[70] Instead, missionaries generally encouraged Basters to resist degrading labour conditions on local farms.

Tension between opposing interests became explosive after 1900 as Leliefontein increasingly exported labour to the British at Boer expense. And labour contracted to Boer employers became that much harder to keep at work, as resident labourers ran off to join parties of Leliefontein migrants. In response, severe disciplinary controls began to be imposed on farmworkers. In turn, scores of agricultural workers reacted to bullying by breaking labour contracts and deserting to the Leliefontein reserve.[71] Received there by the *Raad* as fugitives and refugees, most stayed on at the station only temporarily before moving on in search of better pay and less burdening conditions with the Namaqualand military. Boers accused Methodist clergy of subverting their domestic work force by spreading insubordination, and by instigating them to sever wage and debt relations. A seething Jan van Reenen spoke for many when he wrote from Garies

7 Fortified outpost, Namaqualand.
(Courtesy of the National Army Museum, London)

on 22 February 1901, that 'farmers all around here complain to me ... that their servants and labourers deserted their service, left them in the lurch, and fled into the Institution of Leliefontein, where this appears to be encouraged'.[72]

What we see, then, is a steady and increasingly acute degeneration of relations in the area. Settlers sensed that they were at a crisis, with their capacity to maintain bonds of deference and labour discipline being eroded by insidious pressures emanating from the mission. Groups of Smuts' guerrillas in the locality were enraged by Basters' repudiation of their increasing demands for tax or labour tribute as homage. Commencing mid-way through 1901 as increasing numbers of commandos swarmed into the western area, attacks on Leliefontein auxiliaries began, and agriculturalists on the boundaries of the reserve were harried by armed horsemen riding out from farms bordering the reserve. In skirmishes, agricultural implements were burned and grain pits ransacked. Like so many other mission stations, Leliefontein began living in constant fear of Boer attack. It had good reason to.

On 11 January 1902, a force led by Gerhardus 'Manie' Maritz took the station, cantering up the lower slopes of the Kamiesberg towards a head-on clash with waiting inhabitants at the major settlement of Lilyfountain. The only known published account of what is supposed to have taken place is that provided by Deneys Reitz's classic work, *Commando*, which relates that Maritz 'had ridden into the station with a few men, to interview the European missionaries, when he was set upon by armed Hottentots, he and his escort rapidly escaping with their lives. To avenge the insult, he returned next morning with a stronger force and wiped out the settlement.'[73] What appears to have transpired was a tense meeting between Manie Maritz and the missionaries at which the Boer leader demanded that the Leliefontein burghers swear themselves to peace. Baster *Raadsmen* did not attend; possibly they were against keeping their peace on imposed terms or else were simply nervous about getting themselves hemmed in by horsemen on all sides. After detaining the chief missionary, the Revd J. G. Locke, Maritz ordered Lilyfountain burghers to assemble in front of the parsonage. Handwritten proclamations were distributed, threatening reprisals against anyone caught aiding the British. Carrying the declared allegiance of scores of local farmers, Maritz attempted to repay some of it by ordering all fugitive farmworkers on the reserve to return to their employers on pain of death.[74] The commandant went further, urging the assembled Basters to swear an oath of loyalty to the Republican cause and, unusually, seemed to offer a truce. It was of a rather testing kind. A decree issued by Maritz was read to the attending crowd which 'forbade them, on pain of death, to give any help, information, or forage to the English, and promised them protection. Wounded Bastards by his orders were to be sent to Garies for treatment, and he stated that passes would be given to all to leave the station to assist the Boer cause ... Bastards would be given land and cattle by the Boers.'[75]

This failed to earn Maritz the submissive allegiance of mission burghers. The Lilyfountain crowd grew restive and when two *veldkornets* told the villagers to break up, they were pelted with vegetables and shouted down. Levelling his rifle, the commandant ordered the crowd to disperse. It had no visible effect. Two of those present at this inflammatory moment were Barnabas Links and Jan Dirks, influential members of the *Raad*; the pressing crowd around them quickly hoisted the *Raadsmen* up on their shoulders. The sight of Links came as a rude shock to the commando; according to one member, 'among the encircling audience was recognised . . . the face of Barnabas Links, as one of the Natives captured at Garies in September, 1901 who, it was thought, after a beating . . . had now come back to live in peace at Leliefontein'.[76] Peace was, however, the last thing on Links' mind. He and Dirks, with Willem Bok, Jacob Alias and several other *Raadsmen* had been roving around Lilyfountain for some days, calling burghers by name out of their homes and combing the area for weapons in anticipation of trouble. A small force had been mobilised, sweaty but ready to act, since 3 January. Lines of communication about Boer movements were reliable.

The *Raad* was resolved to do its utmost to protect the reserve's substantial central store of wheat and rye, a portion of which was set aside as food supply for the dozens of refugees squatting at Lilyfountain. The settlement's grain pits not only assured survival during periodic drought crises but now also represented an increasingly valuable capital source during the war period of inflated market prices. The Leliefontein management had good reason for harbouring long-standing suspicion that guerrillas had designs upon its most treasured resources.[77]

Nothing better illustrates this instinctive fear of expropriation than the manner in which Links and Dirks reportedly rose to confront Maritz. 'Why don't you go and leave our goods alone', Dirks shouted in Dutch, while his companion denounced the commando presence, declaring 'by what right do you come here to starve us?' Maritz, evidently maddened beyond words, dismounted and, producing a *sjambok*, made for Links. There was a roar of fury from the crowd and they surged around the *Raadsmen* and Maritz. Clubs were thrust into the hands of Links and Dirks, with which they clumsily attempted to bludgeon the commandant to the ground. Almost simultaneously, a volley crashed out from the mounted commandos, straight into the heaving bodies below them.[78]

Men, women and children ran off in every direction, leaving behind at least a dozen bodies bleeding on the ground. Barnabas Links fell mortally wounded and died in the parsonage garden. Even as the first Boer shots rang out, the small group of armed burghers let fly with their ancient muskets. They had deployed themselves with skill and system, lurking behind the parsonage and lying flat along a high bank which overlooked the scene of confrontation. A short battle raged, in which several Boers and Basters fell. It was said that one Leliefontein burgher, short of shot, got within two yards of a commando to smash a stone into him before he was gunned down. A shaken Maritz decided to pull out to a more secure position on the southern hills at Korenlandskloof above Lilyfountain. In withdrawing, the commandos ran into another disaster. As they came up a ravine, they were ambushed by the Leliefontein force, which rolled boulders down on them and sniped away freely. Thirty Boers were killed, and four of them unhorsed and crushed by tumbling rocks. Seven Basters lost their lives in return fire.[79]

Greatly unnerved by this engagement, a beleaguered and humiliated Maritz sent through a frantic despatch to Commandant Schoeman at Van Rhynsdorp, requesting speedy assistance to help put down the 'Bastard Rebellion'. Schoeman despatched a force at once. In the early afternoon of 13 January it signalled its approach to Maritz who, now on the offensive again, moved down from Korenlandskoof. With

Schoeman's troops streaming in from the north, a vengeful Maritz wheeled into Lily-fountain. There was still plenty of fight left in his opponents and for a further two days the settlement saw scenes of shattering violence as scythes and stones were turned against Mausers. Forty-three Basters were killed. No one can now establish the number of people wounded, but the Intelligence Division of the Namaqualand Field Force made a moderate estimate of one hundred. Some individuals must have perished in secrecy. With resistance crushed, hundreds of panic-stricken burghers melted into the Kamiesbergen, lugging their dead and wounded piggy-back. According to field intel-ligence reports, bodies were found hastily buried in fields as far east as Naaurivier and as far north as Norap, on the fringes of the reserve.[80] Reitz, who arrived at Leliefontein with General Smuts in the wake of the Maritz assault, was much distressed by what he saw. So, if his chronicle is to be believed, were others, including Smuts. 'We found the place sacked and gutted', wrote Reitz, and 'among the rocks beyond the burned houses, lay 20 or 30 dead Hottentots, still clutching their antiquated muzzleloaders . . . Maritz's handiwork . . . wiped out the settlement, which seemed to many of us a ruthless and unjustifiable act . . . We lived in an atmosphere of rotting corpses for some days.'[81]

In Lilyfountain Maritz spared little. Dwellings were gutted, muskets smashed and furniture and sheds consumed as firewood. Any books discovered were burned. Here and elsewhere on the station, the Boer force dismembered the means of production. Fields were razed, grain pits sacked, stock butchered or run off and agricultural tools expropriated. Virtually anything portable, it seemed, wound up on white farms at Garies, O'Okiep and Springbok. Some weeks after the end of the war, Boer producers in Springbok were found to be using over 100 double-furrow ploughs seized from the major reserve settlement of Lilyfountain and another station settlement at Kharkhams.[82] *Bywoners* and other nomadic poor whites trudged across the reserve to capture horses, mules and wagons and supplies of wheat, grain and barley. Like down-trodden whites everywhere, they were often eager and predatory followers of Repub-lican forces, seizing chances to enlarge their meagre resources from the ruin of black competitors. In Leliefontein their sackings were hectic, removing even abandoned clothing and cooking utensils.

As for the Baster refugees, reports between February and May speak of some of them being hunted down and set to work feeding and cooking for the occupying force.[83] At Lilyfountain these forced servants were shackled in iron provided by the parsonage forge, rather an original way for Maritz to support mission industry. Otherwise the station was no longer a centre of production, nor even of habitation. By mid April, some 1,800 weary and despondent inhabitants had trekked to Garies and O'Okiep. In ensuing weeks, several hundred more followed. Other families roamed further, eventually congregating in Lambert's Bay and Port Nolloth, from where the Royal Navy shipped numbers of them to Cape Town as refugees.[84] Criticising an order from General French on 15 May that Leliefontein burghers be ejected from Garies, Concordia and O'Okiep to ease the pressure on garrison grain supplies, the commander of the Namaqualand Field Force retorted, 'the people have nowhere to go. The Boers have burnt Leliefontein.'[85] In breaking the capacity of the mission community to repro-duce itself, Maritz appeared to have succeeded where natural disasters of drought and poor harvests had so repeatedly failed.

Political belligerence

Elsewhere, district tensions exploded into visible struggles between invading commandos, white local collaborators and black communities. Some of these engagements were long, others short-lived, all of them were hard. Individuals both on occupied lands and in threatened neighbouring districts constantly disputed and contested guerrilla demands. Local labour drafts under the direct command of *veldkornets* deserted, maimed horses and stock, poisoned drinking water, slashed harnesses and saddles and, occasionally, fired dwellings on farms on which they were held captive. Africans left to guard the herds of rebel farmers frequently drove them off, disposing of stock to remount depots which generally purchased commodities with no questions asked.

Headmen also pressed the authorities for guns with which to arm followers keen to avenge the deaths of kinfolk.[86] Making their presence felt, scattered groups of Africans inserted their own independent forays into the shifting local balance of direct action and resourceful illegality; if their security was threatened by commandos they issued retaliatory threats against Boer stock and land. In the northeast, to the consternation of rebel farmers, periodic staged withdrawals of regular Boer forces left them wide open to reprisals by armed parties of peasants who not only reclaimed stolen possessions but looted cattle. In some polarised localities order virtually broke down completely. 'In the no-man's land districts of Molteno and Steynsburg', in Warwick's words, 'scoured by patrols from both sides and in which no regularly enforceable authority prevailed, a good deal of raiding and counter-raiding took place between local Afrikaner farmers and black peasants.'[87] Militant Coloured populations in Kenhardt, Prieska, Fraserburg, Upington, Victoria West and Carnarvon were seen as so potentially difficult to subdue that General Wessels, chief commandant of the western district, delayed moving against any of these settlements until he was able to move down troop reinforcements from the Orange Free State.[88]

Some shadowy bands of men in the countryside gave organised expression to their anti-Boer belligerence; they formed themselves into irregular armed levies operating outside the command structure of the army and colonial defence forces, but with the connivance of British agents who supplied them. These untrained, indisciplined and ruffianly gangs displayed a keenness to get at their prey which greatly impressed British officers. Operating in the northwest, Lukas Plaatjie and Pieter Bok, two men from Garies, became celebrated local bounty hunters, bringing in young rebels who were driving cattle seized by commandos. Leading a party of mounted Basters, they hunted down thirty-two Boers between August and November 1900; Bok and Plaatjie were subsequently commended by Colonel Cooper of the Namaqualand Field Force in December 1901, who afterwards recorded his impressions of them:

> These fellows are very keen on upholding justice and the law. Even if their methods are rough, this is all to the good. The infernal low class whites who are so swelled up by the presence of armed Boers in these parts are a great menace ... They seem to think they can steal freely from the Bastards. It pleases me that this bunch of natives will not put up with Boer cheek. Bok and Pladkie [*sic*] have in them the spirit of John Wild and might even teach our English poachers a thing or two.[89]

Relations between the Republican camp and rural blacks were not always an unrelenting test of military violence. But the process of Boer rural conquest proved devastating in other ways. For localities which were overrun and temporarily staked out as Republican enclaves – Aliwal North, Barkly East, Jamestown, Colesberg and Kuruman can be cited as examples – the anguish of occupation was especially marked. Boer confiscations and tribute demands bit deep into the social and political fabric of rural people, bringing unprecedented hard times to many. Yet, in some essential respects, the random plundering of surplus and disruption of patterns of production and accumulation represented merely the topsoil of military conquest. Commandants were sometimes strong enough not just to sack homesteads but to establish a triumphant Republican controlling presence at local levels. For encroaching Boers, politics ran alongside plunder. For, as the external arm of the trekker states, campaigning guerrillas sought powers of political enforcement over newly subjugated peoples. While many of their offensives were of little obvious military importance, they clearly underlined the socio-political motives of the Republican war effort in British territory.

Men like Kritzinger, Smuts, Hertzog and Olivier appeared as the cutting edge of a form of racial power based on the expropriation of Cape peasants, migrants and other workers and on a shrill rhetoric of racial superiority. Shifting layers of local Boer conquest rested unambiguously on force, and the colonising drive for political accumulation bent the backs of rural communities as existing colonial customs and practices were shouldered aside. In dozens of areas, individuals abruptly found themselves subject to the sanctions of what commandants termed Republican Native Law. For those schooled in the rhetoric and rituals of 'British' law, deriving its legitimacy from notional principles of equality and equity, the idea of subordination to a transparently partial and unjust Native law was repellent and degrading. Intended in part to provide a legitimising bureaucratic basis to occupation, 'Native law' served to consolidate the legalistic mumbo-jumbo of Republican political power, ousting the constitutional authority of the colonial order. Subsuming within its rubric all manner of coercive fiscal and work regulations, it defined and enlarged high-handed demands and claims upon resources and labour. In addition to enforcing the carrying of passes, Native law extended local settler prerogatives as it stripped blacks of their existing rights. Sometimes it extinguished customary rights and traditional usages in local economies. Thus, squatters in Hay, De Aar and Douglas found their customary access to timber, water and pasturage curtailed by armed *bywoners*, as parts of the countryside were decreed out of bounds to 'Cape Natives', turning resident Africans into trespassers at a stroke.[90] As happened at Leliefontein, white producers in Kuruman and Douglas profited from the use of scores of ploughshares, wheelbarrows and other implements which commando native commissioners confiscated from peasants between 1899 and 1901. Bloody-minded native commissioners in Aliwal North and Herschel prescribed that Orange Free State 'laws' permitted only one ploughshare per African household.[91] Indian and Muslim traders and pedlars were occasionally also expelled from tracts of proclaimed Republican territory, a measure understandably popular with competing white traders who raced to offer commandants their loyalty and friendship.[92] Republican occupation tried frantically to alter the balance of rural labour relations and the flows of individual accumulation. Its decrees, aimed at tipping the scale of economic forces in parts of the Cape, can perhaps best be seen as a fanciful, blustering attempt to propel local forces along a different historical route or even into a different historic time-scale.

The trajectories of conflict differed from one locality to another. In some, the Cape non-racial franchise was dragged into the arena. While questions of electoral expediency had for some time been restraining settler parliamentary factions from tampering with black franchise rights,[93] conquering commandants seized an exceptional opportunity to snap the constriction of existing equations of political power, electoral coalitions and factions. With a premature whiff of victory in their nostrils, guerrillas made a symbolic lunge at African constitutional and franchise rights. And in few places can Boers have gone more purposefully along the path of symbolic political expropriation than they appear to have done in and around Jamestown, Aliwal North, Dordrecht, Barkly East and Lady Grey towards the end of 1899. Here, as occupying *landdrosts*, *veldkornets*, and other officials reproduced in microcosm some of the paper bureaucratic dimensions of the Boer state, a pattern of confiscation specifically included divesting propertied Africans of political rights.

A rapid glance at events in Jamestown during November 1899 reinforces the point well. On 18 November, Commandant Olivier made a thorough sweep of the settlement, leaning on headmen to supply taxes and mobilise labour drafts and penning all black residents into the native location under curfew.[94] After outlining curfew regulations, tribute claims and the imposition of a pass system, Olivier announced grandly that as Jamestown had now been annexed by the Orange Free State, franchise rights for 'Kaffers en Kleurlingen' would be immediately abolished. Apparently a man of exceptionally small stature, Olivier made up in virulence what he lacked in inches off the ground.

The commandant seems also to have had a keen appreciation of the rituals of exclusion. He devised a humiliating procedure in which registered African voters were ordered to report to a *landdrost* who stamped their hands with ink, issued them with a pass and extracted a pledge of obedience to the law of the Orange Free State *Volksraad*.[95] Scores of glum villagers shuffled forward, compliant for fear of their lives and property. A little vignette of oral remembrance illustrates the tense mix of despair and intransigence which coloured responses to the Republican overturning of settled habits of political conduct. Watutu Mtozi remembered:

> We used to call these Boers 'Free State hyenas' . . . they came upon us in Jamestown and Dordrecht and made trouble for our people in Barkly East and Aliwal North also. Some of them naturally grew up with black people and so they understood our language. They used their own vulgar language towards us because we were causing a lot of trouble for their kind. We were exempted Natives, we voted for Parliament as decent men. We did not want to lose our vote which we were used to . . . they wanted to take it from us, they used to carry heavy *sjamboks* with them which they used for beating us. They shouted 'you Kaffir boys have no more votes'. They did that, you see, because we would not stop fighting back and insulting them.[96]

Most disenfranchisement threats were voiced by forces infiltrating northeastern districts. It can hardly have been coincidental that this region was a vital reservoir of

African political activity in peacetime. Here, the peasant vote was still resilient. Here also, as Trapido, Bundy and Odendaal in particular have shown, the political nexus between the incorporated, 'progressive' peasant producer and the liberal, mercantile appropriator of his product traditionally received its clearest expression.[97] The price of a measure of loyalist understanding and confidence between Africans and English-speaking colonists and officials was a growing rift between them and rural Boer commercial interests, long hostile to liberal merchant advocates of imperial control, and to a competitive, surplus-producing peasantry. These fissures afforded Boer guerrillas a dramatic point of political entry.

During phases of conquest, Boer producers in the triangular region bounded by Aliwal North, Barkly East and Queenstown turned rebel and played a vital role in new relations of domination, assuming a whole range of sub-military functions delegated to them by commandants. In addition to administering passes and collecting taxes, some of them became deeply involved in the theatrical show of stripping Africans of the franchise.[98] An example can be drawn from Barkly East where, in 1898, an alliance between Rhodes and the Colonial Union had brought out the African vote massively against the Afrikaner Bond. In the closing weeks of 1899, an excited band of local rebels, accompanied by Orange Free State *veldkornets*, toured African lands in the locality, boasting of a pending reversal of political fortunes. Several shouted triumphantly that a Barkly East Bondsman would be installed by a new Cape Republican *Volksraad*, and that black men would forfeit what political rights they had.[99] There were similar sallies in Aliwal North and also in the Herschel Reserve which still contained as many as 800 African voters in the late nineteenth century. As a forceful indication of the ambitious intent with which guerrillas were straining to reshape the terrain of local political power, in order to turn its terms ever more decisively against Africans, there was talk in such places as Albert, Dordrecht and Steynsburg of enfranchising illiterate *bywoners* and unskilled white workers to supplant Africans booted beyond the boundaries of citizenship.[100] As an assertive moment, this kind of strutting might be seen as a preliminary warm-up to the great post-1902 reconstruction of poor Afrikaners and their eventual integration into a developing nationalist class alliance, one implacably hostile towards African rights.

The instant suspension of constitutional liberties, however fleeting its impact, came to infuse and shape local perceptions powerfully. If one makes even the most cursory appraisal of rural community responses, it is obvious that people of a little substance and some independence did not make light of the Republican onslaught upon franchise rights. Far from shrugging off commandants' threats as empty bombast, many were unnerved. For talk of extinguishing the common franchise and of founding a *Volksraad* in conquered Cape Town had a claustrophobic impact upon vulnerable communities. To them, Boer encroachment clearly threatened the end of civil liberties and, in the Republicans' scheme of things, their legal assimilation to a common category of ultra-cheap or unpaid servile labour. Above all, as so many Africans repeatedly professed, invasion meant the end of their status and distinctive regional identity as 'Cape' men and British subjects.[101] To Cornelius Olifant, a tenant from Douglas, may be left some appropriately anguished remarks. During September 1900, Olifant related:

I was on my land putting potatoes and pumpkins in bags for sale to the English soldiers when some Free State men rode up about the middle of November last [1899]. With them were Jacobus Maree of the farm 'Witfontein' and Abraham Cronje of the farm 'Wonderfontein'. Maree said my vegetables and fowls and six of my goats would be given to the Boer soldiers. I asked for payment as my goats were worth fully £1.5s. each. He said I would be given about 1s. for each goat as all land was now Orange Free State property and Natives could not make their own prices. Cronje also told me that I was now under the laws of the Orange Free State and made me put my name on a piece of paper with the names of other better class Natives here which was a sign that my vote was taken away. When I did not want to do this thing Maree and the Free State Boers said they would shoot me. I was very afraid to lose my vote as I would then have no rights and just be a common Native and have to work as a slave for these white men. These Boer soldiers who came here to steal our goods and our rights as civilised Natives were not even white men really, but many had some Native blood in them, they were not really white men, just Boer Natives.[102]

Olifant's vocabulary, with its clearly articulated fears and resentments and distaste for 'debased whites', crisply illustrates the way in which tenacious beliefs in independence and class pride among 'progressive' peasants were assailed by the levelling impulse of Republican conquest. Groups of producers lived in permanent tension as Boers usurped local authority and blew away much-prized social freedoms and political rights. And rampaging Orange Free State or Transvaaler *landdrosts* and *veldkornets*, so quick to establish succouring connections with Cape settler allies, became the baleful instruments through which a constellation of Boer agrarian interests played out their racial and class animosities towards their black neighbours.

Conquests and oppositions

Periodic waves of Republican insurgency sought to effect radical shifts in the balance of rural social forces; the coherent identity of the Cape experienced a minor crisis of dissolution. For guerrilla treatment of blacks was not merely to make life unpleasant but to try to break a sturdy and insubordinate spirit of colonial 'separatism'. The conceit of degrees and proclamations carried the indelible mark of Republican hatred of those seen as integrated into a British identity.

With collaborating Cape Boers providing an anchorage from which to launch offensives, Republicans were exempt from the need to cultivate the political and social terrain occupied by African or Coloured villagers. There was, after all, no necessity to reach a working accommodation with large chiefdoms; with Transkeian frontiers tolerably peaceful, the main regional threat of potential African firepower was never drawn. So, the mutual antipathy between a Louwrens Geldenhuys or a Barry Hertzog and local leaderships in small villages and rural areas was hardly surprising. Indeed, a most important element in occupied localities was the constant reverberation of indiscriminate force directed against landless migrant, rural craftsman or wealthier peasant alike. With the dominated classes alternately groaning and sneering at Republicanism's representatives and institutions, commandants were obliged frequently to remind communities through oppressive exactions and curtailments that they were a conquered people.

Far from fighting offensive actions for the improvement of their existing terms of production and dependent labour, many people on white farms found themselves fighting defensive ones against their deterioration. Tenants drawn into defending the properties of English-speaking landowners in places like Rhodes, Wodehouse and Barkly East, were in effect guarding not merely the capital of their landlords but their own productive surplus, which was indistinguishable from that of colonists. Rent and labour tenancy relations marked Africans as clear targets for Boers raiding English farmers.[103] In turning out under arms, tenants' instincts of self-preservation clearly matched those of loyalty and obligation to landowners.

It was a struggle around political hegemony which in large part underlay the disorder and agitation in the countryside. Smallholding and proletarian responses to the guerrilla challenge rested on a rippling unity of popular sentiment and on communal solidarities, characteristically tight at a time of severe crisis. Republican prohibition, eviction and expropriation was a potent threat to already shrinking enclaves of peasant autonomy, to values of petty proprietorship, to a body of – ambiguous and contradictory – ideas and myths about liberal civic and political rights, and to a radiating sense of identity and territoriality as 'free' British subjects. It was above all this consciousness, with its emotional content of an historically tinged regionalism, which helped to make the clash between blacks and commandos so searing and unforgiving.

These were the terms in which great numbers of self-proclaimed 'government' men dug in their heels, clinging doggedly to the familiar meanings of a Cape colonial order. That determination was bred of an outraged sense of moral consciousness and justice. For the aspirations of the ruled were not transformative but essentially conservative; they were desperate for the restoration of old frontiers, arguably their frontiers of illusion, behind which to nurture survival and dignity. Areas like Gordonia and Hay and the localities of the northeastern Cape may well represent cases where a militant and defensive local autonomy was so strong a tradition that, instead of laying a basis for any independent opposition or organisation against the colonial state and colonial ruling class proper, it could perhaps act as a substitute for it.

Hounded by Republicanism, the flinty face which many people turned was tinged by the still lively colours of what Beinart has termed 'the African variant of Cape liberalism'.[104] To its social consciousness of entitlement to 'a larger common society', they added a few self-evident and brusque definitions of their own. In the words of Johannes Mugubisa, a Barkly East police constable who had a scrape with Barry Hertzog over a tribute demand, 'I told him Kruger is not *baas* here and I am not going to pay him a penny, he can do what he wish. I said I am a Government man and not yours, and I am under the English Government, not him. I am sick of these Boers with their nuisance towards me.'[105] To Mugubisa and others as touchy, commandos were about as welcome as a visitation of locusts. The class and class culture which the constable embodied may not have owned its own self as yet, but it was, as it demonstrated through struggle and social fracture, its own self. And with self-knowledge, buttressed identities and undeferential dispositions could emerge. Far from collapsing, these old identities have continued to connect with popular life and aspirations, sometimes vicariously lifting and renovating the fading hopes of subordinated subjects. In 1988, as part of their ultimately successful struggle against state plans to subdivide

Namaqualand's communal reserves into smaller 'economic units', Leliefontein small-holders poignantly petitioned Queen Elizabeth to intercede on their behalf. The Crown was asked to call the South African state to account and to confirm 'their rights to land' granted by Britain in the nineteenth century.[106] One seemed to be lurching abruptly from one century to another, and thereby sighting what Gramsci has called the 'traces' of previous historical connections, the 'stratified deposits in popular philosophy'.[107]

7

Martyrdom, myth and memory: Abraham Esau's war

On 5 January 1901, Abraham Esau, a citizen of Calvinia, was murdered on the outskirts of this small rural settlement by Republican guerrillas. He was part of the hasty and desperate local mobilisations, assemblies and defensive occupations by neighbours, friends and kinsmen and women against Republican conquest. In a war which had its excesses, Esau's killing was in one respect yet another act of reprisal and personal vengeance. Yet a striking feature of Boer rebel conduct towards black civilians is that it did not consist only of a mass of randomly directed vendettas; actions and demands carried the flavour of a generalised repressive determination. In another important sense, therefore, the peculiarly intense personal tragedy of Abraham Esau speaks for some of the ways in which the war challenged the bases of the lives of many black civilians. The historical authenticity of Esau's personal clash with the Republicans serves as a guide to the shaping of some of the essential material actualities of these years. For locked up in the drama of Esau's experience of resistance, incarceration and execution are realities of crisis and conflict that are central to an understanding of the ways in which a war between British imperialism and Boer republicanism turned with abrupt and explosive force into a desperate, undeclared civil war between rural whites and rural blacks.

In one obvious sense, this chapter tries to trace a formative moment in the history of Abraham Esau, through a reconstruction based both on those folk memories which are part of inherited collective tradition in the rural Namaqualand area in which he lived, and on conventional written sources. In another related sense, this exploration is not just an attempt to reconstruct a sequence of events 'as they actually happened' but a consideration of how qualities of martyrdom, myth and legend have come to cluster around a man who became one of many civilian victims of the war. For the construction and sporadic remaking of a local and particularist Esau folk mythology, and its continuing persistence and strength in more recent times, has come to infect social relations and political and cultural identities in the life of a small rural South African town. As war martyr, Esau has had, to borrow a phrase from Thompson, 'the impertinence, and the imperfect sense of historical perspective',[1] to live on in the memory of Namaqualand.

Background and identity

Abraham Esau was born in Kenhardt in the northwestern Cape Colony around 1865, the eldest of several children of Adam Esau and his wife, Martha April. The elder Esaus lived a sedentary existence for a number of years, making a living by alternating casual jobbing in small market settlements with agricultural fieldwork. They came from a class of what Raphael Samuel in another context has termed, 'half-rural labourers who looked to both town and country for their livelihood.'[2] Eventually, the family settled down as living-in servants on the land of one William Seton, a wealthy stock farmer. Seton is recalled as having been 'an Englishman whose farm was great'.[3] As part of the Coloured rural proletariat, the Esau household was poor, but its position on the Seton farm appears to have placed it in a special and close relationship with its settler master. His incremental paternalism ran beyond the provision of housing, food, clothing and other small gratuities, to weekly Bible readings and outings for the Esau children, with whom he is remembered as having had fond ties: 'they remember Abraham had a book from the *baas*, a book about the King'.[4]

Oral history evidence also suggests that the attachment to Seton made the Esaus culturally imitative. Impregnated with Anglicanism, they conversed in English and sought to provide a respectable English mission schooling for their children. Increasingly distanced from the localised formation of Cape Boer social relations and cultural practices, the character of the Esau family stood out as separate from those Coloured labouring households which were customarily bound into Boer culture. As a Jewish trader's daughter born in 1901 remembers of a story transmitted to her by her father: 'Some of the Esau people would come to the store twice each month. Sometimes they had ostrich feathers and always asked a fair price. They were a cut above ordinary Coloureds there, always decent, and with good English. They called my father *Mr* Murinik, and he would give them old Cape Town newspapers he had kept.'[5]

With English and Anglicanism important guiding influences, Abraham Esau sought, as a young man, to behave as an *Englische* or *Engelse Kleurling*. A crucial element in the reservoir of Esau anecdotes in Calvinia folk memory is the image of him having been a 'Coloured Englishman', free of the grip of the master culture and customs of the dominant local Boer community.[6] A few interrupted years shuffling through an elementary mission schooling in the Prieska district made him literate and further defined his status. And, as an adult, Esau developed a self-conscious and expressive 'British' social and cultural identity.[7]

For a number of years Esau worked as a carpenter, flitting from job to job in Kenhardt, Prieska and Carnarvon. At some unknown point in the 1880s, he switched trades and settled in Calvinia as a blacksmith. There, as part of the village's small resident artisanry, the story goes that he achieved some mild prosperity. He built up his own busy smithy and put capital into a small hauling and distribution business. The blacksmith's world was recognisably that of a late-nineteenth-century Coloured artisan class, sustained by the small market town and village economies of the rural Cape. Their numbers were small, but their townsmen standing and small-propertied identity as a 'respectable' or 'sober' rural petty bourgeoisie set them apart from the 'rough' values and behaviour of the mass of unskilled Coloured wage labourers, as Trapido has well illustrated.[8]

These tiny tribes of artisans and independent craftsmen were imbued with both individual and collective class aspirations and civic virtues of hard work, respectability and self-improvement. Limited and subordinate apprenticeship under the paternalist controls of the colonial political order provided this small artisan class with a passionate constituent attachment to the rights and identities of Cape liberalism. Artisan aspirations and ideals fed off political liberalism, with its felt associations with British rule. Paradoxically, at the very turn of the century when the arteries of segregation in South Africa were hardening, rooted social ideals of assimilation still persisted strongly in the Cape. The hopeful vision of small propertied blacks lived on, even as its material prospects were receding. Most important of all was a profound respect for a stable 'British' law and order; a consciousness of inherited rights in citizenship, customary freedoms and constitutional liberties underwritten by a sense of natural justice was a feature of life even in remote rural areas.

War crisis and war preparation

The outbreak of war ruptured social peace and threatened the continued stability of the dominant English-speaking settler political and economic bloc in the Cape. For individuals beneath, like Abraham Esau, living in the midst of large concentrations of disaffected Boers in the north, there was, from the outset, little cause to misapprehend the force, purpose and intentions of Republican guerrillas who began swarming over large parts of the countryside by 1900. Commando incursions southwards from the Orange Free State pitched Namaqualand into a crisis of wartime hysteria. For vulnerable black civilians, the spreading violence and disorder proved painful and traumatic. As a Kenhardt inhabitant recalled, 'Although I was only about ten at that time I can still remember it. When the Boers came they came with whips to beat us. We used to call them the "hungry animals". To save what we had we would pull out the stem of old fallen trees and hide things inside'.[9] Acting like warlords, commando commandants expropriated and confiscated property, promulgated ferociously racist laws in occupied districts and flogged, shot or banished resisters.

In Calvinia, as in neighbouring areas like Clanwilliam, Sutherland and Fraserburg, feelings smouldered during this tense and menacing period. With Republican power rolling over Namaqualand, the village became gripped by an emergency atmosphere; it wintered uneasily in 1900, living in daily expectation of assault and occupation. With British power enfeebled, constituted colonial authority in the region found itself under intolerable strain, unable to curb Boer aggression and enforce peace. Around Calvinia, guerrilla bands fanned out, rationing themselves from the lands of local settler rebels, and making tribute demands upon isolated smallholders and scores of farm servants. There were exemplary executions of any who showed intransigence.[10] From the sandbagged windows of the settlement, the world looked about to fall in.

In response to the specific threat of repression and exaction which confronted them, the Coloured inhabitants of Calvinia turned massively against virtually all Boers. As a populace increasingly under siege, they developed a fierce, sectarian, anti-Boer identity: a defensive fear of conquest produced a militant local consciousness as much as it defined it as British. The force of that movement burned itself into the lingering popular memory of a succeeding generation. 'Man, our people then were born British. They did not want to go under those uncivilised Free State Boers. Here in Calvinia they were afraid. It was a common feeling to hate the Boers. Even those who lived here, most of them, they did not talk to them.'[11]

Inexorably, the Calvinia Coloured community became a hotbed of what one might call 'Cape jingoism', vehemently pro-British and biliously anti-Republican. A species of Cape British 'national' identity bubbled into life, visible in colourful and rowdy pro-imperial petitioning and demonstrating, and in the staging of processions in which effigies of Republican leaders ('they made them out of straw with also bark and leaves')[12] were ritually pelted with dung or scattered in the wind. Time-expired Coloured scouts and muleteers brought back British regimental duties which invited popular participation and local circumstantial and linguistic adaptation in their repetitions. One which has made its way vividly into oral folk tradition includes the lines:

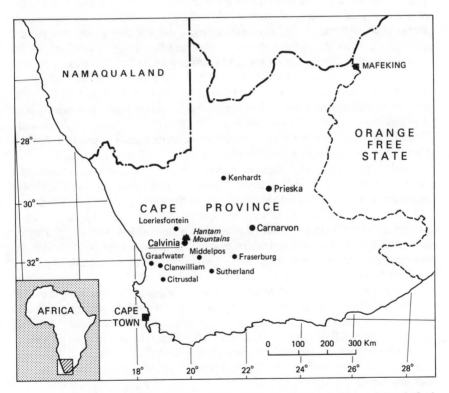

Map 7 Calvinia and neighbouring districts. From S. Godden, *African Affairs* (Oxford University Press, Oxford, 1988).

123

Clearoff Piet	Clearoff Piet
Go away Boer	Weg met jou Boer
Clearoff Piet	Clearoff Piet
Go away Boer	Weg met jou Boer
If you take our bread	As jy vat ons brood
Lord Roberts will see you dead	Maak Lord Roberts jou dood
Clearoff from Calvinia	Clearoff van Calvinia
Free State Boer	Vrystaat Boer
Clearoff from Calvinia	Clearoff van Calvinia
Free State Boer	Vrystaat Boer[13]

Public fear and hatred as 'ritualised popular hatred' – to borrow and adapt a phrase from Olwen Hufton[14] – became a potent expression of community self-definition and solidarity. It worked as a binding force, helping to unify 'respectable' men of small substance like masons or saddlers with unskilled casual labourers.

Out of this turbulent atmosphere Abraham Esau suddenly emerged as a central and influential personality. His conduct crystallised the prevailing political mood. Its defensive radicalism might be seen as roughly akin to that of the interplay between the general historical universe of 'political shoemakers' and plebeian and proletarian people, in which those strategically located, literate and articulate artisans became the 'poor man's advocate, spokesman and leader' and the craggy 'ideologists of the common people'.[15] Oral tradition, backed by written sources, has Esau making his first major public appearance on 19 May 1900, at the head of a victory parade and rally to celebrate the relief of Mafeking on the far northern border of the Colony. Characteristically, in Calvinia, awareness of national struggle and crisis ran concurrently with local sentiment and imagination. 'Mafficking' in the village involved predominantly Coloured men and women with a sprinkling of Africans, and a few pro-British white colonists who turned out for a speech by the visiting Clanwilliam magistrate. Some two hundred people, holding aloft flags and ribbons, assembled to hear Esau denounce the enemy. An attending British Army intelligence agent noted that the blacksmith possessed 'a big voice, of which he enjoys greatly the sound'.[16]

A scare four months later pushed Esau dramatically into the foreground of local resistance. Several labourers came panting into Calvinia with news that commandos encamped in the area were mustering for an assault on the settlement. With excitement mounting and rumour flying thick and fast, a large group of men, headed by Esau, clamoured for firearms outside the magistracy. The Resident Magistrate, Peter Dreyer, turned a deaf ear; he considered the issue of guns to Coloured civilians likely to lead to 'mischief'.[17] On the part of local authority there was considerable apprehension that arming an untrained militia might stir up social indiscipline. There was also fear that with an embittered Boer population itching for any pretext to rebel, any open move to arm black collaborators risked playing straight into Republican hands. And the magistrate appeared fairly confident that Calvinia's puny white guard would be able to cope with any threat.

Calvinia's Coloured tenants, employees and other subordinates were not so sanguine. Esau countered his official rebuff by rallying his anxious and impatient

124

followers and readying them to resist attack with their own meagre resources. His motley band drilled itself into readiness and posted outlying pickets with cattle horns and bells to sound warnings. Perhaps nothing speaks so eloquently of active and sustained community solidarity in the village as the involvement of children and women in flurries of defensive preparation. Transmitted memory recalls in sharp detail how 'children would take big sacks and fill them with sharp stones'.[18] Women also acted as ammunition carriers, using aprons; in addition they collected wooden clubs, carried food, and 'made sharp some swords which Abraham got from skirt soldiers who were once by Middelpos'.[19] In some sense they might perhaps be seen as counterparts of the small numbers of Boer women who served as commando auxiliaries, both actively sharing in struggle and the dangers of frontline service.[20] What commenced as a generalised panic in the face of external force rapidly became structured into a collective resistance, with a sense of common purpose and a developing organisation.

But it had a distinct element of personal leadership which gave it its bubbling tone and undeniably mad heroic character. There was only one candidate. The village blacksmith was becoming a warrior; men and women not only listened to him but were ready to stand with him against rifles, whips and horses. Of the danger of his growing stature local Boer rebels had no doubts. On the mid-September morning after Esau's force began parading, a sheep farmer named Louw sent a secret message to his brother who was in the field nearby with an Orange Free State commando. Its warning was directed wholly at one man, 'the English Coloured Esau', who was 'being the biggest troublemaker here'.[21]

When anticipated enemy action failed to materialise, Esau's followers stood down. But vigilance remained high. Early in October, the blacksmith was out once again, hoping to capture the magistracy mind with the formal dignity of a petition for weapons with which to defend the rural municipality. An urgent address was signed by thirty-seven men, including two Coloured men of the Calvinia constabulary, Christian Manel and Carolus Pretorius, and despatched to the Acting Resident Magistrate of Clanwilliam, the senior area official. A copy was sent separately to Lieutenant James Preston, the British special military secret agent stationed there. Another one was also sent to Milner as Lieutenant-Governor of the Cape Colony and British High Commissioner. On behalf of 'the Coloured Residents of Calvinia', it pledged loyalty to the imperial cause and pleaded 'we beg to petition that the Government may supply us with arms and ammunition, so as to place us in a position to defend the Town, ourselves and families ... A Coloured man who falls into the hands of the Boers receives most brutal treatment from them; in view of this we shall only be too glad to assist in our own protection.'[22] An intelligence meeting between Dreyer and Preston on 13 October was dramatically interrupted mid-way by the blacksmith who is reported to have denounced the magistrate for his inaction, and to have demanded the right, as a British subject, to weapons for himself and his followers. He exclaimed, 'we know good what these Boers are, they are Pharoah's men. I will lead that we may fight them if they come near our doors.' But Dreyer stood firm against such radical Old Testament temper. And, after a bitter exchange, Esau stalked out in contempt.[23] But the immediate response of authority was again brusque rejection. Thereafter, it was recalled, 'Esau came to many houses to say that the government said that this war is a white man's business and the trouble had nothing to do with the Coloureds.'[24] One tale has him 'standing with Barend Smit and old Christian Manel, striking matches to burn the government's letter to him. It was burnt in the open, there in front of Archell's shop. He wanted the magistrate and the English whites to see it done, to see how bad it was.'[25] So began the real forging of Abraham Esau in collective memory as a kind of budding local Emiliano Zapata, and the celebration of that image in the historical commemoration of village crisis and village resistance.

British collaborator

At some point after the ignominy of the failed petition, Esau is known to have slipped out of Calvinia; a weekly field-activity report by the Intelligence Department of the Namaqualand Field Force placed him in the vicinity of Williston on 25 October, riding a Basuto pony, clad in army greatcoat and hat and accompanied by two armed, 'ruffianly Cape Boys'. These turned out to be a pair of ex Coldstream Guards despatch riders, Piet Skilpad and Hendrik Albertus. Evidence then suggests that with the help of local guides, this trio undertook a secret, meandering journey across unsettled open countryside to Clanwilliam.[26]

There, the decisive moment for Abraham Esau was winning a confidential interview with Lieutenant James Preston. Several successive meetings, the content of which went unrecorded, were described by the officer as 'cordial and most useful'. Preston had responded warmly to the October petition by declaring in a confidential letter to Esau that 'the forming of a natives' guard such as you so sensibly propose would set an excellent example. My regret is that circumstances at present are such as to prevent such a desirable force being raised.'[27] And the two men appear to have developed a cosy personal relationship. The Lieutenant recorded in his private journal on 10 November that 'this Abraham is a quite uncommon fellow. Certainly not the type of low Cape Boy who will live on bread and water. He has taken my Tennyson and has filled his head with "Locksley Hall" which he is forever reciting.'[28] For his part, it did not take Esau long to detect that Preston could most easily be reached through his stomach. The Lieutenant was partial to game and the blacksmith only too eager to oblige by sending Skilpad whooping through the veld after buck.

While the documentary record confirms that Esau wormed his way into Preston's confidence, direct written information on war-related actions and activities which developed from this relationship is virtually non-existent. The picture which emerges is essentially suggestive, leaving us to rely on inference. There are reasonable grounds for believing that the special agent's intelligence reference on 14 November to 'my new secret detective' concerned Esau. Equally, the blacksmith would in all probability have been the shadowy 'A' who prepared reports on Boer rebel meetings for the Namaqualand Field Force Intelligence Department. Under the heading, 'Quarterly Information on Suspicious Boer Actions, 1900', he was awarded £10.15s. on 21 November, and under that of 'Intelligence Sundries (Natives)', 'A' received £12 as a 'bonus' a week later.[29]

Beyond this, the trickle of written sources dries up. Further reconstruction and interpretation of Esau's conduct in and around Calvinia in the period up to its occupation by Republican forces in January 1901 has to draw entirely on a wealth of oral tradition still resonant in popular memory.

What emerges is that Esau became a large and provocative presence in Clanwilliam. Riding the countryside upon a large black horse and brandishing a sabre, he rallied Coloured support for the imperial war effort, exhorting, encouraging and advising at every turn. Sleeping rough and working with demonic energy, he also proceeded to hold clandestine night meetings with labourers on abandoned farms in nearby Citrusdal and Graafwater. Under the light of guttering torches they melted away before dawn, supposedly sworn to acts of impenetrable secrecy and unspeakable dirty work.

Esau's exertions brought scores of men and women to his side; their number included domestic workers, migratory labourers, road workers and village artisans. Tradition records that he spoke of them as his 'faithful children'. After his permanent return to Calvinia some time in November, he kept a secret register of their names in his smithy. One typically apocryphal story is that he sealed the incriminating list in a metal casket at the bottom of a brick kiln. Knitted together by a sense of collective identity and a combative spirit, and sworn to secrecy by oath, Esau's followers formed a solid core of spies, snoops and informers. Accumulating a mixture of incriminating hard information, petty gossip and slander about the character, opinions and actions of suspect Boer rebels, this cell poured names and details of suspicious incidents into the bulging files of British Army intelligence.

The centre from which farmers were being fingered was a cellar beneath Esau's stables where the blacksmith transcribed oral reports, rewarded informants with perks (tinned meat and tea) and arranged safe hill routes for runners and riders. To secure the passage of men and women carrying information across open country thick with guerrillas, there was a rhythmic routine of signals by cattle horn, warning stones and marking of farm gateposts. At places close to Calvinia, like Middelpos and Graafwater, haystacks were sometimes fired at night as a spectacular way of warning runners of the proximity of armed Boers.[30] What are popularly believed to be surviving material traces of Esau's cell have come to light in more recent years. In 1947 for instance, some rusted cattle horns were found underneath a pile of stones in a field alongside the road to Middelpos. 'Even though the rain was coming down, people walked out to see it. They all said it was a relic from Abraham Esau's time with the Boers. Some of them wanted a priest there so there could be a blessing.'[31]

In the very short time that it was active, the degree of discipline and tight management in Esau's half-hidden organisation must clearly have been remarkable. Its proportions – as remembered in oral tradition – suggest that it bore many of the archetypal characteristics of a rural secret movement. With its coherent and systematic form of organisation, solidarity through oath, secret codes, night activities and warning signals, one is irresistibly reminded of such nineteenth-century, largely proletarian rural secret societies as the Welsh Scotch Cattle and the Irish Terryalts.

The blacksmith's anti-Boer adventure was both a silent, independent war against the threat of a new acquisition of oppressive power and an attempt to bolster a protective form of association and allegiance directly with imperial power. As the locality's best-known British collaborator, a vigilant Esau acted as a kind of clandestine broker; the priceless asset of carefully gathered local intelligence was to be traded against British readiness to turn out to defend Calvinia against Republican depredation. The blacksmith's activities certainly appear to have been moulded in part by an expectation of access to British military assistance – in the person of James Preston. Preston was clearly a key figure, and a glimpse of the misguided terms of Esau's relationship with him is to be found in a crucial, isolated piece of evidence. A letter from 'A' to Preston in December 1900 spoke of the writer's joy at knowing that if 'Boer locists' advanced upon the people of Calvinia, they would 'suffer as like the Egiptions in the sea' (sic) at the hands of 'our brave British soldiers'.[32] In this confidence Esau had been led completely and tragically astray; there were no nearby British forces in the area ready to come growling over the horizon to see off Boer invaders.

As days passed, Esau's known role as a British agent made his presence in the eyes of local Republican sympathisers an increasing affront. Frightened by the reputed size and menacing nature of his personal following, most colonists in Calvinia wanted to have his influence snuffed out. In mid December, Esau complained of stones being thrown at him and of dead rats being thrown into his home by three farmers.[33] Generalised hostility metamorphosed into improbable fact. Improbable fact dissolved into dark visions of unimaginable mayhem. Rumour grew that Esau's 'movement' was receiving secret arms training, so as to settle scores with farmers and hoarders of grain. It was said that the blacksmith was stockpiling an underground arsenal in readiness for an anti-settler rising on 1 January 1901. There were growing beliefs, based entirely on hearsay, that Esau was being showered with horses and Krugerrands by army agents.[34] There was also much in stories spread by labourers to stimulate alarm in their masters. These celebrated Esau's capacity to penetrate settler circles to eavesdrop upon seditious utterances against the Crown. And they built him into a mythic individual. From a number of tales there was, for instance, Esau's cunning ability to assume 'whiteness' for deception. At times he was 'covered in white clay so that farmers could not see that there was a Coloured man riding near their land'.[35] Another powerful and emotive story said that he had shaved off his moustache, grown his hair and bundled himself up in women's clothing to snoop around farmers' kitchens.[36]

By the end of 1900, according to British intelligence in Namaqualand, Abraham Esau had provoked 'great suspicion and hostility' and was regarded as 'abominable' by guerrilla commandants riding as far afield as Prieska and Carnarvon.[37] And this enmity, helped along by popular imagination, was nothing if not sulphurous. For example, 'Oupa', an African agterryer taken captive by a British patrol at Fraserburg, testified that his masters had spoken regularly of an 'Isak' as 'the most poisonous Hottentot from Calvinia'.[38]

Invasion and occupation

It was just before six o'clock on the evening of 7 January 1901 that Calvinia fell suddenly to a light force of some fifty Orange Free State commandos, led by a Veldkornet Scholtz. An hour later one hundred horsemen under Commandant Pretorius came clattering in to reinforce them. Before nightfall, 'one of their veldkornets got up on top of Dreyer's roof and ripped down the Union Jack'.[39] Villagers did not scramble to make their peace with the invaders. Assembled at one end of Calvinia, Pretorius' squad was for a time subjected to catcalls and pelting with various missiles in the dark, before successfully scattering hostile inhabitants. For a little while Calvinia reverberated with the occasional crack of gunshots, showering stones, the clip of hooves and the thump of *sjamboks*. But sporadic, ragged resistance soon crumpled. As Boer Mausers fell silent, Calvinia passed into the grip of garrison control.

With its position secured, the Orange Free State force set to work establishing a new abrasive layer of power. Commandos began flooding in and by 13 January there were almost six hundred men billeted in the village. With the arrival of a senior officer, Judge J. B. M. Hertzog, and Commandant Charles Niewoudt, martial law was declared; buildings, bedding, food, clothing, tools, horses and personal valuables were requisitioned at gunpoint from sullen inhabitants. Local residents and refugees lost herds of cattle, goats, sheep, and in all some 600 horses, according to the *Midland News* of 16 February 1901. Niewoudt in particular trod swiftly. On 12 January, a day after his entry into Calvinia, he launched a manhunt of those specially marked down for retribution, and for whom an arrest warrant had been issued prior to the occupation. A total of fourteen men were rounded up, nine of whom were 'loyal Coloured men'. Chief among them was predictably Abraham Esau, believed to have been ferreted out of a hiding place 'which was in a cellar underneath the shop of the English Jew Cohen'.[40] In gaol the Coloured prisoners were joined by several colonists viewed as having the position and will to do mischief - Peter Dreyer, his assistant acting magistrate, Charles Dük, and two English-speaking and one pro-British Boer trader.

With this sweep complete, Niewoudt proceeded to proclaim himself *Landdrost* of Calvinia and thereby symbolically to take possession of the village as Orange Free State land. The story is told that he 'stood in front of the magistrate's office. With him he had four *sjamboks* which he turned around and around above his head and he threw them in different directions. "Look, you people", he shouted, "this is now our land".'[41] The display of force soon turned into the enforcement of criminal sanction. As had become customary in conquered Cape districts, the new *Landdrost* lost little time in enacting Republican Native law, with its burdening tribute demands and explicit racial insult.

Oral sources paint a picture of this new overbearing authority quite as harrowing as those to be found in contemporary newspaper reports. Niewoudt is remembered as an invader who 'had no real law, no rules, only the *sjambok*'.[42] A new Republican colonial domination was expressed through the local tyranny of a predatory and parasitic standing army. Commandos strutted about Calvinia with their weapons cocked. Bystanders who neglected to jump aside risked having their heads split. Rounding upon *Hottentots en Kaffers*, Veldkornet Carl van der Merwe (fresh from flogging farmworkers in Philipstown and Britstown) extracted tax payments and labour tribute, and despatched messengers to nearby farmers, urging them to march 'insubordinate' and 'troublesome' labourers into the village for punishment. According to the *Diamond Fields Advertiser* and the *Graaff-Reinet Advertiser*, over one hundred farm labourers were eventually hauled before the *Landdrost* as 'every Dutchman in the District who had a grudge against his Native employees brought them'.[43] Culprits 'were beaten on the backs and also made to work for the Free Staters. For our mothers and fathers what was worst was when Niewoudt took their children away and sent them off to be servants for his Boers.'[44] All unmarried male labourers were summarily bound to yearly service.

What the Coloured inhabitants of Calvinia found themselves confronting was the apparent transplantation of an unfree and bullying political culture which brusquely overrode their inherited sense of natural justice, seemingly turning them into chattels without civic rights. Under the frightening enclosure of curfew, their lives were being forcibly reconstructed around them, overturning their 'free-born' British colonial status and stamping upon their common self-definition. A typically vivid oral confirmation of *why* Republican rule was experienced as such an abomination comes from the recollection of a father, a harness-maker, who used to express rage at having had 'to stand before a Boer magistrate who was not of our land' and at the illegality of 'Free State Native laws' being imposed upon 'free Coloured men of the Cape who were then British subjects, the same as white people born there'.[45]

Resistance and martyrdom

The most immediate and direct embodiment of the 'British' and 'free' identity to which a conquered community clung was naturally Abraham Esau. In so tense, strained and confused an atmosphere, there are obviously details of the blacksmith's imprisonment which can never be fully recovered from either living oral tradition or written clues. Such memory as we have, even if largely anecdotal, celebrates an appropriate moment of tough resistance. First, Esau could not be bludgeoned into giving away the secrets of his cell. Second, demands that he divulge the whereabouts of his rumoured arms cache drew only an assertion of innocence. Third, attempts to force him publicly to renounce his British allegiance met with scorn. The narrative which probably best commemorates Esau's legendary qualities of truculence and obstinacy came from an old woman informant who, beside herself with laughter, claimed that 'you know Abraham carried in his pocket a dead Boer's ear which he showed to the Free Staters and said that he was as deaf as that ear'.[46] Drenched in the spittle of Republican venom, the question of his execution had never really been more than one of timing. His last days were especially wretched. At dawn on 15 January he was dragged before Veldkornet van der Merwe and sentenced, according to Dreyer's well-informed eyewitness account, 'to twenty-five lashes for having spoken against the Boers and for having attempted to arm the Natives'.[47] Obdurate to the last, Esau was a most fit political example to be made under freshly minted occupation laws. His experience seems aptly illustrative of Michel Foucault's notion that 'in the excesses of torture, a whole economy of power is invested'.[48]

Roping Esau to a gum tree in an open square, van der Merwe administered the flogging himself, proceeding 'to lash him on the bare back. Abraham Esau fainted as he received the seventeenth lash. He was then untied and fell to the ground.' Yanked to his feet, one 'Abraham Louw struck Esau between the eyes with a stick. He fell to the ground, and some other men kicked him.'[49] Once again there is a circulating symbolic story – now grisly – about the blacksmith's ear, which relates that 'in the big pool of his blood which ran down from his ears the children came when it was night to put flowers'.[50]

On 5 February, the end came. Evidently acting under instructions from van der Merwe, a Stephanus Strydom had Esau clapped into leg-irons, strapped between two horses and bumped and scraped along at a brisk canter before being dumped about five miles east of the Calvinia municipal boundary. There, after another beating, he was shot dead by Strydom. As the evening of the execution darkened the village, three of Esau's associates, John Driscoll, Jan Draghoender and Jongie Galant stole out to retrieve his body. Loaded on a mule, it was brought back and laid out for the gaze of a stream of mourners. Mounted commandos attempted to beat back crying and hissing onlookers; a number of them had come ready for trouble, carrying sticks and sharpened cart-wheel spokes. Niewoudt got up on his horse and bellowed an order that they return to their homes. His adversaries replied with a rattle of their wooden weapons, prompting a *veldkornet* to fire warning shots into the air. It was a tense, heartstopping moment, but it passed.[51] The following day the Republican occupation of Calvinia suddenly ended with the arrival of a British column under Lieutenant-Colonel Herbert de Lisle.

Twelve British soldiers officiated at Esau's burial, firing a volley over the grave. Driscoll and Galant's descendants recall being told that a sudden thunderstorm scattered mourners and that the Union Jack draping the coffin was torn to shreds by a fierce gust of wind. A further, almost predictable element to the subsequent making of a rooted popular 'tradition' is the story that the coffin was splintered by a bolt of lightning, exposing Esau's shattered face.[52] For a man who saw himself as another of God's Englishmen, the Almighty appeared to have made an appropriate last-minute intervention.

While Esau''s corpse had slipped into the ground, its shadow remained. News of the killing spread rapidly. On 8 February, Captain Thomas Eyre-Lloyd entered a note in his diary, 'there has been a fearful commotion in Calvinia and the Boers have killed Esau, a most loyal coloured figure. They have little propriety. This is truly a most outrageous and evil act. It is likely that there will be the most awful fuss.'[53] Captain Eyre-Lloyd's sense of political realities did not fail him. Discomfited by outrage in the columns of English-language Cape newspapers such as the *Cape Daily Telegraph* and *Cape Mercury*, and by condemnatory press coverage in Britain in papers like *Lloyds Weekly Newspaper* ('Esau's fate calls for retribution. He has suffered cruel martyrdom for no worse crime than loyalty to the British'),[54] the pro-Republican press virtually fell over itself trying to explain away the execution. Versions cooked up by the *South African News* and *Het Zuid-Oosten* claimed that the commando escort had been forced to shoot a berserk Esau in self-defence, after he had charged down upon it with a knife. 'Abraham Esau', the *News* blustered, had been 'a man of great physical strength.'[55] Echoes of the affair actually bounced high enough to catch the attention of the Cape Colonial Secretary (who ordered an investigation) and also that of Chamberlain, as well as Milner. The High Commissioner made a great show of revulsion and immediately seized upon the atrocity story as a suitably decent stick with which to beat the Boer Republics as bloody and barbarous. Milner declared:

> Nothing more disgraceful has happened in modern war than the treatment of the coloured man Esau at Calvinia. What I do know is that they flogged him till he fainted, for the offence of being loyal to the British Crown, he being born and bred a British Subject. The man is well known to me by correspondence, and is known to my staff personally.

> Though Coloured, he was a most respectable, upstanding, and for his class in life (a village blacksmith) superior man – far more civilised than the average Boer farmer.[56]

In the decade of post-war reconstruction, shrewd English-language settler politicians also chose to remember Abraham Esau. Several candidates of the pro-imperialist Progressives made the most of the Esau story in bidding for the votes of Coloured electors in the northern and northwestern Cape in the Colony's 1904 general election. With over 10,500 disfranchised Boers still silenced politically by the taint of treason, the constituency thrust of black grievance and aspiration was of decisive importance in an area like Namaqualand, where Coloured voters still formed at least one quarter of the electorate. Here, in an atmosphere crackling with local village talk of Esau's heroics and Boer rapacity, rural Progressives reminded black voters that a cross for the opposing Bond was a vote for the forces which had killed the blacksmith.[57] A bitter and vituperative political contest was a good moment for the creation of martyrdom. And, acknowledged as a man of some symbolic consequence, Esau ran close to being canonised as a Coloured martyr. In this movement the cult of Esau became detached from a modest village martyrdom. Raised by a section of the Cape's ruling class he became, for a brief moment, visibly a martyr of a Cape liberal political culture.

Central to the manner in which Progressives celebrated him was the image of Esau as a loyal and steadfast Coloured British patriot, an embodiment of the specifically imperial formation of Cape society. The trusty artisan had found a role and identity in natural combat with northern Republicanism, dying in the struggle to maintain a free life and place in the sun. Esau's sacrifice and suffering had been in defence of a natural triangular political symbiosis between 'civilised' men, the rights and protections of Cape constitutionalism and the British empire. The harnessing of citizenship 'rights' and 'freedoms' to the imperial interest could scarcely have been more explicit – nor more electorally successful for the Progressives.[58] Significantly, this recognition of Esau's historic British identity was also how many of Calvinia's Coloured populace chose to see it. And their identification was not simply a passive acting out of imperialist values prescribed from above; it was a means of promoting class pride, dignity and a tenacious sense of local independence. As one woman remembers of her family's turn-of-the-century political traditions, 'you see, we Andersons were jingoes. Also Abraham Esau's people, the Esaus, they were jingoes. Abraham Esau, he was also educated, his English was full. He knew what it was to be a British citizen. The Free Staters hated his kind of "kleurling mense".'[59] It was Esau's stirring up of a British patriotism to oppose Boer encroachment that gave his dramatic experience and martyrdom much of its popular meaning.

In the making and remaking of the Esau tradition, an obvious question to consider is what kind of martyr was Abraham Esau? With his execution, he became and has remained the first martyr of a poor and subordinate rural community. At one level, martyrdom was related to leadership: the war certainly made Esau a leader. His was a leadership legitimised neither by exclusive class following nor by committee mandate but by *populist action*, a willingness to organise against an enemy. But it was not exclusively leadership which made Esau a martyr. As Williams has so succinctly put it in the instance of the Dic Penderyn legend in Welsh working-class history, 'What makes a man a martyr? Death of course – but *unjust* death. It is his innocence, his representative character; it is the sense of injustice.'[60] Bereaved and enraged Coloured men and women in Calvinia needed a symbol of injustice and persecution and they made a martyr out of Abraham Esau. And if it was not so much the sense of the unwitting innocent which made him a martyr it was surely his markedly representative and historically specific identity.

A memory and tradition of Britishness

In the context of the 1900s it is essential to emphasise that the cult of Esau as war hero, with its thickening crust of mythology, did not grip individuals because they wanted to see, or perhaps could only see, their political choices and limits in terms of prominent leadership above them. For the face of Abraham Esau was the face which the Calvinia villagers chose as their own. The unbowed back confronting Stephanus Strydom was the back they chose as their own. The voice of the blacksmith on that grim, shuttered afternoon in February 1901 was *their* voice. Predictably, when in 1906 some local Afrikaner Bondsmen decided to commemorate the legendary Gideon Scheepers, the rebel leader executed by the British in 1901, there was trouble and ill-feeling between Coloured and Boer inhabitants. For the former naturally did not find the dead Scheepers so arresting and memorable a figure:

> Man, it was a scandal for the people who knew how Abraham Esau had just been treated by the *Vrystaters*. So it happened that one old boy, Gert Lubbe, whose mother had actually been sold on the slave table there, ripped off the *vierkleur* they put up outside the Dutch Church for the memorial service for Gideon Scheepers. He set the flag on fire. And other Coloureds came with bottles and tins to rattle them loudly and to shout insults at the congregation inside. They had a cry, they said it was like a chant, 'We also have our dead', 'We also have our dead'.[61]

The remembered symbolic language of the crowd can best be read as the instinctively defiant and despairing language it was: what people were shouting was that the man they were choosing to remember and respect was Abraham Esau. And it was Esau they made into *their* martyr.

In the years following the South African War, the martyrdom of Abraham Esau served a recognisable function. Not only did its contagious mélange of fact and fancy meet some psychological need in a bruised community adjusting to post-war restabilisation and readjustment; it was itself the grain of the inheritance of a particular historical conjuncture. Esau became the mythic symbol of a revivified British patriotism in Calvinia village life. Thus, craftsmen who constructed an annexe to the Anglican Mission Church which became the Abraham Esau Memorial Chapel and the Abraham Esau Memorial Hall were:

> jingoes, you see. I remember old Jan Nortjie with us, he had an old Black Watch kilt, he used to work in this kilt . . . Yes, old Jan, he said he got the kilt from Abraham Esau who had it as a present from the Queen when he met her in Cape Town. He was terribly proud of himself. He made the stone plaque for Esau . . . when it was put down I remember how we all sang 'God Save the King'.[62]

An outbreak of Esau 'fever' accompanying the erection of the memorial building in the

1910s saw a folklorish scramble after artefacts with which to adorn a living and sedimenting tradition:

> There are those little hills around the town, 'koppies', and a bit of a big hill that we call 'Revunie'. That's a Hottentot word. It was a Hottentot secret place. Everybody knew that Esau used to go up there with his spies. That's where those Boers couldn't find them. Many days as children we used to go up there to see what we could find. In manure one time we found Esau''s bullet. I took it down to the chapel where they kept it in a box. The wood for Esau's altar they also brought down from 'Revunie'.[63]

A crucial dimension which has characterised the long post-war march of an Esau folk mythology has been its interaction with events and processes linked to the growth and consolidation of an increasingly segregationist – and Afrikaner dominated – South African state. Displaying a consciousness of connections between seemingly discrete events, Calvinia villagers have seen a relationship between the individual life story of Abraham Esau and historical events like the formation of Union in 1910, the emergence of Afrikaner *apartheid* rule in 1948, and the establishment of South Africa as a Republic in 1961. Although the orbit in which Esau is remembered and celebrated reflects shifts in meaning and perceptions over time, those who consider themselves the common inheritors of that cultural tradition have sustained a core connection which is both a memory of a past voice and identity and the composition of a present one. For Esau and his story have been assimilated as a means of registering an historical identity. The martyr legend and the man are melted back the one into the other. Indeed, the persistence of the Esau mythology may perhaps be seen as focusing fears of an actual loss of historical identity. 'Myth-making', as Gwen Davies has put it, 'can be perceived as a means to survival.'[64]

That survival has been the inward continuity of a peculiarly British thread in the lives of Coloured villagers in and around Calvinia. One Anglican priest remembers being told 'the Esau story' at his first meeting with his congregants after his arrival at the mission church in 1937. He learned how 'the Afrikaners sewed him up in an ox-skin until he was stretched and suffocated to death in the sun. There was lots of bitter feeling towards Afrikaners. They did have an extraordinarily strong British connection ... Oh yes, there was a very strong jingoistic element, among even the common labourers.'[65] His successor in 1946 took his ministry to a small community of Baster pastoralists at the nearby settlement of Loeriesfontein. There he found 'beautifully cool reed houses' with fading symbols of patriotic eccentricity, an idealised desire for a British line: 'None of them had clocks so I had to be there to conduct services according to the dawn. Yet in many of those houses I saw pictures of British Royalty. Even in April last [1986] when I went back visiting, I saw photographs of Queen Victoria and Edward VII, still there.' At outdoor services at:

> the Esau Memorial Chapel, the people wouldn't allow me to take mass in Afrikaans, even though I was fluent. They were an overwhelmingly Afrikaans-speaking congregation, but they insisted on conducting business in English. They didn't mind the Coloured Catechist doing it in Afrikaans now and again, but they demanded that the *Engelse Predikant* always take them in English. I soon learned that it was part of their feeling of protest, over all those years, for Abraham Esau. *His* chapel had to be an *English* chapel.[66]

A rich and amazing folklore persisted alongside these rituals. Towards the end of the 1940s the resident Anglican priest recalls being told:

> a quite fantastic yarn by Martha Baartman, one of the oldest women in Loeriesfontein. Her story was about how two old and well-known Afrikaner farm women who were completely dumb came to lose their voices. It so happened that as children they were out at night on the Clanwilliam Road when the Free Staters were about, when they saw Abraham Esau and his spies galloping past in the dark. When he turned his eyes upon them they were so overcome with fright that they could no longer speak. I was also regaled with another peculiar story about how Esau used to drive sheep into the deep waters at Brandvlei. As they floated, their bodies rotted and turned into Afrikaners. These stories were told to me in pretty ropey English . . . These Basters were all terribly proud of the fact that they had these connections with Abraham Esau.[67]

Here an Esau folklore is expressed directly as myth, in the sense of a fantasy told in an especially powerful and vivid way. The accumulated working of myth is not to diminish its content nor to constrict its telling, but to expand upon them. It is to unharness the implausible or fantastic and to project it into the world as an enactment of power. With the capacity of that power for transformation, the world of Afrikaner rural domination is turned upside down. The invention of a superhuman Esau allowed the devotee of the tradition to reach back to relive and celebrate a miraculous moment in the past which crystallises, at its very origins, the contradiction at the heart of this body of folklore. For Esau is remembered not only as victim and martyr but also as a full-blooded opponent of Boer masters.

As already noted, national events also played their part in sharpening local divisions and enmities. When the old Boer Republics were incorporated as provinces alongside the established British colonies of the Cape and Natal in the new Union of South Africa in 1910, there was strain in relations between some Coloured and white villagers. At the Anglican mission church people drew the memory of their martyr around them like some rough blanket against the winds of a new enclosing state. Across Union was seen to fall the ominous shadow of 'Freestater' and 'Transvaaler' leadership. A teacher remembers learning from his family that:

It just wasn't right to have the Union. Our people were bitter then about the situation as it was turning out after the war. My father spoke at a special service for Abraham Esau that year, he was a Catechist. He said the Union would help the Boers, that it was an insult to the memory of those who had died for the British. He said that we in the Cape, we who were Esau's people, would find life hard.[68]

Across in landed Boer society there were objections to the bitterness with which Coloured villagers were reacting to Union. Here the Esau tradition also became politically operative in memory, although it acquired a different bite and fabrication in consciousness:

> For instance, The Afrikaner Bond didn't want to hear about the Esau affair. The way I first heard it was that he was a spy for the British who betrayed his Afrikaner masters. He also put poison in their food and did other terrible things . . . it was all a bad business. A lot of our farmers were against the Esaus and the Manels, Coloured troublemakers you see, they were making a fuss about the Union because they were born British subjects. They were called Esau big mouths, a bit too big for their station in life.[69]

Simmering hostilities around 1910 were as nothing compared to the disturbance centred around the election of 1948 and the subsequent Nationalist victory. At this time a conspicuous element in Calvinia's social life was the presence of an unusually ener getic and fiery Dutch Reformed Mission Church mission pastor, *Eerwaarde* Uys. He is remembered as a big man, 'an amateur boxer or wrestler', with a loud voice and strong temperament. In zealous pursuit of the Nationalist cause, his pastoral duties became bound up with the election issues of 1948. In Calvinia the Afrikaner nationalist class alliance turned upon vestiges of 'Britishness' which had long affronted them. Displaying a rather cavalier attitude towards electoral propriety, Uys for instance:

> went to the Esau Memorial Chapel where the Union Jack always flew, and tore it down and tore it in half. He said Esau had committed treason against the *volk*, and that respectable Coloured people would not honour murderers. What followed was a forceful appeal to 'so-called Coloured' members of his congregation, that the National Party was the party that really cared about the 'kleurling mense' and that old memories and grievances should be buried . . . now they were part of them and therefore they must vote for them. In those days some had the vote . . . it was common knowledge that Uys was up to no good standing at the polling booth, next to the police, without saying a word.[70]

Uys' attempts to force a new paternalist consensus between an ascendant Afrikaner nationalism in 1948 and a chivvied and cajoled Coloured community foundered on the back of a politically combative young schoolteacher named Leslie Carelse. With his moralistic radicalism of rights and freedoms, Carelse seemed to be renewing old traditions and aspirations; a shopworker, then in her twenties, thought 'he was a fighter for our people, another Abraham Esau'.[71] In this perception she was neither alone nor unrepresentative. In popular imagination the Carelse drama caught echoes of the Esau episode, bouncing off a popular tradition which had hardened into memory. Among those who bore witness, what characterises accounts of Carelse's clash with Uys is an historical awareness of the Esau inheritance in Calvinia. As a local doctor remembers:

> Mr Carelse said that he had been accused of being a communist by the *Sendingkerk* missionary, Uys . . . he was supposed to have said something out loud, at a meeting some where, which Uys interpreted as communism, and as an attack on the Church of the Afrikaner people. So he got a group of his elders to waylay Mr Carelse and they took him out – this was the first time – and assaulted him very badly. He said he was going to sue Uys. Then, things began to build up . . . Afrikaans speaking people in the town came together to take action . . . they said they'd given cheeky boys like Abraham Esau many a hiding in their time, so Carelse should expect one now. Finally, in the night, while Carelse was asleep, a group of whites went and got him out of his bed. They took him by car, right out into the veldt, they took all his clothes off and they *sjambokked* him within an inch of his life and left him there. He was found, naked and bleeding, trying to crawl his way back into Calvinia. Of course there was a sort of token search for his attackers, 'token' being the operative word. It was a tough sort of area. I had the sad experience of being taken to see where Carelse had been whipped, it was near to the spot where Abraham Esau was said to have been murdered . . . people said they did that *deliberately*. The case really caused terrible upheaval at that time, opening up old wounds. Many people felt the connection with the events of the Boer War . . . some of my older patients wanted a plaque for Lesley Carelse put up in the Esau Chapel. He had a bad mental break down, you see, and then died.[72]

Twelve years later came the white referendum over the Nationalist government pro-posal to reconstitute South Africa as a Republic, breaking with the British Common-wealth. In Calvinia, as elsewhere, Afrikaner Nationalists poised to write *finis* to the tradition of constitutional connection with the British Crown. Prime Minister Hendrik Verwoerd was perfectly candid about Nationalist objectives in the elections which were to follow the plebiscite of October 1960: 'We want to make South Africa white ... Keeping it white can only mean one thing, namely domination not leadership, not guidance, but control, supremacy.'[73] The Calvinia referendum campaign excited a wave of popular enthusiasm amongst Afrikaans-speaking whites of different classes. Schools, for instance, staged playground pageants celebrating unity, while wealthy farmers funded activities undertaken by cultural organisations to express organic *volk* solidarity and national pride.

There were no roles for Coloured actors in this cultural and political theatre. The daughter of an Afrikaner landowner remembers that 'we worked for a new country but we were not honoured by our Coloured people. That was our atmosphere. From my personal experience of those in our service they wanted this country to stay with the British.'[74] Peter Manel, a direct descendant of Christian Manel who had been incarcer-ated with Abraham Esau, recalls the referendum campaign as having been 'a bad time for many of our people in Calvinia. I remember that there were some sheep farmers who would get drunk and drive around at night, shouting "we'll shoot you, bloody *rooinek* Coloureds", and "where's your Queen now?"'[75]

In opposition to the orgy of white Republicanism, Calvinia's dominated classes resorted to the continuous tradition of a particularist patriotism of their own. In drawing on the ghost of Abraham Esau, it was characterised both by an introspective localism and by a reaching out in perception and historical consciousness to a language and an older colonising and controlling political culture never completely eroded by a domi-nating Afrikaner nationalism:

> Well, Daantjie Scholtz, he was the chief of the National Party there in 1960, he came to the school to brag that 'we've got our new Republic, we shall be a new, proud nation'. And he was actually shouted down by the teachers and some of the pupils. One of them got up to say that he had a murderers' Republic, which was stained with the British blood of Abraham Esau. He was very brave. He hissed at Scholtz that the Boers were making slaves of people, that they had been robbed of their rights left to them by the British. As you'll imagine, Scholtz was absolutely furious. He said, 'if I hear that man's name again, there'll be trouble for you people. You are traitors, just as he was. You and the English-speakers, those Cape liberal types.'[76]

We can see the Esau story remaining as an active, self-conscious and enduring historical legacy in Calvinia life, illuminated by episodes such as the simmering ten-sion over Republicanism in 1960–1. And the cleavage produced by this historic melo-drama has equipped Coloured and Afrikaner people in Namaqualand with two different histories and two different memories. The force with which the Esau legend has worked through the changing contexts of history has helped to make those histories and those memories almost hallucinatory. Indeed, oral history provides a vivid example of a literal hallucinatory spasm, in the case of one individual's fevered recollection. An informant remembers moving to Calvinia as a nurse a month after South Africa became a Republic:

> I went there in June 1961 and was introduced to the patients as the new *rooinek* sister. An elderly woman muttered something about the damn British. Well, when I was next on night duty she flew at me about the Boer War, about the British sending that Coloured Esau to spy on them and poison their children. She screamed that it was right that he was shot, they should have burned his body. Well, I can tell you I was totally dumbfounded by this woman's hysterics. After a doctor came in to sedate her because she was so uncontrollable, I learned that she was having hysterics about an incident that related to sixty years before . . . it was just as if it was happening right there, there and then.[77]

Here, felt historical emotion was a spring from which it was impossible to break free; folk legend was a nightmare into which one awoke.

In 1901 Calvinia had roughly 300 white and 600 Coloured inhabitants. Today its population has grown but in many respects a 1980s visitor is struck by an apparent absence of change, a sense of continuity. The village boundaries and streetscape of white houses, shops, post office and hotel remain substantially the same, except for some post-1960s housing development on the northern outskirts, behind the low hills of the Hantam Mountains. The Coloured housing location of 'New Town' has been consolidated on the Calvinia periphery, appropriately hidden from white citizens' gaze by the hill associated with the Esau legend, 'Revunie'. The forced population removals of *apartheid* have also seen the flattening of the old Esau Memorial Chapel.

But Abraham Esau remains stubbornly rooted in popular memory: 'Now we've got this multi-purpose hall where they have meetings, dances, and things like that, and the Esau Memorial Chapel has now become a little underground room. But the old plaque is still there, and people respect it.'[78] The neighbouring Clanwilliam Museum is to acquire Charles Niewoudt's original arrest warrant which lists, among others, the name of Abraham Esau. It is expected to be framed below a torn half of the Union Jack ripped down from the Calvinia Magistracy in January 1901. While it may not be the intention of the museum's curator, the symbolic effect will be to remember a martyr and honour a victim of 'a white man's war'. And remembrance continues to be enacted at other levels. It is the annual memorial mass for Abraham Esau that draws everyone to the Anglican Church. On Calvinia sheep farms, herders and shearers still talk animatedly of the events and atmosphere of the South African War, with a relish for adding to the inventions of the Esau folklore. Oral tradition carries the mirrors of their own past, the yoke of Free State Boer conquest and the settled paternalistic rule of a Victorian Cape liberalism. We can still glimpse some of them as the bearers of a half-hidden identity ultimately derived from an old and dead British order, reliving through gesture, sign and symbol, that moment when conquest seemed about to remake their lives and historical future:

> Coloured chaps on the colonial side called themselves 'Rooi Esaus', that name is still heard today. There's also a dance called 'Rooi-rooi' which the older workers do on the farms. One old man I know does this party piece for his fellow shearers when he's tight, as his father taught him. Kind of folk dance I suppose, about Abraham Esau driving off the Boers and then being captured by them, and then having to dig his own grave. When he's finished he stands up to salute and sing to Queen Victoria before they shoot him.[79]

Myth, history and representation

Within Calvinia, the folkloric presence of Abraham Esau has lodged within a deeply ingrained structure of popular memory and popular feeling. Formed in the siege atmosphere of the war, the Esau story has come to play an ideologically inflected role in historical remembering. However much oral invention has come to cluster around it, the texture of its formation in human memory is structured by what Isidore Okpewho terms 'an historicist faith'.[80] The adornments of a spoken Esau tradition are used to enhance rather than replace an historical reality. Abraham Esau therefore lives as much in history as in folk mythology. He came out of a moment of local solidarity and militant resistance. And in considering the experiences and struggles of the war in Calvinia, it is therefore essential to emphasise that the story of Esau – with all its associations and meanings – emerged not from the usual marginality of Calvinia's labouring community but, on the contrary, from their momentary centrality. Poor villagers who were trapped by the limits of their historical situation took self-assertive steps to protect their petty yet precious rights and liberties. The depth of the crisis *forced* an historical awareness of themselves as a people defined *against* Boer or Afrikaner political conquest. And this was passed down as a substantial legacy, simmering in oral tradition even as the temporary terror of the *sjambok* in 1901 seemed to be hardening inexorably into permanent political domination in later decades.

The invocation of an Esau 'tradition' of a Cape British 'patriotism' in oral remembrance and storytelling is the projection of an alternative identity which has continued to reside in the – often hushed – consciousness of Calvinia inhabitants. It has come to mark off a scrap of collective popular memory of resistance and oppression from the ways in which memory has been, and continues to be, officially mythologised, organised and celebrated through ruling white political forces in the state.[81] Indeed, the periodic jostling between blacks and whites in Namaqualand to establish one kind of heroic Esau legend over a demonic one can be seen as a tiny yet integral part of historically shifting and contested relations of moral hegemony in South African society. It is in this sense that the nourishing of an Esau mythology can be seen as acting as a form of social and moral accountancy in which memory and a lingering older identity are established and renewed. As contemporary martyr-history, it seems to appear as the inner exile of the dispossessed.

Accordingly, it is important to note that the potency of orally circulated narratives and interpretations of the Esau story lies in its particular illumination of a community's view of its own past and historical fate. Its force lies in its collective as well as its singular shape. It is apparent that the oral making and remaking of Esau's mythic qualities shapes a consciousness of history in informants as a morally dramatic and episodic force. As threads from 1948 or 1960 loop back to the conjuncture of 1899 to 1902, contemporary popular historical consciousness in Calvinia becomes, to use Ron Grele's reflection, 'a dramatic view of eternally contending binary oppositions'.[82] For in the final analysis, the strength and texture of Esau remembrance has meaning not in terms of empirical fidelity but in terms of its ideologically indicative content. That martyrdom and mythologising has become part of the inherited fibre of lives in the post-war Cape. In the ignition of a folk tradition it is these ideological accretions which are deeply grounded in the conjunction of memory, interpretation, disjunction and continuity.

The story of Esau's martyrdom may be seen as one which essentially 'threw into deeper shadow the actuality of his own society, in which both the values and the artefacts of the past were doomed to decay'.[83] Yet something of that past continues to reside in localised pockets of consciousness. Subjective visions of some of the old moments of regional or particularist community resistance to external settler intrusion and dispossession have not been entirely obliterated by the forces of political, social and economic change in contemporary South Africa. Within the single South African social formation, the Cape may be a post-British colonial society, but it is one in which not all have decolonised themselves. Their attachment to the British past of Cape 'exceptionalism' has sustained understanding and explanation of the values of the present on their own terms. This imagination has been made by the social and political cognition of a local culture and given weight by a history. In the oral history remembrance of many older black people, the expressive moral significance of Abraham Esau as figure and martyr has come to rest primarily in the emotional representation of myth, and in cultural modes and meanings.[84] As Beinart has recently suggested, in South Africa the march of white domination 'has indeed produced some highly instrumental historical myths. But struggles against oppression produce their own historical myths, symbols of resistance and interpretations of the past . . . It is important that they too be explored and understood.'[85] Any such exploration would need to fix not only on the real geological shifts in conquest and capitalist incorporation, but also to be sensitive to the small change of South African history, the diversities of local experience and their forms of political representation in every historical conjuncture. In their 'symbols of resistance and interpretations of the past', black subordinate classes are not bound by identical objective determinations and a single, common consciousness.

From these perspectives, the life of Abraham Esau may help us to answer a key question of the 1899 to 1902 conflict: what sort of war was it? For if the war settled some questions pretty conclusively, it left a residue of unresolved – and contested – meanings. Of crucial importance are the ways in which myth-creating events or incidents actively constitutive of social identities and political sensibilities have worked themselves out over time in specific historical contexts. While the coalescing anti-imperialist liberation mythologies of black South Africa in the 1980s are bidding for the hearts of half the nation, the resonant popular appropriations of the Esau folk tradition speak for antecedents in earlier, defensive radicalisms. The iconography of Abraham Esau the martyr can be seen as an active and influencing survival of one such radical moment. And can also remind us that not all tales and myths of historical struggles against oppression are anti-imperialist in origin and ancestry. Inasmuch as some have helped to constitute identity in the Cape, they have also been imperialist in memories, interpretations and projections. Goldin has shown that the formation of modern Coloured identity was anchored 'in the white heat of the years surrounding the South African War', years of major change in the equilibrium of class forces in the Western Cape, as the productive circuits of capital were reshaped by industrialisation.[86] The location of Abraham Esau, martyr of Calvinia, suggests that a further determining factor of identity has been little less than the sheer historic melodrama of

140

the experience of war itself. For that past remains a battlefield in which contending moralities compete.

The dead of that old battlefield have been buried. But some have remained warm with the blood, breath and gesture of war mythology. This has found expression in moving memory and its particularistic cycles of telling and retelling, production and consumption; these well-rehearsed regularities might well be seen as the narrative equivalent of what Marx called 'simple reproduction' in the economic sphere.[87] Yet their loaded historical alchemy is also suggestive of more than this. For the creation of such 'powerful myths and legends', to quote Samuel, should not be seen as separate from 'the actual retrieval of the material past and the retrieval of vanished mental states and our own need for the symbolic, and the metaphorical and the imaginary'.[88]

8

Treason offenders and their antagonists

In order to appreciate the conduct and meaning of the Cape war it is essential to understand the conduct and meaning of social antagonisms in the countryside. The central theme of this chapter is that agrarian civil conflict should be seen as a crucial component of the deep divisions and bitter dissensions which stamped relations between blacks and factious white settlers. What is particularly striking is the degree to which the countryside became a cradle of civil conflict between black and white as relations between African and Coloured people and colonists degenerated. Away from the battlefields and set-piece sieges of Stormberg, Mafeking and Kimberley so repeatedly depicted by war historians, a kind of irregular civilian warfare was being played out, with continual, muffled skirmishing over alternative sets of rights and assumptions. The atmosphere in white farming districts thus became clouded by smouldering enmities and ideological divisions between angry Boers and equally rancorous black labourers, servants and tenants. To Anglo-Boer conflict was added the radical impetus of flaring Boer–black hostilities. This chapter explores one crucial dimension of the friction and polarisation which permeated all levels of rural social relations. It is concerned with the manner in which treason law became a resonant medium within which a range of social and political conflicts were fought out.

The effect of Republican invasion and local rebellion upon the ordering of relations on settler farms was twofold. First, Republican forays created conditions of disorder and agitation in which emboldened Boer agricultural communities found themselves locking horns with numbers of increasingly truculent labourers, tenants, squatters and neighbouring free independent smallholders. Second, British reaction to the Republican challenge – the introduction of emergency laws to suppress sedition – became one of the most powerful forces making for rural confrontation, as black men and women became the local cogs upon which the treason machinery turned. The threat which public witnesses and anonymous informers posed to the position of Boer colonists proved to be a new and distinctly alarming experience for those with settled habits of authority and superiority. And assumptions of control and obedience were suddenly made to seem very brittle. An examination of this pattern of escalating disruption provides a first-class illustration of the way in which the shock of war led discontented servants and labourers to act as agents of British interests and to strike against employers and landowners. For the peril which confronted rural settlers was not so much a frontal

African onslaught from the surrounding countryside as disloyalty and malice within the ranks of their own household and field labour.

Treason: definition and responses

Several historians have made passing reference to the role of African informants, informers and prosecution witnesses in Cape treason trials. T. R. H. Davenport writes that by mid 1900, Afrikaner Bond spokesmen were becoming incensed by the brusque practice of arraigning farmers 'on the evidence of Kaffirs'.[1] 'The acceptance of evidence, sometimes without corroboration, from Coloureds and Natives, and the rewarding of informers' ranked among 'the most common grievances related to the detention of Afrikaners on suspicion', according to G. H. L. Le May.[2] Warwick has noted that 'the use made by Britain of African witnesses . . . was bitterly condemned by the Boers', and has pointed out that landowners used the issue of rights of tenure as a lever to try to intimidate or silence African tenants listed as prosecution witnesses at treason trials.[3] J. H. Snyman has depicted witnesses as incorrigible liars, easily cajoled by the British into impugning the honour, standing and motives of Boer settlers.[4] However, none of these authors provides us with more than a brief glimpse of these irregularities. There seems to be a clear need to consider the social context of individual people and situations in some detail, in order to try to capture something of the layers of reality of individual experience. For an atmosphere of treason stirred individual struggles of quite dramatic power. An exploration of individuals, relationships and incidents helps to throw light on the feelings of hatred and vengeance which pulsed through agrarian districts. Notwithstanding the influence of locality and other variations in experience, the conflict around law provides clear, in some instances classic, examples of shifts or 'fractures' in attitudes, behaviour and class relations.

There are several questions of particular interest. Who were the men and women who became principal actors and protagonists at treason trials? What factors prompted them to testify against colonists in such considerable numbers? Were they driven to inform and testify because of individual grievances and disputes, or because of some general sense of hostility towards Republicanism? Was their denunciation of rebel suspects solely a consequence of the malign influence brought to bear upon them by army officers, as observers frequently alleged? Was the packing of judicial hearings with 'morose Natives, open to all manner of bias and influence',[5] invariably facilitated by bribes, as settlers habitually claimed? Or were disaffected farm labourers and squatters acting independently, and according to their own interests? If this was so, what were their motivations and objectives? And if British reliance upon black witnesses was regarded by Boer colonists as illegitimate, what was the nature of the settler response? It is questions such as these which make an analysis of the conduct of witnesses and informers a useful exercise.

If we are to understand why colonists were so panicky about the harnessing of blacks to treason proceedings, some preliminary remarks about the workings of martial law are necessary. The provision of severe emergency statutes between 1900 and 1902, to be used against individuals suspected of seditious offences, is a lengthy topic. For present purposes, it will suffice to set out briefly the context within which emergency

143

procedures were drafted, and to note what the offences were. As we have already noted, it did not take long after the declaration of war for the Schreiner administration, with its Afrikaner Bond connection growing daily more unhappy, to find itself in a tight spot. Called upon to fulfil imperial military obligations while at the same time maintaining peaceable relations with a restive Cape Boer constituency, the colonial state faced uncomfortably contradictory imperatives. In the eyes of colonial Boers, the state's imperial alliance stamped it indelibly as partisan. With rebel disturbances becoming increasingly numerous and severe, the administration's relations with Boer communities deteriorated; it soon faced losing civil control of the disaffected rural settler population. Between November 1899 and January 1900, large tracts of the northern and northeastern Cape crackled into flame, as invading Orange Free State commandos and colonial rebels seized power in places such as Aliwal North, Burghersdorp, Philipstown, Colesberg, Upington, Kuruman and Douglas. With colonial authority dangerously eroded in a number of areas, the Schreiner ministry was obliged to take action. Treading gingerly at first, the government authorised the proclamation of martial law in specified, unsettled, rural districts. It feared that any general proclamation to cover the whole colony would further deepen anti-British hostilities among Boers, which were already running at threateningly high levels.

However, the imperial military command had absolutely no doubt after the first wave of Republican incursions that drastic summary legal measures were called for in response to a breakdown of order and a crisis of Boer obedience. There was certainly no shortage of British observers who believed that only a liberal quota of exemplary public executions would check rebel defiance of colonial rule. Both Schreiner and Sprigg were heavily criticised for their lukewarm approach to the prosecution of Cape rebels.[6] The second major Republican offensive of 1900 to 1901, combined with renewed local insurrection, proved a decisive turning point. The crisis provided a heaven-sent opportunity to those who, like Milner and Kitchener, had been clamouring for months for a blanket declaration of martial law. With growing numbers of farmers taking to arms, the Commander-in-Chief's insistence on draconian provisions to deal with rebels carried the day and the Sprigg ministry became a reluctant and unhappy party to a fiercer martial law policy.[7] Kitchener was particularly keen for an armoury of sanctions against virtually anything which could be construed as sedition and treasonable communication with, and support of, the enemy. The pace of events was such that, before the end of 1901, draconian statutes had the force of law throughout the Cape, with the exception of the ports and the Transkeian Territories.

Which offences led to prosecution? Chamberlain issued a general identification of colonial rebels on 4 May 1900, in which the offending categories were: ringleaders; looters and those who committed outrages; individuals responsible for 'acts contrary to the usages of civilised warfare'; those who had 'openly and willingly waged war'; those who had supplied intelligence to, and had rationed, Republican troops and those who claimed to be able to prove that their collaboration with the enemy had been under duress.[8] A range of heavy penalties was imposed on persons convicted of these offences. Conviction on the most serious charges brought the death sentence for principals, while transportation and lengthy periods of imprisonment (up to fifteen years) were meted out to leading accessories. At the other end of the scale (offences such as provisioning commandos and the stockpiling of guns), there were sanctions of shorter terms of imprisonment with hard labour provisions, stiff fines which ranged from £300 to £1,000, property confiscations and periods of disfranchisement.[9] For suspects against whom a credible prosecution case could not easily be mounted, there was the bleak prospect of many months in civil or military detention. Numbers of Boer 'undesirables' were also deported to specified rural districts, and to refugee camps on the coast.

The Cape Treason Court, set up as special district criminal commissions under the civil judiciary, handled hundreds of treason cases between 1900 and 1903, when its work was finally wound up. Adopting a discretionary approach, the commissions tried to moderate the severity of treason law by imposing lesser penalties whenever there was room for latitude.[10] The reluctance of the Treason Court to send men to death, or to impose long prison sentences, irked army officers who were disinclined to be merciful towards Boer rebels. In their view, the intention of treason law was not to become bogged down in technicalities, or to become an arena of debate around the occasional flimsiness of prosecution evidence. Nor was it to pick out extenuating circumstances and to give prisoners the benefit of any doubt. 'The purpose of these trials is to set an example, not to interpret the law in the interests of Boer felons', wrote Lieutenant-Colonel Francis Fremantle, voicing a common viewpoint.[11] Fearing leniency by Cape civil courts, the British Army established open military tribunals (to which resident magistrates and Cape justice officials were sometimes assigned) to enforce laws free of civil hindrance. Juries, which by custom were male and all-white, were not empanelled; attempts by magistrates to call out juries were invariably blocked by British commandants.[12] Not to be thwarted in their desire to punish severely, British district commandants also resorted to the agreeable expedient of convening special courts martial, at which hundreds of Boers were summarily condemned to death.[13] Military prosecutors were, as J. S. Galbraith has suggested, obsessed with the belief that 'the entire Afrikaans-speaking section of the population was tainted with treason'[14] and determined to exact a heavy price from farming communities for their civilian support of the Republican campaign.

The callous and menacing conduct of British commandants appears to have accurately reflected the overbearing style of regular soldiers who find themselves confronting stubborn civil disaffection from a population from which its guerrilla enemy is drawn. To cite Geoffrey Best, troops embroiled in such inflamed conditions develop 'a prickly dislike' of civilians and more specifically 'an obsessive desire' for ferocious punitive measures in reprisal for perceived damages, threats, political slights and suspicious behaviour.[15]

With individual British officers able to alter the rules of the game as it went along, according to their personal prejudices and vendettas, the costs of falling foul of the law could be frighteningly high, as hapless Steynsburg or Cradock *bywoners* discovered when by bad luck or worse judgement they got caught up in looting charges, for local commandants had defined even the theft of the odd sheep or goat from English-speaking landowners as a war crime.[16] Fear of falling under suspicion of treason thus began to strike deep into the core of both poor and propertied Boer society. Settlers considered the mandatory severity of treason penalties a miscarriage of justice, and the passing over of the jury principle an outrage. Violation of basic constitutional expectations left aching wounds. The salt came in the shape of an overwhelming predominance of African and Coloured prosecution witnesses.

As in the Cape, Boer colonists in the occupied Transvaal and Orange River Colony were greatly discomfited by the appearance of African witnesses at trials. The climate for rebel suspects was chilly, and many farmers were vulnerable to damaging testimony by hostile tenants. Initially, there appears to have been some caution about the admissibility of African evidence, with British officers finding district commissioners reluctant to assist them in the collecting of incriminating depositions.[17] Civil officials were squeamish about bringing farmers to account on the basis of identifications made by Africans. Thus, for example, the Kroonstad district commissioner warned Roberts in July 1900 that he 'did not consider it advisable that native evidence against a white man should be taken ... as it might lead to perjury for purposes of revenge, and perhaps to trouble with the Africans concerned'.[18] But, given rural settler alienation, officials had no option but to run the risk of inflaming Boer sensibilities by enlisting African aid. Officers carrying out treason investigations everywhere would, more often than not, run up against a wall of silence when trying to make enquiries among farmers; rural Boer communities generally closed ranks whenever intelligence officers tried to sniff out Republican sympathisers or collaborators. The antagonism was such that it was mostly only on the basis of detailed information supplied by Africans that settlers could be tried in the courts.

Once it had become clear that the support of Africans was being sought in bringing whites to trial, newspapers lost no time in sounding the alarm. In London, *The Times* did not mince words, denouncing a situation in which 'malicious' and 'idle' servants were being encouraged to betray their masters.[19] If the correspondence columns of *Ons Land*, *De Graaff-Reinetter* and the pro-Afrikaner Bond *South African News* are a typical reflection of the popular temper, farmers were beside themselves with rage. 'Many innocent men', wrote a Steynsburg correspondent in June 1900, 'are imprisoned for High Treason on the basis of evidence from Native cranks.'[20] Another correspondent from Colesberg asked, 'Who is safe? Wives and children live in terror, as nobody knows what a drunken native might go and testify.'[21] For the price of a few pounds, intelligence officers were bribing domestic servants into implicating innocent farmers, declared *Ons Land*.[22] Even the pro-imperial settler press was edgy about the issue.[23]

The stiff Treason Bill introduced by the Sprigg administration in July 1900 heightened Boer anxieties to fever pitch. Described in the *South African News* as a measure which 'placed one section of the superior race in this country at the mercy of an inferior race', the Bill was viewed by many hostile whites as the last straw in a British campaign to erode their standing over Africans. At farmers' meetings speakers were clearly rattled by the manner in which embittered servants were seemingly becoming the beneficiaries of war legislation. It appeared to many as if the law was deliberately being brought into play to advantage African parties against one sector of the settler population. And colonists were naturally deeply and incurably suspicious of a situation in which their liberties and even lives could be jeopardised by the word of a disgruntled farm servant.

The pro-Republican press painted a chilling picture of the fate of upright, law-abiding farmers being fingered by unfaithful servants. Under the heading 'Martial Law Scandals', the *South African News* championed the case of three Hope Town farmers who, during April 1900, were sentenced to two years with hard labour for consorting with the enemy, on the basis of evidence furnished by four goatherds. The episode was cited as an exemplary illustration of the 'danger of acting upon native evidence', as the incriminating depositions which clinched the convictions came from 'servants who had been taken away by the Rimington Scouts and kept until the trial, a proceeding hardly calculated to impart to the native mind the need for giving impartial evidence'.[24]

The political assault upon martial law was naturally led by the Bond. In parliament, members of rural constituencies endlessly denounced the 'pernicious consequences' of involving blacks in prosecutions. While a good many Bond parliamentarians were rather carried away by indignation, the scores of verifiable, African-related martial law cases they chose to publicise still tell us a good deal about the extent to which African witnesses were playing influential roles in prosecutions. According to the member for Albert, for instance, events there were taking a serious turn by 1900 when even local *veldkornets* were being committed to prison on the strength of affidavits bought for a few shillings. Similar cases were reported from Calvinia, Aliwal North, Lady Grey, Burghersdorp, Barkly West, Molteno and Steynsburg. Several Bond MPs busied themselves assisting dozens of prosecuted and persecuted constituents who, they protested, stood to lose all on the basis of theatrical depositions obtained through favour and money. One, A. S. du Plessis, ventured that he 'did not wish to assert that a Kafir was incapable of giving evidence. What he would point out was that there were hundreds of them who could do nothing better than drink brandy, and if they saw a chance to earn a few shillings, they would not hesitate to swear to any affidavit.'[25]

During the course of 1900 several instances came to light in which it was legally proven that African witnesses had been encouraged to perjure themselves. This brought to their judicial role an even greater notoriety.[26] Bond rhetoric was consistently sharp and aggressive: the party conference at Paarl in June 1900, for example, produced exactly the kind of impassioned outcry that was required. Enraged delegates heard that with rewards of up to £100 on offer to servants, evidence was being faked and trials were being rigged on a massive scale. Africans everywhere were being offered the opportunity to enrich themselves by spreading false stories and were becoming daily more brazen. According to speakers, the mendacity of farm servants was creating a triangular spectre of panic running through Gordonia in the northwest, Worcester in the southwest and Herschel in the northeast. There was also talk of witnesses acting under duress; in Hopetown and Albert for example, there were allegations that 'poor Coloured boys' were being pressed at gunpoint into giving false testimony against their employers.[27]

For those arraigned, attributes of property, racial status and respectability carried little weight with prosecuting authority. The powerful now felt less secure. For the law now felt less of an instrument of their local propertied and other class interests. A perceived shift in the boundaries of class sharpened the boundaries of conflict and bitterness; the latitude allowed to the labouring poor rankled deeply with landowners. 'Men of character and standing', protested a rural observer, 'are imprisoned on High Treason Charges on the flimsiest evidence from the lowest of half-bred blacks.'[28] In the press, there was a shrill and growing chorus of complaints that 'influential' and 'substantial' farmers were being arrested on the information of 'mere Native servants'.[29] A typical case was that of a 'Mr W.', a prosperous landowner in Rouxville who, in July 1901, was 'sentenced on Native evidence alone . . . no reputable witnesses were called on his side, nor even any of his white *bywoners*, who might have sworn fairly. Two men and one woman Kafir were the only witnesses, and people all said they had been bribed by British soldiers.'[30] Equally disconcerting was the case of Stephanus Nienaber two months later; this prosperous Cradock farmer was indicted *in absentia* for treason on the sole basis of affidavits supplied by Martha Dampers and Sara van der Ventel, former domestic servants of his who had taken up as washerwomen for the Wiltshire Regiment.[31]

Martial law – the hated *Krijgswet* – thus trod sharply on the corns of propertied settlers, men more used to having the law serve their interests than to facing the law as victims. Momentarily, settled habits and relations of power and subordination between propertied and propertyless were shaken. And there were other points of friction. In addition to the vexing problem of informers and witnesses, there was also a growing tendency after 1900 for African special constables to be used to guard martial law prisoners. This practice presented an intolerable affront to many colonists. The sight of constables supervising white hard-labour prisoners at stone quarries, earthworks and other work sites seemed, if anything, to add ignominy to injury. Moreover, special constables appear to have taken to their punitive duties with some relish. Boer prisoners were bullied and humiliated by African guards, being periodically deprived of food rations and clothing and sometimes beaten. At Tulbagh during April 1901 for instance, 'specials' forced a work gang to empty the nightsoil buckets of a detachment of Coloured militiamen; two Boers who protested at their treatment were struck for 'cheekiness' with such force by a notoriously irascible Sergeant Booi that they were hospitalised.[32]

For the government, the outcry over judicial procedures was distressing and disagreeable. To a man, the administration deplored the fuss created by leading Bondsmen like N. F. de Waal and H. C. van Heerden and anxious South African Party voices, such as those of J. W. Sauer and T. N. G. Te Water. As Attorney General, it fell to James Rose Innes to fend off criticism during the later half of 1900. J. X. Merriman, for instance, told parliament that in his Wodehouse constituency, 'The principal evidence as to inciting the rebellion came in most cases from Natives', many of whose motives were highly suspect. While not wishing to 'generally denounce Native evidence', Merriman felt impelled to point out that 'the present circumstances had brought out the bad natives to the very fullest extent. It was a cruel thing to think that the white population of this country should be at the mercy of the lowest class in the community.'[33] Rose Innes countered vigorously, insisting that Africans' trial depositions were being used with extreme caution, as 'where a servant gave evidence against his master, whether that servant was a native or a white man, they looked into the relations that existed between the servant and the master to see if there had been any quarrel that would discredit the evidence of the man'. The Attorney General was adamant that the government was not to be stampeded into tampering with the legal and customary right of Africans to present evidence in the colony's courts. This, he argued, applied to new emergency 'justice' as much as to traditional civil legal forms. Rose Innes tried to legitimise state prosecution practice by reference to principles of legal equity for all citizens which had historical roots in the Cape; the forms, procedures and values of law in the colony ran against the exclusion of any category of person. In parliament, he exclaimed that he 'was not going to be a party to saying that the evidence of a native *because* he was a native should be rejected', and described demands for the debarring of African testimony as 'a very mischievous doctrine'.[34]

Witnesses, infiltrations and grievances

African martial law actions against white farmers were not only pursued and shaped through the courts. Republican sympathisers and active collaborators were rudely shaken by the infiltration of their farms by bands of Africans, sniffing for hidden guns. Household servants often led the way. Feelings against Boers were running high, and their hidden arsenals were an obvious target. For informers, an additional satisfaction was money. The British offered lucrative rewards for information leading to the uncovering of arms caches. At £25 per rifle, and £1 per 1,000 cartridges, Africans did not require much bidding to come forward. To the task of implicating farmers small

8 African men and women and colonists surrendering weapons under martial law regulations, Worcester. (Courtesy of the Cape Archives Depot)

149

groups of workers brought their detailed knowledge of local farm conditions and employers' inclinations. For example, Ciskeian or Transkeian seasonal sheepshearers who customarily contracted as migrant labour teams in Wodehouse or Steynsburg would complement clipping with digging on selected farms. They would subsequently make flurried departures from districts, flush with substantial British reward money.[35] Armed with spades, picks and shovels, other enterprising resident labourers teamed up, locating and digging up many hundreds of arms stockpiles for intelligence officers. Reward monies were usually subdivided, with headmen who bargained with officers apportioning the lion's share for themselves. Tramping provocatively across fields, labourers threw down fences, dug under barns and tore down hayricks; their resolve had a frenzied edge. At Colesberg during September 1900, one observer reported that Africans were 'in imminent danger of falling into pits dug in their feverish search for concealed guns'.[36] In Matjiesfontein in the following year, another soldier observed that 'to hear the Kaffirs talk and to see them dig, one would fancy the subsoil of this district to be a sort of arsenal'.[37] Conviction of offenders blown in this way was a mere formality.

It was in the public and often brutalising atmosphere of High Treason Trials that blacks undoubtedly had a most forceful and unnerving impact upon whites. While there are no adequate crime statistics which might enable one to say in precisely what proportion of High Treason proceedings the intervention of black witnesses proved critical, from patchy local evidence it does seem clear that levels of participation were often startlingly high. For example, about 90 per cent of prosecution witnesses at the Malmesbury Treason Trials of April to May 1902 were Coloured farm workers and female household servants.[38] Sessional returns for Barkly East, Wodehouse and Aliwal North following local Republican rebellion reveal that resident and migrant Africans served as principal witnesses at virtually every treason hearing. Similarly, in troubled Dordrecht, Bedford, Somerset East and Fort Beaufort agricultural workers and tenants turned out massively for military prosecutors; taking newspaper evidence, between July 1901 and May 1902 over 80 per cent of cases listed involved specific court appearances by Africans or the admission of their pre-trial depositions and affidavits. In the individual districts of Sutherland, Fraserburg, Carnarvon, Richmond, Molteno, Steytlerville, Uniondale and Willowmore, black rural dwellers were similarly preponderant in the ranks of prosecution witnesses, with levels of sessional involvement running at 75–90 per cent.

Entire peasant communities were sometimes mobilised. In Griqualand West, scores of Tlhaping from the Taung Reserve streamed to the Vryburg Treason Trials in 1902 to testify against some of the around 900 local Boers who had participated in the insurrection and occupation of October 1899. Court records reveal the souring of relations between rebel colonists and the Southern Tswana as Taung headmen removed labourers from farmers' fields, transport riders refused to carry produce marketed by known Republican collaborators and Vryburg traders who rationed rebels were boycotted. The beckoning allegiances of the war defined a new mood towards traders in this area; in this new, determining context, the links of service and obligation which, as Kevin Shillington has noted,[39] sometimes bound local Africans and traders together fairly amicably, were broken. John McGeer, one of several rural traders indicted for treason, claimed in his pre-trial defence that the Tlhaping Chief, Molala, had happily acquiesced in rebel rule. The chief, stung by this slur, issued a dignified and lengthy rebuttal:

> I speak as Chief of the Batlapins, residing at Taung. I have been informed that John McGeer is going to be tried at Vryburg for High Treason, and that he is going to produce a document purporting to be signed by me, allowing him to open another shop at Taung Station to sell to the Boers during the occupation. This is not true. I never signed any document... He said he would give me money and also some cattle if I signed his document, but I refused. My counsellors witnessed all these talks. Later he came back with some Boers from Vryburg and said to me, 'you Natives have got no power now, the Commandant of Vryburg has given me permission'. As McGeer was always very friendly with these Boers of the Free State, I called a secret *pitso* of all my people and told them not to buy from John McGeer or any of the other white men who are so friendly with these Boers. The Batlapins did not have transactions with those who were friendly with the Boers.[40]

Several prosecution witnesses (including some English colonists) attested to the truth of Molala's deposition.

Trials rapidly won the attention, not to say boisterous approval, of rural inhabitants, who were egged on by soldiers to attend court sessions and witness the enforcement of British justice. Military special courts frequently met publicly and sessions were held in the open: the identity of indicted rebels was rapidly made known throughout the district, and even farther afield. Trials at which Boers were charged with war crimes against black civilians or those on the imperial military payroll were undoubtedly a principal attraction. So, too, were hangings and shootings. Large crowds from miles around would assemble on foot, in carts and on horseback, to gawp at and cheer on these grisly proceedings. In February 1901, an officer in Loxton reported encountering 'wagonloads of Coloured yeomen' who had travelled twenty miles to witness a rebel execution. Public disorder seems to have been a permanent feature of these occasions. Trial sessions and the carrying out of sentences generally took place in an unruly, almost carnivalesque atmosphere, with excited and demonstrative crowds jostling to taunt Boer prisoners, occasionally pelting them with dung and rotten fruit. Hucksters and vendors of sweets and cakes moved through the swirl of the crowd; at Williston a hot spot was occupied by one Mohamed Allie who offered haircuts and shaves to watchers awaiting the spectacle of executions.[41]

Ill-feeling between watching farm workers and distraught relatives of those indicted sometimes erupted in ugly brawling. Efforts by local constabularies to keep order were mostly ineffectual; anxious Chief Detective Officers faced crowds hanging around treason sessions which simply refused to budge. A senior British officer's plea during April 1901, for stricter segregation at hearings ('to check cheeky natives from meddling with prisoners') fell on deaf ears. Indeed, there was eager commingling between court crowds and British troops on court duties. Relations were often openly fraternal, with firing squads being feted by women, and spectators bestowing poultry, eggs and fruit upon infantrymen. At the lowest levels, within the immediate social experience of ordinary labourers, these small gestures and friendly noises were pregnant with larger meaning. For in the mediation of relations in this shared public domain, they can be seen as cementing a level of reciprocity between parties of Cape blacks and the British.

To recognise and illuminate the full realities of black historical experience during this period we must acknowledge that beside the traumas of inevitable racism from imperial troops, pointed to by Trapido and Lewis among others,[42] there was hospitable interplay and consent between soldiers and civilians. For the mass of rural people, popular volatility and anti-Boer sentiment made for a natural alliance with the power and also the culture of imperial forces. The maintenance of peace and defence of liberty was firmly identified with the army. British soldiers, as army chaplains piously assured some groups of prosecution witnesses, were in the colony not just to suppress Republican rebellion but to check Boer encroachment upon local 'freedoms' and to fight for those rights and liberties nationally.[43]

What most aroused the wrath of many hostile observers was the fact that, as already noted, British money had a habit of finding its way into the pockets of informers and witnesses. The practice of paying reward monies scandalised newspapers which denounced it as a crude bait to induce witnesses into perjury. Sensational rumours about the size of sums on offer were circulated; *Ons Land* and the *Worcester Standard*, for example, carried exaggerated accounts of shifty British officers travelling the countryside, offering as much as £500 for depositions incriminating farmers.[44] If rather more modestly, some labourers and servants certainly profited out of the business of swearing depositions. For most ordinary trial witnesses, meals, travel allowances, blankets and other clothing and a daily subsistence allowance of 30s. certainly represented fairly generous terms. Army auxiliaries summonsed to provide trial evidence also appear to have fared rather well. Apart from drawing witness attendance benefits, they were entitled to draw full military pay during periods of absence on court duties. Faced with the tedium of lengthy spells between treason sessions, some men looked to part-time ways of securing work and income. One such individual was January Myakatza, a munitions cart driver who gave evidence at Adelaide treason trial sessions between January and April 1902. In addition to accumulating his monthly regimental pay of £5.10s. and drawing his daily witness subsistence payment, Myakatza engaged as a transport rider in Adelaide for four months, netting £29.[45] For informing against Boers who had taken up arms or were rationing guerrillas, *agterryers* were granted reduced sentences and, occasionally, indemnity against prosecution.

While relatively few witnesses pocketed really hefty sums of money, the presence of well-endowed intelligence officers was unquestionably an influential factor in certain instances. Soldiers and compliant magistracy officials were sometimes able to muster together large groups of witnesses whose co-operation had been secured primarily through the promise of financial reward. At Griquatown, in addition to laying out pounds among informers and 'correspondents', officials saw to it that no fewer than thirty-seven Coloured labourers shared in a £250 reward awarded following the treason conviction of one F. K. van Broeksteen in July 1901.[46] From as early as November 1899, the authorities began advertising as much as £250 for evidence leading to the capture of anyone abducting or murdering black informants or trial witnesses.[47] These were substantial prospective sums for anyone to turn down. The frequency of Boer revenge missions, which we will consider shortly in more detail, became a persistent and troublesome source of counterattack in the countryside. Some individual intelligence officers had the authorisation and the means to pay handsomely for sworn affidavits. In the belief that 'judicious rewards to potential witnesses would assure better results', a Lieutenant Aubrey of the Grenadier Guards personally paid one man, Stephanus Maseti, £260 for information concerning a gang of armed *bywoners* who were 'daily threatening' the families of Coloured auxiliaries in the Graaff-Reinet district. Aubrey also paid Martha Buys, a domestic servant employed by John Wiid, the sum of £92 for swearing treasonable practices against her employer at Somerset East trial sessions during March 1902. Furthermore, no fewer than forty-seven men and women from Alexandria and Jansenville were provided with large rewards by an open-handed Aubrey and furnished with immediate monies for horse hire and other expenses.[48]

Publicly posted rewards were most common in those areas (such as Namaqualand–Gordonia and Barkly East–Aliwal North) where rural conflict was reaching a most intense and open phase by 1900. Sizeable sums were offered by frustrated intelligence officers in an effort to counter intimidation and fear of Republican reprisals among servants and other workers. In parts of the northwest, like Prieska and Kenhardt, Boer pressure against informing was particularly menacing and sustained, and there can be little doubt that terror must have kept many labourers quiet, in a silence born of fear and calculation. Here, many individuals had their backs pressed to the wall, and those who risked speaking publicly against their employers clearly did so as aggrieved and apprehensive victims of abuse rather than as wilful aggressors.

In a situation of violent hostilities between labourers and farmers, the prospect of reward money was undoubtedly a powerful inducement, spurring on the hesitant and the frightened to dare to inform. But this is not to suggest that it was always and primarily money and favour which turned normally fainthearted servants against their masters. Rather, it can be argued that British perks and fees generally worked with the grain of popular anti-Boer anger, a lure to persuade wary witnesses to wriggle forward and finger their antagonists. What we see, then, is a stark battle between agricultural workers and farmers who sought to muzzle them. And the stakes were savagely high.

Those who challenged Boers were immediately at risk and the authorities faced a very real problem of ensuring that trial witnesses stayed alive until the start of treason sessions and that they survived it. For once known, witnesses were always vulnerable to reprisals and some individuals paid a heavy price for their temerity in making identifications to military investigators and prosecutors. Beaufort West, De Aar, Graaff-Reinet, Stormberg, Queenstown, Molteno, Herschel and Aliwal North were typical of districts in which Boers acted with the utmost ruthlessness against blacks suspected of conniving against them.[49] In the northeastern districts of Albert, Lady Grey and Barkly East, quarterly military intelligence summaries for 1901 pointed out that the mortality rate among African informers was 'fearfully high'. Something of the grim reality of this situation can be gauged from a brief glimpse at two typical incidents. At Cradock, on 23 February 1901, a group of witnesses (including several juveniles) at a forthcoming treason trial were rounded up at night by several relatives of the accused, driven to a remote farm and hanged there.[50] In the second episode, Solomon April, a Somerset East shepherd who had testified separately against six farmers at hearings between November 1900 and February 1901, was murdered by a band of rebels on 4 March 1901. Led by a Johan Stafelberg, the Boers apparently then 'rode to all the Natives' huts, and told the occupants that all Natives would be shot who assisted the English with Treason business'.[51] In many instances, floggings were also administered as part of a virtual campaign of rural intimidation. There were cases of children being taken hostage for the duration of a judicial hearing, in an effort to muzzle particular witnesses.[52] Aside from actual physical violence, threats of revenge and injury were widespread. Shooting at labourers' and tenants' huts, not always to injure or kill occupants, was a common gesture of aggression and ill-will. Threats might also be issued to intimidate labourers who were known to have been privy to criminal activity by farmers, even before official investigations had commenced. Or, once trials were under way, witnesses and their families might be menaced in order to get damaging testimonies withdrawn.

Local magistrates were always anxious for witnesses, and a number of them took active practical steps to try to ensure their security. In Klipdam, for example, witnesses were placed under constant, armed police protection, and labourers in the area were reassured that any person who came forward to assist the authorities would enjoy the full and constant protection of the law.[53] For trial witnesses in Kuruman, there was twenty-four hour protection by British troops.[54] Intelligence officers were often also willing to quarter individuals at camps and in barracks, a practice which, naturally, did little to inspire trust in witnesses' integrity among Boer observers. In Griquatown, Graaff-Reinet, Vryburg and Aliwal North, Cape Police special constables who collected depositions from labourers were instructed to assure them that identities need not be revealed.[55] An army labour contract far afield was often a good way for trial witnesses to escape the wrath of local Boers, following treason convictions. With individuals removing themselves to safer areas, hasty movement and migration became an explicit indication of insecurity and apprehension. An illustrative case was that of Carolus Seldon, a Tulbagh goatherd, whose damning testimony gaoled five local farmers during September 1900. Seldon's prudent flight from the district was eased by the 5th Lancers, who provided him with transport, work and assisted him to resettle in Uitenhage during December 1900, out of harm's way.[56]

It is evident that when the opportunity arose, blacks sometimes reacted venomously against the families of Boers known to have been involved in the victimising of witnesses. Women on isolated farms were especially vulnerable to acts of revenge. For example, at Barkly East in December 1901, three women were beaten and stabbed on adjacent farms. Two Coloured men detained following the assaults confessed their guilt, but showed no remorse. They told an army court that their families were having to bear the malice of friends of some rebels they had helped to convict, and that it was therefore only fair that some reprisal of their own be taken.[57] In a similar incident at Sutherland during February 1902, a Mfengu scout assaulted a farmer's wife, convinced by rumour of her part in the disposal of the body of a relative who had mysteriously vanished following his testimony at a local trial.[58] Some episodes were particularly tragic ones. On 11 January 1901, Lukas September, a muleteer with the East Kent Regiment, left a Queenstown camp with the declared intention of settling a grievance with a Boer family in the neighbourhood. He cut down fences and fired some haystacks, mutilated several goats and then entered the farmhouse and attacked the absent owner's wife. According to an investigating army officer, 'he attempted to murder the woman by strangulation, then got a rifle and shot her. He then shot himself.' At an inquiry, fellow transport workers revealed that September's wife, Anna, had disappeared four months previously, following her testimony at a Molteno treason trial. The muleteer believed the family, named Snyman, to have been implicated in her abduction. An official report into the affair concluded that September's violence had arisen from 'grief, and a disturbed disposition'.[59] From scattered reports one senses that such incidents were not casual, indiscriminate acts of violence, but were selective encounters, bearing the marks of a particular, personal note of anger and vengeance. They were the desperate actions of embittered men.

For the most part, however, hostilities did not spill over into extremes of personal violence. As stock was naturally the most vulnerable portion of a farmer's capital, there was killing and maiming of Boer cattle in many districts in which tensions were running high. Albertus Haasforther, an Aliwal North landowner who evicted several Sotho families from tenancies as punishment for having made incriminating statements against his brother, lost dozens of sheep, killed at night by having wool stuffed down their throats.[60] Farmers were also the victims of arson and the poisoning of drinking water. In Bedford, in a list of possible reasons for seventy-eight cases of incendiarism and malicious wounding between January and April 1902, the district Martial Law Administrator mentioned 'revenge following bad feeling over the trials being held here', in no fewer than sixty-nine instances.[61]

For informers, a most obvious tactic to escape the consequences of Boer enmity was to try to keep their identities hidden. The anonymous, informing letter appears to have been one useful way for literate or semi-literate individuals to pass on damaging information to the authorities, or to make allegations, without fear of their identity becoming public. Distant anonymity was undoubtedly the best insurance against possible persecution by irate rebels. Both army officers and colonial officials seem to have taken these letters quite seriously, even though the incriminating evidence they provided was often thin and circumstantial. In Herbert, Molteno, and Griquatown, African special constables and civilian interpreters were employed for considerable lengths of time on the processing of informers' letters.[62] In Somerset East, the magistrate's advice was to have all allegations by letter thoroughly investigated. And at Hanover, a senior Naval Brigade Officer who believed letters to be 'of the utmost usefulness', personally posted one John Ramanana (modestly described as 'a native of genius') to undertake English transcriptions, owing to his 'famous fluency in English, Dutch, and most of the Native tongues such as Basuto'.[63] Anonymous letters despatched to the Tulbagh magistracy between May 1900 and June 1901 provided evidence substantial enough for the initiation of a number of successful prosecutions.[64] Contents of anonymous letters were sometimes cited as trial depositions, and served as documents crucial to the prosecution case in military courts.

Letter writing was a shadowy, remote and predatory sphere of activity and, predictably, there is no hard information as to the identity of authors. Some letters were quite polished, and signed with a pseudonym, while others were barely literate, and were signed with a squiggle.[65] Of the very few which have survived, it may be useful to cite one or two as examples. In January 1901, a correspondent identifying himself as 'a loyal and respectable Coloured gentleman' advised the Somerset East magistrate that several strange *bywoners* were making visits to a local farm at night. 'I don't know if I am interfering or not', the informer concluded, 'but I think I can drop you a line about this farmer.'[66] Another correspondent, signing himself 'Friend', wrote to the prosecutor of the Middelburg Special Military Court, recounting 'We natives have just been about in the country. On the farm "potfontein" I spyed about four Boers with guns, drinking coffee and talking with this farmer who is named Malan. The servant of this man tells me she now has to cook food for Boer strangers. I do believe Malan is helping the Free Staters.'[67] The Commandant of Kuruman heard from a 'Loyal Native Subject' that one Hans Schuiters was provisioning strange horsemen in the district. This informer had also taken to snooping around Schuiters' barn, and claimed to have sighted Republican flags secreted there. 'I do not know what business they have there, but it is not good', he wrote.[68] Cradock intelligence received a letter which advised, 'I take the libbertie to rite to tell you that the man Hoffman is making his natives low. He say he have nuthing to do with the Inglish.'[69] The discordant world revealed by these anonymous letters, expertly flighted with the most damaging gossip, can perhaps be viewed as an interesting variation on Thompson's portrayal of 'the anonymous tradition' in plebeian outrage in eighteenth-century rural English society.[70] These incendiary eruptions coursed through their own threatening channels of calculation and careful forethought; and like the classic anonymous threatening letter despatched by a Hampshire villager to summon a rich man to right an injustice, the presumptuous letter which sprang up from the lower depths of Kuruman illuminated the limits of rural deference and the brittle texture of relations in a highly charged political atmosphere.

For Boer farmers the threat of exposure was ever present, and time and again we see bold employees conducting a grim war of insinuation and character assassination against them. The actions, contacts, discussions and motives of employers and masters were noted and commented upon. Household servants in particular, had a sharp eye and an attentive ear to seditious utterances, however trivial or inflated by drink. As early as January 1900 we see Boer communities beginning to show signs of edginess. In Jansenville, Steytlerville and Willowmore, for instance, farmers advised one another to curb loose talk in front of their servants. At Cradock, during April 1900, Marthinus Hattingh found himself in trouble when Sarah Katyn, Stephanus Ngindane and Jonas Maseti denounced him for swearing against Chamberlain, and for storing portraits of the Boer presidents.[71] Andries Kyster, a shepherd, had his suspicions aroused by an unusually large supply of corn being held by his employer, Jan du Plessis.[72] Isaac Manganane, a Thembu squatter on the farm of Alick de Bruin in Barkly East, thought it odd that the landowner should try to purchase horses and grain from him with foreign gold sovereigns which were 'not English', and reported him.[73] Many Boers had brushes with authority as the result of a simple lack of discretion.

Employers who refused to accede to workers' demands that they be released from service to take up military labour contracts were sometimes snared by disgruntled employees who resorted to the simple expedient of denouncing them as Republican collaborators. The belief among hostile observers that trial evidence was often trumped-up was not without some basis in fact. Military courts undoubtedly had their share of venality and crooked deals, with the occasional loyal servant listed for the defence being bought off or coerced by unscrupulous officers, and prosecutors becoming scheming accomplices in perjury. That evidence was sometimes falsified cannot be discounted: on occasion, questionable allegations proved too much, even for flexible military judges. Neither can we ignore the fact that some witnesses would have spoken from a biased position. Treason trials were undoubtedly a convenient means whereby pre-war grudges or other slights unrelated to war conditions could be pursued. Needing no underhand instigation from British officials, individual malcontents animated by malice and a feverish desire for private vengeance chanced their hand. In doing so, they risked a possible mandatory six-month gaol sentence for perjury. In March 1900, for example, 'Adonis' and 'Jacob', two Queenstown detective constables, had their trial testimonies disallowed and perjury charges entered against them. They had been conspiring against the accused in question, one Jacobus Venter, in order to topple him for a personal injury they had suffered at his hands in July 1898.[74] The Klipdam magistrate was obliged to set aside a martial law conviction when it was disclosed that the most incriminating piece of material evidence, a Mauser rifle, had been planted by three disgruntled servants.[75] There were a number of other bungled attempts at incriminating farmers innocent of any criminal offence, with implicated witnesses fleeing districts following acquittals. Several 'evilly disposed' labourers from Tulbagh and Swellendam, magistrates recorded, joined the army as remount workers, 'being afraid to return to their former service'.[76]

The process of black intervention in the infamous workings of 'Martie Louw' provides a remarkably clear illumination of the forcible, day-by-day determinations of relations of pressure and protest between Boers and neighbouring black civilians. One antagonistic display was the nature of encounters and transactions between black people and the British. Labourers and tenants openly assisted the imperial forces in a great variety of ways, from supplying mounted patrols with foodstuffs to accommodating and feeding army despatch riders and runners. This allegiance to the British war effort could not be anything other than provocative in the eyes of beleaguered Boer farming communities. But attempts to bring wilful employees to heel proved a troublesome business. For many farmers, expressions of displeasure and arrogant attempts to impose their will through warnings and menaces proved their undoing. For wherever steaming dissensions came to a head, large numbers of the poor and the powerless often seemed to have at least half an eye on the safety valve of treason law. A focus of individual – and sometimes communal – initiative, the threat of denunciation for treason could certainly keep some farmers in check. Servants quickly learned and assimilated the menacing meaning of treason and used the threat of betrayal to curb the conduct of masters and employers.

Popular politicisation

Another source of popular conflict with Boer purposes and aims was the increasing demands and pressures upon farm residents' lives as landowners became more domineering domestically. In the high noon of Republicanism in districts like Douglas, De Aar, Prieska and Upington, the trend towards a tightening of servile ties on farms was unmistakable. Growing numbers of individuals found themselves at odds with landowners who seemed almost universally to be trying to make their lives more harsh and humiliating. Owners became more belligerent in their dealings with the work and leisure habits of their labourers; the accumulating bitterness of this period rubbed away what thin thread of paternalism might have ordinarily mitigated the brutalities of daily relations. One episode which exemplifies the smouldering resentments on both sides of the social divide is worth recording in some detail. In November 1900, Jacobus du Plessis and Jacobus Maree were indicted for High Treason in the Douglas Special Treason Court. The chief prosecution witness, Abraham van der Berg, had been employed by du Plessis as a goatherd for several years prior to the outbreak of war. During this time, the goatherd and his family had been housed, had been permitted a regular quota of grain and firewood and had been free to graze their own modest herd of animals on farm pasture without limitation. These were benefits to which van der Berg felt that he had established some customary right.

With the outbreak of war, du Plessis suddenly began to assert a more rapacious and bullying presence. On 10 August 1900, he demanded that van der Berg sell him three of his goats for 10s. each. With wartime market rates, this was clearly a derisory sum. 'I refused this offer', van der Berg declared indignantly, 'as now the war was on, my goats were worth fully £2.10s. each.' Angered, du Plessis produced a revolver and threatened van der Berg with a beating if he did not comply. The following day, du Plessis, accompanied by Jacobus Maree, accosted van der Berg and began threatening him, claiming that as all farms in the Douglas district had become the property of the Orange Free State, 'Kaffirs' and 'Hottentots' no longer had rights to command market prices. However, van der Berg stood his ground. The quarrel ground on until the night of 15 August, when van der Berg returned to his hut, to find du Plessis and Maree remonstrating with his wife, Sarah, who was refusing to supply them with milk. 'Du Plessis again told me I was to give him the goats', van der Berg told the court, 'saying that Oom Paul would pay me the price after the war. He then warned me that . . . if I did not give them, he would shoot me dead.' At dawn the following day, the goatherd was hauled before du Plessis' wife, Maria, and according to his testimony, 'she was very angry. She said to me in Dutch, "My husband and Jacobus Maree are now *veldkornets* with power from the Free State Government. You Cape Hottentots and Kaffirs who are cheeky will now get it hard. The good time is over".'

Changed, explicitly punitive conditions of employment and oppressive conditions of tenure were introduced, to take immediate effect with the withdrawal of grazing rights and wood allowances for the van der Bergs. The family found the world changing literally above their heads as du Plessis pulled down their hut and ordered them to rebuild a habitation on wasteland at the farm boundary. Offended, van der Berg protested that du Plessis had no legitimate cause to tamper with his customary rights, nor to treat him and his wife with contempt. The festering dispute grew exceedingly bitter, and on 19 August, the goatherd found the carcass of one of his goats, slit open. This stung him into action. 'I fled away that night with my goats to Hope Town', he testified, 'and returned to my hut with some troops. I found all my household goods taken away. I discovered that these goods were at Maree's farm . . . so I went with the soldiers and took them. I then took the soldiers to my master and to Maree.'[77]

With Republican masters firmly in the saddle on numerous farms, a severe political shock was administered to groups of rural blacks. Farmers' celebration of the South African Republic and Orange Free State as representative of a sterner social and political ideology became a constant theme. In Cradock, during August 1900, for example, the Cradock Special Treason Court heard from Hans Vennell and Salabisi Musi that their landlord, Marthinus Steyn, had forcibly broken up a beer drink organised by tenants to celebrate the fall of Pretoria. According to Vennell, Steyn then threatened, 'I don't want English rebels such as you staying on my farm . . . You . . . must not think that the English will stay in this land, they are going to their ruin soon. Our times are coming, and the English and you natives will get it hot.' The festering dispute between Steyn and his tenants did not end there. From January 1900 Vennell had been on a £6 monthly retainer from the Cradock Commandant to feed and temporarily house a district army despatch runner named John Palmer. Towards the beginning of July, Vennell was threatened with flogging and subsequently with eviction for aiding Palmer. Vennell related how 'Steyn shouted I was harbouring his enemies by helping that Bushman "Old Jan", (whose proper English name is John Palmer). Steyn said if I catch Old Jan I will shoot him as he is a Kharkie. I therefore warned John Palmer to be careful. I went to see the English in Cradock about Steyn.'[78]

As the war dragged on, similar commotions became increasingly severe and numerous. In Clanwilliam, Ceres, Prince Albert and Sutherland, recalcitrant 'English Natives' or 'Kharkie Kaffirs' were ordered off lands at gunpoint, and ordered not to return on pain of death. At Rietvlei, northeast of Cradock, Jurie Ross, a Coloured smallholder, described how local Boers careered around during October 1901, flogging 'all Kharkie Hottentots'.[79] Thomas April, a shepherd at Schmidts Drift, west of Kimberley, had a bruising confrontation with a local farmer's wife in February 1900. April, who enjoyed fishing rights at a farm pool, suddenly found his customary access barred by one Hanna Lieuw. 'She pointed a rifle at me', April deposed, 'and said that she did not want to see any English Natives round on her land, and threatened to shoot me in the same manner that her husband would shoot Englishmen.'[80] Emboldened by Republican advances, local Boers rode roughshod over labourers' interests and sensitivities, foreshadowing the realities of life under Republican rule in a multitude of painful ways. Of the ugliness of relations during this disturbed and traumatic period, there can be little doubt, as rebels tried to impoverish, demoralise and dispossess employees.

The war significantly sharpened partisan local tempers. For Cape Republicans, the cycle of waiting and preparing for northern conquest was regularly enlivened by political boasting. Labourers were told that new forms of servility would be their fate. One of the many victims of this was Jan Verwagh, an Upington railway workers who, upon remonstrating with a white ganger for having referred to him insultingly as *zwaartgoed*, was threatened with transportation to Bloemfontein, where, he was assured, he would learn to bow and scrape to his betters.[81] Another was Hans Krynauw, a shearer employed in Douglas by Gys Loots; a desperate Krynauw reported Loots for threatening to have three labourers carted across the border to the Orange Free State.[82] In Herbert, Hans Hoopniet denounced Johann Braun for bragging to his labourers 'that the Boers were coming down from Bloemfontein, as far as was necessary, to teach the natives a lesson'.[83]

With farmers in an increasingly swaggering mood, agricultural workers found themselves living in a threatened world. Beatings and constant, deliberate overwork reached unprecedented heights in certain areas, and all manner of new and onerous demands were imposed. For example, Johannes Ockert and Jacobus van Rensburg cannot have been loved by the Coloured labourers in Fraserburg upon whom they descended early in 1900. Workers did not relish being forced to carry passes on their farms, nor their crude and eccentric attempts at segregation. From a considerable roll of witnesses we can pick out one, Jan Cornelius, to give us a glimpse of what was going on. As Cornelius informed the Fraserburg Treason Court in March 1900:

> About ten days before the end of January last, I was on the farm 'Witfontein' when I saw Ockert and van Rensburg standing at the gate. They were armed with rifles and bandoliers. They told me I was not to come that way again, although it was on the main road to Fraserburg, where all the natives buy goods from the store of Cohen. Ockert said the road was not for natives any more, but only for white men. He warned me that if natives again travelled by that road, which is now for white men, he would shoot them dead.[84]

Yet the muscular exertion of farmers' authority failed to cow agricultural labourers. To Hans Henniker's consternation, four of his Thembu tenants were not frightened into silence following a murder and, in July 1901, entered a treason charge against him at the Albert Special Military Court. At his trial, two months later, it emerged that Henniker, an Afrikaner Bond activist, had been forcing Africans on his property to carry special passes. In February 1901, Henniker had an altercation with one of them, Isaac Malife, who apparently had a reputation for 'insolence' and 'surliness'. According to trial witnesses, 'on being asked where his pass was, he waved his stick and said that was his pass'. For this insolent act of defiance, Malife paid with his life. Albert Africans were no doubt satisfied to see Henniker convicted of treason and sentenced to death for the murder.[85] At a De Beers Company firm just west of Kimberley, Jan Koopman, a shepherd, received a threatening message from a Dirk Visagie on 16 February 1900. The farmer accused Koopman of plotting against him and ordered him to quit De Beers property. 'I at once went to see my wife', Koopman testified, 'but I found that my wife and children had left. On making enquiries, I found that the Boers had made my family leave, and they had gone away to live on the farm of Mr Cook, an Englishman. I visited the farm of Dirk Visagie at Rooidam, Kimberley District, but found that he was at present away, helping the Boers with food and horses'. Koopman encountered Visagie's brother, Gerhardus, who responded threateningly. 'He pointed his rifle', Koopman testified, 'and said I was a low Kharkie Hottentot who should leave that place or I would be shot and put down the dam of Dirk Visagie like some other bad natives'. In response, a frightened Koopman had no hesitation in alerting British field intelligence which had the farm dam dragged by sappers. Three bodies added to Koopman's sworn deposition was more than sufficient to manacle both Visagies.[86]

When examining motives and actions one repeatedly encounters a consciousness of 'treason law' as a source of restraint or control to curb Boer excesses. Even those men and women locked in the closest possible relationship with Boers had a tendency to make use of the law when their ties of custom and right were not honoured and relations

160

began to sour. For example, some *agterryers'* loyalties and allegiance to their masters could prove remarkably dispensable, and many of them provided detailed evidence on secret rebel activity. Undoubtedly, as has been noted earlier, there were those who provided treason identifications in the hope of avoiding prosecution themselves, or of incurring lenient treatment or perhaps even favour. But for the great majority the break, when it came, was over abysmal personal treatment. The derisory rewards offered to many servants meant that they only rarely supported their employers with alibis. Female servants who secretly helped to nurse wounded rebels, and to provision commandos, found their expectations dashed when farmers and *veldkornets* in the field failed to provide good levels of subsistence or remuneration. Lena Mledlo, for instance, who swore an affidavit against Johannes Meiring for harbouring a wounded commando, was furious at Meiring's treatment of his domestic servants who had provided nursing and care. 'For this, we servants were promised meat and more money, but we still always got mealies, never meat or anything else', she stated.[87] Klaas Willem and Carel Aardt were similarly motivated to target Piet Geyer when the farmer suddenly withheld a portion of grain which they felt was rightfully theirs as reward for having helped their employer to provision a rebel party.[88] Individuals who had been colluding with Boers in one or other kind of petty criminal activity found their hopes and aspirations trampled underfoot, hurting both their pockets and their pride. Furious, they ratted on their former leading partners-in-crime. Servants and disenchanted *agterryers* supplied countless incriminating identifications while huddled over mugs of brandy or beer with army intelligence interrogators; some, like 'Black Piet', 'Englishman', 'Adonis Kitchener' and 'Hottentot Chamberlain' who 'made themselves most obnoxious to the white citizens' became star local prosecution witnesses, helping to convict dozens of men.[89]

One Coloured *agterryer* who gave a vast amount of evidence in Somerset East and Cradock investigations and trial sessions was Klaas Buys, of whom we have some interesting detail. Buys was a shepherd on the farm of Piet Heydenrich, who took up arms against the British in December 1900. In the following month Buys and his master joined the Stormberg commando; the shepherd was engaged as a cook, with the promise of money and favour to come. But the *agterryer* found himself being ill-used and after three weeks' service he deserted the commando and gave himself up to the authorities at Steynsburg. A skinny Buys (now beginning to fatten after several huge portions of lamb chops) provided interrogators with identifications leading to the immediate arrest of fourteen Boers. He furthermore speculated on the political inclinations of named farmers, testifying that 'the Boers there do not now trust the natives, that's why they never converse in our presence'. Quickly recognising his value as a trial witness, the Steynsburg military prosecutor struck a deal with Buys. In return for full co-operation with the court, the usual indictment for aiding the enemy was set aside and the army furnished the shepherd's family with a Scotch cart and oxen. With Buys' consent, a bogus charge of sheep theft was then brought forward, for which he was detained for six months, 'so in cases when the military authorities need him, he is kept secure and safe from harm, and can be called upon at any time to appear'.[90]

Life in the vicinity of mission stations also became distinctly uncomfortable for some Boers. Where they had previously met with deferential welcome at church services or at baptisms or funerals involving favoured workers' families, they were now exposed to suspicion, hostile surveillance, insolence and even threats of violence. Paternalistic attendance at rites of passage in the lives of the labouring poor produced feelings of conflict rather than reciprocity.

As the social position of Boers deteriorated, so did their volume of local customary transactions with mission production and distribution. Coloured artisans on Moravian settlements such as those at Mamre and Elim in the southwestern Cape refused to supply certain farmers from their brick-making and saddle-making workshops. E. R. Lemmerz, the Elim missionary, reported in 1901 that while villagers were commonly refusing to greet farmers or work on their lands, the 'worst trouble' came from older children who used 'bad language' against visiting whites, spat upon them as they passed through the village and obstructed their entry to the mission store and granary.[91] At Enon Moravian mission in the Eastern Cape, villagers conspired to exploit the timber and other holdings of known Bond farmers. Led by a harness-maker, Petrus Sampson, Enon pastoralists periodically swarmed over settler land, felling trees and turning their animals loose to graze and forage, occasionally even burning off undergrowth so that beasts might have better pasture. These encroachments were not random, but highly specific; according to Sampson, unfit Boers who were disloyal to the Crown had forfeited their property rights.[92]

Missionaries and malcontents

Relations between certain groups of missionaries and congregations were also put under severe strain. Many non-English-speaking clergymen were politically and culturally well disposed towards the Republican cause and, if not actively pro-Boer, were temperamentally given to adopting positions which were either neutral or ambiguous towards the imperial camp. On Moravian, Rhenish, Berlin Missionary Society and Nederduitse Gereformeerde Kerk missions, clergy tried in vain to discourage men from enlisting as British auxiliaries. They also pleaded with parishioners to treat visiting Boers with respect, as station economies needed the custom and occasional benefactions of local farmers. Such calls for restraint caused villagers to suspect missionary motives. In Paarl, Worcester, Swellendam and Barrydale, relations between leaders and led were ruptured; *Sendingkerk* congregants simply flaked away, disturbed by what they saw as the pro-Republican sentiments of *Boere Kerk* ministers. Outraged villagers were quick to attach themselves to other Christian groups, finding the competing patriotic atmosphere of Anglican or Methodist missions more congenial. Although the evidence is fragmentary and not wholly conclusive, there is certainly a suggestion that the indissolubility of popular political, social, regional – and religious – issues led to a general erosion of the pastoral influence of churches sympathetic to the Boer position.[93]

For these were quickening years when ordinary rural men and women created nests in which a vivid kind of popular and self-assertive local political culture grew. At once intransigent and highly self-conscious, it drew its pugnacious sentiments from a rising anti-Boer consciousness and identity. And missionaries who ignored or set themselves against pro-British enthusiasms amongst their laity could expect to run into trouble. Inevitably, many became embroiled in disputes with their congregations. For example, at Enon between January and March 1901 the resident missionaries, Franz Chleboun and Friedrich Rauch, clashed with villagers over anti-war sermons. The windows of Chleboun's residence were smashed and one of his fruit trees was hacked down. An irate congregation, led by Petrus Sampson, did not stop there. Both missionaries were reported to the Cape Town authorities for treason. When an investigating patrol arrived to question them, the mission congregation turned out in force to heap abuse upon the two Germans, denouncing them as spies and traitors. A triumphant Sampson led troops to what he claimed were trenches dug by Rauch to accommodate commandos (the missionary pleaded that they were for guava trees!). Chleboun and Rauch were eventually hauled off for interrogation and were charged with High Treason at the end of March 1901. Sampson's testimony included allegations that they had ripped down British flags and had stored ammunition in the station granary. But the case was too flimsy to secure a conviction and the ministers were acquitted. They returned to lead unhappy lives at Enon. Inhabitants turned their faces away when they came near, and refused milk supplied by their cows. And Frederick Balie, a teacher, assumed their pastoral functions. 'Feelings between us and our people', Rauch concluded, were 'extremely bad'.[94]

In Elim, Mamre, Genadendal, Bethelsdorp, Goedverwacht and Wittewater, there was comic squabbling over the right to fly the Union Jack, with inhabitants running up flags and missionaries trying to rip them down from houses and along pathways. At Goedverwacht, congregants brushed aside fines and pulpit censure, claiming that as defenders of 'the law' it was their 'duty' to fly its colours and prosecute its enemies, the missionaries.[95]

The relief of Mafeking in May 1900 gripped the consciousness of people all over the colony and seems to have given bursts of flag-waving an even sharper retaliatory edge. British social historians like Richard Price and Gareth Stedman Jones have explored the character of 'mafficking' in the context of urban Britain;[96] what is less well known is the occurrence and meaning of 'mafficking' in black rural settlements in South Africa. Here, villagers took to celebratory dancing and feasting; rowdy, trumpet-blowing gatherings to toast British advances, which had previously been sporadic and isolated, now took on a common and concentrated focus. Mission notices prohibiting Mafeking demonstrations were ignored. At Elim and Mamre there were bonfire parties, while in Goedverwacht revellers conducted by a 'hideously noisy band' completed a circuit of nearby Piquetberg, filling the air with anti-Boer ditties and denunciations of pro-Boer priests.[97] Berlin Missionary Society clergy at Douglas confronted 'fires, feasting, toasts to the bravery of those who defended the walls of Mafeking and consequent malicious feeling against the Boers and Germans'.[98]

Such 'mafficking' can undoubtedly be seen in part as an expression and affirmation of local rural solidarities during a critical period of upheaval. It was, moreover, a means whereby villagers defined their identity against a hectoring mission leadership; it threw into ever sharper relief those who were viewed as Kruger's agents.

Something of the stirrings of a new consciousness and a new hardened identity, struggling within and away from established bonds of parochial loyalties and authority between mission clergy and laity, can be seen in the emergence of small organised groups with distinctive independent actions. Particularly noteworthy was the Coloured Political Association of Mamre, which was launched in June 1900. It was the first known independent Coloured political organisation and preceded the formation of the African Political Organisation in Cape Town by two years. The Association was led by a group of resident evangelists and school teachers, Matthew Heathly, Daniel Joorst, Benjamin Jonas and David Kriel, who had earlier parted company with the chief missionary, F. W. Kunick, over the latter's opposition to 'mafficking' and the display of British flags and Queen Victoria's photograph in the mission yard. With its declared objective of 'driving away all Germans and installing Anglicans', the Coloured Political Association attracted over 500 members of both sexes; in addition to supporting Mamre men on war service, it petitioned for the indictment of all Moravian preachers for treason and for their expulsion from the Cape. Kunick was denounced as a Bondsman and, at Heathly's urging, was carefully investigated by the local magistrate. With the missionary's authority paralysed, the Mamre congregation mostly deserted him for services in English conducted by Heathly, Joorst and Jonas. For his part, Daniel Kriel, a schoolteacher, subverted the Mamre school curriculum, replacing Grimm with Tom Brown and *Terrific Tales*, new reading brought home from the army by discharged muleteers.[99]

In the countryside, scores of Coloured evangelists ceased playing the supportive role customarily assigned to them by station superintendants. At Elim, Abraham Jantjies led the congregation in accusing Moravians of treason during 1901. With its own slogans and meetings, Jantjies' movement spurned the *Bond* or *Boere Kerk*, and attacked the Elim training school as a *Bondschule* teaching *Bondkultur* and *Bond politik*. Distressed missionaries wrung their hands over classroom boycotts, expelled pupils for insubordination and recoiled from provocative, self-composed songs led by young women and girl brass instrumentalists. *Spottlieder* mocked Boers and Germans, while other *Selbsgemachte Lieder* praised the British.[100]

At Wittewater, links in the chain of rumour about the missionary Ernst Schütz were no doubt oiled by some intemperate and unpopular actions on his part. Schütz, for instance, threatened to evict a teacher, Frederick Adams, for spying for British intelligence and for engaging informers; Adams' house was described as 'a nest of spies'. The missionary also withdrew the use of the schoolroom, the usual place for collecting food and money for imperial forces. Angered, Adams and an associate, Petrus Mazwi, spread 'malicious charges' against Schütz and had him investigated for treason.[101]

There were many other signs of organisational vigour among dissidents. At Wittekleibosch in the Eastern Cape, the disaffected congregation was led away by a Solomon Gwe; average attendance at official worship dropped from 800 at the beginning of 1901 to less than 100 by the end of that year. Andreas Benjamin, a Goedverwacht evangelist, turned upon his *Bond* Church and called for the arrest of the priest, Matthias Marx, for treason. On these and other settlements, Moravian leaders were booed away from house visits, taxes were withheld from them, and they were also prevented from officiating at burials;[102] for large funerals, especially those of war dead, were frequently turned into lively demonstrations of community solidarity and war sentiment.

With wartime labour demand draining off so many male villagers, women sometimes found themselves well placed to take up combative public roles. While Sara Baadjies of Pniel and Martha Jantjies of Elim may not have been millenarians in the mould of a Joanna Southcott, they preached impassioned messages of judgement and punishment which would fall upon leaders who served as allies, not enemies, of oppression. At Elim, Jantjies named Lemmerz for committing the 'sin' of High Treason. The station superintendent was in no mood to be damned by a jumped-up Coloured woman and determined to put Jantjies and her band of female followers firmly in their place. Not content with obedience as godliness as a favoured pulpit theme, Lemmerz also obtained leave from the Bredasdorp magistrate to declare that defiance of mission regulations constituted a criminal offence, and that unauthorised meetings in the churchyard amounted to trespassing.[103] Faced with the threat of popular tumult, evangelical and secular ruling interests forged a social disciplinary authority.

The magistrate acted by fining two girls £2 each or one month's imprisonment for breaking regulations. Jantjies' response was to declare, 'Are we British subjects under Queen or Kaiser?' and to persuade an English-speaking farmer to pay the fines.[104] Then, claiming to be in direct communication with Queen Victoria, she led a mass villification of Lemmerz which reached a crescendo of menacing rhythmic clapping, dancing and mocking songs to guitar and banjo accompaniment. A twenty-five page petition was produced, calling for Lemmerz's imprisonment or expulsion. In a powerful speech on 14 December 1900, Jantjies raged at Lemmerz. Girls and young women gathered around Jantjies were instructed to defy the mission ban on flag-flying, to collect treason evidence against Lemmerz and to brew alcohol for troops. As to the future of Elim, Jantjies drew a rosy picture – a British war victory which would bring about the expulsion of all Germans, their replacement by Anglican clergy, the expropriation of Boer property owners, the abolition of taxes, and the opening of taverns;[105] the last aspiration was especially notable in that the fortunes of numbers of rural women were now resting upon the illicit brewing and sale of alcohol to soldiers.

The rapid deterioration in relations between 'neutral' or avowedly pro-Republican missionaries and their unsettled parishioners highlights another facet of the localised, introverted quality of disturbances animated by popular conviction and interpretation of the possibilities generated by treason and martial law. Moravian and other non-British mission discipline was effectively antagonistic towards both the habits of mind and the new framework of action of villagers.

The resulting episodes of treason confrontation might well be taken to reflect personality clashes in a peculiarly bloody-minded time and bloody-minded place. Yet it would be inadequate merely to emphasise the obvious local significance of these disputes. For they also crisply reflected, far beyond their own local confines, the consolidation of rural belligerence; groups and individuals were impelled to adopt their positions by stark ideological and social antagonisms. For an assortment of poor and modest mission villagers, the need to hold fast against the military rebellion of the enemy without was matched by a determination to root out the malignancy of the treasonable enemy within.

165

A forum for a 'counter-culture'

What is striking about the history of this disturbed period is the force with which blacks recognised and opposed seditious currents coursing through the Republican sector of settler society. Recourse to treason law became an extremely common and effective way of proceeding against Boers. As treason statutes and martial law were successively extended and tightened, as penalties were raised, it became more and more difficult for those under suspicion to wriggle out of indictment and conviction. Emergency law was moulded into a sharp and comprehensive instrument of power, at its most frightening when aided by snoops, informers and witnesses.

Treason laws clearly meant different things to different people. To Boers, they were unjust and injurious, imperilling the standing of whites as blacks were allowed to turn the courts towards their own uses. For blacks on the other hand, the rigour of treason law was a boon, making a spontaneous, legalistic mode of opposition especially attractive. While the practice of what was commonly known as 'British justice' in the Cape indisputably 'maintained relations of domination between master and servant', as Albie Sachs has comprehensively demonstrated,[106] blacks still enjoyed common rights of technical equality under the law, and labourers were far from ignorant of this. Even illiterate, uneducated men were aware that the right to present court testimony was a common inheritance. Thus, when Jacob Stoffels, a Cradock shepherd, found his right to testify under challenge by a lawyer during January 1902, he reacted passionately, reminding the Cradock Treason Court that 'even Slaves and Hottentots could speak freely against their masters under British justice'.[107] During the war, this right flourished as never before or since. In fact, as Johannes Snyman has pointed out, the summary powers Africans enjoyed in having white suspects hauled before the courts, gave servants unheard of rights and fresh prerogatives.[108] Defiantly confronting settlers at law, labourers toppled numbers of them with ease.

But treason courts were not simply a congenial theatre for which revenge dramas could be scripted at an individual, personal level. More than this, they provided a medium within which powerful social conflicts could be fought out. In the course of squabbles over the extinguishing of wood, game, hay, pasture and other common rights and perquisites, values, interests, race and class prejudices were displayed in a concentrated fashion. What these high-treason episodes reveal with great clarity are the ways in which the wider divisions and enmities of these years filtered down to the lowest level of relations on individual farms. With sullen servants rebelling against their masters and tenants against their landlords, it is arguable that in some respects war conditions provoked a form of agrarian class conflict, mediated through the treason courts. If yet politically inchoate, some of the furrows of discord between poor servant and propertied settler certainly unearthed the fecund soil of class consciousness; as an extension of citizenship, people were thinking and acting, in Thompson's deft phrase, in 'class ways'.[109] If not quite the fully fledged 'class war-sheathed within the Boer-British conflict',[110] which Jeremy Krikler has asserted for the Transvaal, the Cape's experience of class venom was important and pervasive.

For the Colony's black citizenry embraced a distinctive cluster of social meanings. Taken as a bundle of congruent concepts, it associated the language, cultural representations and politics of the region with the labour system, the social traditions, the popular conception of natural rights; the very products of the duties and functions of understood and assumed British colonial 'freedoms'. From the abiding potency of inherited patterns of thought and practice, and the emerging contours of class sensibilities, ordinary blacks came to terms with what the burdens and opportunities of war meant to them.

The attitudes and self-expression of those who aided emergency judicial procedures were overwhelmingly characterised by a sense of defensive struggle. Their struggle was largely to sustain what Chris Fisher has termed 'incorporeal rights' or 'incorporeal hereditaments', that is, rights and usages conferred and claimed by custom.[111] These were exemplified by Abraham van der Berg's insistence upon a 'just' price for his goats or Thomas April's annoyance at a hindrance upon his fishing rights. When they complained of the attack on their modes of living they were looking backwards to a way of life in which they enjoyed old established practices; it is perhaps appropriate to remember here, from Thompson, that the lived inheritance of the past is one necessary way in which people understand and live the present, even in times of rapid and convulsive social change. The tussles between Republican Boers and black people were thus, in one key dimension sketched by Fisher, a conflict between 'those who would innovate' and those who looked to defending 'the strength of custom to preserve the old ways'.[112] Following from this was the assumption by the 'lower orders' of 'some legitimising notion'; again, it is Thompson's definition which is useful, 'the notion of legitimation' meaning that activated 'men and women . . . were informed by the belief that they were defending traditional rights or customs'.[113] In this regard, the world of Boer Republicanism – brutal, eccentric and haphazard – appeared utterly antithetical to the survival of the mentality and rationality of the Cape's Victorian consciousness. Sour rural workers who became enmeshed in treason investigations did so mainly as an impulsive, protective stand against an abrupt abolition of known frames of reference.

The accessibility of British investigators and prosecutors provided a chance to try to stem the Republican tide, by decisively influencing the outcome of tense conflicts on individual farms. Witnesses were often liable to be bloodied, but every indictment and prosecution spelled a small reversal of Boer pretensions. What emerges very forcibly is the politicisation of material grievances, discontents and disputes. Strains and fissures led injured and angered adversaries to articulate their underlying social and political beliefs, and thereby to reveal their cultural and moral consciousness of their location within a British colonial social order. Black society certainly possessed a dependent, bound and incorporated kind of political culture. But, it was also robust and self-generating. Based upon keen sensibilities of exclusivity and a vigorous assertion of independence, self-respect and justice, it was fiercely resistant to any form of exterior domination. Indeed, what infuriated the Republican landowning constituency most was the grit and assertiveness which distinguished the weak whom they expected to be silent and servile.

In Cape colonial society the precedents and principles of justice were not rooted in wholly segregationist criteria, nor were its procedures transparently punitive towards all blacks and partial towards settlers. Its practice – one thinks for instance of the jury service colour bar or the 1856 Masters and Servants Act and successive amendments – may mostly have belied its ideals, but this did not make the fiction of core legal equality any less potent.[114] In 1899, political and civil rights may have been petty and all the time diminishing, but to those who clung to them they were neither trivial nor worthless. For they still had both an evocative and a substantive, instrumental content. Here we might draw upon Thompson's powerful formulation that the rhetoric and rules of a society 'are something a great deal more than sham. In the same moment they may modify, in profound ways, the behaviour of the powerful and mystify the powerless. They may disguise the true realities of power, but, at the same time, they may curb that power and check its intrusions.'[115] In the Cape, with its own ensemble of colonial relations, they had meaning and legitimacy for those whose perceptions and motivations were animated by a natural sense of law and justice. And it is abundantly evident that the attention of proletarians and smallholders turned as much to rights, liberties and inviolable social privacy as it did to peace. These rights referred not simply to wages or conditions but to some broader cultural notion of a way of life. Accordingly, treason courts naturally became a forum in which those who attended for the prosecution were able to assert their 'free' status and identity.

In conclusion, what the structures and practices of treason and martial law help to demonstrate is that rural black civilians did not wince quietly under acts of petty oppression, victimisation and spite. Nor were they feeble spectators of Republican efforts to subvert the existing order. Instead, they imposed their own distinct mark of opposition at law. For, cast in a new wartime mould, the law became a major lever of defence and retribution. While Boer liberties were throttled from above, shepherds and servants below pondered the toll of treason convictions with grim satisfaction. Fired with anger, passion and a sense of moral outrage, humble men and women fought a bitter war of words against those who sat upon them. The allegiances in social consciousness exposed by the language of treason and martial law matured in a hardening of popular wrath, as informants proceeded against their antagonists, legally shackling those who sought to coffin their meagre liberties. 'Kleinbooi, Gentleman, February, Sixpence or whatever his name is', mused a Coldstream Guards officer a month before the war was ended, 'the native witness is most troublesome to the colonial Boers. He seems quite intent on getting rid of his master, who, for one reason or another, has forfeited his loyalty.'[116] Moreover, the satisfaction of 'doing down their masters',[117] as another observer noted, was undoubtedly considerable.

9

Peace and reconquest

Barrington Moore Jr has recalled telling students for years that an analysis of military institutions and the relationship between military forces and the social order 'provided just as good a way to start the dissection of an "historical" society as did the unravelling of the social relations of production'. As Moore put it, 'where a large sector of production serves military and political purposes, as has been the case throughout much of human history, it pays to understand the social nature of these purposes'.[1] This book has attempted to demonstrate that a study of war and society in the turn-of-the-century Cape can tell us much about the springs of human action and the social, cultural and other material conditions which formed the fabric of South Africa's broad historical development during these crucial post-1870 decades. Indeed, the extraordinary richness of British Army and other war records helps to produce a picture of movement among conquered people which needs to be integrated with the recent wave of South African economic and social histories which have mostly not concentrated attention on the 'internal' popular experiences of ordinary black communities in the South African War. The depth and range of these experiences is suggestive on two counts. First, and most obvious, the upheaval of the war and its part in reconstructing social and economic patterns and relationships formed an integral element of capitalist consolidation as a whole. Second, and most striking for us, is the point that the unique character of the black 'people's war' is of great independent value in understanding the conflict's historical contribution to how and why dominated and dominant South Africans have become what they are. A black South African War stands as testimony to a history of a kind identified by Patrick Wright as 'an open-ended multiplicity of traditions and histories rather than the artificial severity of a single and already completed national lineage'.[2] As Abraham Esau's posthumous claims signify, the war was not a story which ended in 1902. Its more idiosyncratic underlying intoxications have had a rather longer chronological focus.

The creative, expansionary and spontaneous struggles of workers, artisans and peasants in an exceptional period of instability and internal division within settler society have been at the centre of this book. In this concluding chapter, we consider aspects of their post-war adjustment to conditions of peace and confront the vital – and haunting – question of the historical meaning of their activity and consciousness. As conditions in the Cape reveal, it was not just the national resolution of the war crisis in

May 1902 which was significant but the differentiated way regions experienced and adapted to that resolution.[3]

Social peace

The aftermath of war saw a transition from a more-or-less unstable set of relations to the solidification of a more assured, ordered and hegemonic colonial society. In one sense, a compelling phase of transition in the formation of black communities had ended. But echoes of disorder continued to sound through the countryside. Cape pro-Boers who had come out prominently in favour of peace and toleration during the war experienced little toleration from neighbouring blacks after it. Men like David Jones and William Rowland, English merchants and traders from Murraysburg, were snubbed by Coloured townspeople and hissed at on the street.[4] In Fraserburg, in July, a band of young labourers smashed the windows of houses belonging to families who had raised hardship monies for the dependants of convicted rebels.[5] Olive Schreiner, who had been a leading pro-Boer, encountered widespread hostility. Writing from Hanover Road, she reported herself unable to attract a domestic servant despite offering a generous wage, for 'the natives here all boycott me'. On Coronation Day, 16 June, Schreiner was much put out by the conduct of Coloured residents. In the morning, a stick-wielding group of men disrupted a white sports meeting, now intending to 'teach the Boers a lesson', while later that day, 'a Hottentot Boy, who used to be in the town guard, cracked open the head of the wealthiest farmer in the district'. Observing sorrowfully that black people had seemingly changed from dutiful and law-abiding subjects to insolent ones in a few short years, Schreiner concluded gloomily, 'the Natives here are something indescribable'.[6]

If the colony did not topple into a wholesale post-war crisis, the social atmosphere of many agrarian sectors was tense and often menacing. Clashes between farmers and farmworkers or tenants had left festering sores which were unlikely to heal rapidly, and the restoration of a more stable balance of forces on the land ran up against a large legacy of embittered relations. White farmers complained bitterly of restiveness, belligerence, 'impudence' and 'sulkiness' among blacks, particularly those who had been 'demoralised' by military service.[7] Among rural MPs, damage to settler morale was a burning issue. As one of them put it, the war 'had had a bad effect on the native mind . . . The status of the white man had been considerably lowered in the eyes of the natives in consequence of the hostilities, and the former should do everything in their power to rehabilitate themselves in the eyes of the latter.'[8] There certainly seems to have been a plucky determination on the part of many labourers not to knuckle down obediently to their old servitude. Labouring lives which had seemed so utterly determined and constrained in the 1890s had been prised open by the enabling experience of war. Nurturing alternative expectations, and with new modes of work, leisure and other satisfactions under their belt, proletarianised rural dwellers brought back an air of independence which was seen by settlers as directly subversive of the terms of racial and class inequality. Alienation threaded its way through farming communities in places like Fraserburg, Burghersdorp and Cradock, where some of the more brazen amongst Coloured workers were said to have remonstrated vociferously with employers over obligations, roles and conduct. Their rhetorical antagonisms included, 'Why do you want to be called *baas*? Why are you back here? Why should we work for you?'[9] Such snappiness reflected the ambivalent texture of workers' consciousness, contained yet discontented.

Other rural fissures took characteristic forms of hostility, as, for example, arson, other destructive direct action and the continuing usage of Thompson's anonymous tradition, of which more shortly. In the Hay district, ex-rebels were hated men; their marked properties were given a wide berth by migrant shearers. In typical criminal acts, widely regarded locally as war related, prize horses belonging to a Somerset East Bond political agent were poisoned, while in Dordrecht cattle were maimed. Suspicion fell upon some demobilised Mfengu scouts who had apparently boasted of settling scores with disloyal farmers.[10] Scattered incendiarism destroyed hayricks and sheds in the unsettled districts of Bedford, Adelaide, Alexandria and Molteno.

Postal censorship, which had been fleetingly effective during the war, was again cranked up in response to especially threatening letters of vengeance which bobbed up from the seething depths of villages and farm huts. Some letters tested the shaky local intelligence of magistrates and farmers by inflating the strength and intentions of agitators: 'we is hunrids of loyal men and yu will dy now for yore help to the *Vrystaats*'.[11] At Fort Beaufort, the magistrate was warned by the Attorney General of the danger of allowing 'pernicious sentiments' to circulate; in July, African constables were appointed as Receivers of Native Letters to intercept and scrutinise all correspondence for an excitable Chief Detective Officer. Authors (where positively identified) and recipients of 'inflammatory' post were listed for police investigation at Aliwal North, while in Somerset East the postmaster was authorised to open all African correspondence. In Bedford, the issue of travel passes to men on foot was restricted during June 1902 on suspicion that 'malicious' letters were being smuggled and delivered; special piquets were also posted to municipal boundaries to frisk African travellers and check mailbags.[12]

The anonymity and personal nature of the hostile letter gave general anger the intense tangibility of private drama. At Adelaide, for example, there was rough – and menacing – correspondence from tenants over the eviction of their herds from pasture to which they had been granted grazing rights by the army in 1901.[13] Tenants who had seized opportunities to lodge themselves in farm homesteads and to extend areas of cultivation were equally sour over being turfed out by Cape Police.[14] These provided the general context for those who felt victimised to issue anonymous menaces. Thrusts even included one or two predictions that the King would 'burn' or 'be in Hell' for not protecting his subjects' interests.[15] Much of the intimidatory violence of these letters lay, as David Vincent has suggested of nineteenth-century agrarian Britain, in their literary crudeness, for, in essence, 'they belonged to an oral rather than a written tradition'.[16] We see a fine illustration of this in the case of an Alexandria resident, Paul Mrara, who was spotted and hauled in for having sent a threatening letter to a local farmer. From an 'Inglis Boy', it declared: 'de Wet it will be bad for you now. You have shoot a good nativ man ded for Kruger. You will now be shoot ded with a gun one time.'[17] As the tide of settler domination rolled across the countryside, such were the traces of malice and vengeance which flared before waning.

Police unease about the maintenance of good order in the more disturbed localities led to the retention of some bands of militiamen on a reserve footing.[18] In Molteno and Stormberg, rifles were not withdrawn from a picked quota of African guards until October, while in Namaqualand commandants at Garies and Concordia were instructed:

> Lee Metfords and ammunition should be collected from the Black Watch, but you are at liberty to issue Schneiders and Martini Henrys, and a limited amount of ammunition, to such members of the late Black Watch whom you most trust, and consider worthy to carry arms. The name and address of such men is to be carefully recorded so that they can be mustered together rapidly in the event of some emergency.[19]

While the widespread possession of firearms (however old and unuseable in many cases) would perhaps have lent an edge to the menaces, insults and threats to individuals which darkened the post-war atmosphere, no emergencies developed. Indeed, by the end of 1902 things were sufficiently tranquil for Cape officials to disregard the disarmament terms of the Peace Preservation Act. In December, Baster pastoralists were given permanent ownership of their service firearms, the Upington magistrate quite content that 'the retention of these weapons cannot do any harm, and it might be well they should have them to protect their stock'.[20]

Demobilisation and the return of labour

The reabsorption of demobilised auxiliaries into civilian life bears directly on the crisis of authority and social discipline in the colony. Men who had seen months, even years, of active service were sometimes wary of the civilian world to which they were being returned. In Kenhardt and Upington, for example, farm labourers expressed fears of being victimised or blacklisted by aggrieved employers.[21] In particular tense instances, these must have been well founded: work for the British would not have earned workers much credit with Republican-minded farmers. Nervousness among time-expired men at Williston during June was such that Lieutenant C. H. Massey took it upon himself publicly to reassure assembled anxiliaries. The army, he promised, would police farmers' conduct, as the British Government had guaranteed labourers' return to the land, 'in a spirit of goodwill'.[22] Good intentions were perhaps getting a little stretched here.

The manner in which a demobilised man returned to a civilian livelihood was dependent upon the resources and inclinations of his military company. The Namaqualand Field Force tried to take into account the prevailing level of demand in the local economy. Garrisons at Port Nolloth, Springbok and Anenous did not terminate contracts prematurely, partly to shield workers from the deleterious consequences of seasonal unemployment, with its undesirable 'idleness', 'licentiousness' and 'mischief'.[23] Scouts and garrison guards were laid off in staggered batches, taking with them a wheat allowance, or either a cash gratuity or blankets and firewood.[24] The Garies rifle contingent was laid off at the end of June. Hodge, the British commandant, was urged not to pay service gratuities by the Springbok magistrate, as this would discourage smallholders from returning to production promptly and encourage workers to price their labour too highly. Colonel Cooper concurred, instructing Hodge on 19 June:

> The Black Watch should be got rid of as early as possible, with a view to their getting home to resume ploughing . . . you are hereby authorized to grant them a gratuity not exceeding £1 (one pound) per man, to be distributed at your discretion. It is to be clearly understood, that no man is to receive more than £1. A larger amount may provide too much latitude for loafing.[25]

While Cooper was 'extremely anxious that a civil vocation should be resumed everywhere', such vocations were not always within easy reach of small Namaqualand cultivators.[26] According to the Chief Staff Officer of the Namaqualand Field Force, Basters of the Namaqualand Border Scouts would require several hundred ploughshares and a generous quota of seed grain if they were to be properly resettled on land around Garies and Nababeep; as one officer remarked, 'the whole Garies district has been cleared of stock and grain and all horses, leaving Bastards in the lurch'.[27] After just under one hundred Border Scouts had been granted agricultural supplies, it appears that the limits of army generosity to the 'Butterscotch' had been reached. Also in an unpropitious situation were numbers of Coloured artisans in Cape Town, who felt the impact of an influx of demobilised British soldiers whose numbers included highly skilled workers.[28]

The experience of demobbing was varied. Colonial commandants were exceptionally keen to disperse forces without much ado, and even less ceremony. Blacks officially under arms had become more of a political discomfort than ever; militia veterans were left feeling what South African Native Labour Corps members were to feel after the end of the First World War, 'misled, deflated and discarded'.[29] In Richmond, a war gratuity was only paid out to settler volunteers and, in an act of monumental mean-spiritedness, the commandant reduced the final wage of Coloured special constables to recover the cost of equipment breakages. Elsewhere, forces were similarly slighted; with local communities smarting, there were sporadic boycotts of magistrates' victory parades and protests in favour of gratuities and medals for both Coloured and African guardsmen.[30]

Imperial army experience certainly appears to have presented a considerable contrast. Even as auxiliaries relinquished their ties, affirmations of identity and parting ceremonies provided a resoundingly high note. Skilled migrant workers often returned home after being lauded and with something to show for their efforts. In Britstown at the end of May, according to the *Household Brigade Magazine*:

> the Grenadier Guards arranged a great treat for the . . . mule and ox drivers attached to the 2nd Battalion. The boys, 156 in number, each received a share of plum pudding and 2 lb. of tobacco, after which they formed up in grand style under the command of Transport Sergeant Hammond, and gave 3 cheers for the King, Empire, and last but not least, the Colonel Boss who issued good things, i.e., bonuses, rations, warm clothing for the journey back to their villages, and other *baksheesh*.[31]

Merriment and gaiety accompanied many other demobilisations. At Steynsburg, blockhouse units for miles around attended a celebration on 7 June. Riflemen blazed away in competition for bronze medals, Mfengu scouts played polo against a British team, and there were boxing matches between Africans and Tommies. Two muleteers known as Dombey and Pickwick, whose skill as pugilists had earned them the regimental championship of the Scots Guards in 1901, won £27 in contests with fellow transport workers. The raucous occasion was described as a 'great . . . gymkhana' by a laughing cavalry officer who judged a bizarre event in which African workers 'had to put their heads in a pail of whitewash, run half a mile, and then eat a bun tied to a string, without using their hands'.[32] And so the wealth of organised recreational activity associated with war service, its exuberant expressions and carnivalesque repertoire, came to an end.

The other noteworthy element was the advantaged position of some of the better-paid skilled anxiliaries who left service with substantial gifts. Typical of endowments were the Basuto ponies presented to blockhouse guards at Victoria Road and sheep, grain, clothing, tobacco and Kurgerrands presented to Coloured scouts discharged from the Northumberland Fusiliers. In Beaufort West, forty Mfengu scouts attached to the Scots Guards paraded past their commanding officer to the sound of drums and fifes; Colonel Romilly presented each man with a £15 gratuity, five goats, a bronze medal and a certificate of 'Good Conduct and Sobriety'. Known as the 'Black Scots Boys', they elected one of their number as a collector who went from officer to officer, further requesting 'a gift to brighten their humble lives'. Similarly, at Dordrecht, muleteers and teamsters of the Lincolnshire Regiment picked up a range of service bonuses, comprising sheep, turkeys, pigs, goats and hefty cash sums of up to £28. Those who had migrated from distant Western Cape missions had their vehicles stocked for the trip home.[33]

Good employment prospects and high wages during the war were important factors influencing the outlook and position of labourer and farmer or other employer in the post-war period. In South Africa generally, as Warwick has correctly emphasised, workers' improved living standards were undoubtedly vulnerable to the erosions of rising prices.[34] Nonetheless, there were large numbers in the Cape in a situation which, while not without risk, was stable. And there were those who emerged with real gains; thus, for agricultural labourers who had on average spent longer periods of unbroken war service than peasants with seasonal production demands, there were sometimes fat gratuities of up to £15–£20 to add to any accumulated wage savings. A nest egg provided formerly dependent rural workers with a chance to withhold their labour from low-paying employers. Farmers predictably found it difficult to accede to a new independence and bargaining position for their traditional men. In Humansdorp and Uitenhage, for example, landowners were incapable of attracting workmen at reduced, pre-war wages and conditions. Recapture proved difficult. 'The present scarcity of Native labour in agriculture', according to a Humansdorp official in December 1902, was 'entirely due to the recent military service and continuing employment on Railways which causes the natives to become accustomed to higher wages, and they do not now care to resume farm work at former rates.'[35]

In Aliwal North and Jamestown, where the supply of farm labour was particularly irregular throughout 1902–3, farmers attributed the sharp contraction to Africans having grown accustomed to 'living off hoards and lavish wages'.[36] They were joined by some missionaries who had nursed the delusion that war service might teach Africans the virtues of regular wage employment and a disciplined work environment.

174

Clergymen reproached workers for clinging to inflated wage expectations and for making unreasonable demands on employers. Commenting on Africans in Aliwal North, Barkly East and Tarkastad, the Bishop of Grahamstown declared that 'receiving much higher wages than they will have been accustomed to will, I fear, make it somewhat difficult for them to settle down again to their old life'.[37] Indifference to labour demands was also galling to location superintendents and others who had set some store by the possible beneficial influence army nutrition and physical training might have on labour productivity and regularity in peacetime.[38]

Even in deeply proletarianised districts like Clanwilliam, Citrusdal, Worcester, Paarl, Oudtshoorn and Swellendam, many usually poor and trapped Coloured agricultural workers were able to live off accumulated reserves and hold out against a resumption of work at reduced earnings. In Parliament, during 1902 and 1903, the mood among MPs was one of indignation at the spectacle of labourers impertinent enough to expect a continuation of the market value which their labour had commanded during the war years. 'The farmer could not afford to pay 4s.6d. per day', bleated one member, while another bemoaned the existence of 'hundreds of Coloured people who now wanted the same wages the Government had given them during the war'.[39] They were joined by the likes of Merriman who added his industrial anxieties to the attack, pointing out that at the Indwe Coal Mines, 'labour could not be got, although it was in the centre of a large native district, because the natives had been taken up by the military and received from the latter good food and pay, and very little work. There were now all sorts of loose ideas about with regard to production.'[40] The growing clamour over work-shy blacks holding white employers to ransom led to various demands for agricultural labour compulsion, schemes of civil conscription, wage cuts on public works so as to reduce African incomes from 'absurd' and 'abnormal' levels, and a lengthening of working hours.[41]

In some areas, peasant producers were able to buttress their prosperity and independence from wage labour. The national drive to restock the former republics, particularly the Transvaal, created conditions favourable to accumulation in parts of the Transkei which had disposable livestock surpluses. During reconstruction, soaring prices and shortages brought profitable returns to richer peasants; writing from Kroonstad during August 1902, J. F. C. Fuller recorded that great quantities of cattle were being 'sent up by Cape Natives for Boer holdings . . . Fully £15 and more is being paid for these beasts.'[42] In all, 24,000 sheep were supplied to the imperial administration by Transkeian peasants.[43] In view of the twentieth-century history of white capitalist agriculture, the role of African peasant exports in helping to rehabilitate Boer producers must surely represent a particularly cruel kind of irony.

'Since the war, for various causes, the native has grown insolent, and squats on the land, and will not do any work', was Chamberlain's despairing utterance on the postwar labour shortage.[44] While colonial and metropolitan descriptions of well-fed and lounging workers would have had their share of exaggeration, it was clearly impossible to hustle labour straight back to Cape settler farms and diamond and coal mines, as well as to mines on the Rand. While there were obviously regional, class and occupational inequalities and diverging labour outcomes, it is still difficult to resist the conclusion that substantial numbers of blacks became sufficiently well-padded during the war to be able to withhold their labour at its end. They weathered its aftermath with a seemingly resilient capacity for survival. But for how long remained to be seen.

The decline of skilled and migrant independence

The declaration of peace did not bring all military employment to an immediate halt. Indeed, far from curtailing the demand for skilled transport workers, the gradual demobilisation and withdrawal of troops to Cape ports provided a further, if final, stimulus to relatively favourable local conditions of employment. Remount depots continued to attract migrants anxious to maintain their living on Cape wartime wages.[45] As before, Africans' reluctance to labour in the Transvaal was marked. If anything it had intensified with the passing of time. For far from yielding gains for workers, imperial control in the north was characterised by deteriorating labour conditions and increasingly depressed wage levels. While local imperial army service remained a bargaining option, many transport workers were able to maintain – or at least put up a struggle to maintain – their well-being, status and skill exclusivities.

Others came out of the war with a legacy of gradual self-improvement. Here and there, migrant Coloured transport riders were able to convert from pre-war wage dependency to an independent living. For a provident minority who emerged with some sort of nest egg, there were attempts to claw out a living in petty trade and commerce. A few set up as itinerant dealers with wagons purchased from war savings. Others, clutching testimonials and Army Service Corps proficiency certificates, moved into craft and artisanal work, trading on new competencies; oral history in mission settlements like Mamre records the hope and initiative of ex-army wagonmakers, harness-makers and carpenters who never returned but settled in Eastern Cape towns after the war. And there were also reports of muleteers from Bredasdorp, Mossel Bay, Swellendam and Bethelsdorp missions moving into the Knysna region where, cashing in on rising timber prices, they cut a profitable path through forests, stockpiling wood and even hiring local casual poor white woodcutters.[46] This recomposition of some Coloured workers into skilled artisans, craftsmen or wandering petty dealers can be seen as an ingredient in the general growth of a Coloured skilled and small commercial class during this period, recently illuminated by scholars like Goldin and Lewis.[47] Such small-scale market involvement by demobilised transport anxiliaries perhaps also bears some resemblance to post First World War East Africa, where there were attempts by discharged carriers to carve out an independent livelihood in commerce.[48] There may at least be a sense here in which, however contingent and precarious, these little pockets of accumulation are representative of a fertile moment of transition and realignment in the localised determination of class formation and class relations. While daily life and work in the 1900s were sites of intensifying racial discrimination against Coloured people in skilled trades and other urban commercial spheres, there were those still able to inhabit partially autonomous social realms, purposively developed in the context of war experience.

Such concrete actions and social experiences ran against the grain of historical momentum in the Cape. As small manufacturing industry and coastal food processing collapsed by 1904, Coloured craftsmen, fishermen and other skilled workers ran into difficulties. Those groups which had turned their capacities to such good account in the war, as skilled and semi-skilled labour in west coast towns like Vredenburg, Saldanha Bay, St Helena Bay and Darling were hard hit.[49] Depression and unemployment now broke communities more completely than the rampant aggression of Republican commandos which two or three years previously had periodically depopulated fishing settlements. Workplaces became derelict and any spirit of post-war optimism was replaced by an atmosphere of despondency.

Towards the end of 1903, the expanding foundations of transport and related employment had also splintered as trade depression hit the colony, running down ports and railways. The pace at which employment opportunities closed was ruthlessly fast. Coveted job options in the urban carrying sector were suddenly extinguished, plunging tens of thousands of migrants into unemployment, and creating major crises of insecurity for skilled rural communities with newly rejuvenated labouring traditions and recent experiences of improvisation and workplace pride. For them, the break brought by commercial depression was so sharp that it virtually amounted to a rupture. Following the depressive effects of the military departure from the labour market, severe economic decline expelled any mass illusions of lasting post-war job choices and popular preferences for the service sector.

Nevertheless, as Beinart has demonstrated, Cape African migrants did not lightly submit to the inevitable and obligingly buckle down *en masse* to the greedy demands of underground labour on the Witwatersrand. While there was a massive increase in the number of Cape workers drawn into mining employment between 1904 and 1908,[50] for some 20,000 men from migrant communities in the Transkei and Ciskei, with long traditions of exclusivity and skilled independence, the 1904–7 Herero and Nama Rebellions in German South West Africa brought partial arrest of the downturn in job fortunes. It is possible to catch echoes from the South African war experience, as ancillary transport workers moved in, reasserting the kind of skilled identity and sectional work culture they had recently fleshed out. They were joined by Namaqualand muleteers who rode or trudged into German South West Africa to man mule and camel supply columns, and by Baster pastoralists from places like Pofadder, Steinkopf and Leliefontein who offered to service a new imperial army of conquest. Despite the constant misery and brutality of service in this genocidal German colonial war, for experienced and skilled migrants 'South West Africa was a last chance to preserve their particular identity'.[51]

This kind of elite migrant identity did not long outlive the pre-Union decade. By 1912, the demand for Cape labour for South West Africa railway and harbour work had largely ebbed away. The degree of choice on the labour market contracted, levering increasing numbers of Cape migrants on to the mines. German South West Africa was where Eastern Cape and Transkeian 'labour aristocrats' staged their last substantial holding operation against the cheapening of their labour. They resisted as skilled groups with a coherent identity, volition and a developing set of bargaining strategies and tactics in the face of tightening constraints and appropriations.

Peasantries clung to hopes of salvaging something from the padding grown during the South African War. But none of these layers was thick enough to withstand completely the corrosive effects of post-war pressure points – drought in 1904 and 1908, the weakening of labour competition from non-mining employers in the 1903–9 depression, and the expanding conjunction of interests between Cape and Transvaal administrators and mining capital in appropriating Cape labour for production on the Rand.

Yet, proletarianisation remained partial; many men remained migrants with finely calibrated levels of dependence for subsistence upon wage labour and domestic production. Placed in the rich and suggestive perspective sketched by Beinart and Bundy, it is also clear that for all the faltering and fragmented character of migrants' initiatives after the war, work customs and work combinations persisted and periodically reasserted themselves in new industrial settings. Certainly, the peak moment of a labour elite's combination, workplace self-activity and skill, had passed. Yet communities with sectional labour identities and particularist social and ethnic loyalties never ceased to try to exploit whatever material and social space was still left open to them. The early decades of the twentieth century saw new patterns of rural and urban migrant organisation, forms of protest and struggle, work fellowship and subcultures and styles of political consciousness rooted in interlocking rural and urban social and cultural forces.[52] For Cape migrants sucked into what van Onselen has called South Africa's 'cauldron of capitalist development',[53] these were years of continuing shifts and adaptations to try to ease the pain of strategies geared to subdue and accommodate them to new practices of labour exploitation.

Whether one places the accent on abrupt changes or lingering continuities, what comes through clearly is the patchy character of capitalist proletarianisation in the region. The Cape colonial world was not riveted at every point by the remorseless accumulative logic of mining capital. Skilled labouring communities did not all go down like nine-pins under extractive pressures for labour and tax. There were favourable moments and conjunctures, enabling rural groups to refurbish and hold together a distinctively bracing social and working world. The South African War was surely the most weighty of these, illuminating the sagacity, alertness and continuous re-enactment of the independence and 'freedom' of groups who were always contesting their reduction to the status of unskilled and unorganised. In essential respects, the war and post-war experiences of workers and peasants are, naturally, broadly illustrative of themes of class formation, culture and consciousness within capitalist industrialisation which lie at the heart of modern South African historiography. Yet, this intimate and detailed detour into the special significance of the war experience for Cape blacks provides a colouration to the general historical picture which has either been absent from the literature or has been brushed in rather lightly. For the actions and aspirations of the colony's working agrarian communities may be seen as a staging post on the road to constructing and reconstructing work, community and tradition in twentieth-century South Africa. If there is such a thing as a 'mutation of consciousness', the work and supply relationships of local communities surely helped to produce something approaching it, as the war hammered into shape a nucleus of an intensely active, migrant labour elite.

Compensation and relief

Recently scholarship has emphasised just how inadequate were the capital resources set aside as funds for individuals whose property had been destroyed or requisitioned and for communities which had suffered heavy material losses. Warwick has illuminated the appallingly discriminatory approach to funding for African resettlement and reconstruction in the Orange River Colony and the Transvaal, while Willan and Pakenham have shown how the authorities' miserly response to compensation claims by the Baralong and Mfengu of Mafeking aroused great post-war resentment and bitterness.[54]

In comparative terms, the Cape region was clearly not scourged like the Orange Free State or Transvaal; black agrarian society was spared the brutal excesses of Kitchener's 'scorched earth' drives which further north laid waste to peasant as well as settler holdings. But this factor, and the reality of local African accumulation during the war, ought not to be allowed to obscure the high costs of the conflict to some parts of the rural population. During a tour of Cradock in October 1902, a British officer remarked on the sight of Africans 'reduced to eating roots and leaves, although they have compensation claims for quite large sums'.[55] In Gordonia and northern districts like Hay, Herbert and Hope Town, hundreds of uprooted civilians desperately roamed the countryside, foraging for food and fuel. Chronic food shortages during the latter half of 1902, serious drought in 1903 and the onset of post-war depression tightened the screw for those already living a precarious, hand-to-mouth existence. In Humansdorp, where scarcity and high food prices were producing an inflammatory atmosphere by August 1902, a nervous magistrate sought authorisation to advance rations against compensation claims, noting that 'many . . . are kept waiting about until their claims are heard, and cannot go to work in order to buy food'.[56]

The same might be said about other areas which had suffered at the hands of Republican forces. Famished refugees who had been hounded off Namaqualand mission lands found that peace did not bring bread. At the end of June 1902, Leliefontein Basters were given some seed grain and a collection of ploughs by the Namaqualand Field Force in a forlorn attempt to re-root what its commanding officer called 'these sound yeomen who have stood for us so fearlessly'.[57] Pinched circumstances awaited mission inhabitants who had mostly trickled back from refuge in Port Nolloth, Lambert's Bay, Concordia and O'Okiep by the end of 1902. Guerrilla razing of arable land made the resumption of wheat cultivation difficult and yields were pitifully low. The Leliefontein *Raad* authorised communal grain distribution but there was barely sufficient to go round. By 1903, missionaries were reporting a continuing, general deterioration in the position of Leliefontein inhabitants and increasingly obligatory labour migration to urban work centres as far distant as Cape Town. War destruction also accelerated proletarianisation in other Namaqualand settlements. Blighted lands around Steinkopf, for example, were thronged with local war heroes with empty bellies. Seed grain and a few sacks of flour from the Namaqualand Field Force provided scant assistance to villagers to restart cultivation on scorched soil. Many drifted off despondently into wage labour on nearby settler farms. Those who tried to knit together a meagre existence on the mission experienced declining production, distress and hunger during 1902 and 1903.[58] For clusters of weakened pastoralists and agriculturalists, already being pushed inexorably into wage labour and migration by the forces of capitalist transformation, injurious war conditions provided a further, concentrated shock of dispossession.

While conceding common rights to compensation for war losses, the Cape administration was operating under constraints on public relief expenditure in a critical reconstruction phase. Strategic political choices were having to be made which conformed to the national pattern of reconstruction. With multiplying fiscal demands upon the local colonial state, intensified from the end of 1903 by the falling off of revenue under the impact of depression, the rebuilding of settler lives and the needs of settler accumulation were a priority. African and Coloured needs played second fiddle. Nationally, as Milner conceded in July 1902, 'compensation to Natives must needs be a very rough and ready affair'.[59] Rough and ready it certainly was. There was little overall coordination by the Cape Division of the War Losses Compensation Commission, and its administrative machinery was sluggish and creaky. Ways of handling applications and of distributing relief funds varied considerably from district to district; everything hinged upon the relief decisions of district officials who were allowed enormous latitude in determining appropriate 'standards' and 'tests' to inform their judgements. What most marked their administration of public aid was deterrence and economy. In areas like Rhodes, Barkly East, Vryburg and Burghersdorp, magistrates and assisting officials aggressively stiffened requirements for compensation, on the grounds that 'indiscriminate charity' would encourage 'begging' or 'malingering' at a time of acute farm labour shortage. 'Labour is the antidote for these natives', declared a Barkly East official in August 1902.[60] The favoured approach was spelled out crisply by the Cradock magistrate, who wrote in the following month, 'if the urgent demand for native labour in most parts of the Colony is taken into consideration, there is really very little necessity to allow too many native claims. It is common knowledge that the natives are now more independent and work-shy than ever, and the provision of lavish compensation can only encourage further idleness.'[61] Never one to disregard his own advice, the magistrate discontinued hearings at the end of September.

Stringent residence conditions for claimants operated against the interests of thousands of Africans displaced from the Boer Republics during the war. With no claim on resources, the plight of groups of refugee peasants who had lost stock in places like Albert, Klipdam and Somerset East was desperate.[62] Dismayed and demoralised Africans lumped into the category of Non-Resident Native Refugees found themselves at the very bottom of the heap; flight to the Cape may have secured their lives but not their assets.

Separate compensation hearings handled by British Army Paymasters interlocked with those of district officials directing local relief budgets. For its part, the military also kept an obligingly tight purse. Paymasters made the most of the army's haphazard wartime requisitioning practices to frustrate claimants; sundry, changing ad hoc demands of proof meant that the only beneficiaries were those able to lodge cast-iron paper claims, attested to by military men or colonial officials. Invariably, these tended to be more wealthy 'progressives' rather than poorer, illiterate squatters or labourers from whom a predatory sergeant had extracted a goat or pig or two with a blurted promise of recompense. In Vryburg, Burghersdorp and Jamestown, substantial compensation was – reluctantly – paid to peasants; the examples of Zwartbooi Jack, Piet Motisani and Jimson Kasa, who secured sums of £373.10s., £558.9s. and £680.14s. respectively, provide some small indication of the re-capitalising of well-to-do African producers.[63] But even for this relatively fortunate compensated minority, the scarcity value of cattle during reconstruction would have made the rebuilding of herds a long and costly haul.

Providing the more general background were untold numbers of persons embroiled in weeks or months of acrimonious haggling with soldiers over chits which had underestimated the market value or quantity of commandeered supplies.[64] Others who tackled the often formidable physical difficulties of lodging a compensation application by travelling many miles to hearings, discovered that unsigned chits provided for foodstuffs were rejected as invalid. Those who had accepted officers' promises that inventories of requisitioned goods would be deposited with magistrates, clamoured in vain for accountability from irritable officials who were in any event unsympathetic to what were commonly defined as 'fanciable claims'. Aggrieved individuals who occasionally succeeded in tracking down neglectful regiments before they decamped found that contracting officers now had amnesia.

Popular discontent was never far below the surface and when and where it crackled into open hospitality, the anger of the dispossessed was vehement and deeply felt. Rejection of claims occasioned outbreaks of brawling between civilians and soldiers, the stoppage of supply wagons on the road and numerous repeated attempts to run off stock in military hands. At Beaufort West, troops drew bayonets to disperse Africans on 10 June 1902 as, according to a senior officer, 'it was necessary to get rid of a good many . . . who have been squealing about their losses and pestering us for recompense'.[65] In Queenstown, to cite a further instance, a squad of soldiers found itself hemmed in by furious claimants. According to a British participant in the fracas, a large crowd of Africans 'lost their tempers and had a go at us. For almost an hour they chucked oranges, stones and abuse at us. We finally managed to drive them off with difficulty.'[66] In these new relations, the imperial army, once seen as a protector, had now become a betrayer. It was breaking the moral economy of reconstruction.

Here and there, civic sentiment and a nostalgia for paternalist principles prompted Cape officials to champion the interests of impoverished men. Distressed by the military's rough handling of several Coloured herders, the Tulbagh magistrate, for example, issued a forceful rebuke, declaring that 'they are all poor, Coloured men, and it seems strange that in spite of every exertion on their part, they have been quite unable to secure the sums to which they are so justly entitled. It seems that very bad faith has been kept.'[67]

Aside from such flickering instances of sensitivity to the predicament of compensation claimants, the overall picture seems clear: virtual consensus existed on the broader need to minimise disbursements to black victims of sporadic imperial requisitioning or Republican depredation. Cases contested by the War Losses Compensation Commission dragged on unresolved until as late as 1911, when it wound up its work, finally crushing the waning hopes of unknown numbers of applicants. In the view of Lawrence Richardson of the Society of Friends' South African Relief Committee, 'Natives everywhere got a great deal from receipts which were freely given to them.'[68] Yet the very opposite appears to have been true for the majority of compensation claimants who were forced to come to terms with a more modest future.

What little discussion there has been of black compensation in the literature on the war has tended to emphasise the privileged claims of rural settler society on the post-war social dividend. As Keegan has asserted for the Orange Free State, even the 'supposedly non-discriminatory compensation payments for losses during the Anglo-Boer War were seriously skewed in practice in favour of white rehabilitation at the expense of black tenant farmers'.[69] While focus on the discriminatory terms of settler salvation is clearly warranted, these tell only part of the story of post-war reward and the consolidation of dominant political forces. It is the salience of the deterrent, disciplinary character of relief administration that has been rather underrated by historians. Obviously, the deliberate curtailment of expenditure on black claimants acted as a subsidisation of larger shares for recovering colonists. But what needs to be further emphasised is that the disposition of the War Losses Compensation Commission and its role in the definition of rights and allotment of needs meant that it took on some significance in the settlement of outstanding class issues at the end of the war.

As in other parts of the country, the Cape was, as we have already stressed, the scene of a growing volume of propertied settler complaints, concerning the 'idleness', 'insolence' and 'independence' of a labouring population which had been 'spoiled' or 'pampered' by the war. For farmers confronting the consequences of an apparent corrosion of social cohesion and social discipline, to say nothing of a shortage of cheap hands at harvest time, the stinginess of relief dispensation was cause for some celebration. Producers certainly welcomed compensation exclusion as a means of restoring a sense of 'industry' in workers and of enforcing work on their terms, although whether it actually increased the availability and regularity of agricultural labour is not easy to gauge. But, regardless of consequences, the approach to rehabilitation illustrates that those who controlled power were agreed that reconstruction assistance should be doled out in such a way as to bring 'loose' or 'idle' able-bodied males to heel.[70] And the purgative strategy played a role in the containment of a challenging spirit in which non-wage labouring subjects cast themselves as claimants for justice rather than as supplicants for subsistence. In these class-infected terms, a necessary 'reconquest' of black society involved freeing relations between owners and workers from the influence of a war economy of provision, in which non-capitalist regulation of work and remuneration formed an essential determining element.

Population, segregation and mortality

Natural growth and especially migration in the late nineteenth century had been swelling the population of Cape Town and other urban centres; under the displacing pressures of war conditions, the influx grew into a minor flood. Areas which emerged from the war with the most notable aggregate increase in population were towns perceived as sanctuaries by refugees, and port cities and railway junctions where roller-coaster growth in the local economy increased demand for dockers and transport workers. Cape Town, Port Elizabeth, East London, King William's Town, Naauwpoort, De Aar and Queenstown were typical of urban areas with greatly augmented black populations. The steep rise in the official size of the urban Cape Coloured population – from 106,273 in 1891 to 193,648 in 1904 – can be seen as a direct consequence of agrarian upheavals which ran people off the land; as Lewis has confirmed the war's 'disruptive effects helped speed up the urban drift'.[71] In Graaff-Reinet, to take but one local example, the Native Location which had contained 1,000 inhabitants at the last pre-war count in March 1899, became congested with farm-servants, shepherds, goatherds and lime-burners, not a few of them the dregs of poor-white groups who helped to constitute what Iliffe has termed the 'multiracialism of South African poverty in the late nineteenth and early twentieth centuries'.[72] In May 1904, the town census recorded 3,594 black location dwellers.[73]

Where distinct 'indigent' migratory groups were visible within swollen urban African populations, they drew the opprobrium of settlers who demanded that such surplus 'alien Natives' be ejected and railed back to their former homes. But refugees who had settled in districts like Aliwal North, Colesberg, Britstown, Prieska and De Aar were deeply apprehensive of conditions further north and were not to be lightly budged. Reporting ruefully on attempts to induce Africans to return to an Orange River Colony from which they had bolted early in 1900, a baffled Aliwal North missionary reflected:

> The native mind is slow to accept new conditions. The news that the Colony is henceforth always to be under British Rule is to them too good to be true . . . We have tried to induce them to return, but they shake their heads and say, 'It is too soon yet, we will wait and see what power the Boers have before we return.'[74]

Ex-army camp followers, some of them involved in petty criminality and prostitution and, therefore, 'not of the best class of Native', were also singled out for removal, on moral and sanitary grounds.[75]

African refugees and workers in Aliwal North and other small northeastern towns such as Barkly East and Jamestown, established themselves as squatters in 'irregular' locations on the municipal margins. While local administrations were agreed that something should be done, tactics of exclusion encountered determined opposition. As yet short of appropriate racially discriminatory legislation, municipal officials were obliged to fall back on housing and sanitary regulations; these Africans were able to evade by moving, in Aliwal North for instance, to unused white land bordering the town boundaries on which they rented sites from landowners or leaseholders.[76] There, defying efforts to shunt them into an official 'sanitary' native location, where their lives might be more closely regulated, shanty-dwellers tried to go their own way, in settlements whose equilibrium owed nothing to the intrusions of magistrate or police.

In a sense, the volatile, confrontationist atmosphere of the war had seen the climax of popular licence; at the local level, black people were suddenly distressingly obdurate, sharp-tongued, alert and 'free'. For white rulers, subjugation and containment was an urgent objective. A key element of the drive to assert – or reassert – control was the tackling of enlarged urban social danger through increasingly common and rigorous segregationist practices. For settler politics, the issue of urban segregation, over which there were increasingly strong rumblings by the end of the nineteenth century, was now given greatly increased impetus. For this period, Maynard Swanson and also Colin Bundy have shown how dominant interests looked to the increasingly important Department of Public Health and its 'sanitation-syndrome' philosophy for corrective action against urban slums.[77] During the minor plague crisis in the colony, exaggerated settler panic about contamination and public health imperatives added weight to ideological pressures to have black labour dispersed from urban centres and rehoused in outlying municipal locations. As Swanson has put it, 'Cape Town and Port Elizabeth's experience with bubonic plague transcended its purely epidemiological dimensions. The plague had been identified with their black populations, and they with it ... Sanitation and public health provided the legal means to effect quick removals of African populations; they then provided and sustained the rationale for permanent urban segregation.'[78] Stabilisation of social control in the post-war Cape therefore usefully amplifies Marks and Trapido's recent underlining of the point that 'the ideology of segregation did not only speak to the needs of the mining industry'.[79] Within the overall defining context of developing industrial capitalism in South Africa, it had its own significant local appropriations and couplings.

To consider populations and war is also to write about death. Due to the lack of statistical documentation, it is impossible to provide even approximately accurate totals for deaths of all kinds attributable to the conflict. While both Peter Warwick and Burridge Spies have revealed the high death-rates of African refugee camps in the Transvaal and Orange River Colony, they have also acknowledged the flawed nature of the Native Refugee Department statistics from which their figures were drawn.[80] For the Cape Colony, as elsewhere, we simply do not have even a rudimentary statistical record from which to consider war mortality or the demographic consequences of bloodshed, stress and exhaustion.

As a legacy of the war, the evidence on human loss is illuminating in only a limited qualitative sense. All we can conclude with certainty is that conflict in the Cape did not produce major casualties; the effect on the actual population structure does not appear to have been significant. Related to this, there is also the obvious question of war and disease; as J. M. Winter has noted, 'the relationship between war and disease is time-honoured and well-documented'.[81] The only epidemic was, as we know, the Cape Town bubonic plague of 1901, in which the unloading of army forage housing infected rats and fleas triggered an outbreak of disease which cut a lethal path through slums inhabited by the city's black workers, causing several hundred deaths. The urban historian Elizabeth van Heyningen has pointed to 'the unquestioned part played by the military in introducing and spreading the plague'.[82] It is, however, equally evident that excess morbidity attributable to the plague in Cape Town and other parts of the Colony was slight.

Yet, behind such blunt calculations is the untold human sorrow of bereavement and the suffering of families swept up in the conflict. Memories of the brusque disposal of war dead weighed heavily on the minds of the living. Small rural communities had a highly developed sense of obligations and honours due to men who had fallen as combatants or as civilian victims; what irked and in many cases outraged them, was the indecent haste with which the colonial authorities had generally disposed of bodies in unconsecrated ground. It must have seemed as if magistrates were seeking to eradicate any popular commemoration of struggle and resistance, and thereby popular memory: perhaps they needed to. In Cradock, for example, burials were a particularly shoddy affair. Shocked by the absence of any Coloured names from official district war-dead returns, several teachers, tradesmen and churchmen mounted an investigation towards the end of June 1902. Faced with the result of a head count of local Coloured casualties, the Cradock Civil Commissioner reluctantly disclosed that the bodies of district scouts had been dumped in unmarked graves on nearby white farmland. To official consternation, this led to a night attempt to disinter the corpses. Although the grisly action was stopped by the police, this was not before the remains of thirty-nine men had been

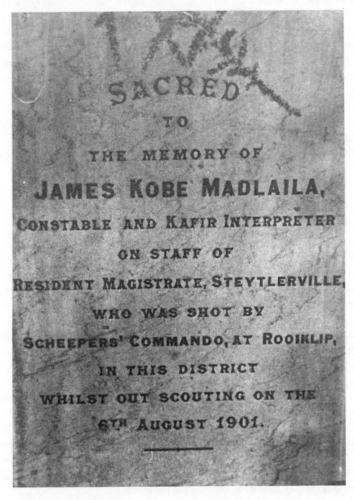

9 Grave of Constable James Kobe Madlaila, Steytlerville.
(Courtesy of Mrs Taffy Shearing)

uncovered on one farm alone. Impassioned pleas that war dead be accorded official burial fell on deaf ears. A scandalised community leadership persisted in articulating a deeply felt hurt in the months and years that followed. 'I may just mention', wrote a teacher to the magistrate in May 1904, 'that the business of our dead is not forgotten. Our Brave Men will still have to be buried respectable, as there are remarks still now passed. Our enemy the Dutch had all good coffins.'[83]

Everywhere memory was rampant. Jan Begomba, a Bedford peasant, was horrified to learn that bodies had been, and were being, buried in secret. He immediately circulated a petition asking for proper military burials for all 'Hottentot Scouts, Pondo Scouts and other Kaffir soldiers', and for the compilation and publication of a roll of war dead in recognition of their loyal service. 'They have no right to do away with them as if they are convicts', he wrote, 'they were British Subjects, and should be buried respectable'.[84] Begomba's call was characteristic of many locally discrete contributions to the 'making' of South Africa's dense and rich network of, to borrow Benedict Anderson's riveting phrase, 'imagined communities'.[85] Within a key historical conjuncture of rapidly separating ethnic and political identities between 'Coloured' and African people in the Cape, the war experience itself provided a vocabulary of political inclusion, drawing on the verities of a constituency of citizenship. Whatever happened to an African tenant in Adelaide or a Coloured artisan in Calvinia, it was *citizens*, and not communities or even classes, who died in the Cape war.

The war had made citizenship the commonest assertion of radicalism or local sovereignty. Little wonder, then, that when its proprieties or civic recognitions were not bestowed, people struggled to reclaim them.

Political aftermath

The debilitating aftermath of the war meant that British imperialism may have lost some of its shine in colonial politics but, as exemplified in Abraham Esau's martyrdom, in the tense and bitter decade leading up to Union it remained a substantive force around which popular Cape passions continued to be mobilised. Indeed, it is arguable that the exceptional historical circumstances of this phase – memories of Republican invasion, anti-Boer rural unrest and the discrediting of Cape Boers generally – worked to strengthen greatly the hold of imperial sentiment upon the loyalties of many ordinary African and Coloured citizens. In this condition of society and politics it was still relatively easy for Progressive office-seekers to gratify anxious Coloured voters with convincing rhetorical displays of 'British justice', while handing the solid political outcomes in 1904 and 1908 to dominant class interests.[86] While small groups of alienated urban Coloured workers in Cape Town were being attracted to John Tobin's 'Stone' movement brand of incipient anti-imperialist and anti-capitalist labour politics based on common working-class interests, this following was of very modest dimensions.[87] While their doubts and frustrations about imperial intentions piled up, the response of the organised Coloured petty bourgeoisie and skilled workers was continued adherence to the bona fides of liberal social actors in the dominant elite.

The perspective within which historians – from G. B. Pyrah and Leonard Thompson through to Odendaal and Willan – have been accustomed to view this pre-Union period is, quite properly, the crushing of African hopes of political representation in the newly emerging national state. 'The goal of British policy in Southern Africa', as Marks and Trapido have emphasised, 'had little to do with granting Africans' political rights or with "freedom" and "justice".'[88] It was certainly no part of the reconstruction to distribute political or other favours to black people whose strategic wartime loyalty and collaboration had helped Britain to secure victory. 'The contribution of black South Africans to the war effort', to quote Willan, 'was to be without tangible political reward.'[89] The empire had certainly clothed itself in the beguiling rhetoric of rights and justice for all civilised men, but that rhetoric was sham.

But there is another possible perspective which may coexist with this bleak conclusion. This necessarily involves a view of the Cape as more than merely a weak and declining tributary formation in the national reconstruction of South Africa as a segregationist, labour-exploitative and politically discriminatory industrial state. Transition there certainly was, but the survivals and continuities through that transition call for careful consideration. This view involves seeing the changing Cape at the same time as in a sense not in transition at all; instead, it should be seen as a society in its own right, with its own inner logic of labour and property relations, class and cultural texture, and expressions of accommodation, constraint, consent and coercion. These formed the ramparts behind which people struggled to conserve their lives, their means and their values.

This prism is one through which we may gain a fuller appreciation of the meaning of 'Abraham Esau's War' in terms of Davidson's definition of 'a people's war', namely that of armed struggle to defend modes of customary living against external aggression.[90] If we judge the Cape 'people's war' in terms of its own self-sufficient purposes and values, then what would have mattered to many was possibly not so much Britain's deafness to pleas from the black elite to extend the Cape franchise north, but the reality of its preservation in the south. For what had been most vitally at stake for both the rural propertied and the rural poor was the survival of a colonial system with known structure, habits and order, against the perceived threat of its authoritarian dismemberment. And it was in significant measure a battle of workers to hold on to their own, distinctive Cape identity, a sense of an active and influencing inheritance, which assumed quite remarkable pre-eminence in these crisis years. For it was 'not only the Eastern Cape elite who had internalised the values associated with the "little tradition" of Eastern Cape liberalism'.[91]

We face, then, something of a post-war paradox. Paul Rich, Martin Legassick, John Cell, Colin Bundy and others have argued cogently that the years between the war and the 1913 Land Act witnessed a growing assertion of segregationist doctrines in social and administrative practices, and a toughening of the colour line in political and territorial matters. To cite Paul Rich's observation, 'racialisation in political dialogue within white settler society escalated in the period up to and after the Anglo-Boer War of 1899–1902, and pushed the more paternalistic mode of Victorian Cape liberalism on to the defensive'.[92] Yet, while the rivets of Cape liberalism were popping, the substantial legacy of a defended political culture and struggle over its claims and rights was being simultaneously passed down by black people.

Far from falling apart, the entrenched common values and perceptions associated with that regional identity and culture, now magnified by war experiences, were borne into the post-war decade with an enhanced sense of adherence and legitimacy. Those who had appropriated for themselves a self-conscious definition as 'Cape British' on their own militant terms did not cease to be the people they had shown themselves to be. For in some ways, the war had been a successful defensive struggle over the fundamental identity or rhetorical ideological formation of a region. Its old liberal synthesis of citizenship rights and limited political freedoms survived the Peace of Vereeniging.

Thus, the minority black electors of Victoria East or Aliwal North went to the polls in the 1900s in customary anticipation that their votes might yet play some competitive part in defining the political future. Settler politics, after all, had come out of the war scarred and fragmented; disfranchisement of thousands of mostly poorer rural Boer rebels had advantaged Coloured and African voters who usually held the balance of power in a number of crucial constituencies.[93] Their electoral muscle increased the discomfiture of Boers struggling to extricate themselves from the damaging consequences of their wartime provocations against colonial security.

The war had greatly sharpened local factionalism and hostility between English settler and Boer interests.[92] Boer 'traitors' had embraced peace, but the terms were not immediately lenient. They emerged from the war as criminalised survivors, stigmatised and voteless; while qualified black men mobilised to play their dependent allotted role in constituency outcomes, ex-rebels faced continued exclusion from political power. In the re-establishment of the equilibriums of public authority, power and personal security, so profoundly disturbed by the war, the politics of Cape Boer survival were, for several years at least, perhaps more desperate than those of relatively incorporated black citizens. This relationship of incorporation was, of course, beset with its own intensifying contradictions; it coexisted uneasily with strident pressures against black rights in the pre-Union decade. These were fed by the peace of 1902, when notoriously, 'the British conceded the "Coloured" franchise to the defeated Boer generals'.[95] Nevertheless, in, say, 1905, Boer ascendancy and the construction of an exclusive Anglo-Afrikaner hegemony in the Cape seemed not yet absolutely assured. Eighty-odd years ago, in John Lonsdale's telling observation, 'Afrikaners as well as Africans were a conquered people.'[96] It took the reconstitution of the colonial state in readiness for Union to patch the breach in settler politics, pardoning and incorporating 'disloyal' colonists while pushing Africans to the boundaries of a new racial politics of national culture. To adapt Bill Freund's observation, this was also the price paid by 'capitalists ... to whites outside the ring of successful accumulators to recover an overall hegemony in South Africa. Gradually, those Boers who were too dependent on pre-capitalist relations were brought up or pushed out.'[97] The winning over and incorporation of Boer 'poor whites' in the colony was to be very considerable.

The Cape common roll franchise lingered on after Union, outlasting plaintive Cape liberals like Percy Molteno who, in 1906, had been moved to reflect soberly that 'owing to the late war, our responsibility to the Natives is great'.[98] Far from discharging any debt, the newly stabilised and sealed national state administered the bitter pill of the 1913 Natives' Land Act. The Land Act – its effects most concentrated in the Orange Free State or Transvaal – began rolling back the consequences of African challenge and African gain during the war. A broad case might be made for seeing this Act as prompted at least in part by the strengthening of peasant squatting and sharecropping economies in war conditions. The postwar 'reconquest' of Africans – both economic and political – was as urgent as, and indeed, inseparable from, the politics of national state formation and the reconstitution of South Africa as an imperialist enclave. To take up Lonsdale's perspective on the Natives' Land Act, 'it is worth asking how far the 1913 Natives' Land Act was the culmination of a white reconquest of Africans after the South African War'. For the Act was designed to lay a basis 'to keep blacks not only economically in their place, but politically and militarily as well'.[99]

But at the same time it would be a considerable exaggeration to argue, as Cell has, that in 1913, almost everywhere, 'Africans were proletarianised by a stroke of the pen.'[100] As Keegan and many other of South Africa's new agrarian historians have been demonstrating, the recapture and dispersal of African labour resources through 'rural social-engineering legislation' was not to be so swift and easy a process.[101] For various forms of sustained, bitter resistance to that unfolding second 'conquest' stretched into decades.

Conclusion

The stabilisation and realignment of the Cape Colony after 1902 can be seen as an obvious manifestation of what Stanley Greenberg has depicted as the post-1890s 'intensification of racial discrimination', an era when 'racial domination was given a "modern" form . . . where repressive features were elaborated and institutionalised', and when there was a hardening 'elaboration of the state racial apparatus'.[102] Struggles over survival, rights and citizenship – human needs which shaped the meanings of the South African War in the colony – were to be resolved by guaranteeing their repro-duction for whites and confiscating or diminishing those of blacks. The mounting dis-illusion of African and Coloured elites with a post-war outcome which saw the specific regional configurations of the Cape merging inexorably into the overarching political culture of a repressive racial state, is now one of the most thoroughly documented and analysed issues in South African history. Any further recapitulation would be superfluous.

Instead of again dwelling on painful compositional moments in the dwindling political hopes of a Sol Plaatje or an Abdullah Abdurahman, it is worth recalling the significance of the terrain of wartime experience for the black population. If it brought anything, it brought both fright and excitement, both anxiety and exhilaration. The decline and defeat of the expansive energies of whole sectors of popular life, indeed the brevity and limits of their movement, does not diminish their importance to an under-standing of the outcomes of specific struggles and historic regional divisions which have profoundly influenced 'the complexity of political consciousness and com-munity construction in twentieth-century South Africa'.[103] This book has sought to stress a dramatic human history of mostly common 'actors' with intentionality and realisation, within the particularities and peculiarities of Cape colonial 'exceptional-ism'. For the Anglicised and other infusing local cultures that informed individual and community responses to war conditions were mostly markedly different from those in other areas of Southern Africa; it is now surely evident that a fuller appreciation of black social history in the war years requires a move beyond the synthetic, national account so ably provided by Warwick, to the particularities of the local study.

If there was something irreducibly local about the character of black participation in the crisis, it was a vigorously assertive and polarising kind of localism. Against adversity, it created its own social heroes in the shape of Abraham Esau, its decorated mission muleteers and its celebrated town militia. And we return to the recurrent theme of a society of workers, peasants and petty bourgeoisie resting on a common and articulate recognition of a social polity rooted in the righteousness of patriotism and liberty. This lingering mode of thought was characteristically a cross-class phenomenon; it was also invested, to use Tom Nairn's phrase, with 'the glamour of backwardness'.[104] In that vision there was meaning, with which Cape workers and artisans alike strove to interpret and order their unsettled world so that they could act within it. As the British historian Robert Colls has reflected, 'fact, myth and image, are grit to the oyster; and when the shell is broken, consciousness is the pearl, or the stone'.[105] In men marching through villages, or in skilled migrants riding wagons in boisterous combination, a consciousness of where subordinated people's popular priorities, associations and countervailing powers were residing blew up in breathless waves of feeling and action. That consciousness could not yet act in independence; it ran under the controlling hegemony of British imperialism. But its protean capacity to sustain and enrich the spaces which people created for themselves was momentous enough.

None of this is to overlook the material distress caused by the war's economic effects upon the productive base of a community like Leliefontein, or the sorrow and anguish resulting from a husband, lover, brother, son or father departing for the Army Service Corps sometimes never to be heard of again. Nor is it to overlook the disappointment especially of time-expired Coloured and African auxiliaries as they faded into a civilian presence. Indeed, their soldiering sense of anti-climax at the transition from the corporate, brassy world of regiments, colours and patrolling to the ordinary and the routine, reflected what is possibly a fairly universal historical condition. No doubt, like 'demobbed' troops of the World Wars, US veterans of the Vietnam War, perhaps even demobilised East and West African carriers after the First World War, experience of the present and anticipation of the future now carried a feeling of deflation. These structures of feeling, to use Raymond Williams' striking historical concept, were bound up with how Cape society itself was changing and was being changed. And its direction, after the sacrifices of the war, produced little cause for euphoria. Yet, whatever the final tally, it was the movement of individuals and groups – often divided in terms of their class and cultural experiences and concerns – who came together to assert some sense of commonly held interest. This not only changed the texture of a 'white man's war' but helped determine what shape it would take.

However regulated in militia or other corporate forms, it is worth emphasising again that the labourers of Namaqualand and elsewhere also drilled on their own terms. Their risks, privations, opportunities and strengths, as well as their mettle, form a fascinating part of South Africa's past. That pluck is occasionally still recalled in 'Rooi-Rooi Jare' ('Red-Red Years') and 'Rooi Lewensmoed' ('Red Courage') 'resistance' folksongs among older Coloured farmworkers in the Karroo. Their original context of flash and smoke has gone; the shearers of Fraserburg or Graaff-Reinet are no longer thumbing a nose at Smuts or Lötter. Instead, out of the earshot of landowners, workers dip into an historical inheritance for a displacing song which not only pushes back the pain of exploitation but provides a sardonic yet visceral relieving laugh:

> We Cape men of the farms
> Stand with the khakis and their arms.
> We are spies, we are sheep,
> We live in the mud.
> We are scouts, we are dogs,
> We bark for Boer blood.
>
> We Cape Hottentots are smart you see
> Not white men, but now we are free
> Not too hot, and not too cold,
> But the best thing, we're told
> Is that in their arms the Freestaters us will hold.[106]

It is a voice which, in testing times, imprinted itself upon the moving and shaping forces of modern South African history. And it forms part of the haunting historical patrimony of its dominated classes, the residue of language from a lightning-flash moment when artisans and rural proletarians were enthused and combative and peasants militant. In many respects that rallying language empowered them by giving them definition and consciousness. It provided a transitory tinge of triumphalism. As they found, however, while it contested the terms of their domination, it did not change society to their advantage. If, in their stance towards the world, they struggled within limits to make themselves, 'consciousness was not power'.[107]

After 1902, the Cape's dominated blacks found the world closing in; what lay ahead of them was a blizzard. But what has also to be registered is the element of palpable achievement, the increment of an articulate social being. This is not a matter of finding something to be inflated or idealised, for it is important to remember the bruising reality of disengagement and 'reconquest'. Yet the convulsions of the war experience produced certain advances and certain clarifications of the degree of growth and initiative which this generation was able to achieve within a subaltern existence.

These perspectives are crucial to any understanding of the differential social and communal history and geography which was then, and is now, the brutally unequal and oppressive world of South Africa. For necessarily alongside the historical panoramas of industrialisation and agricultural dispossession, alongside the subjection of proletarians or tenants to national economic fluctuations, or alongside the grand constructions of nationalism, are the smaller, more episodic and diffuse scenes. In these, the bare but possible chances for cultural determination, consciousness and resolution also occur. In these were formulated the sectional emblems of both symbolic and material interest with which the common people of the Cape inscribed their own local rhythms into the cadence of national life.

Whatever its other outcomes, the South African War did not put an end to Cape 'exceptionalism'. What it did was greatly to change the world in which that force was to try to play out its old roles to the end.

In this, it continued to assimilate into local society a varied human legacy of that imperialist war. A scatter of British soldiers, cocky, 'red-faced boys' who had transcended the routine racism and prejudice of their social setting, did establish affective and stable human linkages with black inhabitants. Like other sinful metropolitan troops who were to disregard the segregationist habits and beliefs of colonial societies, they were looked at askance by most local settlers. But these men found an anchorage after 1902. Those in particular who had struck up relationships with Coloured women or who had married them after demobilisation, were absorbed into Cape Town's customarily Coloured residential areas, or found an agreeable spot within that city's tenuously surviving 'special tradition of multiracialism'.[108] As socially integrated craftsmen or as British 'bobbies', ex-soldiers were woven into the fabric of an Anglicised Cape 'exceptionalism'. Such intersections, too, helped to ensure that some memory of the war experience survived into the later years of the century; and also that that memory was rooted in the assumptions of an active and eloquent humanity, driven by the needs of identity and respect. Abraham Esau's war was bound up with a certain way of looking at the British soldier; that did not dissipate with the artisan's last gasps. Remembered fragments, like ex-Fusilier Albert Thomas, remained embedded in an expectant, optimistic imperial consciousness: ' "British Bert" he was called. He lived right in here, here with us. He was like the other Irish and those cockneys ... they came out in the army to Cape Town first ... and then they came back down here after the Boer War ... He wasn't all mighty and standoffish like he was European and we was Coloured.'[109]

Notes

Preface

1 A. Sher, *Middlepost*, London, 1988, p. 363.
2 S. Sontag (ed.), *Barthes: Selected Writings*, London, 1982, p. 104.
3 See M. Rediker, *Between the Devil and the Deep Blue Sea: Merchant Seamen, Pirates, and the Anglo-American Maritime World, 1700–1780*, New York, 1987, p. 151; R. Skidelsky, 'Only Connect: Biography and Truth', in E. Homberger and J. Charmley (eds.), *The Troubled Face of Biography*, London, 1988, p. 15.
4 For a recent, useful synthesis, see I. E. Smith, 'The Origins of the South African War (1899–1902) in the Context of the Recent Historiography of South Africa', Africa Seminar Paper, Centre for African Studies, University of Cape Town, 1989.
5 R. Fraser, *Blood of Spain: The Experience of Civil War 1936–1939*, Harmondsworth, 1979, p. 29.
6 J. Iliffe, 'Hidden Struggles' (review), *Journal of African History*, 29, 1 (1988), p. 125.
7 S. Marks and R. Rathbone (eds.), *Industrialisation and Social Change in South Africa: African Class Formation, Culture and Consciousness 1870–1930*, London, 1982, p. 9.
8 M. Howard, *The Causes of War*, London, 1984, p. 217.

1 Introduction: perspectives and place

1 S. Marks and A. Atmore (eds.), *Economy and Society in Pre-Industrial South Africa*, London, 1980; S. Marks and R. Rathbone (eds.), *Industrialisation and Social Change in South Africa: African Class Formation, Culture and Consciousness 1870–1930*, London, 1982; S. Marks and S. Trapido (eds.), *The Politics of Race, Class and Nationalism in Twentieth Century South Africa*, London, 1987; C. Bundy, *The Rise and Fall of the South African Peasantry*, London, 1979; W. Beinart, *The Political Economy of Pondoland, 1860–1930*, Johannesburg, 1982; W. Beinart and C. Bundy, *Hidden Struggles in Rural South Africa: Politics and Popular Movements in the Transkei and Eastern Cape 1890–1930*, Johannesburg, 1987; C. van Onselen, *Studies in the Social and Economic History of the Witwatersrand, 1886–1914*, 2 vols., Johannesburg, 1982; B. Bozzoli (ed.), *Labour, Townships and Protest*, Johannesburg, 1979; *Town and Countryside in the Transvaal: Capitalist Penetration and Popular Response*, Johannesburg, 1983; *Class, Community and Conflict: South African Perspectives*, Johannesburg, 1987; P. Bonner, I. Hofmeyr, D. James and T. Lodge (eds.), *Holding Their Ground: Class, Locality and Culture in 19th and 20th Century South Africa*, Johannesburg, 1989. The emergence of this movement is usefully evaluated in C. C. Saunders, *The Making of the South African Past: Major Historians on Race and Class*, Cape Town, 1988, part 5.
2 E. P. Thompson, *The Poverty of Theory and Other Essays*, London, 1979, p. 194.
3 But for a crude and intemperate critique of the 'new' agrarian social history and an attempt to rehabili-

tate more 'classical' Marxist theory, see M. Morris, 'Social History and the Transition to Capitalism in the South African Countryside', *Africa Perspective* (new series), 1, 5/6 (1987), pp. 7–23.

4 S. Yeo, 'Whose Story? An Argument from within Current Historical Practice in Britain', *Journal of Contemporary History*, 21, 1 (1986), p. 305.

5 'Introduction', in W. Beinart, P. Delius and S. Trapido (eds.), *Putting a Plough to the Ground: Accumulation and Dispossession in Rural South Africa, 1850–1930*, Johannesburg, 1986, p. 49.

6 van Onselen, *Studies*, vol. I: *New Babylon*, Johannesburg, 1982, p. xvi.

7 G. Lewis, *Between the Wire and the Wall: A History of South African 'Coloured' Politics*, Cape Town, 1987; I. Goldin, *Making Race: The Politics and Economics of Coloured Identity in South Africa*, Cape Town, 1987.

8 P. Maylam, *A History of the African People of South Africa: From the Early Iron Age to the 1970s*, Cape Town, 1986, pp. 136–8; A. Odendaal, *Vukani Bantu! The Beginnings of Black Protest Politics in South Africa to 1912*, Cape Town, 1984, pp. 30–9.

9 A. Grundlingh, *Fighting their Own War: South African Blacks and the First World War*, Johannesburg, 1987; see also his 'The Impact of the First World War on South African Blacks', in M. E. Page (ed.), *Africa and the First World War*, London, 1987, pp. 54–80.

10 For some suggestive interpretation of war as a catalyst for social, economic and other change in colonial African societies, see *Journal of African History*, 19, 1 (1978), thematic issue: 'World War I and Africa', especially introduction by Rathbone, pp. 1–9; D. Killingray and R. Rathbone (eds.), *Africa and the Second World War*, London, 1986, esp. 'Introduction', pp. 1–19; D. Killingray, 'War and Society in British Colonial Africa: Themes and Prospects', in D. L. Ray, P. Shinnie and D. Williams (eds.), *Into the 80s: Proceedings of the Eleventh Annual Conference of the Canadian Association of African Studies*, Vancouver, 1981, pp. 250–63.

11 S. Andreski, *Military Organisation and Society*, 2nd edn, London, 1968.

12 For World War II, see L. Grundlingh, 'The Recruitment of South African Blacks for Participation in the Second World War', in Killingray and Rathbone (eds.), *Africa and the Second World War*, pp. 181–203; M. Roth, '"If you give us rights we will fight": Black Involvement in the Second World War', *South African Historical Journal*, 15 (1983), pp. 85–104.

13 B. Porter, *The Lion's Share: A Short History of British Imperialism, 1850–1970*, London, 1975, p. 250.

14 See J. Krikler, 'The Transvaal Agrarian Class Struggle in the South African War 1899–1902', *Social Dynamics*, 12, 1 (1986), pp. 1–30.

15 Fraser, *Blood of Spain*, p. 29.

16 P. Warwick, *Black People and the South African War*, Cambridge, 1983, pp. 30–8; T. Pakenham, *The Boer War*, London, 1979, pp. 396–418; B. Willan, 'The Siege of Mafeking', in P. Warwick (ed.), *The South African War: The Anglo-Boer War, 1899–1902*, London, 1980, especially pp. 150–60; B. Willan, *Sol Plaatje: A Biography, 1876–1932*, Johannesburg, 1984, pp. 77–103; and, of course, the classic J. L. Comaroff (ed.), *The Boer War Diary of Sol Plaatje, an African at Mafeking*, London, 1973. For Kimberley, see Pakenham, *Boer War*, pp. 325–6; Warwick, *Black People*, pp. 129–30.

17 V. Bickford-Smith, 'Black Labour at the Docks at the Beginning of the Twentieth Century', in C. C. Saunders and H. Phillips (eds.), *Studies in the History of Cape Town*, vol. II, University of Cape Town, 1980, pp. 75–125; S. Dubow, 'African Labour at the Cape Town Docks, 1900–1904: Processes of Transition', in C. C. Saunders, H. Phillips and E. van Heyningen (eds.), *Studies in the History of Cape Town*, vol,. IV, 1981, pp. 108–34; C. C. Saunders, 'Segregation in Cape Town: The Creation of Ndabeni', *Africa Seminar, Collected Papers*, vol. I, University of Cape Town, 1978, pp. 43–63.

18 'The Politics of Race, Class and Nationalism', in Marks and Trapido (eds.), *Politics of Race*, p. 3.

19 'Waiting for something to turn up? The Cape Colony in the 1880s', in A. Mabin (ed.), *Organisation and Economic Change*, Southern African Studies, vol. V, Johannesburg, 1989, p. 37.

20 See B. Freund, 'Development and Underdevelopment in Southern Africa: An Historical Overview', *Geoforum*, 17, 2 (1986), pp. 133–40.

21 Beinart and Bundy, 'Introduction: "Away in the Locations"', in *Hidden Struggles*, pp. 2–3.

22 W. H. Worger, *South Africa's City of Diamonds: Mine Workers and Mining Capital in Kimberley*,

1867–1895, New Haven and London, 1987, especially chs. 3, 6; R. V. Turrell, *Capital and Labour on the Kimberley Diamond Fields 1871–1890*, Cambridge, 1987, especially ch. 8.

23 Beinart and Bundy, 'Introduction: "Away in the Locations"', in *Hidden Struggles*, p. 10.

24 J. Lonsdale, 'The European Scramble and Conquest in African History',. in R. Oliver and G. N. Sanderson (eds.), *The Cambridge History of Africa*, vol. VI, 1870–1905, Cambridge, 1985, p. 760.

25 'Settler Accumulation in East Griqualand from the Demise of the Griqua to the Natives Land Act', in Beinart, Delius and Trapido (eds.), *Plough to the Ground*, p. 278; and also C. Bundy, 'Dissidents, Detectives, and the Dipping Revolt: Social Control and Collaboration in East Griqualand in 1914', in A. V. Akeroyd and C. R. Hill (eds.), *Southern African Research in Progress, Collected Papers*, vol. V, University of York, 1980, pp. 4–5; '"We don't want your rain, we won't dip": Popular Opposition, Collaboration and Social Control in the Anti-Dipping Movement, *c.* 1908–16', in Beinart and Bundy, *Hidden Struggles*, p. 208.

26 For what Kenneth W. Grundy has called 'a confusion of organizational forms and uses for diverse black and mixed fighting groups' in eighteenth and nineteenth-century Cape colonial warfare, see his *Soldiers without Politics: Blacks in the South African Armed Forces*, Berkeley and Los Angeles, 1983, pp. 32–8; Warwick, *Black People*, pp. 10–15; Grundlingh, *Own War*, p. 4.

27 Beinart, 'Settler Accumulation', p. 279.

28 A. Sachs, *Justice in South Africa*, London, 1973, p. 55.

29 'The Military Defence Forces of the Colonies', *Report of Proceedings of the Royal Colonial Institute*, 27, 1898–1899, Appendix 5, p. 284.

30 N. Etherington, 'Labour Supply and the Genesis of South African Confederation in the 1870s', *Journal of African History*, 20, 2 (1979), p. 245.

31 'Firearms in Southern Africa: A Survey', *Journal of African History*, 12, 4 (1971), p. 520.

32 Lewis, *Between the Wire*, p. 24.

33 S. Trapido, 'African Divisional Politics in the Cape Colony 1884–1910', *Journal of African History*, 9, 1 (1968), pp. 78–98; T. R. H. Davenport, *South Africa: A Modern History*, London, 1977, p. 83.

34 E. A. Walker, 'The Franchise in South Africa', *Cambridge Historical Journal*, 11, 1 (1953), p. 99.

35 Marks and Trapido, 'The Politics of Race, Class and Nationalism', pp. 13–14; see also H. Giliomee, 'The Beginnings of Afrikaner Nationalism, 1870–1915', *South African Historical Journal*, 19 (1987), pp. 133–4.

36 P. Rich, 'Segregation and the Cape Liberal Tradition', *Collected Seminar Papers on the Societies of Southern Africa in the 19th and 20th Centuries*, vol. X, Institute of Commonwealth Studies, University of London, 1981, p. 33; T. R. H. Davenport, *The Afrikaner Bond: The History of a South African Political Party, 1880–1911*, Cape Town, 1966, pp. 119–20.

37 'Liberalism in the Cape in the Nineteenth and Twentieth Centuries', *Collected Seminar Papers on the Societies of Southern Africa in the 19th and 20th Centuries*, vol. IV, Institute of Commonwealth Studies, University of London, 1974, p. 55; Trapido, '"The Friends of the Natives": Merchants, Peasants and the Political and Ideological Structure of Liberalism in the Cape, 1854–1910', in Marks and Atmore (eds.), *Economy and Society*, p. 255.

38 'Friends of the Natives', p. 255.

39 S. Marks, *The Ambiguities of Dependence in South Africa: Class, Nationalism, and the State in Twentieth-Century Natal*, Johannesburg, 1986, p. 57.

40 S. Dubow, 'Race, Civilisation and Culture: The Elaboration of Segregationist Discourse in the Inter-War Years', in Marks and Trapido (eds.), *Politics of Race*, p. 74.

41 W. Beinart and C. Bundy, 'State Intervention and Rural Resistance: The Transkei, 1900–1965', in M. A. Klein (ed.), *Peasants in Africa: Historical and Contemporary Perspectives*, Beverly Hills and London, 1980, p. 275.

42 J. W. Cell, *The Highest Stage of White Supremacy: The Origins of Segregation in South Africa and the American South*, Cambridge, 1982, p. 25.

43 Cited in P. Lewsen, 'Cape Liberalism in its Terminal Phase', in D. C. Hindson (ed.), *Working Papers in Southern African Studies*, vol. III, Johannesburg, 1983, p. 41.

44 As shown, for example, by Goldin, *Making Race*, pp. 19–27; Dubow, 'Race, civilisation and culture', pp. 73–5; Lewis, *Between the Wire*, pp. 10–14; Cell, *White Supremacy*, pp. 196–212; Rich, 'Segregation', pp. 31–41; R. Parry, '"In a Sense Citizens but not altogether Citizens" . . . Rhodes, Race and the Ideology of Segregation at the Cape in the Late Nineteenth Century', *Canadian Journal of African Studies*, 17, 2 (1983), pp. 377–91; V. Bickford-Smith, 'Class, Colour and Production in Cape Town on the Eve of the Mineral Revolution (*c.* 1875)', *Social Dynamics*, 13, 2 (1987), pp. 32–45.

45 S. Trapido, 'White Conflict and Non-White Participation in the Politics of the Cape of Good Hope, 1853–1910', Ph.D. thesis, University of London, 1970. On the dire legal standing of blacks in the Boer Republics, see for example H. J. van Aswegen, 'Die Posisie van die Nie-Blanke in die Oranje-Vrystaat, 1854–1902', *South African Historical Journal*, 5 (1973), pp. 41–60.

46 Marks and Trapido, 'The Politics of Race', p. 5.

47 Goldin, *Making Race*, p. 27.

48 R. Ross, *Adam Kok's Griquas: A Study in the Development of Stratification in South Africa*, Cambridge, 1976, p. 136.

49 To use Tim Keegan's broad categorisation: 'Race, Class and Economic Development in South Africa', *Social Dynamics*, 15, 1 (1989), p. 115.

50 C. Bundy, 'Vagabond Hollanders and Runaway Englishmen: White Poverty in the Cape before Poor Whiteism', in Beinart, Delius and Trapido (eds.), *Plough to the Ground*, p. 117.

51 C. Bundy, 'The Transkei Peasantry, *c.* 1890–1914: "Passing through a Period of Stress"', in R. Palmer and N. Parsons (eds.), *The Roots of Rural Poverty in Central and Southern Africa*, London, 1977, p. 206; Beinart and Bundy, 'Introduction: "Away in the Locations"', in *Hidden Struggles*, p. 18.

52 Beinart, '"Jamani": Cape workers in German South West Africa, 1904–12', in Beinart and Bundy, *Hidden Struggles*, p. 167; see also J. Butler, 'Thomas Pakenham's *The Boer War*: A Good Read, but Poor History', *Africa Seminar, Collected Papers*, vol. II, University of Cape Town, 1981, p. 108.

2 Colonial state, imperial army and peacekeeping

1 'Participation in the "Boer War": People's War, People's Non-War, or Non-People's War?', in B. A. Ogot (ed.), *War and Society in Africa*, London, 1972, pp. 109, 111.

2 'Black People', in Warwick (ed.), *South African War*, p. 195.

3 *The People's Cause: A History of Guerrillas in Africa*, London, 1981, p. 31.

4 D. Killingray, 'The Idea of a British Imperial African Army', *Journal of African History*, 20, 3 (1979), p. 422.

5 'Colonial Africa and its Armies', in B. Bond and I. Roy (eds.), *War and Society*, vol. II, London, 1977, p. 27.

6 CO 179/206/26305 desp., 28 Sept. 1899, Minutes by Sir H. Just, Sir F. Graham and J. Chamberlain.

7 NMM, Limpus Papers, Mss. 75/139/2/B, Journal of HMS *Terrible*, entry for 2 April 1900; *Black and White Budget*, 29 Sept. 1900.

8 *Ons Land*, 12 July 1900, 22 Sept. 1900; *Worcester Advertiser*, 8 April 1900; *South African News*, 27 Jan. 1901.

9 SAL, Schreiner Papers, section B, Rev. W. P. de Villiers to W. P. Schreiner, 17 Jan. 1900.

10 *Navy and Army Gazette*, 19 May 1900, 28 Sept. 1900; *Oxfordshire Light Infantry Chronicle* (1900), p. 108.

11 NAM, 7208/8, Cpl J. Paterson, Letters, 1899–1901, Paterson to his brother, 17 April 1900.

12 CO 48/551/2411 encl. 6 in Milner to Chamberlain, 3 Jan. 1901, Sprigg to Milner, 31 Dec. 1900.

13 'Introduction: "Away in the Locations"', in *Hidden Struggles*, p. 8.

14 See for example, 'The Crying Need of South Africa', *Quarterly Review*, 196, 391 (1902), p. 297; L. Golding, 'Quaint South African Beliefs and Customs', *Chambers's Journal*, 11, 101 (1899), pp. 822–4; M. J. Farrelly, 'Our Hold on South Africa After the War', *Macmillan's Magazine*, 512 (1902), p. 157; H. L. Bellot, 'The Problem in South Africa: Boer v. Briton', *Westminster Review*, 154,

1 (1900), p. 27; Sir G. Lagden, *Basutoland and the Basutos*, Report of Proceedings of the Royal Colonial Institute, 37 (1900–1901), p. 272; *Navy and Army Illustrated*, 13 June 1900.
15 'The First Chapter of the War', *Scottish Review*, 35 (1900), pp. 357–8
16 As in the case of the rebel chief, Mhlonhlo, in the East Griqualand and Pondoland areas, who was rumoured to be again plotting mischief when Republican forces obligingly overturned colonial authority in northeastern Cape districts in 1899: W. Beinart, 'The Anatomy of a Rural Scare: East Griqualand in the 1890s', in Beinart and Bundy, *Hidden Struggles*, pp. 68–9; Warwick, *Black People*, pp. 114–15.
17 See for example, LHC, Aston Papers, 1/1, Special Service Diary, 1899–1900, entry for 20 May 1900; 6/1, Maj. G. G. Aston to M. Aston, 7 May 1900; WSCRO, Maxse Papers, 511, Lt F. I. Maxse to P. Wyndham, 20 Jan. 1900; *Naval and Military Record*, 30 Dec. 1899.
18 USPG, Reports, E series, Africa, 1900(B), 45661, The Bishop of St John's Kaffraria on the War and the Attitude of the Natives, unpublished typescript, n.d. See also, Reports, E series, Africa, 1900(A), 2974, Revd J. Pattison, Report for Lady Frere, Dec. 1900; Reports, E series, Africa, 1900(B), 45661, Revd E. Lancaster, Report for Kokstad, Dec. 1900; Reports, E series, Africa, 1900(E), Revd D. Dodd, Report for St Peter's Grahamstown, Dec. 1899; Letters Received, D series, 9204, Africa, vol. V, Revd J. Watt to Revd W. Tucker, 20.1.1900.
19 *Foreign Mission Chronicle of the Episcopal Church in Scotland*, 1, 2 (1900), p. 38.
20 SAL, Schreiner Papers, section B, Letterbook, 1899, Schreiner to M. du Plessis, 8 December 1899; *Cape Mercury*, 17 Oct. 1899. See also E. A. Walker, *W. P. Schreiner: A South African*, London, 1937, p. 203.
21 CO 48/551/2411 encl. 6 in Milner to Chamberlain, 3 Jan. 1901, Sprigg to Milner, 31 Dec. 1900.
22 SAL, Schreiner Papers, Letterbook, 1899, Schreiner to J. Molteno, 22 Dec. 1899.
23 SAL, Schreiner Papers, Mss. 782 (1899–1900), Letterbook, 1900, Schreiner to Milner, 24 Nov. 1899; Schreiner to Milner, 20 Nov. 1899; Folio 252, Letterbook, 1900, Schreiner to Milner, 18 April 1900; T. Bothma, 'The Conciliation Movement in the Cape Colony during the Anglo-Boer War, 1899–1902', M.A. thesis, University of Cape Town, 1974, p. 49; E. van Heyningen, 'The Relations Between Sir Alfred Milner and W. P. Schreiner's Ministry, 1898–1900', M.A. thesis, University of Cape Town, 1971, p. 90.
24 *Lloyds Weekly Newspaper*, 10 Dec. 1899. See also SAL, Schreiner Papers, Schreiner to Sauer, 27 Nov. 1899; van Heyningen, 'Sir Alfred Milner', pp. 90–1; B. Ten Kate, *De Oorlog in Zuid-Afrika en de Zending*, Rotterdam, 1901, pp. 42–3.
25 SAL, Merriman Papers, No. 405, Merriman to J. de Wet, 21 Nov. 1899; see also Merriman Papers, No. 405, Merriman to J. Hugo, 16 Nov. 1899; No. 403, Merriman to B. Coetzee, 18 Nov. 1899. On 18 Dec. 1899, Merriman told James Bryce, the British Liberal, 'as regards the Natives . . . I consider this an even more real danger than the Dutch population': P. Lewsen (ed.), *Selections from the Correspondence of John X. Merriman*, Cape Town, 1966, p. 121.
26 SAL, Schreiner Papers, section B, Steyn to Schreiner (tel.), 20 Nov. 1899.
27 Ibid., Schreiner to Hofmeyr, 15 Dec. 1899; Mss. 782, Letterbook, 1899–1900, Schreiner to Milner, 24 Nov. 1899.
28 CA, AG 2013, Schreiner to RM, Barkly East, 10 Nov. 1899; 1/ALN 4/1/1/1, Schreiner to RM (conf. tel.), 19 Nov. 1899. Van Heyningen, 'Sir Alfred Milner', p. 92, has noted that on 'rare occasions when Schreiner found that natives had been used in any capacity, he was quick to investigate the matter and put an end to it before it became a critical issue'.
29 ACG, RO.14/9/13, Lt J. Everard, Diary, 1899–1902, entry for 11 Dec. 1899; RO.14/9/11, Col. A. S. Henniker, Diary, 1900–1902, entry for 9 Jan. 1900; *Navy and Army Gazette*, 4 Jan. 1900; 'The Second Chapter of the War', *Scottish Review*, 25 (1900), p. 356.
30 SAL, Schreiner Papers, section B, Private Secretary's Letterbook, 1898–1899, Schreiner to Milner, 24 Nov. 1899; see also *James Rose-Innes, Autobiography*, Oxford, 1949, p. 187.
31 CO 417/269/33058 encl. in Milner to Chamberlain (conf.), 9 Nov. 1899, Milner, Diary of Events, 6 Nov. 1899.

32 SAL, Schreiner Papers, Mss. 782, Letterbook, 1899, Schreiner to Milner, 24 Nov. 1899. For responses, see *Cape Hansard*, 1900, p. 92; W. E. Stanford, *The Reminiscences of Sir Walter Stanford*, vol. I, Cape Town, 1958, pp. 203–4. Milner conceded that 'the civil or political principle, not to use Natives, except in emergency is clearly laid down': for which, see Schreiner Papers, Milner to Schreiner, 29 Nov. 1899; Schreiner, conf. draft minute, 15 Dec. 1899; SLD to I. Davies, 4 Jan. 1900.

33 UCTL, Stanford Papers, F(x)19, J. B. Moffat to Stanford, 23 Dec. 1899.

34 SAL, Schreiner Papers, D.63/406, B3B(15), Milner to Schreiner, 24 Nov. 1899.

35 CO 48/545/2483 encl. 1 in Milner to Chamberlain (secret), 3 Jan. 1900, Elliot to SNA (tel.), 25 Dec. 1899; CA, NA 445, Elliot to SNA (tel. 1333), 17 Dec. 1899; Scott to SNA (tel. 1215), 27 Nov. 1899; 1/CMK 2/163, Scott to SNA (tel. 1314), 29 Nov. 1899; B. Holt, 'Sir Henry Elliot', *Africana Notes and News*, 11, 5 (1954), pp. 158–60.

36 See Warwick, *Black People*, pp. 114–19, for a concise and detailed account of the mobilising of Transkeian levies and for useful discussion of social conditions, politics and security in the Territories generally.

37 CO 179/210/7726 encl. 5, H. Nourse to F. R. Moor, 10 Jan. 1900.

38 *Cape Hansard*, 1900, p. 103. An equally sanguine Sprigg advised the House of Assembly that as the Territories 'were the natural home of the Natives ... it was quite proper to employ them in defence'.

39 UCTL, Stanford Papers, F(2)2, Elliot to Stanford, 5 May 1901, 7 July 1901; D.30, 18 July 1901, 3 Sept. 1901; CA, 1/CMK 2/52, Stanford to Scott, 22 July 1901; *South African News*, 2 Oct. 1901; *Umtata Herald*, 4 Jan. 1901, 19 May 1901, 25 May 1901.

40 'Conflict in Qumbu: Rural Consciousness, Ethnicity and Violence in the Colonial Transkei', in Beinart and Bundy, *Hidden Struggles*, p. 115. See also C. C. Saunders, 'Tile and the Thembu Church: Politics and Independence on the Cape Eastern Frontier in the Late Nineteenth Century', *Journal of African History*, 11, 4 (1970), p. 567; B. M. Flournoy, 'The Relationship of the African Methodist Church to its South African Members, 1896–1906', *Journal of African Studies*, 4, 1 (1975), pp. 544–5.

41 CA, 1/EOT 6/1/1/1/17, 2488/89, Elliot to Field Cornets, Elliot District, 4 Dec. 1899. For examples of 'panics' and the calm official response, see CO 48/545/2483 encl. 10 in Milner to Chamberlain (secret), 3 Jan. 1900, Elliot to SNA (tel.), 23 Dec. 1899; CA, 1/CMT 3/157, 598/99, RM, St Johns, to Elliot, 16 Oct. 1899, Petitions encl., 13 Oct. 1899, 14 Oct. 1899; 1/CMK 1/236, RM, Maclear, to Scott (tel.), 14 Oct. 1899; AG, 687, SNA to Spl JP, Rhodes, 15 Nov. 1899; DD, 1/66, SNA to Elliot (tel.), 11 April 1901; Elliot to SNA, 12 April 1901.

42 CA, 1/JTN B1, Notes on South Africa Colonial Forces, 31 Dec. 1901; CO 48/555/42296 encl. 1 in Hely-Hutchinson to Chamberlain (conf.), Lt McIntyre to General Officer Commanding Cape Colony (tel.), 26 Oct. 1901; CO 48/543/786 encls. 1 and 2 in Milner to Chamberlain, 14 Dec. 1899, Hook to Schreiner and reply (tels.), 8 Dec. 1899; CA, 1/ALN 4/8/1, 4/397, Lt Richardson to OC, Colonial Forces, Aliwal North, 7 Feb. 1902. For a partial list of levies, see, CA, DD 7/175, Native Levies and Intelligence, 1900; G. Tylden, 'Further Addenda and Corrigenda to the "Armed Forces of South Africa"', *Africana Notes and News*, 13, 4 (1958), pp. 151–66.

43 CO 48/543/5422, RM, Barkly West, to Under Colonial Secretary, 31 Oct. 1899; CA, NA 263, 91/00, RM, Taung, to SNA, 23 June 1900; *Graaff-Reinet Advertiser*, 7 Jan. 1901; *Colesberg Advertiser*, 18 Feb. 1900.

44 *South African News*, 27 June 1900.

45 'Shepherds, limeburners, sundry peddlers and woodcutters', according to army intelligence: NAM, 6807/189, Confidential Weekly Intelligence Report No. 352/C, 5 May 1900.

46 NAM, 6807/187, Cmdt, De Aar, to Intelligence (Western), 22 Dec. 1901.

47 CA, 1/TBH 5/1/4/4, Cmdt, Piquetberg to RM, 28 Nov. 1901.

48 CO 48/560, Anonymous Letter to RM, encl. in RM, Victoria West, to Under Colonial Secretary, 9 April 1902.

49 NAM, 6807/187, Sloman to Intelligence Officer, Beaufort West, 28 Jan. 1900.

50 RSR, Mss. 1/120, Bidder, Letterbooks, vol. III, Lt H. F. Bidder to his parents, 2 Jan. 1901.

51 CA, 1/SSE 10/75, Deputy Admr to H. Lombard, 3 Jan. 1901; 1/KMN 10/24, C. T. David to Ag RM,

6 Nov. 1899, 19 Oct. 1900; NAM, 6807/188, file 46, statement by C. van Wyk, 3 Jan. 1902; *Lloyds Weekly Newspaper*, 21 July 1901.

52 Beinart and Delius, 'Introduction', in *Plough to the Ground*, p. 43.

53 *Cape Hansard*, 1900, pp. 103, 108; *Midland News and Karoo Farmer*, 10 Dec. 1899.

54 CA, 1/ALN 4/9/1/2, Cmdt to Spl JP, Jamestown, 16 Nov. 1899.

55 CA, AG 273, Buller to D. B. Hook (tel.), 4 Nov. 1899; AG 2015, Under Colonial Secretary to Hook, 6 Nov. 1899.

56 CA, 1/BKE 1/1/2/2/2, Affidavit by W. A. Cronje, 28 Nov. 1899; *Cape Times*, 6 Dec. 1899.

57 J. H. Snyman, *Die Afrikaner in Kaapland, 1899–1902*, Pretoria, 1979, p. 61; I. A. James, 'The Rebellion in Barkly East and Dordrecht in 1899', B.A. Hons. thesis, University of Cape Town, 1964, pp. 7, 30–1.

58 *Cape Times*, 6 Jan. 1900.

59 *Cape Mercury*, 5 Feb. 1900.

60 CO 48/553/29712 encl. 2 in Hely-Hutchinson to Chamberlain, 5 Aug. 1901; Kitchener to Hely-Hutchinson, 31 July 1901; Boer Proclamation by P. H. Kitzinger, November 1901, *Further Correspondence Relating to Affairs in South Africa, Cd. 903, 1902*, p. 137.

61 Kitchener Papers, PRO 30/57/22, Brodrick to Kitchener, 7 March 1902. Contrary to Kitchener's claims, hundreds of armed men were manning blockhouses in the west, midlands and northeast: ACG, R.A.13/1/H.9, Grenadier Guards, 3rd Battalion Records, entry for 31 June 1901; *Highland Light Infantry Chronicle*, 3/4, 3 (1901), pp. 652, 654; anonymous, 'The Relief of O'Okiep', *Royal Engineers Journal*, 2 (1903), p. 3; *Household Brigade Magazine*, 45, 4 (1901), p. 613.

62 Kitchener Papers, PRO 30/57/22, Brodrick to Kitchener, 22 March 1901.

63 G. H. L. Le May, *British Supremacy in South Africa, 1899–1907*, Oxford, 1965, p. 101.

64 CA, 1/JTN B1, Defence Force Orders, nos. 33–6, 17 Aug. 1902. Camp followers were paid 2s.6d. per day, and received a daily ration allowance valued at 1s.3d. Clothing was sometimes issued.

65 *Navy and Army Illustrated*, 13 Dec. 1899.

66 *Black People*, pp. 21–2.

67 *South African News*, 21 Aug. 1901; *Household Brigade Magazine*, 48, 4 (1901), pp. 806–7; 56, 5 (1902), p. 532.

68 ACG, A.103/2, Col. C. A. Codrington, Diary, 1902, entry for 24 March 1902.

69 RSR, Mss. 4/33, Beale Letters, Lt W. Beale to his sister, 30 Sept. 1901. For other accounts of the 'Scots Boys', see SGR/A.43, Maj. C. H. Willoughby, Blockhouse Notes, 1901–2, 25 Oct. 1901; SGR/A.44, Col. A. H. Royds, Blockhouse Standing Orders, 1901–2, 16 Feb. 1902; *Household Brigade Magazine*, 46, 4 (1901), p. 667.

70 NAM, 702/4/2/3/2, Royal Dragoons, Diary Letters, 1900–1902, entry for 30 Nov. 1901; *Lancashire Fusiliers Annual*, 11 (1901), p. 124.

71 NAM, 7510/30/2, Lt-Col. A. Perry, Service Diary, entry for 25 Jan. 1901.

72 CA, 1/AXA 6/3/1/4, 212/77, OC, 5th Royal Warwickshire, to RM, 11 Aug. 1901.

73 NAM, 6112/190/14, Col. H. Cooper to Staff Officers, Cape Colony No. 3 District, 30 Jan. 1902; 6112/190/6, Cooper, Confidential Letterbook, 1901–2, Cooper to Intelligence Sections (tel.), 17 Feb. 1902. One despatch rider, Moses Damara, 'a most financially-minded Christian', was able to draw as much as £12 per month, carrying despatches between Port Nolloth and Anenous during 1902: NAM, 6112/190/2, Capt. Christie to Cmdt, Steinkopf, 7 May 1902; Field Force Native Paylist, 25 March 1902.

74 NAM, 6807/186, Capt. S. L. Barry to Intelligence Officers (conf.), 5 Oct. 1901. Local mule drivers earned an average of £4.10s. per month.

75 Calculations from NAM, 6807/188, Barry to Intelligence, Middelburg, 27 Jan. 1901; 6112/190/5, Cooper to Intelligence, Calvinia, 16 Feb. 1901; RHF/D.127(2), Col. H. R. Kelham, 1st Battalion, Highland Light Infantry in South Africa, 1900–2, entry for 11 Dec. 1901; CA, 1/AXA 6/3/1/4, 211/76, Capt. N. Macdonald to RM, 15 Dec. 1901.

76 Girouard, a railway engineer, had been one of Kitchener's protégés in the Sudan, where he had worked

extensively with labour levies: Pakenham, *Boer War*, p. 454. He went on to become Governor of the East African Protectorate.

77 *CBBNA*, G.52-1901, pp. 2, 17; CA, 1/TAM 7/31, SM to Cmdt, 4 March 1902; Warwick, *Black People*, p. 133.

78 *CBBNA*, G.52-1901, pp. 21, 16. For revealing reports on conditions, see for example CA, 1/CMK 1/137, RM, Mount Ayliff District Report, 31 Jan. 1900; 1/CMK 1/139, RM, Umzimkulu District Report, 31 Mar. 1900; 1/TAM 9/10, SM to CC, 31 July 1900; USPG, Reports, Africa, E Series, St Luke's Mission Report, 31 Dec. 1899; 6384, St Thomas' Mission Report, 9 Dec. 1900; *South African News*, 21 Nov. 1900; *Umtata Herald*, 7 April 1900; *Cape Mercury*, 14 Aug. 1900; *Imvo Zabantsundu*, 17 Feb. 1900; *Izwi Labantu*, 20 March 1900; *Mission Field*, 532, 1900, p. 157; *Foreign Mission Chronicle*, 1, 2 (1900), pp. 64–5.

79 Beinart and Bundy, 'Introduction: "Away in the Locations"', in *Hidden Struggles*, p. 10.

80 CA, I/MBY 6/3/4, RM to Under Colonial Secretary, Statistical Branch, 5 Nov. 1901; NA 406, Folio 52, CC, Tulbagh, to SNA, 4 Feb. 1900; *Graaff-Reinet Advertiser*, 16 Jan. 1901; *Cape Mercury*, 15 Oct. 1901. In 1899, cash wages on Eastern Cape farms averaged 12s.6d. per month, while in other regions earnings fluctuated from 10s. to 20s.: M. Wilson and L. Thompson (eds.), *The Oxford History of South Africa*, vol. II, Oxford, 1971, pp. 122, 160.

81 *Thistle*, 6, 7 (1900), pp. 73–4; *Cape Hansard*, 1900, p. 25.

82 NAM, 6807/188, J. van Breede to Col. H. de Lisle, 16 Aug., 1901, encl. in de Lisle to Intelligence, Middelburg, 1 Sept. 1901.

83 *South African News*, 23 May 1900.

84 CA, 1/BED C1/1/6/1, Chief Const, Special Police, to RM, 14 April 1901; *South African News*, 10 Oct. 1900; *Diamond Fields Advertiser*, 29 May 1900.

85 *Cape Mercury*, 1 Jan. 1901.

86 CA, NA 633, RM, East London, to SNA, 30 May 1902.

87 *Cape Hansard*, 1900, p. 44; *Mossel Bay Advertiser*, 28 Dec. 1899.

88 SAL, Schreiner Papers, Folio 9, Letterbook, 1900, Schreiner to Milner, 8 Jan. 1900.

89 NAM, 7005/30, Sgt C. Drury, Diary of the Boer War, 1899–1900, entry for 21 Feb. 1900; 6807/187, Col. McCracken to Col. Hickman (conf.), 27 Jan. 1901; 6112/190/14, Col. Sullivan to SO, Namaqualand Field Force, 23 April 1901; 6810/1/19, Lt C. L. Veal, Diary of the Boer War, 1899–1901, entry for 6 Dec. 1900.

90 SAL, Schreiner Papers, No. 192, Schreiner to Capt. Hook, 7 Jan. 1900; NAM, 6807/187, Col. Sullivan to Intelligence, Middelburg, 16 Aug. 1900; *South African News*, 1 May 1901.

91 *Umtata Herald*, 21 Sept. 1901.

92 *Cape Mercury*, 3 July 1901.

93 By 1901 dock earnings had risen to a minimum of 3s.6d. and a maximum of 4s.6d. per day in Cape Town, while the Public Works Department paid from 2s.6d. to 3s.6d. per day, with the provision of rations and tents on site: CA, 1/TAM 7/31, RM to Cmdt, 27 May 1901; *Cape Times*, 6 Sept. 1901; *Midland News and Karoo Farmer*, 18 June 1901.

94 ACG, RO.14/9/17, Capt. E. Hanburey-Tracey, Diary, 1900–2, entry for 14 June 1901; CA, 1/BKE A/2/1/1, M. Kalodi to RM, 27 May 1900; 1/TAM 7/31, Cmdt to SM, 3 March 1902; 1/ALN 4/9/10, 1040/01, RM to Capt. Dickson (tel.), 3 July 1901.

95 See for example, CA, 1/BED C1/1/2/1, Deputy Admr to OC, Nesbitt's Horse, 11 Oct. 1901; *Oakleaf*, 11, 5, 1900, p. 184; *Cape Daily Telegraph*, 18 Jan. 1900.

96 NAM, 6807/187, RM, De Aar to Gen. Hart (conf.), 11 Sept. 1901; *Kings Royal Rifle Corps Chronicle* (1902), p. 33.

97 NAM, 6807/187, Capt. Christie to Col. T. E. Llewellyn, 16 April 1902.

98 CA, 1/BED C1/1/1/1, Deputy Admr to Cmdt, No. 3 Area, Grahamstown, 13 Feb. 1902; 1/ADE B1, Deputy Admr to Cmdt, Fort Beaufort, 3 April 1902.

99 *Household Brigade Magazine*, 44, 4, 1901, p. 547.

100 AGG, Lt Spencer Churchill, Diary, 1900, entry for 8 Nov. 1900.

101 CA, AG 786, J. A. van Zyl to Prime Minister, 5 Oct. 1900, encl. in SLD to SNA, 20 Oct. 1900.

102 Ibid., RM, Richmond, to SNA, 27 Oct. 1900.

103 Ibid., SNA to SLD, 23 Oct. 1900.

104 CA, 1/BKE A/2/1/1, CC, Rhodes, to RM, Barkly East, 28 Jan. 1901; 1/CWM 4/1/2/1, RM to SNA, 14 Feb. 1902; 1/TBH 5/1/4/4, RM to OC, Troops, Tulbagh, 7 Nov. 1900; 1/MBY 6/3/4, RM to SLD, 6 Nov. 1901; 1/HDP 5/1/1/2/4, Cmdt to RM, 10 May 1901.

105 CA, 1/SSE 8/103, W. M. Moolman to RM, 28 Feb. 1901.

106 CA, 1/CAL 4/1/1/3, W. Bain to M. Breda, 5 Aug. 1901.

107. CA, 1/ALN 1/4/01, N. J. de Wet to RM, 18 Nov. 1901. For further glimpses of such feeling, see, for example, CA, 1/FBG 4/1/8/1/17, A. Bell to CC, 8 March 1901; 1/BED Add. 1/1/2/2, Cmdt to RM, 4 Feb. 1901; 1/GR 6/84, J. W. Fowler to Chief Const, 27 April 1901; *Cape Mercury*, 17 July 1901; *South African News*, 4 Sept. 1901.

108 *Light Bob Gazette*, 2, 9 (1901), p. 17.

3 The politics of patriotism

1 *Vukani Bantu!*, p. 30.

2 *Cape Argus*, 20 Nov. 1897; *Cape Times*, 23 Nov. 1897; G. H. L. Le May, *British Supremacy in South Africa, 1899–1907*, Oxford, 1965, p. 16; J. S. Marais, *The Cape Coloured People, 1652–1937*, London, 1937, pp. 180–1, 235–7.

3 *Parliamentary Debates* (Commons), 4th Series, 77, 19 Oct. 1899.

4 Ibid. (Lords), col. 257, 1 Feb. 1900.

5 *Cape Mercury*, 8 Jan. 1901; *Cape Times*, 9 Jan. 1901; *Further Correspondence relating to Affairs in South Africa*, Cd. 547, 1901, p. 34.

6 *South African Spectator*, 20 April 1902. See also Lewis, *Between the Wire*, p. 15.

7 The most important standard works include P. Walshe, 'The Origins of African Political Consciousness in South Africa', *Journal of Modern African Studies*, 7, 4 (1969), pp. 598–602; *The Rise of African Nationalism in South Africa: The African National Congress, 1912–1952*, London, 1970, pp. 15–25. For more recent treatment, see Odendaal, *Vukani Bantu!*, pp. 30–9; Lewis, *Between the Wire*, pp. 15–16; Goldin, *Making Race*, pp. 19–20.

8 CO 417/266/27246, encl. 1 in Milner to Chamberlain, 20 Sept. 1899, resolutions passed at a meeting of Coloured Men, Cape Town, 6 Sept. 1899.

9 CO 48/543/31479, encl. 2 in Milner to Chamberlain, 24 Oct. 1899, A. Mangena and T. B. Skenjana to Milner, 3 Oct. 1899; LMS, Box 57, Folder 2, Revd W. B. Rubusana to Revd R. W. Thompson, 20 Jan. 1900.

10 CO 48/551/3277, encl. in Milner to Chamberlain, Petition from representatives of 100,000 Coloured inhabitants of Cape Colony, 5 Jan. 1900.

11 *St George's Gazette*, 17, 204 (1900), p. 181; *Naval and Military Record*, 22 Oct. 1901. For the establishment and aims of these bodies, see Lewis, *Between the Wire*, p. 17; Goldin, *Making Race*, p. 30.

12 NAM, 6707/53, Lt J. Walsh, Notebook, 1900, entry for 26 July 1900.

13 *Cape Times*, 17 Oct. 1900.

14 NAM, 7203/42/1, Royal Dragoons Regimental Diaries, entries for 15 Jan. 1900, 4 Dec. 1900; RAMC, 2/23/2, Col. H. M. Morton, Letters, 1901–2, Morton to his brother, 9 Jan. 1900; *Cape Daily Telegraph*, 13 July 1900; *Black and White Budget*, 28 July 1900.

15 *Imvo Zabantsundu*, 30 Oct. 1899.

16 See for example, *South African Spectator*, 25 Jan. 1902; 17 March 1902; 19 July 1902.

17 Ibid., 5 Oct. 1901.

18 Ibid., 31 May 1902. Peregrino and the Coloured People's Vigilance Society, which he had founded in 1901, were resentful of having to negotiate aid for Coloured refugees through the Native Affairs Department, which they regarded as a slight against their identity as a superior ethnic stratum: CA, NA 527, Folio 14, Petition of Coloured People's Vigilance Committee, 25 April 1902; van Heyningen,

'Refugees and Relief in Cape Town, 1899–1902', in C. Saunders and H. Phillips (eds.), *Studies in the History of Cape Town*, vol. III, Cape Town, 1980, p. 107. For discussion of Peregrino's interesting life and political career, see C. C. Saunders, 'F. Z. S. Peregrino and the "South African Spectator"', *Quarterly Bulletin of the South African Library*, 32, 3 (1978), pp. 81–90; Lewis, *Between the Wire*, pp. 16–20.

19 Odendaal, *Vukani Bantu!*, p. 11, describes J. T. Jabavu as 'the outstanding political figure of his place and time'. For other appraisals of his political life, see L. D. Ngcongco, 'John Tengo Jabavu, 1859–1921', in C. C. Saunders (ed.), *Black Leaders in Southern African History*, London, 1979, pp. 142–55; T. Karis and G. M. Carter (eds.), *From Protest to Challenge: A Documentary History of African Politics in South Africa*, vol. IV, *Political Profiles, 1882–1964*, Stanford, 1977.

20 *Imvo Zabantsundu*, 16 Oct. 1899.

21 Ibid., 20 Dec. 1899.

22 Ibid., 15 May 1900.

23 Ibid., 15 April 1900; 28 May 1900, 22 Feb. 1901.

24 Quoted in A. J. Lee, *The Origins of the Popular Press, 1855–1914*, London, 1976, p. 173.

25 Odendaal, *Vukani Bantu!*, pp. 13–14, 31–2; Ngcongco, 'John Tengo Jabavu', p. 151; Davenport, *Afrikaner Bond*, p. 185.

26 Alan Soga's militarism was renowned; he even took time off from editing *Izwi Labantu* to enlist temporarily in Brabant's Horse, coming under fire in the northern Cape: Odendaal, *Vukani Bantu!*, p. 31.

27 *Izwi Labantu*, 13 Aug. 1901; Denoon, 'Participation in the Boer War', p. 114.

28 *Cape Mercury*, 6 Jan. 1900; *Cape Daily Telegraph*, 8 Jan. 1900; *Izwi Labantu*, 28 Jan. 1900.

29 *Cape Daily Telegraph*, 23 Aug. 1900.

30 *Umtata Herald*, 16 Oct. 1900; 14 June 1900; 7 Feb. 1901; *Cape Mercury*, 8 July 1901; *Graaff-Reinet Advertiser*, 14 July 1901; *Imvo Zabantsundu*, 22 July 1901.

31 *Umtata Herald*, 21 Jan. 1900.

32 *Cape Mercury*, 22 Dec. 1899.

33 *Cape Mercury*, 4 Jan. 1900; 14 Jan. 1900.

34 Ibid., 30 Dec. 1899; *Imvo Zabantsundu*, 12 March 1900. Lord's grudging retraction appeared in several papers, including the *Cape Daily Telegraph* and *Umtata Herald*.

35 *Cape Mercury*, 16 Oct. 1900. For more in this genre, see also *Umtata Herald*, 25 Aug. 1900; *Diamond Fields Advertiser*, 12 June 1900.

36 *Imvo Zabantsundu*, 24 Jan. 1900.

37 SGR, P/A.36, Col. H. Pulteney, Staff Diary, 1901–2, entry for 3 Feb. 1900; *Thistle*, 9, 7 (1900), pp. 126–7.

38 CA, I/JTN B/I/I/I, Maj. J. Walter to RM, 10 Oct. 1900; *Household Brigade Magazine*, 37, 4 (1901), p. 30.

39 *Imvo Zabantsundu*, 3 Jan. 1900.

40 L. D. Ngcongco, 'Jabavu and the Anglo-Boer War', *Kleio*, 11, 2 (1970), p. 16.

41 *Imvo Zabantsundu*, 28 Jan. 1901. On the importance of temperance issues in Cape African politics, see W. G. Mills, 'The Roots of African Nationalism in The Cape Colony: Temperance, 1866–1898', *International Journal of African Historical Studies*, 13, 2 (1980), pp. 197–213.

42 *Izwi Labantu*, 27 Aug. 1901.

43 *South African Review*, 22 Aug. 1901. For similar comment, see *Umtata Herald*, 26 Aug. 1901; *Cape Argus*, 25 Aug. 1901; *Cape Daily Telegraph*, 22 Aug. 1901.

44 NAM, 7709/28, Lt J. Morgan, Diary, 1900, entry for 9 Sept. 1900.

45 *Lloyds Weekly Newspaper*, 28 April 1901.

46 NAM, 6807/189, 36/17, Lt Drury to RM, Alexandria, 22 July 1901; CA, I/BED CI/1/2, Cmdt to Drury (conf.), 7 Aug. 1901.

47 *Izwi Labantu*, 3 Sept. 1901.

48 NAM, 7607/49, Lt S. G. Francis, Letters and Diaries, Francis to unknown recipient, 27 Jan. 1901.

49 Examples from a large general literature on the background to Article Eight and state unification are R. Hyam, 'African Interests and the South Africa Act, 1908–1910', *Historical Journal*, 13, 1 (1970), pp. 85–105; 'British Imperial Policy and South Africa, 1906–1910', in Warwick (ed.), *South African War*, pp. 375–8; L. M. Thompson, *The Unification of South Africa, 1902–1910*, Oxford, 1960; G. B. Pyrah, *Imperial Policy and South Africa, 1902–1910*, Oxford, 1955; P. Lewsen, 'Merriman as Last Cape Prime Minister', *South African Historical Journal*, 7 (1975), pp. 65–9; for black political responses, Odendaal, *Vukani Bantu!*, pp. 37–9, 64–81; Lewis, *Between the Wire*, pp. 15–16, 34–63; Willan, *Sol Plaatje*, pp. 123–4, 139–42; R. E. van der Ross, *The Rise and Decline of Apartheid: A Study of Political Movements among the Coloured People of South Africa, 1880–1985*, Cape Town, 1986, pp. 22–55; P. Walshe and A. Roberts, 'Southern Africa', in A. D. Roberts (ed.), *Cambridge History of Africa*, vol. VII, Cambridge, 1986, p. 552.
50 '"A Voice in the Big House": The Career of Headman Enoch Mamba', in Beinart and Bundy, *Hidden Struggles*, p. 100.
51 *Ambiguities of Dependence*, pp. 60–1. See also, P. Maylam, *A History of the African People of South Africa: From the Early Iron Age to the 1970s*, Cape Town, 1986, pp. 154–6.
52 *Own War*, p. 15.
53 R. N. Price, 'Society, Status and Jingoism: The Social Roots of Lower Middle Class Patriotism, 1870–1900', in G. Crossick (ed.), *The Lower Middle Class in Britain, 1870–1914*, London, 1977, pp. 89–112; *An Imperial War and the British Working Class*, London, 1972, pp. 176, 241.

4 Arms and patriotism: town guards and district militia

1 *Green Howards Gazette*, 88, 8 (1900), p. 52.
2 *South African News*, 20 Oct. 1899; *Graaff-Reinet Advertiser*, 27 Oct. 1899. Johannes Job, one of Harmsworth's original recruits, commanded a detachment of the Klipdam guard until his capture and execution by Boers on 5 Dec. 1901. He was personally credited with having shot seven commandos: 1/KDM 3/1/1/7/6, RM to Assistant RM, 7 Dec. 1901.
3 LMS, South Africa, Letters, Box 58, Folder 3, Revd J. Brown to Revd W. Thompson, 26 Feb. 1900; *Black and White Budget*, 6 Dec. 1899.
4 CO 48/545/10422, encls. 6 and 24 in Milner to Chamberlain (secret), 14 March 1900, RM, Calvinia, to SLD, 6 March 1900, 7 March 1900; CO 48/543/13216, encl. 1 in Milner to Chamberlain (secret), 11 April 1900, Statement by F. Jooste, prisoner-of-war, 3 April 1900; *Graaff-Reinet Advertiser*, 20 March 1900.
5 CA, 1/CDP A/1/1/2, Ag RM to L. Louw, 16 Dec. 1899; Churchward Papers, Acc. 762(2)1–5, P. R. Churchward to G. Churchward, 15 Jan. 1900; *Light Bob Gazette*, 6, 9 (1901), p. 5; *Black and White Budget*, 26 May 1900; *Globe and Laurel*, 59, 7 (1900), p. 115; *Bandolier*, 2, 26 (1902), p. 14.
6 NMM, Porter Papers, PTR/6/2, A. Wills to J. R. Porter, 16 Nov. 1900.
7 CA, 1/GR 6/84, Ag RM to Gaoler, 14 Feb. 1901.
8 *South African News*, 18 Oct. 1899.
9 *Cape Daily Telegraph*, 18 Oct. 1899; *Midland News and Karoo Farmer*, 2 Nov. 1899.
10 NAM, 6807/186, Weekly Report of Capt. F. Barry (conf.), 15 Dec. 1899.
11 *Green Howards Gazette*, 90, 8 (1900), p. 101.
12 *South African News*, 29 May 1901.
13 *Graaff-Reinet Advertiser*, 6 March 1901.
14 RSR, du Moulin Papers, Intelligence Notebook, entry for 28 July 1900.
15 CA, 1/CDK 8/23, Intelligence Agt to Cmdt, 20 Feb. 1900; SGR, A/38/1, Capt. W. H. Nash, Diary, 1900–1, entry for 24 June 1900.
16 RSR, du Moulin Papers, Intelligence Notebook, entry for 12 Oct. 1900.
17 *Lloyds Weekly Newspaper*, 10, 17 March 1901. Following these clashes, headmen posted watchers with horns on the outskirts of Cradock, ready to sound the alarm in the event of further incursions.
18 *Imvo Zabantsundu*, 23 March 1901.

19 ACG, RO./23/8/3/3, Col. A. S. Henniker, Diary, entry for 12 March 1901. Cradock Africans were forced at gunpoint to accept Republican native passes: *South African News*, 6 March 1901.

20 ACG, RO./23/8/3/3, Heniker, Diary, entry for 20 April 1901; see also CA, 1/CDK 8/23, Cmdt to RM, Maraisburg, 23 April 1901.

21 CA, DD 1/66, 52/1901, Petition from Coloured men to assist in the Defence of Richmond, 3 April 1901; *Graaff-Reinet Advertiser*, 27 Feb. 1902.

22 NMM, Stokes Rees Paper, STR/6/3, Capt. F. Halkett to Lt O. Palmer, 9 Nov. 1899, encl. in W. Rees to R. Harris (conf.), 18 Dec. 1900.

23 AGG, R.16/H.15/3, Gurdon-Rebow Letters, Capt. Phillips to Lt W. Gurdon-Rebow, 2 Dec. 1899.

24 V. Bickford-Smith, 'Commerce, Class and Ethnicity in Cape Town, 1875–1902', Ph.D., University of Cambridge, 1989, p. 145.

25 RSR, du Moulin Papers, Intelligence Notebook, 1899–1901, entry for 7 Jan. 1900.

26 *Green Howards Gazette*, 88, 8 (1900), p. 77.

27 NAM, 7805/66/3, Dundas Papers, P. Bell to Lt J. R. Dundas, encl. in Dundas to C. Doondy, 22 March 1900.

28 CA, 1/UPT 5/3/1/1, SLD to RM, Upington, 26 Nov. 1899.

29 CA, 1/ADE B1, Letterbook, 1901–2, Confidential Circular from Admr, 12 Feb. 1901.

30 CA, 1/GR 6/84, Ag RM to Cmdt, 8 March 1901.

31 *South African News*, 22 Aug. 1900; *Globe and Laurel*, 69, 9 (1901), p. 74.

32 CA, 1/JTN B/1/1, Cape Colony District Orders, 3 Jan. 1902; District Mounted Troops and Town Guard Orders and Papers, February–July 1901; NAM, 6807/189, Notes on Town Garrison Native Specials, August, 1901.

33 Data drawn from: CA, 1/JTN B/1/1/2, Cape Colony, District Orders, No. 3 Region, 14 July 1901; NAM, 6112/190/3, Namaqualand Garrison Numerical Rolls, Garies Return, April 1902; ibid., Col. White to Col. Shelton (conf.), 17 April 1902; 6112/190/1/15, Col. Shelton to Gen. Settle (tel), No. 3411, 27 Feb. 1902; 6112/190/15, C.1/510565, Col. H. Cooper to Gen. French (secret), 21 April 1902; 6112/190/8, Col. Shelton to SO, Namaqualand Field Force, 7 May 1902; L. C. M. S. Amery (ed.), *The Times History of the War in South Africa 1899–1902*, vol. V, London, 1906, pp. 550–1; G. Tylden, *The Armed Forces of South Africa*, Frank Connock Publications No. 2, Africana Museum, Johannesburg, 1954, p. 118; J. M. Smalberger, *Aspects of the History of Copper Mining in Namaqualand, 1846–1931*, Cape Town, 1975, p. 111.

34 NAM, 5603/10, Col. H. F. N. Jourdain, Diaries, vol. VI, entry for 8 Aug. 1901; *South African News*, 20 Dec. 1899.

35 SGR, A.3/2, Lt C. H. Willoughby, Notes on Blockhouse Defences, 1901–2, Report on conversation with Sgt Donald, 22 Aug. 1900.

36 'European Scramble and Conquest', p. 758.

37 See for example, *Naval and Military Record*, 17 June 1900; *Globe and Laurel*, 75, 9 (1902), p. 6; *Cape Mercury*, 4 Jan. 1902.

38 ACG, RO.10/9/10, Digest of Movements, 1st Battalion, Coldstream Guards, January—March, 1902, Sgt A. Dye, entry for 12 Jan. 1902; *Suffolk Gazette*, 135 (June 1902), p. 62.

39 CA, 1/CDK 8/23, 2/66/00, RM to Col. Henderson, 19 April 1900; *Foreign Mission Chronicle*, 2, 4 (1901), p. 112

40 NAM, 6112/190/15, Col. White to Senior Naval Officer, Lambert's Bay, 26 March 1900.

41 NAM, 6112/190/14, Capt. A. Parker to Col. Cooper, 5 June 1900.

42 NAM, 6807/186, Capt. Barry to SO, Namaqualand Field Force, 5 Aug. 1900.

43 CA, 1/GR 14/90, Special Police Notebook, 1901, Collection of Natives for Town Companies, 19 June 1901.

44 CA, DD 7/13, Colonial Defence Force Orders, Nos. I and II, Instructions relating to European Town Guards and Coloured Town Guards, 27 April 1901; 7/15, Colonial Defence Department to Cmdt, No. 9 Area, Beaufort West, 19 July 1901.

45 NAM, 6807/187, Capt. Sloman to Intelligence Officer, Beaufort West, 28 Jan. 1901, 2 Aug, 1901.

46 RHF/D.128/(3), Col. H. R. Kelham, Service Diaries, vol. II, entry for 13 Aug. 1901; *Highland Light Infantry Chronicle*, 3/4, 8 (1901), p. 583.
47 NAM, 6807/187, Capt. Halse to Col. B. Donovan, 24 April 1901.
48 NAM, 600/45/4, Lt P. Mitford, Diary, 1901, entry for 20 Jan. 1901.
49 *Naval and Military Record*, 8 March 1901.
50 *Household Brigade Magazine*, 45, 4 (1901), pp. 621–2.
51 *South African News*, 22 Aug. 1900.
52 NAM, 6807/186, Col. Levey to Capt. Barry, 19 Sept. 1900.
53 'Another Victorian Paradox: Anti-Militarism in a Jingoistic Society', *Historical Reflections*, 8, 2 (1981), p. 171; P. Morton, 'The New Police Historiography' (review article), *Historical Reflections*, 12, 1 (1985), pp. 307–9; see also H. Cunningham, *The Volunteer Force: A Social and Political History 1859–1908*, London, 1975, pp. 75–8; R. Reinders, 'Militia and Public Order in Nineteenth Century America', *Journal of American Studies*, 2, 1 (1977), pp. 96–7.
54 *Navy and Army Illustrated*, 23 Aug. 1901.
55 *Lloyds Weekly Newspaper*, 6 Jan. 1901.
56 CA, 1/AXA 5/2/2/1. Capt. B. Sullivan to Ag RM, 18 Sept. 1901.
57 NAM, 6112/190/8, Capt. A. Parker to Col. Shelton, 17 May 1901.
58 *South African News*, 16 Jan. 1901. 180 railway guards were enrolled at Cradock and 220 at Willowmore.
59 *Navy and Army Gazette*, 19 April 1901.
60 *South African News*, 16 Jan. 1901.
61 NAM, 6112/190/1, Col. Cooper to Gen. French (conf.), 4 May 1902.
62 'Colonial Africa and Its Armies', in B. Bond and I. Roy (eds.), *War and Society*, vol. II, London, 1977, p. 31.
63 RHF/D.129(1), Kelham, Service Diaries, vol. I, entry for 15 Feb. 1901; *Highland Light Infantry Chronicle*, 3/4, 8 (1901), p. 661.
64 *Globe and Laurel*, 69, 9 (1901), p. 64.
65 CA, 1/ALN 4/9/7, Special Police Notebook, entry for 27 April 1901; NAM, 5603/10, Jourdain Diaries, vol. VII, entry for 7 Oct. 1901; see also NAM, 7208/73, W. G. Ransley, 'On Service, or Barracks, Bivouacs and Battles: Being Some Experiences in the Army as a Soldier and Scripture Reader', ms. typescript. Ransley recorded the importance of regalia to African town guards, as a means not only of providing a touch of glamour to company drill, but as a mark of group identification. Feathers, coloured handkerchiefs and brass buttons were all used by different garrisons as unofficial insignia.
66 See, for example, *Highland Light Infantry Chronicle*, 3/4, 8 (1901), p. 660.
67 NAM, 6112/190/7, Col. Cooper to Col. Donald, 3 April 1902.
68 *Black and White Budget*, 9 Dec. 1900.
69 *Highland Light Infantry Chronicle*, 6, 9 (1902), p. 766.
70 NAM, 6112/190/15, Gen. Settle to Gen. French (conf.), 4 April 1902.
71 Ibid., Col. Cooper, circular (conf.), 26 March 1902.
72 *South African News*, 6 March 1901; *Midland News*, 19 Feb. 1901.
73 LMS, Box 58, Folder 3, Revd J. Brown to Revd W. Thompson, 14 Nov. 1900; *Graaff-Reinet Advertiser*, 12 Aug. 1901.
74 *Graaff-Reinet Advertiser*, 20 March 1901.
75 NAM, 6112/190/14, Capt. A. K. Taunton to Shelton, 28 April 1902; CA, 1/SBK 3/1/3, Evidence of Trooper M. Dixon to Inquest Proceedings, 7 May 1902.
76 *Graaff-Reinet Advertiser*, 16 Jan. 1901; *Cape Mercury*, 21 July 1901.
77 CA, 1/ADE B1, Martial Law Admr's Letterbook, 1901–2, Admr to RM, 21 Jan. 1902.
78 CA, 1/BED C1/1/2/1, Deputy Admr to Nesbitt's Horse, 20 Dec. 1900.
79 CA, 1/GR 4/90, Police Station Notebook, entry for 2. Nov. 1900; *Graaff-Reinet Advertiser*, 13 Jan. 1901.
80 CA, 1/GR 6/84, Ag RM to Chief Const, 12 Feb. 1901; see also, 1/GR 4/90, Police Station Notebook,

Orders for Special Duties in collecting Native Boys for the Military, entries for 19 June 1901, 2 July 1901, 19 Sept. 1901.

81 NAM, 6807/186, Capt. H. S. Sloman to Capt. C. Fay, 26 Feb. 1901.

82 *Globe and Laurel*, 69, 9 (1901), p. 74.

83 Ibid., p. 72. It is interesting to note that at the beginning of the Spanish Civil War Madrid domestic workers were used to staff clothing workshops set up to supply republican militias; Fraser, *Blood of Spain*, p. 290.

84 CA, DD 7/13, Draft Orders, Coloured Companies, 2 April 1901.

85 CA, 1/ADE 5/2/2/1, Assistant RM to SO, Namaqualand Field Force (conf.), 2 Jan. 1902.

86 CA, 1/JTN B1, Col. T. H. Lukin, Divisional Orders No. 9, No. 1 Division, Cape Colony, 13 March 1901.

87 RSR, Mss. 4/34/1–43/3, Beale Papers, Native Pay Slips, November–December 1901.

88 *Naval and Military Record*, 8 Nov. 1900.

89 CA, 1/GR 6/84, Ag RM to Chief Const., 12 Feb. 1901.

90 CA, 1/AXA 6/3/1/5, 2/692/02, Ag RM to Under Colonial Secretary, 15 Jan. 1902.

91 ACG, RO./23/8/3/3, Henniker, Diary, entry for 11 Nov. 1900.

92 *South African News*, 14 Feb. 1900.

93 CA, 1/BED Add. 1/2/2/1, Col. Haig to Cmdt, Bedford (conf.), 10 June 1901; AGG, 1st Battalion, Grenadier Guards, Order Books, vol. III, 1900, entry for 7 March 1900; *Rifle Brigade Chronicle*, 1901, p. 86.

94 NAM, 6001/45/4, Mitford, Diary, entry for 17 May 1901; *South African News*, 17 April 1901; *Imvo Zabantsundu*, 12 April 1901.

95 CA, 1/AXA 6/3/1/5, 2/768/00, Ag RM to Under Colonial Secretary, 15 Jan. 1900.

96 CA, 1/SSE 12/12, Cmdt, Middelburg, to Ag RM (conf.), 9 Sept. 1901.

97 *Lloyds Weekly Newspaper*, 19 Sept. 1901.

98 *Cape Hansard*, 1902, pp. 177–8.

99 See J. M. Winter, *The Great War and the British People*, London, 1986, pp. 30–3.

100 C. Steedman, *Policing the Victorian Community*, London, 1984, pp. 3–4.

101 NAM, 7304/29/25, Hopwood Letters, Cpl H. Hopwood to family, 17 Nov. 1900.

5 Moving Lord Kitchener: military transport and supply work

1 RSR, Mss. 1/98, P. Mahlungu to Lt B. F. Fletcher, 22 Aug. 1900.

2 Preface, *South African Peasantry*, 2nd edn, Cape Town, 1988.

3 'Agrarian Social Structure and Rural Class Relations: Class Struggle in the Orange Free State and the Transvaal, *c*. 1890–1920', *Rural Africana*, 4–5 (1979), p. 88.

4 T. Keegan, 'Trade, Accumulation and Impoverishment: Mercantile Capital and the Economic Transformation of Lesotho and the Conquered Territory, 1870–1920', *Journal of Southern African Studies*, 12, 2 (1986), p. 211.

5 Sir J. Fortescue, *The Royal Army Service Corps*, vol. I, Cambridge, 1930, pp. 229–65; Pakenham, *Boer War*, pp. 318–19.

6 D. Porch, 'Military History' (review article), *Historical Journal*, 24, 4 (1981), p. 986.

7 *Bugle*, 19, 2 (1900), p. 7; *Rifle Brigade Chronicle* (1900), p. 207; *Navy and Army Gazette*, 20 April 1901.

8 *Administration of the Army Remount Department, 1899–1902: Proceedings of Court of Enquiry, 1902, Cd. 993*, p. 363; *Umtata Herald*, 5 May 1900; *Naval and Military Record*, 15 Nov. 1900; *Morning Post*, 24 April 1901.

9 *Light Bob Gazette*, 5, 8 (1900), p. 5.

10 C. N. Connolly, 'Class, Birthplace, Loyalty: Australian Attitudes to the Boer War', *Historical Studies*, 71, 18 (1978), pp. 221–2; Trapido, 'African Political Organisation, p. 104; *Cape Mercury*, 6 Jan. 1900; *St George's Gazette*, 19, 218 (1901), p. 234. For the mythology of colonial Australian 'bushmen', see

R. Pascoe, *The Manufacture of Australian History*, Oxford, 1979, pp. 13–14; M. Taussig, 'An Australian Hero', *History Workshop Journal*, 24 (1987), pp. 120–3.

11 van Onselen, 'The Main Reef Road into the Working Class: Proletarianisation, Unemployment, and Class Consciousness amongst Johannesburg's Afrikaner Poor, 1890–1914', in *Studies*, vol. II: *New Nineveh*, p. 121; see also F. A. Johnstone, *Class, Race and Gold*, London, 1976, pp. 52–3.

12 Warwick, *Black People*, p. 21.

13 *Black and White Budget*, Transvaal Special, Dec. 1899, p. 4.

14 NAM, 7708/42/7, Lt S. M. Rowlandson, Service Diary, 1900, entry for 26 June 1900.

15 ACG, RO.10/9/10/22, 1st Battalion, Digest of Movements, entries for 15 March 1902, 13 April 1902; RO.8/4/18, Col. C. A. Codrington, Diary, entry for 22 April 1902.

16 See for instance, *Mission Field*, 529 (1900), pp. 27–8, 92; *Primitive Methodist Quarterly Review*, 22 (1900), p. 572; *Foreign Mission Chronicle of the Episcopal Church in Scotland*, 2, 3 (1902), pp. 26–8.

17 P. Carstens, *The Social Structure of a Cape Coloured Reserve: A Study of Racial Integration and Segregation in South Africa*, Cape Town, 1966, p. 37; M. J. Price, 'Leliefontein: History and Structure of a Coloured Mission Community, 1870–1913', B.A. Hons dissertation, University of Cape Town, 1976, p. 19.

18 CA, SGE 5/116, Revd J. Lundie to M. Solomon, 8 Nov. 1899; SGE 2/74, Report on Wesleyan Mission School, Naauwpoort, 1 Nov. 1900.

19 CA, 1/CAL 5/1/3/3/3, CC to Capt. O. Black, 6 Jan. 1900; 1/BRE 4/1/3/2/2, RM to SO, Remounts, Stellenbosch, 12 July 1901; *South African News*, 1 Nov. 1900.

20 *Mission Field*, 549 (1901), p. 340. Hunting-dog packs were popularly known among troops as 'bobberies'. It was common practice for soldiers to hire 'bobberies' from workers, paying in cash or game: *Green Howards Gazette*, 92, 8 (1900), p. 141.

21 *Mission Field*, 531 (1900), p. 92.

22 Bundy, *South African Peasantry*, pp. 76–7; D. M. Goodfellow, *A Modern Economic History of South Africa*, London, 1931, p. 122; S. T. van der Horst, *Native Labour in South Africa*, Oxford, 1942, pp. 105–6.

23 CA, 1/CMK 1/137, RM, Mount Ayliff, District Report, 31 Jan. 1900; 1/CMK 1/139, RM, Umzimkulu, District Report, 31 March 1900; 1/TAM 9/10, SM to CC, 31 July 1900; *Mission Field*, 532 (1900), p. 157; *Foreign Mission Chronicle*, 1, 2 (1900), pp. 64–5; *Umtata Herald*, 7 April 1900; *Imvo Zabantsundu*, 12 March 1900.

24 See, for instance, USPG, Reports Africa, E Series Mss., St Luke's Mission Report, 31 Dec. 1899.

25 *CBBNA*, G.52–1901, pp. 16, 21.

26 P. Warwick, 'African Labour during the South African War 1899–1902', *Collected Seminar Papers on the Societies of Southern Africa in the 19th and 20th Centuries*, vol. VII, Institute of Commonwealth Studies, University of London, 1977, p. 110.

27 CA, 1/TAM 7/31, SM to Cmdt, 4 March 1902; *CBBNA* G.52–1901, pp. 2, 17.

28 *Mission Field*, 549 (1901), pp. 339–40.

29 CA, 1/UIT 16/33, 186/07, Native Inspector's Notebook, entry for 29 Jan. 1901; *Cape Times*, 24 Oct. 1900; *Cape Mercury*, 18 Feb. 1901; *Mossel Bay Advertiser*, 29 Jan. 1901.

30 Warwick, *Black People*, p. 137.

31 *CBBNA*, G.25–1902, pp. 21–2, 31, 33; Warwick, *Black People*, p. 137.

32 CA, 1/BED C1/1/1/2, OC Remounts to Cmdt, 17 Jan. 1900; 1/ADE, B/1, Admr's Report, 18 Jan. 1902; *Umtata Herald*, 3 Feb. 1900.

33 *Cape Daily Telegraph*, 31 July 1900; *Umtata Herald*, 27 Jan. 1900; *Basutoland Annual Report, 1900–1901, Cd. 788–13*, pp. 33, 38; 'Sport with the Army in South Africa', *Bailey's Magazine*, 494, 74 (1901), pp. 281–2.

34 CA, 1/BED C1/1/4/1, Area Admr to Col. Hewett (tel.), 15 Jan. 1901; *Thistle*, 6, 7 (1900), p. 77; *Oakleaf*, 11, 4 (1901), p. 184.

35 CA, 1/BED Add. 1/1/2/2, Cmdt to Martial Law Admr, 20 Jan. 1901; *Cape Daily Telegraph*, 17 April 1900; *Cape Mercury*, 30 Jan. 1901.

36 *Lancashire Fusiliers Annual*, 1901, p. 154.
37 *CBBNA*, G.25–1902, p. 6; G.29–1903, p. 10.
38 CA, 1/BED Add. 1/1/2/2. Cmdt's Martial Law Notices, No. 3, 7 Nov. 1901; *CBBNA*, G.25–1902, p. 8; Bundy, 'The Transkei Peasantry, *c.* 1890–1914: "Passing through a period of stress"', in R. Palmer and N. Parsons (eds.), *The Roots of Rural Poverty in Central and Southern Africa*, London, 1977, p. 207.
39 *Naval and Military Record*, 19 Feb. 1900, 11 Apr. 1901.
40 *Navy and Army Illustrated*, 28 Sept. 1901.
41 AGG, R.15/H.19/3, Battalion Order Books, vol. III, 1901, entry for 12 Nov. 1901; *Household Brigade Magazine*, 49, 4 (1901), p. 197.
42 CA, 1/BED C/1/1/5/1, 3/18/02, Deputy Admr to Remount Agt, 22 Jan. 1902.
43 ACG, RO.10/1/22, Digest of 1st Battalion Movements, entry for 22 Feb. 1902.
44 NAM, 6112/190/15, Capt. C. B. Macdonald to Col. White, 17 March 1902; *South African News*, 6 June 1900.
45 *Cape Times*, 23 Aug. 1901.
46 *Rifle Brigade Chronicle* (1901), p. 48.
47 P. Scully, 'Whining farmers: Stellenbosch District, 1870–1900', unpublished postgraduate seminar paper, Department of History, University of Cape Town, 1985.
48 *Albert Times and Molteno Advertiser*, 22 Oct. 1900; *Mossel Bay Advertiser*, 14 March 1901.
49 See NAM, 7510/30/2, Capt. A. Perry, Service Diary, entry for 29 March 1900; AGG, 7th and 8th Companies, Native Labour Roll Books and Pay Slips, Sections 1–4, 15 Jan. 1900 to 15 May 1900; CA, NA 496, folio 102, Senior Veterinary Officer to SNA, 10 Jan. 1902; 1/CAL 5/1/3/3/3, 11/24/99, RM to Col. Bridge, 31 Dec. 1899; 1/TAM 7/31, RM to SM, 24 March 1902; 1/GSD 6/6, Table of Wages, rations and clothing, 6 July 1901.
50 On workplace injuries, see RAMC, Porter Papers, Medical Officer's Order Book, Cape Colony, entries for January–March 1900; Mss. 2/80, No. 11 General Hospital Record Book, 1900–2, Mss. 7/5, No. 6 General Hospital Casualty Registers, 1901–2; CA, 1/CMK 2/12, 17011/423, CM to SNA, 2 April 1901.
51 *Light Bob Gazette*, 6, 9 (1901), p. 11.
52 *Navy and Army Gazette*, 14 Aug. 1900.
53 CA, NA 500, folio 103, E. Stubbs to SNA, 31 Dec. 1901.
54 India Office Library, Military Files, South Africa, IOL/MIL/7/L5620, OC Cape Colony (Western District), to OC Natal (conf.), 30 May 1900.
55 CA, NA 500, folio 103, SO, Remounts, to SNA, 14 Jan. 1902.
56 W. Beinart, '"Jamani"': Cape Workers in German Southwest Africa, 1904–12', in Beinart and Bundy, *Hidden Struggles*, p. 184.
57 For the Mvuso affair, see CA, 1/CMT 3/68, Lt J. W. Flemmer to OC, Remounts, Bowker's Park, 22 Oct. 1901; Statement by Chief Mvuso Matanzima, 3 Jan. 1902; Major C. Etheridge, Statement re: Native Labour at Bowker's Park, 4 Jan. 1902; NA 496, Folio 92, F. J. Evens to SNA, 5 Jan. 1902; Etheridge to Acting SO, Remounts, Eastern, 2 Feb. 1902.
58 CA, NA 500, folio 879, RM, Engcobo, to SNA, 12 Dec. 1900.
59 Pakenham, *Boer War*, p. 420.
60 WSCRO, Maxse Papers, 50, Lt-Col. F. A. Maxse to H. A. Wyndham, 31 May 1900.
61 For colourful accounts of nineteenth- and twentieth-century animal transportation, see J. F. Victorin, *Travels in the Cape, The Years 1853–1855*, Cape Town, 1968 edn; S. P. Hyatt, *The Northward Trek*, London, 1909, pp. 185–6, 196–7; *The Old Transport Road*, London, 1914; H. V. Morton, *In Search of South Africa*, London, 1948, pp. 81–4, 358; W. Steenkamp, *Land of the Thirst King*, Cape Town, 1975, pp. 121–4.
62 For typical work descriptions, see RAMC, Maidment Deposit, Mss. 1/1011, Pte C. G. Maidment, Diary, 1899–1901, entry for 19 Oct. 1901; *Suffolk Gazette*, 134 (1901), p. 84; *Morning Post*, 17 April 1901; *St George's Gazette*, 20, 234 (1902), p. 116.

63 *Highland Light Infantry Chronicle*, 2, 16 (1900), p. 514. For a British analogy, see P. Bagwell, *The Transport Revolution since 1770*, London, 1974, p. 35.

64 *Highland Light Infantry Chronicle*, 2, 16 (1900), p. 528.

65 For wages and service benefits, see for example, CA, 1/SBK 4/2/1, 1/52/01, RM to OC, Transport, Kimberley, 24 Aug. 1901; NA 500, Folio 132, Capt. C. H. Bridge, memo, Oct. 1899; *Black and White Budget*, 7 April 1900; *Oakleaf*, 11, 6 (1900), p. 185; *Light Bob Gazette*, 10, 8 (1900), p. 6; *Official Records of the Guards Brigade in South Africa*, London, 1904, p. 143.

66 AIG, Douglas-Scott Letters, Capt. H. M. Douglas-Scott to Earl of Kerry, 13 July 1902.

67 CA, 1/BED C/1/1/2/1, OC, 3rd Battery, RFA, to Cmdt, 17 Dec. 1901.

68 WSCRO, Maxse Papers, 333, Senior Transport Officer to Col. Maxse, 3 April 1901.

69 NAM, 6807/186, Folio 7, Transport Documents, memo on transport funds, 1 May 1901.

70 NAM, 6112/190/14, SO to Capt. Macdonald, 6 May 1901.

71 NMM, STR/6, Stokes Rees Papers, Cmdr R. Harris, *Minute* No. 128, 11 April 1901, encl. in Naval Brigade Transport Orders, Colesberg, March–July 1901.

72 CA, 1/CMK 2/51, CM to OC, Pietermaritzburg, 18 Sept. 1900; 1/KMN 11/3, RM to OC, 5th Lancers, 5 Nov. 1900; *Foreign Mission Chronicle*, 2, 1 (1901), p. 29; *Mission Field*, 549 (1901), pp. 339–40.

73 *Thistle*, 9, 7 (1900), p. 118.

74 RAMC, Mss. 1/162, Hewitt Letters, Lt E. C. Hewitt to Col. J. Capson, 5 April 1901; *Lancashire Fusiliers Annual*, 11 (1901), p. 163.

75 *Kings Royal Rifle Corps Chronicle*, 1901, p. 38.

76 NAM, 7709/43/98, Lloyd Letters, Lt T. N. Lloyd to Capt. E. Cottingham, 28 Nov. 1900.

77 LHC, Aston Papers, 6/1, P. Aston to I. Aston, 12 May 1900; Capt. P. A. Clive, Diaries, vol. III, entry for 11 April 1901; NAM, 7503/82, Lt E. Craig-Brown, Diary, entry for 11 June 1901; *Navy and Army Gazette*, 11 May 1901.

78 *Black and White Budget*, 3 Feb. 1900.

79 *Rifle Brigade Chronicle* (1901), p. 187; *Household Brigade Magazine*, 56, 5 (1902), p. 531.

80 *Household Brigade Magazine*, 55, 5 (1902), p. 440.

81 H. J. Whigham, 'The First Stage of the Boer War', *Scribner's Magazine*, 27, 2 (1900), p. 212; *Navy and Army Illustrated*, 7 Sept. 1901; *Highland Light Infantry Chronicle*, 1, 3 (1900), p. 522; *Black and White Budget*, 3 Dec. 1901.

82 'The African Musician and the Development of the Johannesburg Entertainment Industry, 1900–1960', *Journal of Southern African Studies*, 5, 2 (1979), p. 142; D. Coplan, 'The Emergence of an African Working Class Culture', in Marks and Rathbone (eds.), *Industrialisation*, pp. 359–60; *In Township Tonight!: South Africa's Black City Music and Theatre*, Johannesburg, 1985, pp. 13–14.

83 See J. L. Hanna, 'African Dance and the Warrior Tradition', *Journal of Asian and African Studies*, 12, 1–4 (1977), pp. 124–5; M. E. Page, 'The Great War and *Chewa* Society in Malawi', *Journal of Southern African Studies*, 6, 2 (1980), p. 181; A. Clayton and D. C. Savage, *Government and Labour in Kenya, 1895–1963*, London, 1974, p. 181; J. Iliffe, *A Modern History of Tanganyika*, Cambridge, 1979, pp. 238–9. They are perhaps also reminiscent of the mixture of colonial and military-based mockery and aspiration in West African carnivalesque: D. Birmingham, 'Carnival at Luanda', *Journal of African History*, 29, 1 (1988), p. 99.

84 *Rifle Brigade Chronicle* (1901), p. 185.

85 C. van Onselen, 'The Witches of Suburbia: Domestic Service on the Witwatersrand, 1890–1914', in *Studies*, vol. II: *New Nineveh*, p. 39.

86 *Kings Royal Rifle Corps Chronicle* (1901), p. 37.

87 K. Thomas, 'Work and Leisure in Pre-Industrial Society', *Past and Present*, 29 (1964), p. 53; see also W. F. Mandle, 'Games People Played: Cricket and Football in England and Victoria in the Late Nineteenth Century', *Historical Studies*, 15 (1973), p. 523; K. A. P. Sandiford, 'Cricket and Victorian Society', *Journal of Social History*, 17, 2 (1983), p. 305.

88 T. Couzens, 'An Introduction to the History of Football in South Africa', in Bozzoli (ed.), *Town and Countryside*, p. 200.

89 NAM, 7208/8, Paterson Letters, Cpl J. Paterson to his brother, 11 May 1901.
90 NAM, 6112/190/15, Capt. Macdonald to SO, 2 July 1900.
91 See D. Rubinstein, 'Cycling in the 1890s', *Victorian Studies*, 21, 1 (1977), p. 59; H. Cunningham, *Leisure in the Industrial Revolution, c. 1780–1880*, London, 1980, pp. 135–6.
92 'Time, Work Discipline and Industrial Capitalism', *Past and Present*, 38 (1967), p. 73.
93 NAM, 7802/4/2, Cobb Letters, Col. R. S. S. Cobb to Spl Agt, Kenhardt, 17 Nov. 1900.
94 NAM, 6112/190/15, Capt. MacDonald to Col. Sullivan, 4 July 1900. 'Cape Smoke' was a notorious crude brandy, distilled mainly in the Western Cape: see 'Cape Viticulture', *Chambers's Journal*, 142, 2 (1900), pp. 665–6.
95 *Oxfordshire Light Infantry Chronicle* (1901), p. 47.
96 *Green Howards Gazette*, 92, 8 (1900), p. 143; *Rifle Brigade Chronicle* (1901), p. 85.
97 *Household Brigade Magazine*, 51, 5 (1902), p. 204.
98 'Work Discipline', p. 60.
99 NAM, 6112/190/5, Capt. Ross to Col. White, 15 Nov. 1901.
100 *Light Bob Gazette*, 2, 9 (1901), p. 9.
101 In addition to leave on full pay, auxiliaries serving as witnesses in lengthy trials received a daily extra-duty stipend and could even earn additional money doing small transport jobbing between trial sessions: see chapter 8.
102 Such as Mathew Thomas, who on 4 April 1901 drove a fully laden munitions cart into a mounted commando, scattering them and capturing four: *Morning Post*, 20 April 1901.
103 See *Globe and Laurel*, 59, 7 (1900), p. 115; *Household Brigade Magazine*, 43, 4 (1901), pp. 461–2.
104 NMM, Mss. 72/3, Limpus Papers, Occasional war notes, 1900–1.
105 CA, 1/TAM 7/28, RM, Cofimvaba to SM, 12 July 1901; DD 7/12, Capt. W. J. Gray to SO, Porterville Road, 15 Aug. 1901; 1/ALN 4/9/8, Capt. A. S. Whiteley to RM, 23 March 1901; 1/CMT 3/9 Statement on Alleged Ill-treatment of Natives at Remount Stations, 11 April 1901.
106 *Oakleaf*, 8, 5 (1900), p. 149.
107 *Household Brigade Magazine*, 43, 4 (1901), pp. 461–2.
108 *Globe and Laurel*, 59, 7 (1900), p. 115.
109 *Light Bob Gazette*, 8, 3 (1900), p. 5; *Lloyds Weekly Newspaper*, 2 Aug. 1900.
110 '"Jamani"', p. 172.
111 For these and similar cases, see ACG, RO.46/1/139, Court Martial Record Books, 1900–1901; RSR, Mss. 1/115, Battalion Punishment Books, vol. II, 1901; *Household Brigade Magazine*, 43, 4 (1901), pp. 461–2; *Light Bob Gazette*, 6, 9 (1901), pp. 8, 11.
112 *Light Bob Gazette*, 6, 9 (1901), p. 11.
113 CA, 1/TAM 7/27 W. D. Soga to SM, 13 March 1900; for similar appeals, see 1/TAM 7/3, 7/29, J. Ngeani to SM, 17 April 1900; J. Seretlo to SM, 25 May 1900.
114 NAM, 7805/66/4, Maj. J. R. Dundas, Letters, Dundas to his wife, 10 Nov. 1900.
115 One of the key themes of their *Hidden Struggles*.
116 NAM, 6807/187, Capt. T. E. Llewellyn to OC, Cheshire Regiment, 11 April 1902; see also *CBBNA*, G.25–1902, pp. 21–2.
117 CA, 1/UIT 16/33, RM to Acting RM, Bredasdorp, 4 Jan. 1903; 1/TBH G/1/1/1, RM to OC, Cheshire Regiment, 4 March 1902; *Berliner Missions Jahresbericht*, 79 (1902), p. 29.
118 *Making Race*, p. 27.
119 As used notably by J. G. Rule, *The Experience of Labour in Eighteenth Century Industry*, London, 1981, esp. ch. 8.
120 NAM, 6807/187, Capt. H. S. Sloman to W. H. Wayland, 19 Nov. 1901.

6 The Republican guerrilla war in the countryside

1 AGG, RO.14/9/16, Lt C. H. Massey, Diary, 1900–2, entry for 19 March 1902.
2 NAM, 7704/5/56, Lt J. S. Preston, Letters, Preston to his mother, 18 Feb. 1901. For similar denials, see

NAM, 6807, 187, Col. J. Kavanagh to J. Gibson, 11 Jan. 1902; 6807/193, Col. Crabbe to Lt Williams, 16 Aug. 1900; Cmdt Opperman to Capt. S. L. Barry, 23 Oct. 1901; *St George's Gazette*, 227, 19 (1901), p. 194.

3 *Oxfordshire Light Infantry Chronicle* (1900), pp. 138–9.

4 NAM, 6807/190/19, Cmdt Conroy to Lt Wheeler, 8 Feb. 1902, encl. in Maj. Kirkpatrick to Gen. French, 21 Feb. 1902.

5 Smuts to W. T. Stead, 4 Feb. 1902, in W. K. Hancock and J. van der Poel (eds.), *Selections from the Smuts Papers*, vol. I, Cambridge, 1966, p. 485.

6 F. Pretorius, *The Anglo-Boer War 1899–1902*, Cape Town, 1985, p. 79; cf. also his earlier 'Life on Commando', in Warwick (ed.), *South African War*, p. 113.

7 *Under the Union Jack*, 24 Jan. 1900.

8 *Black and White Budget*, 2 June 1900.

9 *Under the Union Jack*, 27 Dec. 1899.

10 *Oxfordshire Light Infantry Chronicle* (1902), p. 83.

11 NAM, 6807/187, Col. Calwell to R. H. Massie, 24 April 1902.

12 *Cape Daily Telegraph*, 23 April 1900.

13 NAM, 7802/4/2, Col. R. S. S. Cobb, Anglo-Boer War Letters, Cobb to Spl Agt, Middelburg, Oct.–Nov. 1899.

14 Bundy, 'Vagabond Hollanders', p. 117; I. Hofmeyr, 'Building a Nation from Words: Afrikaans Language, Literature and Ethnic Identity, 1902–24', in Marks and Trapido (eds.), *Politics of Race*, p. 96.

15 ACG, RO.10/9/10, Pte A. Dye, Digest of Movements of the 1st Battalion, 1899–1901, entry for 24 Nov. 1899.

16 RHF/D.124/45544(i), Col. H. R. Kelham, Records of the 1st Battalion, entry for 6 July 1900.

17 Ibid., entry for 23 July 1900.

18 *Green Howards Gazette*, 101, 9 (1901), p. 93. For other examples, see *St George's Gazette*, 20, 218 (1901), p. 51; *Naval and Military Record*, 11 April 1901.

19 *Light Bob Gazette*, 6, 8 (1900), pp. 4–5.

20 NAM, 6112/190/14, Maj. Porter to Col. Cooper, 5 Feb. 1902; RSR, Mss. 1/98, Boer Letters, W. Lubbe to B. de Klerk, 29 Dec. 1899; W. Bekker to Gen. Malan, 19 Oct. 1901.

21 T. Shearing, 'Coloured Involvement in the South African War in the Cape Colony', *Quarterly Bulletin of the South African Library*, 40, 1 (1985), pp. 9–10.

22 See Warwick, *Black People*, p. 11; B. McLennan, *A Proper Degree of Terror: John Graham and the Cape's Eastern Frontier*, Johannesburg, 1986, p. 26.

23 P. Delius and S. Trapido, '*Inboekselings* and *Oorlams*: The Creation and Transformation of a Servile Class', *Journal of Southern African Studies*, 8, 2 (1982), p. 239.

24 NAM, 6807/187, Lt J. R. Gibson, Intelligence Reports on Native Followers, 26 Dec. 1901, 7 Jan. 1902, 12 Jan. 1902; *Light Bob Gazette*, 1, 9 (1901), pp. 5–6. On the whole question of medical treatment of combatants, see E. Lee, *To the Bitter End*, Harmondsworth, 1985, pp. 66–84.

25 Pretorius, *Anglo-Boer War*, p. 79.

26 *Highland Light Infantry Chronicle*, 3/4, 8 (1901).

27 India Office Library, Eur.Mss./D.1900/A/2. Cpl J. J. Butterworth, Diaries, vol. II, entry for 18 Sept. 1900.

28 AGG, Lt E. G. Spencer Churchill, Diary, 1901, entry for 30 June 1902.

29 *Household Brigade Magazine*, 32, 3 (1901), p. 162.

30 T. J. Keegan, *Rural Transformations in Industrializing South Africa: The Southern Highveld to 1914*, Johannesburg, 1986, p. 159.

31 *Anglo-Boer War*, p. 78.

32 D. Roberts, *Paternalism in Early Victorian England*, New Brunswick, 1979, p. 270.

33 P. Delius, *The Land Belongs to Us: The Pedi Polity, the Boers and the British in the Nineteenth Century Transvaal*, Johannesburg, 1983, p. 140.

34 H. Giliomee, 'The South African Frontier: Stages in Development', unpublished seminar paper, Institute of Commonwealth Studies, University of London, 1979.

35 *The Land Belongs to Us*, p. 142.

36 *Green Howards Gazette*, 89, 8 (1900), p. 81.

37 NAM, 6112/190/5, Cmdt Myburgh to Cmdt Theron, encl. in Maj. R. H. Massie, Secret Weekly Intelligence Summary, Cape Colony, District No. 43, 13 April 1902.

38 NAM, 6807/188, Spl Agt, Albert, Weekly Special Report on Conditions of District, 28 Nov. 1901.

39 NAM, 6807/187, D. McKinnon, Special Report on Native Specials, 11 Dec. 1901; *St George's Gazette*, 227, 19 (1901), p. 194.

40 NAM, 6807/189, Confidential Weekly Intelligence Summary, No. 19 District, 11 Jan. 1902.

41 NAM, 6112/190/15, Capt. Ross to Secret Agt, Carnarvon (secret), 2 Jan. 1902.

42 RAMC, Mss. 1/007, Maj. F. J. W. Porter, Anglo-Boer War Diaries, vol. I, entry for 4 April 1900.

43 ACG, RA.10/9/7/1, Capt. T. H. Eyre-Lloyd, Diary, 1899–1901, entry for 13 Dec. 1900. Warwick, *Black People*, p. 199, cites the assessment of the official German General Staff account of the war that intelligence gathered for commandos by African scouts was 'remarkably accurate and . . . transmitted with extraordinary rapidity'.

44 CA, 1/DGS 1/4/1/3, Affidavit by S. Rooibaard, 23 June 1901; *Navy and Army Gazette*, 3 Nov. 1900; *Green Howards Gazette*, 88, 8 (1900), p. 69; *Household Brigade Magazine*, 40, 4 (1901), p. 236.

45 ACG, RA.10/9/7/1, Capt. T. H. Eyre-Lloyd, Diary 1899–1901, entry for 13 June 1901.

46 *Household Brigade Magazine*, 47, 4 (1901), p. 754.

47 CA, 1/BKE 4/1/8/2, Statement by J. Mungawara, encl. in RM to Spl Agt, Dordrecht, 17 Nov. 1901.

48 *Highland Light Infantry Chronicle*, 2, 14 (1900), pp. 568–9.

49 CA, 1/DGS 1/4/1/3, Affidavit by A. Steenkamp, 20 June 1901; 1/FBG 4/1/8/1/1/6, RM to A. Klein, 5 Sept. 1900.

50 RAMC, Mss. 1/007, Maj. F. J. W. Porter, Anglo-Boer War Diaries, vol. II, entry for 2 Dec. 1901.

51 NMM, PTR/6/2/4, Porter Papers, Medical Journal, 1899–1900, entry for 30 Nov. 1900.

52 RAMC, Porter Diaries, vol. II, entry for 23 Dec. 1900. Translated by Porter's personal 'camp follower', Alfred Elias.

53 Delius and Trapido, '*Inboekselings*', p. 226.

54 *Highland Light Infantry Chronicle*, 3/4, 8 (1901), pp. 654–5.

55 NAM, 6112/190/4, Confidential Daily Intelligence Summary, No. MP.92, Cape Colony No. 54 District, 20 May 1902.

56 RSR, Mss. 1/101, du Moulin Papers, Lt E. P. du Moulin, Intelligence Notebook, entry for 20 March 1901.

57 CA, 1/DGS 1/4/1/2, J. Kok to Ag JP, 19 Nov. 1900; 1/4/1/3, H. Kieviet to RM, 2 Jan. 1901.

58 *Highland Light Infantry Chronicle*, 1/2, 3 (1901), pp. 580–1.

59 WCL, Lyttelton Letters, NGL/KL/622e. Gen. N. G. Lyttelton to his wife, 23 Sept. 1901.

60 NAM, 5603/7, Col. H. F. N. Jourdain, Diaries, vol. VII, entry for 23 Sept. 1901.

61 NAM, 6807/187, J. R. Gibson to Col. Kavanagh, 11 Jan. 1902; Sworn Statements by J. Maree, 6 Jan. 1902, 8 Jan. 1902.

62 NAM, 6112/190, Secret Weekly Intelligence Summary, Cape Colony No. 45 District, 13 April 1902; Sworn Statement by M. Louwrens Geldenhuys, 28 March 1902.

63 NAM, 6112/190/17, Col. White to Col. Haig (secret), 1 April 1902.

64 R. Kruger, *Goodbye Dolly Gray: The Story of the Boer War*, London, 1974, pp. 439, 454; A. Schmidt, 'The Life of Gideon Scheepers, 1878–1902', B.A. Hons dissertation, University of Cape Town, 1965, p. 25.

65 NAM, 6807/193, Confidential Secret Agt's Report to Capt. Ross, 20 Jan. 1902.

66 NAM, 6807/187, Translation of Rouxville Commando Proclamation, 14 Oct. 1901.

67 SAL, MCA, Box 25, File No. 4, Revd W. H. Miller to Revd J. G. Locke, 19 July 1902; ACG, RO.10/9/10/22, Digest of Movements of 1st Battalion, entries for 17 Dec. 1901, 2 Jan. 1902.

68 SAL, MCA, Box 37, Leliefontein Church Minute Book, 1887–1911, Report of *Raad* Meeting, 12 Jan.

1901. The mission church council was so chronically short of members during the war that its administrative routines virtually broke down.

69 Price, 'Leliefontein', p. 19.

70 CA, 1/SBK A/1/1/3, S. Viljoen to CC, 22 July 1899; MCA, Leliefontein Church Minute Book, Report of *Raad* meeting, 11 Dec. 1898.

71 *Berliner Missionsbericht*, July 1901, pp. 287–8.

72 CA, 1/SBK 5/4/3, J. J. van Reenen to RM, 22 Dec. 1901. On local Boer anti-mission animosities, see also J. W. Kok, *Sonderlinge Vlug: Die invloed van die Tweedevryheidsoorlog op die Sendingaksie van die N.G. Kerk*, Pretoria, 1971, pp. 20-1.

73 D. Reitz, *Commando: A Boer Journal of the Boer War*, London, 1931, pp. 298–9. See also Steenkamp, *Thirst King*, pp. 176–7.

74 NAM, 6112/190/15, Col H. Cooper to Capt. S. L. Barry, 2 Jan. 1902.

75 NAM, 6807/189, Confidential Weekly Intelligence Summary, No. 43 District, 11 Jan. 1902.

76 SAL, MCA, Box 25, File No. 3, 'Copies with translations of some papers found at Concordia, after its evacuation by the Boers on 2nd May 1902', n.d.

77 NAM, 6112/190/17, Revd Locke to Col. Shelton (conf.), 25 Oct. 1901.

78 Ibid.

79 NAM, 6112/190/17, W. M. Maxwell to Col. H. Cooper (tel.), 21 Jan. 1902; Reitz, *Commando*, p. 298.

80 NAM, 6807/189, Folio 7, Summary of Intelligence Arrangements, Namaqualand, 27 March 1902.

81 *Commando*, p. 299. For further details, see P. A. Pyper, 'General J. C. Smuts en die Tweede Vryheidsoorlog, 1899–1902', M.A. thesis, Potchefstroom Universitiet vir Christelike Hoër Onderwys, 1960, pp. 129–31.

82 NAM, 6807/189, Confidential Weekly Intelligence Summary No. 41, 12 June 1902.

83 SAL, MCA, Box 27, Leliefontein Church Mission Book Reports, Report of Meeting, 10 June 1902.

84 SAL, Moffat Collection, J. Henwood, Ms. Diary of Events in O'Okiep, April 1902–May 1902, entry for 14 April 1902; NAM, 6112/190/16, Col. White to Col. Haig, 18 April 1902.

85 NAM, 6112/190/4, Cooper to French (conf.), 15 May 1902.

86 CA, 1/CMT 3/10, D. Makholiso to RM, Cala, 15 Oct. 1901; SNA to CM, Transkeian Territories, 2 Nov. 1901; 1/BKE 1/1/2/2/1, RM to SLD, n.d.

87 *Black People*, p. 120.

88 *Diamond Fields Advertiser*, 1 Jan. 1901; *Lloyds Weekly Newspaper*, 11 March 1900.

89 NAM, 6112/190/7, Cooper, Confidential Notebook, entry for 13 Dec. 1901. The comparative reference is presumably to Jonathan Wild, a notorious eighteenth-century English bounty-hunter and scourge of poachers: see E. P. Thompson, *Whigs and Hunters: The Origin of the Black Act*, Harmondsworth, 1977, p. 163.

90 CA, 1/DEA 3/1, D. Jafta to R. T. Fitzgerald, 11 Jan. 1901; 1/DGS 1/4/1/3, Affidavit by L. Damara, 21 April 1901; 1/GSD 7/30, 6/1900/D, RM to Under Colonial Secretary, 6 July 1900.

91 CA, 1/DGS 1/4/1/3, H. Hooper to CC, 17 Dec. 1900; 1/DGS 1/4/1/1, Affidavit by Koolovits, 25 Jan. 1901.

92 *Light Bob Gazette*, 2, 9 (1901), p. 13.

93 In the 1898 election, party electoral struggles obliged both British and Boer interests to campaign for the black vote. Fear of alienating strategically important segments of the African electorate forced settler politicians to be circumspect on franchise matters: Trapido, 'Liberalism in the Cape', p. 56.

94 CA, 1/JTN B/1/1, Affidavit by M. Sayedwa, 4 April 1902; B/2/2,. Affidavit by Silas, 3 Aug. 1900; Cory Library, Ms. 11/002, A. J. Kidwell, 'Notes on Jamestown and the Boer War, 1899–1902'.

95 CA, 1/JTN B/1/1, L. J. Brookes to CC, 22 Sept. 1900; 1/FBG 4/1/8/1/17, Copy of Statement by Cmdt Olivier, encl. in Col. D. Mackenzie to CC, 18 March 1901.

96 Interview, Mr Watutu Mtozi (b. 1886), June 1985.

97 Trapido, 'Friends of the Natives', pp. 260–1; Bundy, *South African Peasantry*, p. 137; Odendaal, *Vukani Bantu!*, pp. 6–7.

213

98 CA, 1/ALN 4/9/8, Statement by Ventvogel, 21 Mar 1901; *Bandolier*, 1, 14 (1901), p. 24; *Kokstad Advertiser*, 1 Sept. 1901; *Diamond Fields Advertiser*, 2 July 1901, 9 July 1901.

99 CA, 1/BKE 1/1/2/2/2, Jonas to RM, 16 Jan. 1900.

100 RSR, Boer Letters, B. J. de Klerk to his brother, 29 Dec. 1899; W. Lubbe to B. De Klerk, 25 Dec. 1899.

101 See for instance, CA, 1/DGS 1/4/1/1,. Affidavit by Paulus, 10 Sept. 1900; 1/4/1/2, Affidavit by Jacob, 10 Oct. 1900; AG 3071, Affidavit by E. Marubani, 3 April 1900; NA 258, Folio 103, Statement by Jilose, 4 April 1900.

102 CA, 1/DGS 1/4/1/2, Statement by C. Olifant, 19 Sept. 1900.

103 CA, 1/CDP A/1/1/A/2, Diary of Sgt-in-Charge, Calitzdorp Police, entry for 5 Jan. 1901; 1/VBG 22/13, A. Newman to Cmdt, 12 Feb. 1901; 22/5, R. W. Close to Spl JP, 26 June 1900.

104 '*Amafelandawonye* (the Die-hards): Popular Protest and Women's Movements in Herschel District in the 1920s', in Beinart and Bundy, *Hidden Struggles*, p. 226.

105 CA, 1/BKE A/2/1/1, J. Mugubisa to Spl JP, 11 Jan. 1901.

106 *Sunday Times*, 27 March 1988; *Cape Argus*, 28 March 1988.

107 Cited in S. Hall, 'The Problem of Ideology – Marxism without Guarantees', in B. Matthews (ed.), *Marx: 100 Years on*, London, 1983, p. 81.

7 Martyrdom, myth and memory: Abraham Esau's War

1 *Whigs and Hunters*, p. 268.

2 R. Samuel, 'Village labour', in P. Thane and A. Sutcliffe (eds.), *Essays in Social History*, vol. II, Oxford, 1986, p. 89.

3 Interview, Mrs Wilhemina Isaacs, domestic worker (b. 1900), Sept. 1978.

4 Interview, Mrs Nettie Daniels, dressmaker (b. 1889), Sept. 1978.

5 Interview, Miss Anne Murinik, teacher (b. 1901), March 1983.

6 Interviews, Mrs Florence Malan, teacher (b. 1903), Jan. 1987; Isaacs; Daniels; Murinik.

7 W. R. Nasson and J. M. M. John, 'Abraham Esau: A Calvinia Martyr in the Anglo-Boer War', *Social Dynamics*, 11, 1 (1985), p. 65; K. Schoeman, 'Die Dood van Abraham Esau: Ooggetuieberigte uit die besette Calvinia, 1901', *Quarterly Bulletin of the South African Library*, 40, 2 (1985), p. 62.

8 Trapido, 'African political organisation', p. 90; see also Lewis, *Between the Wire*, pp. 12–15; Goldin, *Making Race*, p. 16.

9 Interview, Nettie Daniels.

10 Nasson and John, 'Abraham Esau', p. 66.

11 Interview, Nettie Daniels.

12 Ibid.

13 Interview, Florence Malan.

14 'Attitudes towards authority in eighteenth-century Languedoc', *Social History*, 3, 3 (1978), pp. 301–2.

15 E. J. Hobsbawm and J. W. Scott, 'Political Shoemakers', *Past and Present*, 89 (1980), pp. 87, 113.

16 NAM, 6807/190, 1st Cavalry Division, Intelligence Papers, District Military Intelligence Reports 1900–2: Section E, 21 May 1900.

17 CA, 1/CWM 4/1/2/1, RM Calvinia to Spl JP (secret), 23 Sept. 1900.

18 Interview, Wilhemina Isaacs.

19 Interview, Nettie Daniels. 'Skirt soldiers' is probably a reference to a battalion of Scottish Fusiliers which was stationed in Namaqualand.

20 For Boer women on war service, see S. B. Spies, 'Women and the War', in Warwick (ed.), *South African War*, esp. pp. 163–4.

21 RSR, Mss. 1/3, Boer Letters Collection. D. Louw to I. Louw (secret), 16 Sept. 1900.

22 CA, 1/CWM 4/1/2/2, Petition from Coloured Men to defend Calvinia, 10 Jan. 1900.

23 NAM, 7704/56/42, Lt J. S. Preston, Diary, 1899–1901, entry for 13 Oct. 1900.

24 Interview, Mr Willem Peters, stonemason (b. 1894), Sept. 1978.

25 Interview, Florence Malan.
26 Nasson and John, 'Abraham Esau', p. 67.
27 NAM, 7704/56/17, Preston Letters, Preston to Esau (secret), 3 Nov. 1900.
28 NAM, 7704/56/42, Preston, Diary, entry for 10 Nov. 1900.
29 NAM, 6112/190/15/4, Namaqualand Field Force Papers, 1900–2, Summaries of Intelligence, June 1900 to January 1901, Confidential Report, 30 Nov. 1900.
30 Nasson and John, 'Abraham Esau', p. 68.
31 Interview, Mr Samuel Anderson, warehouseman (b. 1923), Jan. 1987.
32 NAM, 7704/56/17, Preston Letters, 'A' to Preston, 11 Dec. 1900 encl. in Preston to H. Elphinstone (conf.), 18 Dec. 1900.
33 Preston letters, 'A' to Preston, 14 Dec. 1900.
34 Nasson and John, 'Abraham Esau', p. 68.
35 Interview, Nettie Daniels.
36 Ibid.; Interviews, Willem Peters; Florence Malan.
37 NAM, 6807/190, Military Intelligence Reports, 1900–1, Section C Summaries, 22 Dec. 1900.
38 NAM, 6807/190, Summary of Intelligence, June 1900 to December 1900, Folio 5, Testimony of Solomon Maseti ('Oupa'), 3 Jan. 1901.
39 Interview, Florence Malan.
40 Ibid.
41 Interview, Mr John Esau, carpenter (b. 1911).
42 University of Cape Town, Kaplan Centre for Jewish Studies, Oral Life Histories Collection, Testimony of Mr Jacob Zurne (b. 1887).
43 *Diamond Fields Advertiser*, 7 Feb. 1901; *Graaff-Reinet Advertiser*, 17 Feb. 1901.
44 Interview, John Esau.
45 Interview, Wilhemina Isaacs.
46 Interview, Nettie Daniels.
47 CA, AG 2070, Anglo-Boer War Files, Papers relating to the occupation of Calvinia led by the enemy, RM Calvinia to SLD, 29 Jan. 1902; *Graaff-Reinet Advertiser*, 6 Feb. 1901; *Midland News*, 19 Jan. 1901.
48 *Discipline and Punish*, Harmondsworth, 1979, p. 35.
49 *Cape Times Weekly*, 31 Dec. 1902; Schoeman, 'Dood van Abraham Esau', p. 58.
50 Interview, Nettie Daniels.
51 Miss M. A. Tredgold, 'Calvinia: Events in Connection with the Invasion of Calvinia and Thereafter', unattributed ms. typescript, 30 Jan. 1902; *Rifle Brigade Chronicle* (1902), p. 19.
52 Interviews, Mrs Sarah Erasmus (b. 1919); Mr Nicolaas Galant, clerk (b. 1924), Oct. 1978.
53 ACG, 16/9/1, Capt T. H. Eyre-Lloyd's Diaries, vol. III (1900–3), entry for 8 Feb. 1901.
54 *Lloyds Weekly Newspaper*, 20 Feb. 1901.
55 *South African News*, 18 Sept. 1901. Such a case was indeed made by Afrikaner authors of those many melodramatic accounts of the war published in the 1930s. C. J. Scheepers Strydom, *Kaapland en die Tweede Vryheidsoorlog* (Nasionale Pers, Kaapstad, 1937), p. 156, concocted a version in which Stephanus Strydom, trying to aid an exhausted Esau by carrying him on his horse, was attacked and almost stabbed. Having gone berserk, Esau had to be shot in self-defence; see also J. A. Smith, *Ek Rebelleer*, Kaapstad, 1939, pp. 75–8.
56 CO 48/551/5078, encl. in W. Hely-Hutchinson to J. Chamberlain (conf.), 20 Feb. 1901, Memorandum from G. V. Fiddes, Imperial Secretary, 18 Feb. 1901; *Telegram from Sir A. Milner to the Secretary of State for War, relating to the Reported Outrage on Esau at Calvinia, Cd. 464*, 1901; see also Milner to Lyttelton Gell, 19 Feb. 1901, in C. Headlam (ed.), *The Milner Papers, South Africa, 1897–1905*, vol. II, London, 1933, pp. 233–4; W. Basil Worsfold, *Lord Milner's Work in South Africa, 1897–1902*, London, 1906, p. 427.
57 A. S. Skillicorn, 'The role of the black voter in the 1908 Cape General Election, with particular reference to the Eastern Cape', B.A. Hons. diss., University of Cape Town, 1975, pp. 7–8. For the post-war

atmosphere, see also Trapido, 'White Conflict and Non-White Participation', pp. 416–17; 'African Political Organisation', p. 11; Goldin, *Making Race*, pp. 30–1; Lewis, *Between the Wire*, p. 26.

58 Skillicorn, 'Black Voter'', p. 8.

59 Interview, Samuel Anderson.

60 *The Merthyr Rising*, London, 1978, p. 204.

61 Interview, Nettie Daniels. *Vierkleur*: Boer Republican flag.

62 Interview, Florence Malan.

63 Interview, Wilhemina Isaacs.

64 'The art of self-defence', *Planet*, 57 (1986), p. 107.

65 Interview, Revd Alastair McGregor (b. 1910), Dec. 1986.

66 Interview, Revd Reginald Pearce (b. 1915), Dec. 1986.

67 Ibid.

68 Interview, Mr Leslie Newman, teacher (b. 1913), Jan. 1987.

69 Interview, Miss Anna Spies (b. 1901), Jan. 1987.

70 Interview, Reginald Pearce. For Afrikaner Nationalists and the question of Coloured 'identity' after the late 1940s, see Goldin 'Coloured identity', pp. 166–71.

71 Interview, Mrs Alida Arendse, shopworker (b. 1922), Oct. 1978.

72 Interview, Dr Alfred Biddle (b. 1919), Feb. 1985.

73 Quoted in A. Stadler, *The Political Economy of Modern South Africa*, Cape Town, 1987, p. 78.

74 Interview, Anna Spies.

75 Interview, Mr Peter Manel, motor mechanic (b. 1935), April 1985.

76 Interview, Reginald Pearce.

77 Interview, Mrs Theresa Sharp, nurse (b. 1925), Feb. 1985. *Rooinek*: literally 'redneck', a derogatory Afrikaner term for the British, made popular in the South African War.

78 Interview, Leslie Newman.

79 Interview, Theresa Sharp.

80 I. Okpewho, *Myth in Africa*, Cambridge, 1983, p. 89.

81 For the usage of political myth to embroider official South African versions of historical reality, see L. Thompson, *The Political Mythology of Apartheid*, New Haven, 1985.

82 R. Grele, 'Listen to their voices: Two case studies in the interpretation of oral history interviews', *Oral History*, 7, 1 (1979), p. 40.

83 E. P. Thompson, *William Morris: Romantic to Revolutionary*, London, 1955, p. 809.

84 For a general consideration of oral history as cultural meaning and myth as historical emotion, see L. Passerini, 'Work ideology and consensus under Italian fascism', *History Workshop Journal*, 8 (1979), p. 84; 'Mythbiography in Oral History', paper presented at the Sixth International Oral History Conference, Oxford, 1987; A. Portelli, 'The Peculiarities of Oral History', *History Workshop*, 12 (1981), p. 99; G. S. Kirk, *Myth: Its Meaning and Function in Ancient and other Cultures*, Berkeley and Los Angeles, 1971, p. 257.

85 W. Beinart, 'History of the African People' (review article), *South African Historical Journal*, 18 (1986), p. 228. See also Thompson, *Political Mythology* , p. 243.

86 Goldin, 'Coloured identity', p. 163.

87 A. White, 'Bakhtin, Sociolinguistics and Deconstruction', in F. Gloversmith (ed.), *The Theory of Reading*, Brighton, 1984, p. 130.

88 R. Samuel, 'Myth and History: a First Reading', *Oral History Journal*, 16, 1 (1988), p. 18.

8 Treason offenders and their antagonists

1 Davenport, *Afrikaner Bond*, p. 223. T. P. Theron, Bond Chairman, first voiced his fury in parliament in July of that year: *South African News*, 18 July 1900; *Worcester Advertiser*, 21 July 1900.

2 *British Supremacy*, p. 55.

3 P. Warwick, 'African Societies and the South African War, 1899–1902', Ph.D. thesis, University of York, 1978, p. 186.

4 J. H. Snyman, *Die Afrikaner in Kaapland met verwysing na die Militêre Howe, 1899–1902*, Pretoria, 1979, pp. 71–2.

5 *Midland News and Karoo Farmer*, 17 Feb. 1901.

6 See for example, *Black and White Budget*, 6 Jan. 1900; *Household Brigade Magazine*, 29, 3 (1900), p. 347; A. Conan Doyle, 'A Glimpse of the Army at Work', *Strand Magazine*, 117, 20 (1900), pp. 346–7; 'The War and its Lessons', *Quarterly Review*, 195, 389 (1902), p. 311.

7 C. Townshend, 'Martial Law: Legal and Administrative Problems of Civil Emergency in Britain and the Empire, 1800–1940', *Historical Journal*, 25, 1 (1982), pp. 179–81; Le May, *British Supremacy*, pp. 120–1.

8 Le May, *British Supermacy*, p. 67.

9 For a detailed table of criminal sentences, see *Cape Law Journal* , 17 (1900), pp. 30–42, 132–49.

10 A. Sachs, *Justice in South Africa*, Brighton and London, 1973; J. Dugard, *Human Rights and the South African Legal Order*, Princeton, 1978, p. 209.

11 F. Fremantle, *A Doctor in Khaki*, London, 1901, p. 273. One of a minority of British officers who were unhappy about the extent to which African informers were being used, Fremantle argued that 'too much stress is laid on Kaffirs as informants', p. 463.

12 CA, 1/UPT 5/2/4/3/3, Ag RM to Under Colonial Secretary, 22 Dec. 1900; 1/DEA 3/2/1/1, RM to Cmdt, 4 June 1901; *Albert Times and Molteno Advertiser*, 19 July 1900.

13 Few of those convicted were actually executed, owing to mitigating intervention by the Army High Command: Sachs, *Justice*, p. 125.

14 J. S. Galbraith, 'British War Measures in Cape Colony, 1900–1902: A Study of Miscalculations and Mismanagement', *South African Historical Journal*, 15 (1983), p. 81.

15 G. Best, *Humanity in Warfare: The Modern History of the International Law of Armed Conflicts*, London, 1980, p. 195.

16 NAM, 5603/9, Jourdain Diaries, vol. VI, entry for 13 Sept. 1901.

17 *South African Law Journal*, 18 (1901), p. 416; S. B. Spies, *Methods of Barbarism? Roberts and Kitchener and Civilians in the Boer Republics: January 1900–May 1902*, Cape Town and Pretoria, 1977, p. 109.

18 Cited in Spies, *Methods of Barbarism?*, p. 153.

19 *The Times*, 17 March 1901, 11 Feb. 1902.

20 *South African News*, 13 June 1900.

21 Ibid., 26 Sept. 1900.

22 *Ons Land*, 18 July 1900.

23 See for example, *Cape Daily Telegraph*, 25 April 1901; *Cape Argus*, 17 June 1901.

24 *South African News*, 18 April 1900.

25 *Cape Hansard*, 1900, p. 609.

26 Snyman, *Afrikaner in Kaapland*, pp. 94–5.

27 *Cape Mercury*, 30 June 1900.

28 *Midland News and Karoo Farmer*, 22 Feb. 1900.

29 *South African News*, 17 Jan. 1900; *Umtata Herald*, 16 Aug. 1900; *Graaff-Reinet Advertiser*, 17 Aug. 1901; *Cape Daily Telegraph*, 1 Jan. 1901.

30 *South African News*, 17 July 1901.

31 *Ons Land*, 28 Sept. 1901.

32 CA, 1/TBH 5/1/4/4, S. Booi to RM, 22 April 1900.

33 *Cape Hansard*, 1900, p. 656.

34 Ibid., p. 586.

35 NAM, 7711/1/13, Lt E. Longueville, Diary, 1899–1901, entry for 17 July 1900.

36 *Oakleaf*, 1, 8 (1900), p. 12.

37 *Household Brigade Magazine*, 42, 4 (1901), pp. 375–6.

38 CA, 1/MBY 1/4/1, District Treason Trial Papers, May 1902.
39 *The Colonisation of the Southern Tswana 1870–1900*, Johannesburg, 1985, pp. 220–1.
40 CA, 1/VBG 22/4, Affidavit by Chief Molala, 21 Sept. 1902.
41 NAM, 7602/2, Backhouse Diaries, vol. VI, 16 May 1902; *Navy and Army Gazette*, 11 May 1902.
42 'African Political Organization', p. 111; *Between the Wire*, p. 15. This led to black disenchantment with troops after certain Boer-occupied areas reverted to British control: G. Cuthbertson, 'Missionary Imperialism and Colonial Warfare: London Missionary Attitudes to the South African War, 1899–1902', *South African Historical Journal*, 19 (1987), p. 98.
43 *St George's Gazette*, 19, 206 (1900), pp. 36–7.
44 *Ons Land*, 13 March 1900; *Worcester Standard*, 14 July 1900.
45 CA, 1/ADE B/1, District Administrator to M. Kendrick, 13 May 1902.
46 CA, 1/GSD 7/47, Capt. C. Fay to RM (conf.), 21 Jan. 1901.
47 *South African News*, 5 Sept. 1900, 20 March 1901; *Black and White Budget*, 9 Dec. 1900.
48 AGG, RO.16/H.22, Lt G. Aubrey, Intelligence Notebook, Entries for 19 Oct. 1901, 22 Jan. 1902; CA, 1/SSE 162(a), J. Wiid, Treason Papers, Affidavit by M. Buys, 9 March 1902.
49 *Cape Mercury*, 5 March 1901; *Umtata Herald*, 8 March 1901; *Navy and Army Gazette*, 3 Aug. 1901.
50 *Umtata Herald*, 9 March 1901.
51 CA, 1/SSE 10/17, Capt. Wood to RM, 5 March 1901; *Midland News and Karoo Farmer*, 16 March 1901.
52 CA, 1/ALN 4/9/1/2, Report on J. Joubert, 20 Jan. 1902, encl. in RM to CDO, 24 Jan. 1902.
53 CA, 1/KDM 3/1/1/1/7/4, Ag RM, Police memo., 29 Aug. 1900.
54 CA, 1/KMN 10/24, Ag RM to Cmdt, 19 Nov. 1900.
55 CA, 1/GSD 6/17, RM, Hay, to RM, 1 Jan. 1902.
56 CA, 1/TBH 5/1/4/4, RM to Chief of Police, Wellington, 9 Nov. 1900.
57 NAM, 7704/56/17, Preston Letters, Lt J. S. Preston to his sister, 27 Dec. 1901.
58 NAM, 6807/187, Capt. H. S. Sloman to Lt W. H. Wayland (conf.), 23 Feb. 1902.
59 NAM, 7805/66/4, Dundas Papers, Lt J. R. Dundas to C. Doondy, 12, 18 Jan. 1901.
60 CA, 1/ALN 3/2/2, CDO to RM, 13 Sept. 1901.
61 CA, 1/BED C/1/1/1, Intelligence Report, 15 April 1902.
62 CA, 1/GSD, RM to A. Gossa, 15 Jan. 1900; RM to Capt. M. T. Smith, 4 Feb. 1901.
63 NMM, Mss. 75/139, Limpus Papers, Notebook, 1900, Cmdr A. H. Limpus to Capt. Hamilton, 10 April 1900.
64 CA, 1/TBH 5/1/3/4, RM to AG, 19 May 1900, 19 July 1900, 10 April 1901; 5/1/4/4, RM to Ag RM, Malmesbury, 26 April 1900.
65 *South African Law Journal*, 18 (1902), p. 380.
66 CA, 1/SSE 8/103, Anon. to RM, 30 Jan. 1901.
67 CA, 1/CDK 8/23, 671/1900, 'Native Treason Letter', encl. in Col. B. Henderson to RM, 12 Feb. 1901.
68 CA, 1/KMN 10/24, Anon. to Cmdt, n.d.
69 NAM, 6807/187, encl. in Capt. Sloman to Lt Wayland, 30 Jan. 1902.
70 *Whigs and Hunters*, pp. 164–6; 'The Crime of Anonymity', in D. Hay, P. Linebaugh, J. G. Rule, E. P. Thompson and C. Winslow, *Albion's Fatal Tree: Crime and Society in Eighteenth Century England*, Harmondsworth, 1977, pp. 255–344; E. P. Thompson, 'Eighteenth Century English Society: Class Struggle without Class?', *Social History*, 3, 2 (1978), pp. 144–5, 162.
71 CA, 1/CDK 8/23, G. M. Hattingh, High Treason Papers, Native Affidavits, 29 April 1900, 2 May 1900.
72 CA, 1/CDK 8/24, 685/1900, J. du Plessis, High Treason Papers, Affidavit by A. Kyster, 4 July 1900.
73 CA, 1/BKE 1/1/2/2/2, A. de Bruin, Martial Law Report, Affidavit by I. Manganane, 24 July 1900.
74 *South African News*, 28 March 1900.
75 CA, 1/DGS 1/4/1/3, Affidavits by Jan and David, 5 Dec. 1901; *Diamond Fields Advertiser*, 8 Jan. 1901.
76 CA 1/TBH 5/1/4/4, RM to RM, Uniondale, 19 Sept. 1901.
77 See CA, 1/DGS 1/4/1/2, J. Maree and J. du Plessis, High Treason Papers, Affidavits by A. van den Berg, 11, 12 Nov. 1900; Affidavit by B. Johannes, 12 Nov. 1900. 'Oom Paul': a reference to Paul Kruger.

78 See CA, 1/CDK 8/25, Cradock High Treason Case Papers, 1900, Affidavits by H. Vennell and S. Musi, 10, 11 Aug. 1900.
79 CA, 1/CDK 8/23, Cradock High Treason Case Papers, 1902, Affidavit by J. Ross, 2 Jan. 1902.
80 CA, 1/DGS 1/4/1/2, J. and H. Lieuw, Treason Trial Papers, Affidavits by T. April, 5 Mar. 1900.
81 CA, 1/UPT 5/1/4/3/3, H. Botha, Treason Trial Papers, Affidavits by J. Verwagh, 6, 7 June 1901. 'Zwaartgoed', meaning 'black thing', was a common term of racial abuse.
82 CA, 1/DGS 1/3/1/1, Affidavit by H. Krynauw, 5 Nov. 1900.
83 Ibid., J. Braun, Treason Trial Papers, Affidavit by H. Hoopniet, 15 Nov. 1900.
84 CA, 1/FBG 1/4/1/2, Affidavit by J. Cornelius, 22 March 1900.
85 See CA, 1/ALN 4/1/2/2, H. Henniker, Treason Trial Papers, Affidavits by James, Jonas, Msinga and Isaac, 14, 17 Sept. 1901; *South African Law Journal*, 18 (1901), p. 425.
86 See CA, 1/VBG 22/4, J. Koopman, Trial Affidavits, 22–4 March 1900, encl. in RM to Chief of Police, Kimberley, 23 April 1900.
87 CA, 1/BKE 7/1/2/2/2, J. Meiring, Treason Trial Papers, Affidavit by Lena Mledlo, 25 May 1900.
88 CA, 1/SSE 1/63, P. Geyer, Treason Trial Papers, Affidavits by C. Aardt and K. Willem, 11, 13 Dec. 1901.
89 CA, 1/VBG 22/13, L. D. Wood to RM, 20 Sept. 1902.
90 See CA, 1/CDK 8/23, 3/68/1900, Affidavits by Klaas Buys, 5, 7 Feb. 1900; Statements, 6, 7 Feb. 1900; 1/SSE 1/63, Chief Const. to RM, 8 Feb. 1900; RM, Maraisburg, to Col. Hensall (conf.), 9 Feb. 1900.
91 *Periodical Accounts relating to the Moravian Missions*, 44, 4 (1900), p. 427.
92 Ibid., p. 429.
93 S. P. Engelbrecht, *Geskiedenis van die Nederduitsch Hervormde Kerk in Afrika*, Kaapstad, 1953 p. 268.
94 *Mitteilungen aus der Brüder-Gemeine*, 1 Jan. 1901, pp. 44–6; J. Taylor-Hamilton and K. G. Hamilton, *History of the Moravian Church: The Renewed Unitas Fratrum, 1722–1957*, Moravian Church Board of Christian Education, 1967, p. 580.
95 *Mitteilungen*, 1 Jan, 1902, pp. 51–5.
96 Price, *Imperial War and the British Working Class*, pp. 132–77; G. Stedman Jones, 'Working-Class Culture and Working-Class Politics in London, 1870–1900: Notes on the Remaking of a Working Class', *Journal of Social History*, 7 (1974), p. 461; and also, Cunningham, 'The Language of Patriotism, 1750–1914', *History Workshop Journal*, 12 (1981), p. 25.
97 Taylor-Hamilton and Hamilton, *Moravian Church*, p. 584.
98 *Periodical Accounts relating to the Moravian Missions*, 44, 4 (1900), p. 427.
99 B. Krüger, 'Die Brüdermission in SüdAfrika-West während des Burenkrieges, 1899–1902', in *Unitas Fratrum: Zeitschrift für Geschichte und Gegenwartsfragen der Brüdergemeine*, Hamburg, 1979; *Mitteilungen*, 1 Jan. 1902, p. 54.
100 *Mitteilungen*, 4 April 1902, p. 52.
101 *Mitteilungen*, 4 April 1902, p. 59.
102 Krüger, 'Die Evangelische Brüdergemeine in Süd Afrika", in *Unitas Fratrum Herrnhuten Studien*, Utrecht, 1975, p. 280.
103 *Mitteilungen*, 4 April 1902, pp. 9, 55–60.
104 Taylor-Hamilton and Hamilton, *Moravian Church*, pp. 588–60.
105 *Mitteilungen*, 4 April 1902, p. 55.
106 'Enter the British Legal Machine: Law and Administration at the Cape, 1806–1910', *Collected Seminar Papers on the Societies of Southern Africa in the 19th and 20th Centuries*, vol. I, Institute of Commonwealth Studies, University of London, 1970, p. 34.
107 CA, 1/CDK 8/25, Cradock High Treason Case Summaries, 1902, Affidavit by J. Stoffels, 3 Jan. 1902. On the heritage of Cape colonial law, see R. Ross, 'The Rule of Law at the Cape of Good Hope in the Eighteenth Century', *Journal of Imperial and Commonwealth History*, 9, 1 (1980), p. 8; Sachs, 'British Legal Machine', pp. 8–15.

108 J. Snyman, 'Die Afrikaner in Kaapland, 1899–1902', Ph.D. thesis, University of Potchefstroom, 1973, pp. 230–1.
109 Thompson, 'English Society', p. 147.
110 J. Krikler, 'The Transvaal Agrarian Class Struggle in the South African War 1899–1902', *Social Dynamics*, 12, 2 (1986), p. 23.
111 C. Fisher, *Custom, Work and Market Capitalism*, London, 1981, p. vii.
112 Ibid., p. ix.
113 E. P. Thompson, 'The Moral Economy of the English Crowd in the Eighteenth Century', *Past and Present*, 50 (1971), p. 78.
114 See N. Hogan, 'The Posthumous Vindication of Zachariah Gqishela: Reflections on the Politics of Dependence at the Cape in the Nineteenth Century', in Marks and Atmore (eds.), *Economy and Society*, p. 285; P. Lewsen, 'Cape Liberalism in its Terminal Phase', in D. C. Hindson (ed.), *Working Papers in Southern African Studies*, vol. III, Johannesburg, 1983, p. 41.
115 *Whigs and Hunters*, p. 265.
116 *Household Brigade Magazine*, 49, 5 (1902), p. 31.
117 NAM, 6807/186, Folio 16, Capt. A. Parker to Col. J. F. Shelton, 19 Aug. 1901.

9 Peace and reconquest

1 Review of G. Best, *War and Society in Revolutionary Europe, 1770–1870* (1982) and V. G. Kiernan, *European Empires from Conquest to Collapse, 1815–1960* (1982) in *Social History*, 8, 3 (1983), p. 393.
2 *On Living in An Old Country: The National Past in Contemporary Britain*, London, 1985, p. 129.
3 Thus, for a picture of the Boer states, see J. S. Mohlamme, 'Black People in the Boer Republics during and in the aftermath of the South African War of 1899–1902', Ph.D. thesis, Wisconsin University, 1985.
4 R. First and A. Scott, *Olive Schreiner: A Biography*, New York, 1980, p. 244.
5 *Bandolier*, 2, 25 (1902), p. 22.
6 Olive Schreiner Letters, MMPUS/BC.16/D.60/241, O. Schreiner to F. Schreiner, 30 June 1902.
7 See for instance, CA, I/GSD 7/31, Chief Constable to Ag RM, 17 July 1902; I/SSE 10/17, 296/02, RM to K. Hacker, 12 Aug. 1902; *Midland News and Karoo Farmer*, 5 Aug. 1902.
8 *Cape Hansard*, 1902, p. 469.
9 NAM, 7605/19/2, Lt M. Crayshay, Boer War papers, Capt. H. Peacock to Crayshay, 17 Oct. 1902.
10 CA, I/GSD 7/31, Intelligence Officer to Ag RM, 15 June 1902, 18 June 1902; I/SSE 10/17, 296/02, RM to K. Hacker, 12 Aug. 1902.
11 RSR, I/119, Bidder Letterbooks, vol. III, 'Seditious communication and advice', encl. in R. C. Griffin to Bidder (conf.), 19 Oct. 1902.
12 CA, I/ADE 4/1/2/1,. 50976/2, AG to RM, Fort Beaufort, 25 July 1902; I/SSE 10/16, RM to Postmaster, 28 July 1902; I/BED CI/I/I/I, Intelligence Officer, Grahamstown, to Deputy Admr Bedford, 28 June 1902; *Bandolier*, 2, 25 (1902), p. 19.
13 CA, I/ADE 4/1/2/1, 50977/6/2, RM to Lt Cartwright, 16 July 1902.
14 CA, I/KMN I/1/3, RM to Chief Constable, 5 Sept. 1902; I/TBH 5/1/3/4, RM to RM, Uitenhage, 18 July 1902.
15 CA, I/ADE 4/1/2/1, RM to RM, Bedford, 18 July 1902.
16 'Communication, Community and the State', in C. Emsley and J. Walvin (eds.), *Artisans, Peasants and Proletarians: 1760–1860*, London, 1985, p. 172.
17 RSR, 1/119, Bidder Letterbooks, vol. IV, 'Native letter', encl. in Intelligence Officer, Middelburg, to Bidder (conf.), 2 Nov. 1902.
18 *Oxfordshire Light Infantry Chronicle* (1902), pp. 151, 158.
19 NAM, 6112/190/5, Cooper (conf. memo.), 20 June 1902.
20 CA, 1/UPT 5/2/4/3/3 55/02, Ag RM to Under Colonial Secretary, 22 Dec. 1902.
21 ACG, RO.14/2/9/.15, Capt. W. B. Barttelot, Diary, entry for 3 June 1902; *Midland News and Karoo*

Farmer, 2 July 1902; *Albert Times and Molteno Advertiser*, 19 July 1902; *Cape Mercury*, 24 July 1902.

22 AGG, RO.14/9/16, Massey, Diary, entry for 12 June 1902.

23 NAM, 6112/190/5, Cooper to Cmdt, O'Okiep, 11 June 1902.

24 NAM, 6112/190/14, Col. Shelton to SO, Cape Colony District, 3 June 1902; 6112/190/7, Cooper to Gen. French (tel.), 22 June 1902.

25 NAM, 6112/190/7, Cooper to Cmdt, Garies, 19 June 1902.

26 NAM, 6112/190/9, Cooper to Cmdt, Garies, 9 June 1902.

27 NAM, 6807/193, Capt. Ross to Gen. Haig (tel.), 21 June 1902.

28 Goldin, 'Coloured identity', p. 160; *Making Race*, p. 18.

29 Grundlingh, *Own War*, p. 128.

30 CA, I/BED C/1/1/3/1, Cmdt, Richmond, to Deputy Admr, 10 June 1902; I/ADE B/1/1, Martial Law Admr's Notebook, entry for 9 July 1902; NAM, 5903/1/43, Hanover Station Orders, No. 14/4, 14 July 1902; 7603/70/8, Lt M. P. Holt, 'Why did the South African War take place, and what were its consequences?', unpublished typescript, n.d.; *Albert Times and Molteno Advertiser*, 5 July 1902.

31 *Household Brigade Magazine*, 51, 5 (1902), pp. 206–7.

32 SGR, I/A.72/2, Lt G. Paynter, Diary, entry for 7 June 1902.

33 CA, I/ALN 4/1/1, Capt. Difford to CC, Aliwal North, 18 June 1902; *St George's Gazette*, 20, 234 (1902), p. 116.

34 Warwick, *Black People*, pp. 183–4.

35 CA, I/ALN 1/1/12, H. Moller to RM, 16 October 1902.

36 *Primitive Methodist Missionary Record*, June 1902, p. 84; November 1903, p. 175.

37 USPG, Letters Received, Africa, vol. I, D Series, Bishop of Grahamstown to Archbishop of Cape Town, 1 June 1902.

38 CA, I/KDM 4/1/2/5, 366/02, Ag RM to RM, Barkly West, 10 May 1902; *Naval and Military Record*, 3 June 1902.

39 *Cape Hansard*, 1902, pp. 472–3.

40 Ibid., p. 471.

41 For some of these demands, see CA, I/GSD 7/31, Ag RM to Under Colonial Secretary, 14 Oct. 1902; I/BED CI/I/I/5/I, C/138, R. H. Alcott to P. Hewett, 18 Nov. 1902; S. D. Bayres, 'Markets of the Future: No. 1 – South Africa', *Magazine of Commerce*, 1, 1 (1902), p. 81.

42 Fuller Papers, IV/3/104, Fuller to his father, 10 Aug. 1902.

43 Bundy, *South African Peasantry*, p. 122.

44 *H.C. Debs.*, 4th Series, vol. CXX, col. 104, 24 March 1903. For further varied elaboration of this theme, see SAL, Richardson Papers, Notebook, 1902, Account of conversation with Milner, 22 Oct. 1902; *Cape Daily Telegraph*, 12 July 1902; *Umtata Herald*, 29 Aug. 1902; *Foreign Mission Chronicle*, 3, 4 (1902), p. 137; W. P. Reeves, 'Colonial Ideals', *Independent Review*, 1, 3 (1903), p. 368; Revd J. S. Moffat, 'Native Labour in South Africa', *Independent Review*, 8, 2 (1904), pp. 629–40; D. Hobart Houghton and J. Dagut (eds.), *Source Material on the South African Economy, 1860–1970*, vol. II, Cape Town, 1972, pp. 22–9, 30; D. Denoon, *A Grand Illusion: The Failure of Imperial Policy in the Transvaal Colony during the Period of Reconstruction, 1900–1905*, London, 1973, pp. 127–58; Cell, *White Supremacy*, pp. 78–9.

45 CA, I/AXA 6/3/1/5, 180/12, RM to SNA, 12 June 1902; *Oxfordshire Light Infantry Chronicle*, 1902, p. 117. As before, the transporting of labour out of the Cape provoked desertions: CA, NA 500, Folio 103, 683/A.103, SNA to CMT, 18 June 1902; Folio 101, 684/A.103, SNA to Cmdt, Cape Colony No. 1 District, 16 June 1902.

46 CA, I/UIT 16/33, RM to Ag RM, Bredasdorp, 4 Jan. 1903; I/TBH G/1/1/1, RM to OC, Cheshire Regiment, 4 March 1902; *Berliner Missions Jahresbericht*, 79 (1902), p. 29; *The Bugle*, 19, 5 (1902), pp. 6–7; Grundlingh, '"God Het Ons Arm Mense die Houtjies Gegee": Towards a History of the "Poor White" Woodcutters in the Southern Cape Forest Area, *c.* 1900–1939', University of the Witwatersrand, History Workshop Paper, Conference on the Making of Class, Feb. 1987.

47 Goldin, *Making Race*, p. 16; Lewis, *Between the Wire*, p. 12.

48 See J. M. Lonsdale, 'Some Origins of Nationalism in East Africa', *Journal of African History*, 9, 1 (1968), p. 145; J. Tosh, 'The Economy of the Southern Sudan under the British, 1898–1955', *Journal of Imperial and Commonwealth History*, 9, 3 (1981), p. 284; G. Hodges, 'Military Labour in East Africa and its Impact on Kenya', in Page (ed.), *Africa and the First World War*, p. 141.

49 S. C. Townell, 'The Crawfish Industry of the Cape West Coast, 1874–1947', B.A. Hons dissertation, University of Cape Town, 1977, pp. 28–34; P. Cuthbert, 'The Administration of Dr Jameson as Prime Minister of the Cape Colony, 1904–1908', M.A. thesis, University of Cape Town, 1950, pp. 19, 53.

50 Until the start of the depression, Cape migrants on Rand mines numbered fewer than 4,000 – by 1908 they had increased to over 50,000: W. Beinart, '"Joyini Inkomo": Cattle Advances and the Origins of Migrancy from Pondoland', *Journal of Southern African Studies*, 5, 2 (1979), p. 209; '"Jamani": Cape Workers in German South West Africa, 1904–12', in *Hidden Struggles*, p. 177; A. H. Jeeves, *Migrant Labour in South Africa's Mining Economy: The Struggle for the Gold Mines' Labour Supply, 1890–1920*, Kingston and Montreal, 1985, p. 257, also emphasises the role of the depression in weakening non-mining work options for Cape Africans.

51 Beinart and Bundy, 'Introduction: "Away in the Locations"', in *Hidden Struggles*, p. 20.

52 W. Beinart and C. Bundy, 'State Intervention and Rural Resistance: The Transkei, 1900–1965', in M. Klein (ed.), *Peasants in Africa: Historical and Contemporary Perspectives*, Beverly Hills, 1980, p. 286; Beinart, 'Jamani', pp. 185–6.

53 *Studies*, vol. I: *New Babylon*, p. xv.

54 Warwick, *Black People*, pp. 160–2; Willan, 'Mafeking', pp. 159–60; *Sol Plaatje*, pp. 105, 113–16; Pakenham, *Boer War*, p. 418.

55 RSR, 1/119, Bidder, Letterbooks, vol. II, RM, Cradock, to R. C. Griffin, 22 Sept. 1902, encl. in Griffin to Bidder (conf.), 5 Oct. 1902.

56 CA, I/HDP 5/1/1/2/4, RM to Cmdt, Uitenhage, 12 Aug. 1902.

57 NAM, 6112/190/7, Cooper to Shelton, 14 June 1902.

58 NAM, 6112/190/7, Revd Locke to Cooper, 2 July 1902; 6112/190/15, Revd E. C. Hewitt to Cooper, 7 Feb. 1903; Price, 'Leliefontein', pp. 55–6; Carstens, *Cape Coloured Community*, p. 37.

59 Cited in Denoon, 'Participation in the Boer War', p. 115.

60 *Bandolier*, 2, 24 (1902), p. 12.

61 CA, I/CDK 8/23, 7/12/02, RM to Cmdt, Uitenhage, 19 Sept. 1902.

62 CA, I/ALN 4/1/2/3, Under Secretary, War Department, to RM, 22 Dec. 1902; RAMC, A/459, Lt J. F. Palmer, Diary, entry for 22 Aug. 1902; *Rifle Brigade Chronicle* (1902), p. 62; *Cape Hansard*, 1903, p. 655.

63 CA, I/BDP B/I/I/I, RM to Secretary, War Losses Compensation Commission, 12 Feb. 1903; I/VBG 22/10, 18/3/3, Claim No. 29, War Losses Compensation Commission, Vryburg District, 24 April 1903; Claims Nos. 78 and 82, Vryburg District, 25 June 1903.

64 CA, I/BRE 4/1/3/2/2, RM to Lt P. Milton, 14 Nov. 1902; I/ALN 4/9/1/1, J. Msiki to RM, 16 Sept. 1902.

65 AGG, RO.14/9/16, Massey, Diary, entry for 11 June 1902.

66 Douglas-Scott Letters, Lt Douglas-Scott to H. Francis, 4 July 1902.

67 CA, I/TBH G/1/1/1, 21/1/2, RM to Gen. French (conf.), 22 July 1902. For the mens' case, see I/TBH G/1/1/2, S. Daniels and four others to RM, 10 July 1902.

68 SAL, Richardson Papers, Mss. 661, L. Richardson, Notebook, 1903, entry for 24 Oct. 1903; see also A. Davey (ed.), *Lawrence Richardson: Selected Correspondence*, Cape Town, 1977, p. 21.

69 *Rural Transformations*, p. 109.

70 *Albert Times and Molteno Advertiser*, 22 Sept. 1902; *Graaff-Reinet Advertiser*, 2 Oct. 1902; *Worcester Standard*, 17 Nov. 1902.

71 Lewis, *Between the Wire*, p. 12. See also Trapido, 'African People's Organisation', p. 11; Goldin, *Making Race*, pp. 16–18; Skillicorn, 'Black Voter', p. 10.

72 *The African Poor: A History*, Cambridge, 1987, p. 114.

73 K. Wyndham-Smith, *From Frontier to Midlands: A History of the Graaff-Reinet District from 1786–1910*, Grahamstown, 1976, p. 193.

74 P/MMS, 1139, PM Annual Reports, 1901–2, Annual Report, Aliwal North Mission, 1902.

75 P/MMS, 1138, PM Quarterly Reports, 1901–2, minutes of quarterly meeting, Aliwal North, 5 July 1902.

76 CA, I/ALN 4/3/3, RM to Under Colonial Secretary, 17 June 1902; NA 500, Folio 101, Senior Medical Officer to Cmdt, Aliwal North, 10 July 1902.

77 M. W. Swanson, '"The Sanitation Syndrome": Bubonic Plague and Urban Native Policy in the Cape Colony, 1900–1909', *Journal of African History*, 18, 3 (1977), pp. 387–410; Bundy, 'Vagabond Hollanders', p. 121.

78 Swanson, 'Sanitation Syndrome', p. 409.

79 Marks and Trapido, 'Politics of Race', p. 8.

80 *Black People*, pp. 145, 151; *Methods of Barbarism?*, p. 266.

81 'Some Aspects of the Demographic Consequences of the First World War in Britain', *Population Studies*, 30, 3 (1976), p. 542.

82 'Cape Town and the Plague of 1901', in Saunders, Phillips and van Heyningen (eds.), *Studies in the History of Cape Town*, vol. IV, p. 84.

83 CA, I/CDK 8/23, Letter from 'Coloured school teacher', 9 May 1904, encl. in RM to RM, Somerset East, 11 June 1904.

84 CA, I/BED CI/I/I/I, J. Begomba to District Administrator, 31 May 1902.

85 B. Anderson, *Imagined Communities*, London, 1983.

86 Trapido, 'White Conflict', pp. 416–17.

87 Lewis, *Between the Wire*, pp. 18–19; Goldin, *Making Race*, pp. 30–1.

88 S. Marks and S. Trapido, 'Lord Milner and the South African State', *History Workshop Journal*, 8 (1979), p. 52.

89 *Sol Plaatje*, p. 105.

90 Davidson, *The People's Cause*. See also D. Killingray, 'People's Warfare' (review), *Journal of African History*, 24, 4 (1983), p. 544.

91 Beinart, 'Jamani', p. 184.

92 *White Power and the Liberal Conscience: Racial Segregation and South African Liberalism*, Johannesburg, 1984, p. 3. For a summary of the views of other historians making the same general point, see Cell, *White Supremacy*.

93 Cuthbert, 'Administration of Dr Jameson', pp. 7–8, 58–63; E. D. Thielscher, 'The Suspension Movement in the Cape Colony and its Effects, 1901–1904', B.A. Hons. dissertation, University of Cape Town, 1962, pp. 79–80; Skillicorn, 'Black Voter', pp. 7–8; Trapido, 'African Political Organisation', p. 11; E. A Walker, *Lord de Villiers and His Times: South Africa, 1842–1914*, London, 1925, p. 413.

94 H. Giliomee, 'Western Cape Farmers and the Beginnings of Afrikaner Nationalism, 1870–1915', *Journal of Southern African Studies*, 14, 1 (1988), p. 59.

95 Marks and Trapido, 'Politics of Race', p. 28.

96 J. Lonsdale, 'From Colony to Industrial State: South African Historiography as seen from England', *Social Dynamics*, 9, 1 (1983), p. 67.

97 'Rural Struggles and Transformations' (review article), *South African Historical Journal*, 19 (1987), p. 167.

98 P. A. Molteno to Lord Loreburn, 20 March 1906, cited in V. Solomon (ed.), *Selections from the Correspondence of Percy Alport Molteno, 1892–1914*, Cape Town, 1981, p. 254.

99 'Colony to Industrial State', p. 78.

100 Cell, *White Supremacy*, p. 116.

101 For this contrasting perspective, see Keegan, *Rural Transformations*, p. 58; *Facing the Storm: Portraits of Black Lives in Rural South Africa*, Cape Town, 1988; Beinart and Delius, 'Introduction', in *A Plough to the Ground*, p. 38. The Act influenced land practices in the Cape, although it was of no

legal effect there because of the Province's constitutionally entrenched non-racial franchise: Maylam, *African People*, p. 143.

102 S. Greenberg, *Race and State in Capitalist Development: South Africa in Comparative Perspective*, Johannesburg, 1980, pp. 386–7.

103 Marks and Trapido, 'Politics of Race', p. 1.

104 Cited by R. Samuel, 'Patriotic Fantasy', *New Statesman*, 18 July 1986.

105 *The Collier's Rant: Song and Culture in the Industrial Village*, London, 1977, p. 198.

106 Song celebrating 'Die Bruin Rooinekryers' ('The Brown Redneck Riders'), performed by 'Oom' Attie Hendricks, Fraserburg, March 1979. Transcribed and translated by the author. Born in 1903, 'Oom' Attie was the son of an agricultural worker who had scouted for the West Kent Regiment, 'The Buffs'; the regiment's scout company was apparently known, appropriately, as the 'Brown Buffs'.

107 C. Clark, 'Politics, Language and Class' (review article), *Radical History Review*, 34 (1986), p. 85.

108 G. M. Fredrickson, *White Supremacy: A Comparative Study on American and South African History*, New York, 1981, p. 260.

109 Cited in W. R. Nasson, 'Bobbies to Boers: Police, People, and Social Control in Cape Town, *ca.* 1880–1960', in D. Anderson and D. Killingray (eds.), *Policing the Empire: Government, Authority and Control, 1780–1940*, Manchester, forthcoming.

Select bibliography

I Unpublished sources

A Official

    South Africa

State Archives Depot, Cape Town
AG   Attorney-General's Department, Anglo-Boer War Files
DD   Colonial Defence Department, Papers relating to Native Levies and Intelligence Work, Anglo-Boer War
NAD   Native Affairs Department, Correspondence Files
SGE   Archive of the Superintendent-General of Education, Cape Colony
CHB   Papers of the Table Bay Harbour Board
I/BED   Anglo-Boer War Papers of the Commandant, Native Commissioner and Deputy Administrator of Martial Law, Bedford
I/CDK   Anglo-Boer War Papers of the Civil Commissioner and Resident Magistrate, Cradock
I/CMT   Archive of the Chief Magistrate, Transkeian Territories
I/CMK   Archive of the Chief Magistrate, Griqualand East
I/TAM   Archive of the Special Magistrate, King William's Town (Tamacha)

The following Resident Magistrates' Archives were consulted:
I/ADE Adelaide; I/ALN Aliwal North; I/AXA Alexandria; I/BDP Burghersdorp; I/BKE Barkly East; I/BRE Bredasdorp; I/CAL Caledon; I/CDP Calitzdorp; I/CWM Clanwilliam; I/DEA De Aaar; I/DGS Douglas; I/EOT Elliott; I/FBG Fraserburg; I/GR Graaff-Reinet; I/GSD Griquatown; I/HDP Humansdorp; I/JTN Jamestown; I/KDM Klipdam; I/KMN Kuruman; I/LDG Lady Grey; I/MBY Malmesbury; I/SSE Somerset East; I/SBK Springbok; I/TBH Tulbagh; I/UIT Uitenhage; I/UPT Upington; I/VBG Vryburg.

Great Britain

    Public Records Office, London
CO 417 Africa South, Despatches and Correspondence, 1899–1902
CO 48 Cape Colony, Despatches and Correspondence, 1899–1902
WO 32 South African War, Despatches and Correspondence, 1899–1902

Bibliography

B Non-official

South Africa

Cory Library for Historical Research, Rhodes University, Grahamstown
A. J. Kidwell, Notes on the Boer War, original typescript (Mss. 11/002)

J. W. Jagger Library, University of Cape Town
Olive Schreiner Letters: Murray Parker, Ursula Scott Collections
W. P. Schreiner Papers
W. E. Stanford Papers

South African Public Library, Cape Town
J. X. Merriman Papers
J. Rose-Innes Papers
Lawrence Richardson Papers
W. P. Schreiner Papers (Mss. S.A. Section B)
    Methodist Church Archives:
J. Henwood, Diary of the Siege of O'Okiep, 1902
J. G. Locke Papers
Miscellaneous Records of Methodist Missions in Namaqualand, 1901–2

Oral interviews, 1978–87
Mr Watutu Mtozi; Mrs Wilhemina Isaacs; Mrs Nettie Daniels; Mr Jacob Zurne (UCT Kaplan Centre for Jewish Studies, Oral Collection); Miss Anne Murinik; Mr Willem Peters; Mrs Florence Malan; Mrs Teresa Sharp; Mr Peter Manel; Mr Arthur ('Attie') Hendricks; Mrs Jessie Qakamfana; Mrs Emily Fosa; Dr Alfred Biddle; Mrs Alida Arendse; Miss Anna Spies; Mr Leslie Newman; Revd Reginald Pearce; Revd Alastair McGregor; Mr Nicholas Galant; Mrs Sarah Erasmus; Mr Samuel Anderson; Mr John Esau.

Great Britain

Archives of the United Society for the Propagation of the Gospel, London
D Series Mss. Letters Received, Africa, 1899–1902
E Series Mss. Missionaries' Field Reports, Africa, 1899–1902

Greater London Record Office, Middlesex Records Division
Churchward Papers

Imperial War Museum, London
Coney Diaries

India Office Library and Records, London
Butterworth Diaries (Mss. Eur. D. 1900)
Sir G. White Collection (Mss. Eur. F. 108)

Library and Archives of the Royal Army Medical College, London
Army Field Hospital Reports, 1900–2
Maidment Deposit
Palmer Diaries
Porter Diaries
Wilson Diaries

Hewitt Letters
Beach Papers
Morton Papers

Library of the School of Oriental and African Studies, University of London
Archives of the Council for World Mission (incorporating the London Missionary Society)
    Archives of the London Missionary Society:
LMS South Africa, Incoming Letters, 1899–1902
LMS South Africa, Reports, 1899–1902
    Archives of the Wesleyan Methodist Missionary Society:
MMS Records of the South African Conference, 1897–9, 1900–1
    Archives of the Primitive Methodist Missionary Society:
P/MMS South African Correspondence, 1899–1902
P/MMS South Africa, Quarterly Mission Reports, 1899–1902

Liddell Hart Centre for Military Archives, King's College Library, University of London
Aston Papers
Burnaby Papers
Clive Papers
Fuller Papers
Hamilton Papers

Museum of the Royal Highland Fusiliers, Glasgow
Battalion Service Diaries, 1899–1901
Battalion Service Digests, 1899–1901
Kelham Service Diaries

National Army Museum, London
This contains a substantial holding of relevant military journals, diaries, notebooks, letters and other ephemera. As the collection is far too large to list here, a glance at my notes and attributions will indicate the range of manuscript sources to which I am most directly indebted. This bibliography entry is therefore confined to two major collections:
NAM 6807/187/190 1st Cavalry Division, Intelligence Papers, South African Campaign
NAM 6112/190/15 Namaqualand Field Force Papers, 1900–2

National Library of Scotland, Edinburgh
Mission Records, United Free Church of Scotland: Kaffraria and North Kaffraria, Cape Colony, 1899–1902

National Maritime Museum, London
Limpus Papers
Porter Papers
Stokes Rees Papers

Public Records Office
Kitchener Papers (PRO 30/57)
Roberts Papers (WO 105)

Record Office, Regimental Headquarters, Coldstream Guards, London
Codrington Diaries
Everard Diaries
Eyre-Lloyd Diaries

Bibliography

Henniker Diaries
Battalion Service Digests, 1899–1902
Regiment's Court Martial and Punishment Books, 1899–1902
C. H. Burtachaell, 'The Medical Service with Lord Methuen's Force during the Advance on Kimberley', original typescript.

Record Office, Regimental Headquarters, Grenadier Guards, London
W. Burke, Diary, 1899–1902
V. Russell, Diary, 1899–1902
Spencer-Churchill Diaries, 1900–2
Gurdon-Rebow Letters
Aubrey Notebooks, 1900–2
Battalion Native Labour Roll Books, 1901
Battalion Order Books, 1899–1901
Battalion Records, 1899–1901
Regiment's Court Martial and Punishment Books, 1900–2

Record Office, Regimental Headquarters, Irish Guards, London
Douglas-Scott Diaries and Letters, 1901–2
H. J. Lerner, South African War Scrapbooks, 2 vols.

Record Office, Regimental Headquarters, Scots Guards, London
Barttelot Diaries, 1899–1902
W. Nash, Diary, 1900–1
G. Paynter, Diary, 1900–2
W. Cuthbert, 2nd Battalion Notes
C. H. Willoughby, Intelligence Notebooks

Westfield College Library, University of London
Lyttelton Letters

West Sussex County Record Office, Chichester
Archives of the Royal Sussex Regiment
Maxse Papers

II Published contemporary sources

A Official

South Africa

Cape Colony, *Blue Books on Native Affairs, 1899–1903, G.50, G.52, G.25, G.29*
Cape Colony, *Legislative Assembly Debates, Hansard, 1899–1902*
South African Native Affairs Commission, 1903–1905, Minutes of Evidence (1905), 5 vols.

Great Britain

Parliamentary Debates, 1899–1902
Parliamentary Papers, 1899–1902

British Parliamentary Papers:

Administration of the Army Remount Department, 1899–1902, Proceedings of Court of Enquiry, 1902, Cd 993

Basutoland Annual Reports, 1899–1902

Further Correspondence relating to Affairs in South Africa, 1900–1903, Cd 43, Cd 261, Cd 420, Cd 547 Cd 903, Cd 1163, Cd 1463

Report of the South African Native Affairs Commission, 1905, Cd 2399

Report, together with Minutes of Evidence (2 Vols.) and Appendices of the Commissioners Appointed to Enquire into the Military Preparations and Other Matters Connected with the War in South Africa, 1904, Cd 1789, Cd 1790, Cd 1791, Cd 1792

South Africa, Despatches, Vol. 1, 1901, Cd 457

Telegram from Sir Alfred Milner to the Secretary of State for War, relating to the Reported Outrage on Esau at Calvinia, 1901, Cd 464

B Non-official

Newspapers and Periodicals

South Africa

Albert Times and Molteno Advertiser
Cape Argus
Cape Daily Telegraph
Cape Law Journal
Cape Mercury
Cape Times
Colesberg Advertiser
De Graaff-Reinetter
Diamond Fields Advertiser
Graaff-Reinet Advertiser
Het Zuid-Oosten
Kokstad Advertiser
Midland News and Karoo Farmer
Ons Land
Mossel Bay Advertiser
Imvo Zabantsundu
Izwi Labantu
South African Law Journal
South African News
South African Spectator
Umtata Herald
Worcester Advertiser
Worcester Standard

Great Britain

Edinburgh Review
Fortnightly Review
Lloyds Weekly Newspaper
Morning Post

Bibliography

Nineteenth Century
Quarterly Review
The Times

Army Journals
Black and White Budget
Navy and Army Gazette
Navy and Army Illustrated
Naval and Military Record
Under the Union Jack
United Service Gazette

Regimental magazines
Bandolier (Cape Police); *Bugle* (Yorkshire Light Infantry); *Donegal's Own* (Inniskilling Fusiliers); *Globe and Laurel* (Royal Marines); *Green Howards Gazette*; *Highland Light Infantry Chronicle*; *Household Brigade Magazine*; *King's Royal Rifle Corps Chronicle*; *Lancashire Fusiliers Annual*; *Light Bob Gazette* (Somerset Light Infantry); *Oakleaf* (Cheshire Regiment); *Oxfordshire Light Infantry Chronicle*; *Rifle Brigade Chronicle*; *Royal Engineers Journal*; *St George's Gazette* (Northumberland Fusiliers); *Suffolk Gazette* (Suffolk Regiment); *Thistle* (Royal Scots Regiment)

Mission journals
Berliner Missionsgesellschaft, Jahresberichte
Berliner Missionsgesellschaft, Missionsberichte
Mitteilungen aus der Brüder-Gemeine
All the World
All Nations
Foreign Mission Chronicle of the Episcopal Church in Scotland
Methodist Monthly
Mission Field
Periodical Accounts relating to the Moravian Missions
Primitive Methodist Quarterly Review
Primitive Methodist Missionary Record

C Contemporary books, articles, pamphlets and unofficial reports

'A Horse's Experience of the South African War: Told by Itself', *Bailey's Magazine*, 501 (1901), pp. 361–6
Bayres, S. D. 'Markets of the Future: No. I – South Africa', *Magazine of Commerce*, 1 (1902), pp. 75–83
Bigelow, P. 'The Latter Day Fighting Animal', *Anglo-Saxon Review*, 5 (1900), pp. 186–92
Billington, R. C. *A Mule Driver at the Front*, Chapman and Hall, London, 1901
Blackburn, D. 'Some South African Prejudices', *Chambers's Journal*, 5, 254 (1902), pp. 812–16
Blackburn, D. and W. Waithmann Cadell. *Secret Service in South Africa*, Cassell, London, 1911
Bridge, C. H. 'A Short Lecture on Military Vehicles', *Army Service Corps Quarterly* (July, 1907), pp. 167–89
Brief History of the Transvaal Secret Service System, Taylor, Cape Town, 1899
Brooks, S. 'British and Dutch in South Africa', *Harper's Monthly Magazine* (January, 1900), pp. 304–10
Calwell, C. E. *Small Wars, Their Principles and Practice*, 2nd edn, HMSO, London, 1899
Conan Doyle, A. *The Great Boer War*, Smith and Elder, London, 1903
de Wet, C. R. *Three Years War*, Constable, London, 1902
Dickinson, W. K. L. *The Biograph in Battle: Its Story in the South African War*, Fisher Unwin, London, 1901
Easton, E. E. 'Inside the Boer Lines', *Harper's Monthly Magazine* (May, 1900), pp. 815–29
'First Chapter of the War', *Scottish Review*, 35 (1900), pp. 129–61

Fuller, J. F. C. *The Last of the Gentleman's Wars, a Subaltern's Journal of the War in South Africa*, Faber, London, 1937

Golding, L. 'Looting a Boer Camp', *Chambers's Journal*, 4, 161 (1900), pp. 94–6

Hartland, E. S. 'The Native Problem in our New Colonies', *Monthly Review* (April, 1901), pp. 73–90

Hillier, A. P. 'The Native Races of South Africa', *Report of Proceedings of the Royal Colonial Institute*, 30 (1898–9), pp. 30–51

Hook, D. B. *With Sword and Statute on the Cape of Good Hope Frontier*, Greaves, London, 1906

How to Read War News: Notes and Hints to Readers of Despatches and Intelligence from the Seat of War, with a Glossary of Military Technical Terms, African and Dutch Phrases, Fisher Unwin, London, 1900

Howe, Countess (Lady Georgina Curzon). *Imperial Yeomanry Hospitals in South Africa, 1900–1902*, 3 vols., Humphrey, London, 1902

Mackarness, F. *Martial Law in the Cape Colony during 1901*, National Press Agency, London, 1901

'Martial Law', *Edinburgh Review*, 105, 399 (1902), pp. 98–106

Moffat, J. S. 'Native Labour in South Africa', *Independent Review*, 1, 4 (1904), pp. 629–40

The Black Man and The War, Vigilance Paper No. 8, South African Vigilance Committee, Cape Town, c. 1900–1

Moffett, E. C. *With the 8th Division*, Knapp and Drewett, London, 1903

Molema, S. M. *The Bantu Past and Present*, Green, Edinburgh, 1920

Molteno, P. A. *The South African Crisis: A Plain Statement of Facts*, South African Conciliation Committee, Cape Town, c. 1900–1

Morgan, B. H. 'The Trade and Industry of South Africa', *Report of Proceedings of the Royal Colonial Institute*, 34 (1902–3), pp. 130–61

Official Records of the Guards Brigade in South Africa, Kelliher, London, 1904

Owen, J. F. 'The Military Defence Forces of the Colonies', *Report of Proceedings of the Royal Colonial Institute*, 21 (1889–90), pp. 277–302

Parker, S. J. 'The Evolution of the Method of Supply from a War to a Normal Peace System, South Africa, 1902–1907', *Army Service Corps Quarterly* (July 1907), pp. 140–50

Plaatje, S. T. *Native Life in South Africa*, King, London, 1916

Ralph, J. *Towards Pretoria*, Pearson, London, 1900

Reeves, W. P. 'Colonial Ideals', *Independent Review*, 1, 3 (1903), pp. 365–79

Reitz, D. *Commando: A Boer Journal of the Boer War*, Faber and Faber, London, 1929

'Relief of O'Okiep', *Royal Engineers Journal*, 2 (1903), pp. 1–4

Royal Engineers Institute, *Detailed History of the Railways in the South African War 1899–1902*, Royal Engineers Institute, Chatham, 1904

Scully, W. C. *Further Reminiscences of a South African Pioneer*, Fisher Unwin, London, 1913

'Second Chapter of the War', *Scottish Review*, 36 (1900), pp. 353–78

'South African Journalist'. 'The Boers and Poor Whites', *Chambers's Journal*, 3, 131 (1900), pp. 462–7

South African Native Races Committee. *The Natives of South Africa, Their Economic and Social Conditions*, Murray, London, 1901

The South African Natives, Their Progress and Present Condition, Murray, London, 1909

Spoelstra, C. 'Are the Boers Hostile to Mission Work?', *New Age*, London, 1902

'Sport with the Army in South Africa', *Bailey's Magazine*, 494, 75 (1901), pp. 281–2

St Cuthbert's Mission in the Diocese of St John's Kaffraria, Report for 1902, and Occasional News, 4th Series (1902)

Treatment of the Natives in South Africa, Pamphlet No. 41, South African Conciliation Committee, Cape Town, 1900

van Warmelo, D. *On Commando*, Methuen, London, 1902

Viljoen, B. *My Reminiscences of the Anglo-Boer War*, Hood, Howard and Douglas, London, 1902

'Vindex Justitae'. 'A Message from the Cape', *Westminster Review*, 155, 4 (1901), pp. 359–60

Wallace, R. 'Agriculture in South Africa', *Report of Proceedings of the Royal Colonial Institute*, 32 (1900–1), pp. 139–65

231

Bibliography

Wyncoll, C. E. 'South African Railway Transport: Notes on Railway Transport during the South African Campaign', *Army Service Corps Quarterly* (July 1906), pp. 432–63

Young, F. 'A Winter Tour in South Africa', *Report of Proceedings of the Royal Colonial Institute*, 28 (1899–1900), pp. 26–33

D Documentary records subsequently published

Comaroff, J. L. (ed.) *The Boer War Diary of Sol T. Plaatje, an African at Mafeking*, Macmillan, London, 1973

Davey, A. M. (ed.) *Lawrence Richardson: Selected Correspondence, 1902–1903*, Van Riebeeck Society, Cape Town, 1977

Hancock, W. K. and J. van der Poel (eds.) *Selections from the Smuts Papers*, vol. I, Cambridge University Press, London, 1966

Headlam, C. (ed.) *The Milner Papers, South Africa, 1897–1905*, 2 vols., Cassell, London, 1933

Hobart Houghton, D. and J. Dagut (eds.) *Source Material on the South African Economy, 1860–1899 and 1899–1919*, 2 vols., Oxford University Press, Cape Town, 1972

Karis, T. and G. M. Carter (eds.) *From Protest to Challenge: A Documentary History of African Politics in South Africa*, vol. I: *Protest and Hope, 1882–1934*, Hoover Institution Press, Stanford, 1972

Gerhart, G. M. and T. Karis (eds.) *From Protest to Challenge: A Documentary History of African Politics in South Africa*, vol. IV: *Political Profiles, 1882–1964*, Hoover Institution Press, Stanford, 1977

Lewsen, P. (ed.) *Selections from the Correspondence of John X. Merriman*, vol. III, Van Riebeeck Society, Cape Town, 1966

Macquarrie, J. W. (ed.) *The Reminiscences of Sir Walter Stanford*, 2 vols., Van Riebeeck Society, Cape Town, 1958 and 1962

Solomon, V. (ed.) *Selections from the Correspondence of Percy Alport Molteno, 1892–1914*, Van Riebeeck Society, Cape Town, 1981

Wright, H. M. (ed.) *Sir James Rose-Innes: Selected Correspondence, 1884–1902*, Van Riebeeck Society, Cape Town, 1975

III Secondary sources

A Books

Amery, L. C. M. S. (ed.), *The Times History of the War in South Africa 1899–1902*, 7 vols. Sampson, Low and Marston, London, 1900–9

Beinart, W. *The Political Economy of Pondoland, 1860–1930*, Ravan, Johannesburg, 1983

Beinart, W. and C. Bundy. *Hidden Struggles in Rural South Africa: Politics and Popular Movements in the Transkei and Eastern Cape, 1890–1930*, Ravan, Johannesburg, 1987

Beinart, W., P. Delius and S. Trapido (eds.) *Putting a Plough to the Ground: Accumulation and Dispossession in Rural Africa, 1850–1930*, Ravan, Johannesburg, 1986

Best, G. *Humanity in Warfare: The Modern History of the International Law of Armed Conflicts*, Weidenfeld and Nicholson, London, 1980

Breytenbach, J. H. *Die Geskiedenis van die Tweede Vryheidsoorlog in Suid-Afrika, 1899–1902*, 3 vols., Die Staatsdrukker, Pretoria, 1969–1974

Bundy, C. *The Rise and Fall of the South African Peasantry*, Heinemann, London, 1979 and new edn., Cape Town and London, 1988

Carstens, P. *The Social Structure of a Cape Coloured Reserve: A Study of Racial Integration and Segregation in South Africa*, Oxford University Press, Cape Town, 1966

Cell, J. W. *The Highest Stage of White Supremacy: The Origins of Segregation in South Africa and the American South*, Cambridge University Press, Cambridge, 1982

Davenport, T. R. H. *The Afrikaner Bond: The History of a South African Political Party, 1880–1911*, Oxford University Press, Cape Town, 1966

South Africa: A Modern History, Macmillan, London, 1977

Davidson, B. *The People's Cause: A History of Guerrillas in Africa*, Longman, London, 1981

de Kiewiet, C. W. *A History of South Africa, Social and Economic*, Oxford University Press, Oxford, 1941

Denoon, D. *Southern Africa since 1800*, Longman, London, 1972

Enloe, C. H. *Ethnic Soldiers: State Security in a Divided Society*, Penguin, Harmondsworth, 1980

Farwell, B. *The Great Anglo-Boer War*, Allen Lane, London, 1977

Goldin, I. *Making Race: The Politics and Economics of Coloured Identity in South Africa*, Maskew Miller Longman, Cape Town, 1987

Goodfellow, D. M. *A Modern Economic History of South Africa*, George Routledge, London, 1931

Greenberg, S. B. *Race and State in Capitalist Development: South Africa in Comparative Perspective*, Ravan, Johannesburg, 1980

Grundlingh, A. *Fighting their Own War: South African Blacks and the First World War*, Ravan, Johannesburg, 1987

Grundy, K. W. *Soldiers without Politics: Blacks in the South African Armed Forces*, University of California Press, Berkeley and Los Angeles, 1983

Jabavu, D. D. T. *The Life of John Tengo Jabavu, Editor of Imvo Zabantsundu, 1884–1921*, Lovedale Press, Lovedale, 1922

Keegan, T. J. *Rural Transformations in Industrializing South Africa: The Southern Highveld to 1914*, Ravan, Johannesburg, 1986

Facing the Storm: Portraits of Black Lives in Rural South Africa, David Philip, Cape Town, 1988

Krüger, B. and P. W. Schäberg. *The Pear Tree Bears Fruit: The History of the Moravian Church in South Africa, Western Cape Province, 1869–1980*, Genadendal, 1984

Le May, G. H. L. *British Supremacy in South Africa, 1899–1907*, Oxford University Press, Oxford, 1965

Lewis, G. *Between the Wire and the Wall: A History of South African 'Coloured' Politics*, David Philip, Cape Town, 1987

Macmillan, W. M. *The Cape Colour Question: A Historical Survey*, Faber and Gwyer, London, 1927

Bantu, Boer, and Briton: The Making of the South African Native Problem, Oxford University Press, Oxford, 1963

Marais, J. S. *The Cape Coloured People, 1652–1937*, Longman, London, 1937

Marks, S. *The Ambiguities of Dependence in South Africa: Class, Nationalism, and the State in Twentieth-Century Natal*, Ravan, Johannesburg, 1986

Marks, S. and A. Atmore (eds.) *Economy and Society in Pre-Industrial South Africa*, Longman, London, 1980

Marks, S. and R. Rathbone (eds.) *Industrialisation and Social Change in South Africa: African Class Formation, Culture and Consciousness 1870–1930*, Longman, London, 1982

Marks. S. and S. Trapido (eds.). *The Politics of Race, Class and Nationalism in Twentieth Century South Africa*, Longman, London, 1987

Maylam, P. *A History of the African People of South Africa: From the Early Iron Age to the 1970s*, David Philip, Cape Town, 1986

McCracken, J. L. *The Cape Parliament, 1854–1910*, Oxford University Press, Oxford, 1967

Odendaal, A. *Vukani Bantu!: The Beginnings of Black Protest Politics in South Africa to 1912*, David Philip, Cape Town, 1984

Omer-Cooper, J. D. *History of Southern Africa*, James Currey, London, 1987

Pakenham, T. *The Boer War*, Weidenfeld and Nicholson, London, 1979

Palmer, R. and N. Parsons (eds.) *The Roots of Rural Poverty in Central and Southern Africa*, Heinemann, London, 1977

Pretorius, F. *The Anglo-Boer War 1899–1902*, Nelson, Cape Town, 1985

Pyrah, G. B. *Imperial Policy and South Africa, 1902–1910*, Oxford University Press, Oxford, 1955

Reader, D. H. *The Black Man's Portion*, Oxford University Press, Cape Town, 1961

Sachs, A. *Justice in South Africa*, Sussex University Press and Heinemann, London, 1973

Bibliography

Saunders, C. C. (ed.) *Black Leaders in Southern African History*, Heinemann, London, 1979
  The Making of the South African Past: Major Historians on Race and Class, David Philip, Cape Town, 1988
Simons, H. J. and R. E. Simons. *Class and Colour in South Africa, 1850–1950*, Penguin, Harmondsworth, 1969
Taylor-Hamilton, J. and K. G. Hamilton. *History of the Moravian Church: The Renewed Unitas Fratrum, 1722–1957*, Board of Christian Education, Moravian Church of America, 1967
Thompson, L. M. *The Political Mythology of Apartheid*, Yale University Press, New Haven, 1985
  The Unification of South Africa, 1902–1910, Oxford University Press, Oxford, 1960
Tylden, G. *The Armed Forces of South Africa*, Frank Cannock Publications no. 2, Africana Museum, Johannesburg, 1954
van der Horst, S. T. *Native Labour in South Africa*, Oxford University Press, Oxford, 1942
van der Poel, J. *Railways and Customs Policies in South Africa, 1885–1910*, Royal Empire Society, London, 1933
van der Ross, R. E. *The Rise and Decline of Apartheid: A Study of Political Movements among the Coloured People of South Africa, 1880–1985*, Tafelberg, Cape Town, 1986
Walker, E. A. *W. P. Schreiner: A South African*, Oxford University Press, Oxford, 1937
Walshe, P. *The Rise of African Nationalism in South Africa: The African National Congress, 1912–1952*, Hurst, London, 1970
Warwick, P. (ed.) *The South African War: The Anglo-Boer War, 1899–1902*, Longman, London, 1980
  Black People and the South African War, 1899–1902, Cambridge University Press, Cambridge, 1983
Willan, B. *Sol Plaatje: A Biography, 1876–1932*, Ravan, Johannesburg, 1984
Wilson, M. and L. M. Thompson (eds.) *The Oxford History of South Africa*, 2 vols., Oxford University Press, 1969 and 1971

B Articles

Atmore, A. with M. J. Chirenje and S. I. Mudenge. 'Firearms in South Central Africa', *Journal of African History*, 12, 4 (1971), pp. 545–56
Atmore, A. and S. Marks. 'The Imperial Factor in South Africa: Towards a Reassessment', *Journal of Imperial and Commonwealth History*, 3, 1 (1974), pp. 105–39
Bailes, H. 'Technology and Imperialism: A Case Study of the Victorian Army in Africa', *Victorian Studies*, 24, 2 (1980), pp. 82–104
Bayo, 'Adekson J. 'Ethnicity and Army Recruitment in Colonial Plural Societies', *Ethnic and Racial Studies*, 2, 2 (1979), pp. 151–65
Beinart, W. and C. Bundy. 'State Intervention and Rural Resistance: The Transkei, 1900–1965', in M. A. Klein (ed.), *Peasants in Africa: Historical and Contemporary Perspectives*, Sage, Beverly Hills and London, 1980, pp. 271–315
Bundy, C. and W. Beinart. 'Rural Political Movements in South Africa: Transkei and Eastern Cape, 1890–1930', in *Agrarian Unrest in British and French Africa, British India and French Indo-China in the 19th and 20th Centuries*, Past and Present Society Conference Papers, London, 1982, pp. 1–24
Cuthbertson, G. 'Missionary Imperialism and Colonial Warfare: London Missionary Society Attitudes to the South African War, 1899–1901', *South African Historical Journal*, 19 (1987), pp. 93–114
Davies, R. 'The Political Economy of White Labour in South Africa: Some Preliminary Notes', in T. Adler (ed.), *Perspectives on South Africa: A Collection of Working Papers*, Communication No. 4, African Studies Institute, University of the Witwatersrand, 1977, pp. 132–94
Delius, P. and S. Trapido. '*Inboekselings* and *Oorlams*: The Creation and Transformation of a Servile Class', *Journal of Southern African Studies*, 8, 2 (1982), pp. 214–42
Denoon, D. 'Participation in the "Boer War": People's War, People's Non-War, or Non-People's War?', in B. A. Ogot (ed.), *War and Society in Africa*, Cass, London, 1972, pp. 109–23
Freund, B. 'Rural Struggles and Transformations' (review article), *South African Historical Journal*, 19 (1987), pp. 167–73

234

Galbraith, J. S. 'British War Measures in Cape Colony, 1900–1902: A Study of Miscalculations and Mismanagement', *South African Historical Journal*, 15 (1983), pp. 68–84

Giliomee, H. 'The Beginnings of Afrikaner Nationalism, 1870–1915', *South African Historical Journal*, 19 (1987), pp. 115–42

Hanna, J. L. 'African Dance and the Warrior Tradition', *Journal of Asian and African Studies*, 12, 1–4 (1977), pp. 111–33

Hyam, R. 'African Interests and the South Africa Act, 1908–1910', *Historical Journal*, 13, 1 (1970), pp. 85–105

Kiernan, V. G. 'Colonial Africa and its Armies', in B. Bond and I. Roy (eds.), *War and Society*, vol. II, Croom Helm, London, 1977, pp. 3–35

Killingray, D. 'The Idea of a British Imperial African Army', *Journal of African History*, 20, 3 (1979), pp. 421–36

Krikler, J. 'The Transvaal Agrarian Class Struggle in the South African War 1899–1902', *Social Dynamics*, 12, 2 (1986), pp. 1–30

Krüger, B. 'Die Brüdermission in SüdAfrika-West während des Burenkrieges, 1899–1902', in *Unitas Fratrum: Zeitschrift für Geschichte und Gegenwartsfragen der Brüdergemeine*, Wittij, Hamburg, 1979, pp. 126–44

Lewsen, P. 'The Cape Liberal Tradition – Myth or Reality?', *Race*, 13, 1 (1971), pp. 65–80

'Merriman as Last Cape Prime Minister', *South African Historical Journal*, 7 (1975), pp. 61–87

'Cape Liberalism in its Terminal Phase', in D. C. Hindson (ed.), *Working Papers in Southern African Studies*, vol. III, Ravan, Johannesburg, 1983, pp. 33–50

Lonsdale, J. 'South African Historiography as seen from England', *Social Dynamics*, 9, 1 (1983), pp. 67–82

Marks, S. 'The Historiography of South Africa', in D. Newbury and B. Jewsiewicki (eds.), *African Historiographies*, Sage, Beverly Hills, 1986, pp. 165–76

Marks S. and A. Atmore. 'Firearms in Southern Africa: A Survey', *Journal of African History*, 12, 4 (1971), pp. 517–30

Marks, S. and S. Trapido. 'Lord Milner and the South African State', *History Workshop Journal*, 8 (1979), pp. 50–80

Murray, M. 'Agrarian Social Structure and Rural Class Relations: Class Struggle in the Orange Free State and the Transvaal, *c.* 1890–1920', *Rural Africana*, 4–5 (1979), pp. 82–96

Nasson, W. R. '"These Natives think this War to be Their Own": Reflections on Blacks in the Cape Colony and the South African War, 1899–1902', in *Collected Seminar Papers on the Societies of Southern Africa in the 19th and 20th Centuries*, vol. II, Institute of Commonwealth Studies, University of London, 1981, pp. 36–47

'"Doing down Their Masters": Africans, Boers, and Treason in the Cape Colony during the South African War of 1899–1902', *Journal of Imperial and Commonwealth History*, 12, 1 (1983), pp. 29–53

'Moving Lord Kitchener: Black Military Transport and Supply Work in the South African War, 1899–1902, with particular reference to the Cape Colony', *Journal of Southern African Studies*, 11, 1 (1984), pp. 25–51

'Warriors without Spears: Africans in the South African War, 1899–1902' (review article), *Social Dynamics*, 9, 1 (1983), pp. 91–4

Nasson, W. R. and J. M. M. John. 'Abraham Esau: A Calvinia Martyr in the Anglo-Boer War', *Social Dynamics*, 2, 1 (1985), pp. 65–73

'The War of Abraham Esau 1899–1901: Martyrdom, Myth and Folk Memory in Calvinia, South Africa, *African Affairs*, 87, 347 (1988), pp. 239–65

'Abraham Esau's War', in P. Thompson and R. Samuel (eds.), *The Myths We Live By*, Routledge, London (in press)

Ngcongco, L. D. 'Jabavu and the Anglo-Boer War', *Kleio*, 11, 2 (1970), pp. 6–18

Parry, R. '"In a Sense Citizens but not Altogether Citizens . . . ": Rhodes, Race, and the Ideology of Segregation at the Cape in the Late Nineteenth Century', *Canadian Journal of African Studies*, 17, 2 (1983), pp. 377–91

Ranger, T. 'The Invention of Tradition in Colonial Africa', in E. Hobsbawm and T. Ranger (eds.), *The Invention of Tradition*, Cambridge University Press, Cambridge, 1984, pp. 211–59

Rich, P. 'Segregation and the Cape Liberal Tradition', *Collected Seminar Papers on the Societies of Southern Africa in the 19th and 20th Centuries*, vol. X, Institute of Commonwealth Studies, University of London, 1981, pp. 31–41

Saunders, C. C. 'F. Z. S. Peregrino and the "South African Spectator"', *Quarterly Bulletin of the South African Library*, 32, 3 (1978), pp. 81–90

'Segregation in Cape Town: The Creation of Ndabeni', *Africa Seminar, Collected Papers*, vol. I, Centre for African Studies, University of Cape Town, 1978, pp. 43–63

Schoeman, K. 'Die Dood van Abraham Esau: Ooggetuieberigte uit die Besette Calvinia, 1901', *Quarterly Bulletin of the South African Library*, 40, 2 (1985), pp. 56–66

Shearing, T. 'Coloured Involvement in the South African War in the Cape Colony', *Quarterly Bulletin of the South African Library*, 40, 1 (1985), pp. 7–11

Snyman, J. H. 'Rebelle Verhoor in Kaapland Gedurende Die Tweede Vryheidsoorlog, met Spesiale Verwysing na die Militêre Howe, 1899–1902', *Argief Jaarboek vir Suidafrikaanse Geskiedenis*, Die Staatsdrukker, Pretoria, 1963, pp. 1–74

'Die Afrikaner in Kaapland met verwysing na die Militêre Howe, 1899–1902', *Argief Jaarboek vir Suidafrikaanse Geskiedenis*, Die Staatsdrukker, Pretoria, 1979

Swanson, M. W. '"The Sanitation Syndrome": Bubonic Plague and Urban Native Policy in the Cape Colony, 1900–1909', *Journal of African History*, 18, 3 (1977), pp. 387–410

Thompson, E. P. 'Time, Work Discipline and Industrial Capitalism', *Past and Present*, 38 (1967), pp. 56–97

Trapido, S. 'The Origin and Development of the African Political Organisation', *Collected Seminar Papers on the Societies of Southern Africa in the 19th and 20th Centuries*, vol. I, Institute of Commonwealth Studies, University of London, 1970, pp. 89–111

'African Divisional Politics in the Cape Colony, 1884–1910', *Journal of African History*, 9, 1 (1968), pp. 79–98

'Liberalism in the Cape in the Nineteenth and Twentieth Centuries', *Collected Seminar Papers on the Societies of Southern Africa in the 19th and 20th Centuries*, vol. IV, Institute of Commonwealth Studies, University of London, 1974, pp. 53–66

Tylden, G. 'The Development of the Commando System in South Africa, 1715–1922', *Africana Notes and News*, 13, 8 (1959), pp. 303–15

van Heyningen, E. 'Refugees and Relief in Cape Town, 1899–1902', in C. Saunders and H. Phillips (eds.), *Studies in the History of Cape Town*, vol. III, Centre for African Studies and Department of History, University of Cape Town, 1980, pp. 64–113

C Unpublished papers, dissertations and theses

Bonner, P. 'African Participation in the Anglo-Boer War of 1899–1902', M.A. dissertation, University of London, 1967

Cuthbert, P. 'The Administration of Dr Jameson as Prime Minister of the Cape Colony, 1904–1908', M.A. thesis, University of Cape Town, 1950

Dickson, P. G. 'The Ideas and Influence of John Tengo Jabavu, Editor of *Imvo Zabantsundu*, 1884–1921', B.A. Hons dissertation, University of Cape Town, 1964

James, I. A. 'The Rebellion in Barkly East and Dordrecht in 1899', B.A. Hons. dissertation, University of Cape Town, 1964

Mabin, A. 'The Underdevelopment of the Western Cape, 1860–1900', Conference Paper, Western Cape Roots and Realities Conference, University of Cape Town, 1986

Nasson, W. R. '"The Bite of the Black Mosquito": Black Participation in the South African War, and Social Control in the Cape Colony', Commonwealth and Overseas History Seminar Paper, Faculty of History, University of Cambridge, 1979

'Black Society in the Cape Colony and the South African War of 1899–1902: A Social History', Ph.D. thesis, University of Cambridge, 1983

Ngcongco, L. D. '*Imvo Zabantsundu* and Cape Native Policy, 1884–1902', M.A. thesis, University of South Africa, 1974

Page, A. H. 'The Supply Services of the British Army in the South African War, 1899–1902', D.Phil. thesis, University of Oxford, 1977

Price, M. J. 'Leliefontein: History and Structure of a Coloured Mission Community, 1870–1913', B.A. Hons. dissertation, University of Cape Town, 1976

Schmidt, A. 'The Life of Gideon Scheepers, 1878–1902', B.A. Hons. dissertation, University of Cape Town, 1965

Skillicorn, A. S. 'The Role of the Black Voter in the 1908 Cape General Election, with particular reference to the Eastern Cape', B.A. Hons. dissertation, University of Cape Town, 1975

Trapido, S. 'White Conflict and Non-White Participation in the Politics of the Cape of Good Hope, 1853–1910', Ph.D. thesis, University of London, 1970

Index

Aberdeen, 20

Adams, Frederick, 164

Adelaide, 71, 171, 186; black auxiliaries in, 29–30, 38, 46, 57, 105: wages, 26, 58, 79; treason trials, 87, 152

African People's Organisation, 39

African Political Association, 164

Afrikaner Bond, 6–7, 144, 146–8, 164; relations with blacks, 19, 35–6, 52, 116, 132, 135

agterryers, 94–5, 97–103, 128; as informers, 101–2, 152, 161

Albany, 27, 71, 73

Albert, 74, 82, 103, 116, 180; treason trials, 147, 153, 160

Alexandria, 73, 171; black auxiliaries in, 24, 38, 53, 59, 60

Alice, 24, 27, 53, 70, 71

Aliwal North, 102, 103, 106; black auxiliaries in, 16, 24, 48, 55–6, 74, 82; white reaction to, 20, 21, 29, 31; Boer occupation of, 107–8, 114–16, 144; post-war conditions, 171, 174–5, 183, 186; treason trials, 147, 150, 153–5

Anenous, 172

Baadjies, Sara, 165

Balie, Frederick, 163

Baralong, 179

Barkly East, 21, 28, 30, 99; black auxiliaries in, 16, 31; Boer occupation of, 103, 105, 114–16, 118; post-war conditions, 175, 180, 183; treason trials, 150, 153, 154, 156

Barkly West, 88, 147

Basotho, 5, 14, 71, 106; as auxiliaries, 18, 19, 24, 48, 51, 55, 78, 82, 86

Basters, 68, 74, 81, 134; as auxiliaries, 24, 42, 172, 173, 177; treatment by Boers, 105–6, 108–12

Basutoland, 5, 71, 81

Bathurst, 26, 69

Beaufort West, 101, 153, 174, 181

Bedford, 57, 71, 73, 79, 171, 186; black auxiliaries

in, 26, 29–30, 38, 55, 60; treason trials, 87, 150, 155

Benjamin, Andreas, 164

Berlin Missionary Society, 162, 163

Bethelsdorp mission, 163, 176

Bethune, Lieutenant-Colonel, 27, 70

Bezuidenhout, Commandant, 18, 95, 102

Bhaca, 5, 18, 48, 82

black elite: franchise, 6–7, 187; perception of the war, 32–40

Bloemfontein, 67, 77, 159

Boer army, 20; blacks in, 93–5, 97–103, 105, *see also agterryers*; commando raids, 56–7, 105–19, 122, 142, 177, *see also* names of commandos, e.g. Myburgh commando

Bok, Pieter, 113

Border Scouts, 19

Botha, General Louis, 83

Bowkers Park, 76, 88

Boyes, George, 20, 30

Bredasdorp, 42, 68–9, 165, 176

British Army: use of black troops, 12–23; use of foreign troops, 13, 66, 67, 84, 89, *see also* labour, remount workers, scouts, transport riders

Britstown, 28, 42, 129, 173, 183

Brodrick, St John, 22

Buller, General Sir Redvers, 18

Burghersdorp, 46, 88, 144, 147; black auxiliaries in, 53, 55; post-war conditions, 170, 180–1

Bushmanland Borderers, 19, 23

Butterworth, 19

bywoners, 9, 112, 114, 116; in army, 20, 66; in treason trials, 145, 148, 153, 156; *see also* 'poor whites'

Caledon, 27, 31, 42, 70, 74

Calvinia, 24, 120–40, 147, 186

Cape Boers, 16, 19, 46, 89, 98, 117, 121, 144, 186–7

Cape Copper Company, 54, 68

238

Cape Daily Telegraph, 36, 37, 131
Cape Mercury, 27, 36, 37, 131
Cape Mounted Rifles, 5, 16
Cape Town, 46, 68, 184; labour, 9, 28, 30, 173,
    179, 182–3; politics, 33–4, 164, 186
Carelse, Leslie, 136
Carnarvon, 150; black auxiliaries in, 13, 24, 43, 82;
    Boers in, 97, 106, 107, 113; British army in, 73,
    95
Cathcart, 27, 69, 70
Ceres, 159
Chamberlain, Joseph, 144, 156, 175; views on
    blacks, 13, 33, 131
Chleboun, Franz, 163
Christie, Captain Charles, 29
Ciskei, 4, 37, 70, 73; as labour market, 26, 69,
    177
Citrusdal, 127, 175
Clanwilliam, 73, 92, 175; black auxiliaries in, 31,
    70; Boers in, 122, 159; Abraham Esau, 124,
    126–7
Clarkson, 68
Coal mining, 28, 54, 70, 175
Codrington, Colonel C. A., 24
Colesberg, 65, 77, 146, 150, 183; black auxiliaries
    in, 44, 48; Boers in, 95, 101, 103
Coloured Men's Political and Protectorate
    Association, 34
Coloured People's Vigilance Society, 34
Coloured Political Association, 164
'Coloured War Councils', 34, 44
commandos, *see* Boer army; and specific names of
    commandos, e.g. Myburgh commando
compensation, post-war, 179–82
Concordia, 95, 112, 172, 179; black auxiliaries in,
    47, 54, 55, 57
Conroy, Commandant E. A., 93, 98, 107
Cooper, Colonel H., 24, 26, 56, 113, 173
Cradock: black auxiliaries in, 44–6, 49, 51, 53, 79;
    post-war conditions, 170, 179–80, 185; treason
    trials, 145, 153, 156, 159, 161, 166
Cronje, General P. A., 94

Damon, Silas, 97, 98
Darling, 177
De Aar, 29, 183; Boers in, 107, 114–15; labour
    depot, 20, 26, 30; remount depot, 13, 65, 68, 69,
    74, 77, 82, 88, 91; treason trials, 102, 153, 157
Dean, George, 54
De Beers Company, 28, 70, 160
De Beers Dynamite Works, 28, 70
de Lisle, Colonel H., 27, 70, 131
demobilisation, 172–4, 176
De Waal, N. F., 148
De Wet, General C. R., 64
disarmament, 5; post-war, 61
dock workers, 3, 9, 28

Dordrecht, 150, 171; black auxiliaries in, 16, 48,
    50, 53, 54, 174; Boers in, 21, 103, 106, 115–16
Douglas, 68, 101, 159, 163; Boers in, 114–15, 144;
    treason trials, 157–8
Dreyer, Peter, 124, 125, 128, 130

East Griqualand, 5, 16, 18, 71, 73, 90
East London, 28, 34, 37, 76, 183
Elliot, Sir Henry, 18–19
Elliot, 19
Elim mission, 68, 83, 105, 162–5
Engcobo, 105
Enon mission, 162–3
Esau, Abraham, xvii–xix, 63, 120–2, 124–40, 190
Ethiopianism, 19

farmworkers, 157–61, 166–8, 172, 174–5; as
    auxiliaries, 27–8, 42, 47, 52, 70, 109–10
food, 69, 79, 105, 111–12, 179
Foreign Mission Chronicle, 15
Fort Beaufort, 80, 150, 171; black auxiliaries in,
    24, 27, 70
Fouché, Commandant W. D., 101, 104 map, 107–8
franchise: non-racial, 6–8, 33, 115–17, 188;
    Transvaal, 6, 38–40
Fraserburg, 42, 59, 113, 122, 170; treason trials,
    150, 160
French, General J., 56, 67, 77, 113

Garies, 50, 95, 112–13, 173; black auxiliaries in,
    47, 54, 55, 172
Gatacre, Major-General Sir W. F., 83
Gcaleka, 48
Geldenhuys, Louwrens, 103, 107, 117
Genadendal mission, 68, 105, 163
Girouard, Colonel E. P. C., 26
Goedverwacht mission, 163, 164
Gordonia, 73, 105, 118, 179; treason trials, 147,
    153
Graaff-Reinet, 42, 105, 153, 154, 183; black
    auxiliaries in, 47, 50, 57
Graaff-Reinet Advertiser, 57
De Graaff Reinetter, 146
Graafwater, 127
Graham, John, 46
Green Point, 84
Griqualand West, 5, 150
Griquatown, 152, 154, 155
Gwe, Solomon, 164

Hanover, 46, 47, 70, 155
Harmsworth, Alfred, 41
Hay, 114, 118, 171, 179
Heathly, Matthew, 164
Henniker, Colonel A. S., 45
Herbert, 81, 155, 159, 179
Herero Rebellion, 177

Herschel, 28, 105, 114, 116; black auxiliaries in, 19–21; treason trials, 147, 153
Hertzog, J. B. M., 114, 118–19, 129
Hofmeyr, 30, 44
Hofmeyr, J. H., 16
Hope Town, 43, 47, 90, 147, 179
Hugo, Commandant H. J., 102
Humansdorp, 31, 179

Imvo Zabantsundu, 7, 34–8, 44–5
Indians: cavalrymen, 13, 15 ill, 68, 84, 90; labourers, 76; pedlars, 45, 115
Indwe Colliery, 28, 54, 70, 175
informers, 22, 101–2, 107, 127, 142–3, 155–6, 164; payment of, 149–50, 152–3, 157; *see also* spies
Innes, James Rose, 36, 37, 148–9
Izwi Labantu, 34, 35–8, 40

Jabavu, John Tengo, 7, 34–7, 39, 40
Jamestown, 48, 114, 115–16, 174, 181, 183
Jansenville, 20, 47, 53, 70, 156
Jantjies, Abraham, 164
Jantjies, Martha, 165
Jews in Namaqualand, 121, 129, 160
Jonas, Benjamin, 164
Jones, David, 170
Joorst, Daniel, 164
Julius Weil and Co., 73

Keiskamma Hoek, 69
Kelham, Colonel H. R., 54
Kenhardt, 153, 172; black auxiliaries in, 24, 29, 42, 43; Boers in, 106, 113, 122
Kimberley, 33, 86, 160; mine labour, 4, 7, 28, 70; siege of, 3, 142
King Williams Town, 26, 34, 35–7, 69, 183
Kitchener, General (later Field-Marshal) Lord, 22, 26, 144, 179
Klipdam, 41–2, 154, 157, 180
Klipfontein, 57, 95
Knysna, 69, 176
Kommagas, 68
Kriel, David, 164
Kritzinger, General P. H., 22, 93, 101, 102, 107, 114; commando, 57
Kroonstad, 98, 146, 175
Kruger, President S. J. P., 33, 44, 118, 163
Kunick, F. W., 164
Kuruman: black auxiliaries in, 42, 56, 67; Boers in, 114–15, 144; treason trials, 154, 156
Kyd, Thomas, 36

labour, 7, 9–10; convict, 29, 42, 148; in Boer army, 94, 102–3, 105; in British army, 26–31, 42; migrant, *see* migrant labour; post-war, 174–82; *see also agterryers*, 'poor whites', wages

Lady Frere, 70, 89
Lady Grey, 55, 147, 153; Boers in, 20, 21, 105, 115
Lambert's Bay, 47, 108, 112, 179
Leliefontein mission, 68, 108–10, 119, 177, 179, 190; destruction of, 110–13, 114
Lemmerz, E. R., 162, 165
liberalism, 6–9, 32–3, 61, 132, 138, 187
Locke, Revd J. G., 110
Loeriesfontein, 134–5
Lötter, Commandant J., 93, 107, 191
Loxton, 151
Lydenburg, 98

McGeer, John, 150–1
Machadodorp, 67
Maclear, 18, 82
Mafeking, 73, 179; siege of, 3, 94, 142; relief of, 124, 163, 164
Mafeteng, 48
Malan, General W., 93, 102, 104 map
Malmesbury, 31, 70, 150
Mamre, 68, 176, 162–4
Manel, Christian, 125, 126
Manel family, 135
Manel, Peter, 137
Mantsayi, Robert R., 36
Maraisburg, 57, 103
Maritz, General Gerhardus 'Manie', 95, 102, 106, 110–12
martial law, 30, 143–9, 157, 165–6, 168
Marx, Matthias, 164
Masters and Servants Act (1856), 57, 168
Matanzima, Chief Mvuso, 76
Matjiesfontein, 107, 150
Maxse, Lieutenant-Colonel F., 78
Mazwi, Petrus, 164
Merriman, John X., 16, 35, 148, 175
Methodist missions, 162
Mfengu, 15, 69, 106, 179; as auxiliaries, 5, 18, 21, 48, 55, 56, 67, 82, 107; as scouts, 19, 24, 26, 171, 173, 174; as transport workers, 79, 84, 86
Middelpos, 125, 127
Middelburg, 28, 44, 60
migrant labour, 9–10, 150, 176–8; in army, 26, 67, 69–70, 74, 90–2
militia, *see* town guard
Milner, Sir Alfred (later Lord), 13, 18, 33, 131–2, 144, 180
mine workers, 7, 9, 42, 48, 175, 177; *see also* coal mining; Witwatersrand
missionaries: and black auxiliaries, 15, 67–9, 162–5
Moiletsie, Chief, 21
Molala, Chief, 151
Molteno, 73, 113, 171; black auxiliaries in, 24, 60, 79, 172; Boers in, 57, 93, 99, 101, 103, 105; treason trials, 147, 150, 153, 155

Molteno, Percy A., 188
Moravian missions, 68, 164; *see also* name of mission, e.g. Elim
Mossel Bay, 176
Mount Fletcher, 82
Mount Frere, 82
Mpondomise, 14, 82
Muishond, 57
Murraysburg, 20, 44, 170
Myburgh commando, 20, 93, 101

Naauwpoort, 30, 67, 68, 77, 183; remount depot, 65, 74, 75, 88
Na'babeep, 47, 57, 173
Nama Rebellion, 177
Namaqualand, 70, 78, 81, 119, 120, 132, 172; Boers in, 24, 95, 122, 153; Jews in, 121, 129, 160
Namaqualand Border Scouts, 19, 23, 47, 173, 190
Namaqualand Copper Company, 54
Namaqualand Field Force, 47, 54, 56, 68, 84, 112, 126, 179; recruitment to, 24, 29, 79, 108–9
Native Cycling Corps, 84
Natives' Land Act (1913), 188–9
Naude commando, 99
Nederduitse Gereformeerde Kerk missions, 162
Nel commando, 101
New Cape Collieries, 28, 70
Ngqika, 48
Niewoudt, Commandant C., 105; commando, 129–31, 138

Olivier, Commandant J. H., 21, 114, 115
Ons Land, 146, 152
O'Okiep, 47–8, 54, 95, 112, 179
Orange Free State, 115, 159, 182; commandos, 21, 28, 62, 113, 116–17, 122–3, 125, 128–30, 144
Orange River Colony, 77, 146, 179, 183, 184
Oudtshoorn, 27, 44, 70, 175

Paarl, 88, 147, 162, 175
passes: laws, 8, 33; travel, 29–30, 45, 107–8, 160, 171
Peace Preservation Act (1878), 5, 172
Pearston, 52, 57
peasants, 7, 9, 59, 175; culture, 82, 84; destruction of communities, 105, 114–15; militia, 16–18, 48–9; suppliers to army, 70–1, 73, 79, 91
Peddie, 24, 26, 69
Peregrino, F. Z. S., 34
Philipstown, 46, 59, 129, 144
Pijpers commando, 101
Piquetberg, 20, 163
Plaatjie, Lukas, 113–14
Pniel, 68, 165
Pofadder, 177

Pondoland, 19
'poor whites', 9, 95, 112, 116, 176, 183, 188; recruitment of, 20–1, 43–4; transport conductors, 66, 88–9; *see also* bywoners
Port Elizabeth, 28, 33, 34, 68, 183
Port Nolloth, 47, 50, 108, 113, 172, 179
Porter, Major Frederick, 103, 105
Potchefstroom, 98
Preston, Lieutenant James, 125, 126, 128
Pretoria, 33, 78, 85, 98
Pretorius, Commandant, 128–9
Prieska, 20, 73, 88, 153, 157, 183; black auxiliaries in, 24, 50–1, 59, 95; Boers in, 107, 113, 128
Prince Albert, 47, 90, 159
Progressives, 35–6, 132, 186

Queenstown, 26, 31, 70, 73, 116, 181, 183; black auxiliaries in, 58, 76, 107; remount depot, 13, 68, 82, 88; treason trials, 153, 154, 157
Quthing, 81

Rauch, Friedrich, 163
refugees, 44, 59, 60, 113, 179–80
Reitz, Deneys, 110, 112
remount workers, 23, 64–92, 176–7; sources of supply, 68–70; wages, 73–6, 79, 87–8, 90–1; *see also* transport conductors, transport riders
Rhenish missions, 162
Rhodes, 21, 28, 118, 180
Rhodes, Cecil John, 32, 36, 116
Richardson, Lawrence, 182
Richmond, 44, 45, 105, 150, 173
Rietfontein, 107
Rimington Scouts, 147
Riversdale, 68, 74, 105
Roberts, Lord, 65, 67, 77, 85, 146; use of black auxiliaries, 21–2, 26
Robertson, 27
Rose Innes, James, *see* Innes, James Rose
Rouxville, 148; commando, 101, 107–8
Rowland, William, 170

Saldanha Bay, 177
Salisbury, Lord, 33
Sampson, Petrus, 162, 163
Sauer, J. W., 16, 21, 35, 148
Scheepers, Gideon, 107, 133
Schoeman, Commandant, 112
Scholtz, Daantjie, 137
Schreiner, Olive, 170
Schreiner, W. P., 28, 144; views on black auxiliaries, 13, 15–16, 18
Schütz, Ernst, 164
Scott, John, 18
scouts: with Boers, 93–5; with British army, 21–4, 44–5, 55, 95, 101, 108, 123; treatment by Boers, 106–7; demobilisation, 172–4; burial, 185–6;

scouts (*cont.*)
  wages, 24, 26, 29, 59, 78; *see also* spies, informers
Seton, William, 121
Settle, General H. H., 56
Smuts, General J. C., 83, 112, 114; attacks on blacks, 102, 106, 107, 110; views on black auxiliaries, 93–4, 95
Society of Friends, 182
Soga, A. K., 34, 35, 37, 38, 40
Soga, W. D., 90
Somerset East, 42, 71, 171, 180; black auxiliaries in, 26, 31, 49 ill, 51, 56
Somerset West, 28, 70
South African League, 33
South African Native Congress, 39
South African Native Labour Corps, 173
South African News, 131, 146, 147
South African Party, 35, 148
South African Republic, 33, 94, 99; *see also* Transvaal
South African Review, 37
South African Spectator, 33, 34, 40
South West Africa, 177
spies, 101–2, 106, 127, 164; treatment of, 22, 108; *see also* informers
Sprigg, Sir Gordon, 13, 15–16, 60–1, 144, 146
Springbok, 112, 172
St Helena Bay, 177
Stanford, Sir Walter, 16, 18
Steinkopf German mission, 55, 68, 83, 177
Stellenbosch, 27; remount depot, 13, 69, 70, 74, 76, 84, 87
Sterkstroom, 60, 73
Steyn, President Marthinus, 16, 64
Steynsburg, 44, 57, 93, 173–4; Boers in, 103, 113, 116; treason trials, 145, 146, 147, 150, 161
Steytlerville, 46, 47, 70, 150, 156
'Stone' movement, 186
Stormberg, 65, 83, 153, 172; black auxiliaries in, 48, 59; commando, 106, 107, 161
Strachan and Company, 73
Strydom, Stephanus, 131, 133
Sutherland, 42, 107, 122, 150, 154, 159; black auxiliaries in, 48, 52, 59, 95
Swellendam, 42, 74, 157, 162, 175, 176

Tarkastad, 44, 48, 52, 175
Taung Reserve, 150
Te Water, T. N. G., 148
Thembu, 18, 19, 21, 26, 48, 69, 82
Thembuland, 36, 71
Theron commando, 93, 101
Tlhaping, 71, 150
Tobin, John, 186
town guards, 41–63
Transkeian Territories, 4, 5, 8, 14, 37, 144; levies

raised in, 16, 18–19; migrant labour source, 7, 9, 26, 67, 69, 77, 177; trade, 70, 175; *see also* East Griqualand
transport conductors, 66, 87–90; *see also* remount workers
transport riders, 10, 65, 68, 74–6, 88–90, 92, 101, 150, 176; pace of labour, 86–7; recreation 82–6; wages, 74, 78–81, 85; *see also* remount workers
Transvaal, 35, 38–40, 146, 175, 176, 178, 179, 184; *see also* South African Republic
treason, 142–68
Tulbagh, 70, 92, 105, 181; black auxiliaries in, 31, 42, 148; treason trials, 154, 155, 157

Uitenhage, 27, 70, 154
Umtata Herald, 36, 37
Uniondale, 150
unemployment, 177
Upington, 88, 157, 172; black auxiliaries in, 24–5, 29; Boers in, 105, 113, 144, 159
Uys, *Eerwaarde*, 136

van der Merwe, Carl, 129–31
van der Merwe commando, 98
van Heerden, General, 98
van Heerden, H. C., 148
Vereeniging, Peace of, 39
Verwoerd, Hendrik, 137
Victoria East, 71, 80, 186
Victoria Road, 50, 89, 174
Victoria West, 20, 28, 30, 42, 97, 113
vote, *see* franchise
Vryburg, 29, 52, 150–1, 154, 180–1

wages, 42; farmworkers, 27–8, 174–5; labour levies, 42; remount workers, 73–6, 79, 87–8, 90–1; scouts, 24, 26, 29, 59, 78; transport riders, 74, 78–81, 85
War of the Guns (1880–1), 5
War Losses Compensation Commission, 181–2
Weir, J. W., 37
Wessels, General, 93, 113
White, Colonel, 47, 50, 107
Williston, 73, 95, 107, 151, 172; black auxiliaries in, 24, 29, 43, 48, 82
Willowmore, 57, 70, 150, 156; black auxiliaries in, 47, 49–50, 53
Winburg, 97
Wittekleibosch mission, 164
Wittewater mission, 163, 164
Witwatersrand, 7, 26, 38, 177–8
Wodehouse, 118, 148, 150
women, 91–2, 148, 165; as domestic servants, 58, 148, 161; as laundry-women, 74, 102, 148; war experiences, 3–4, 102, 106, 125
Worcester, 147, 162, 175; remount depot, 69, 70, 74, 75, 76, 84, 88

Worcester Standard, 152
workers, *see* dock workers; farmworkers; mine
    workers; remount workers
Wupperthal, 68, 83, 105

Zuid Afrikaansche Republiek, *see* South African
    Republic
Het Zuid-Oosten, 131
Zulu, 48

OTHER BOOKS IN THE SERIES

6 *Labour in the South African Gold Mines, 1911–1969* Francis Wilson

11 *Islam and Tribal Art in West Africa* René Bravman

14 *Culture, Tradition and Society in the West African Novel* Emmanuel Obiechina

18 *Muslim Brotherhoods in Nineteenth-century Africa* B. G. Martin

23 *West African States: Failure and Promise: A Study in Comparative Politics* edited by John Dunn

25 *A Modern History of Tanganyika* John Iliffe

26 *A History of African Christianity 1950–1975* Adrian Hastings

28 *The Hidden Hippopotamus: Reappraisal in African History: The Early Colonial Experience in Western Zambia* Gwyn Prins

29 *Families Divided: The Impact of Migrant Labour in Lesotho* Colin Murray

30 *Slavery, Colonialism and Economic Growth in Dahomey, 1640–1960* Patrick Manning

31 *Kings, Commoners and Concessionaires: The Evolution and Dissolution of the Nineteenth-century Swazi State* Philip Bonner

32 *Oral Poetry and Somali Nationalism: The Case of Sayyid Mohammed 'Abdille Hasan* Said S. Samatar

33 *The Political Economy of Pondoland 1860–1930: Production, Labour, Migrancy and Chiefs in Rural South Africa* William Beinart

34 *Volkskapitalisme: Class, Capital and Ideology in the Development of Afrikaner Nationalism 1934–1948* Dan O'Meara

35 *The Settler Economies: Studies in the Economic History of Kenya and Rhodesia 1900–1963* Paul Mosley

36 *Transformations in Slavery: A History of Slavery in Africa* Paul E. Lovejoy

37 *Amilcar Cabral: Revolutionary Leadership and People's War* Patrick Chabal

38 *Essays on the Political Economy of Rural Africa* Robert H. Bates

39 *Ijeshas and Nigerians: The Incorporation of a Yoruba Kingdom, 1890s–1970s* J. D. Y. Peel

40 *Black People and the South African War 1899–1902* Peter Warwick

41 *A History of Niger 1850–1960* Finn Fuglestad

42 *Industrialisation and Trade Union Organisation in South Africa 1924–55* Jon Lewis

43 *The Rising of the Red Shawls: A Revolt in Madagascar 1895–1899* Stephen Ellis

44 *Slavery in Dutch South Africa* Nigel Worden

45 *Law, Custom and Social Order: The Colonial Experience in Malawi and Zambia* Martin Chanock

46 *Salt of the Desert Sun: A History of Salt Production and Trade in the Central Sudan* Paul E. Lovejoy

47 *Marrying Well: Marriage Status and Social Change among the Educated Elite in Colonial Lagos* Kristin Mann

48 *Language and Colonial Power: The Appropriation of Swahili in the Former Belgian Congo 1880–1938* Johannes Fabian

49 *The Shell Money of the Slave Trade* Jan Hogendorn and Marion Johnson

50 *Political Domination in Africa: Reflections on the Limits of Power* edited by Patrick Chabal

51 *The Southern Marches of Imperial Ethiopia: Essays in History and Social Anthropology* edited by Donald Donham and Wendy James

52 *Islam and Urban Labor in Northern Nigeria: The Making of a Muslim Working Class* Paul M. Lubeck

53 *Horn and Crescent: Cultural Change and Traditional Islam on the East African Coast, 500–1900* Randall L. Pouwels

54 *Capital and Labour on the Kimberley Diamond Fields 1871–1890* Robert Vicat Turrell

55 *National and Class Conflict in the Horn of Africa* John Markakis

56 *Democracy and Prebendal Politics in Nigeria: The Rise and Fall of the Second Republic* Richard A. Joseph

57 *Entrepreneurs and Parasites: The Struggle for Indigenous Capitalism in Zaire* Janet MacGaffey

58 *The African Poor: A History* John Iliffe

244

59 *Palm Oil and Protest: An Economic History of the Ngwa Region, South-eastern Nigeria 1800–1980*
   Susan M. Martin

60 *France and Islam in West Africa, 1860–1960*   Christopher Harrison

61 *Transformation and Continuity in Revolutionary Ethiopia*   Christopher Clapham

62 *Prelude to the Mahdiya: Peasants and Traders in the Shendi Region, 1821–1885*   Anders Bjørkelo

63 *Wa and the Wala: Islam and Polity in Northwestern Ghana*   Ivor Wilks

64 *Bankole-Bright and Politics in Colonial Sierra Leone: The Passing of the "Krio Era", 1919–1935*
   Akintola Wyse

65 *Contemporary West African States*   edited by Donal Cruise O'Brien, John Dunn, and Richard
   Rathbone

66 *The Oromo of Ethiopia: A History, 1570–1860*   Mohammed Hassen

67 *Slavery and African Life: Occidental, Oriental and African Slave Trades*   Patrick Manning